MORANIFESTO

313.3'45

Also by Caitlin Moran:

Non fiction:
How to Be a Woman

Collections:
Moranthology

Fiction:
How to Build a Girl

CAITLIN
MORANIFESTO
MORAN

EBURY
PRESS

3 5 7 9 10 8 6 4 2

Ebury Press, an imprint of Ebury Publishing
20 Vauxhall Bridge Road
London SW1V 2SA

Ebury Press is part of the Penguin Random House group of companies whose
addresses can be found at global.penguinrandomhouse.com

Penguin
Random House
UK

Copyright © Casa Bevron 2016

Caitlin Moran has asserted her right to be identified as the author of this Work in
accordance with the Copyright, Designs and Patents Act 1988

First published by Ebury Press in 2016

This edition published in 2017

www.penguin.co.uk

A CIP catalogue record for this book is available from the British Library

ISBN 9780091949068

Printed and bound in Great Britain by Clays Ltd, St Ives PLC

MIX
Paper from
responsible sources
FSC® C018179

r our busi-
ɔm Forest

LONDON BOROUGH OF WANDSWORTH	
9030 00005 4446 4	
Askews & Holts	30-Mar-2017
828.9209	£8.99
	WW16018540

To 'Lizzie' and 'Nancy' — HANG THE WET TOWELS UP THEY CANNOT DRY ON THE FLOOR FOR THE LOVE OF BABY JESUS HANG THE TOWELS ON THE TOWEL RAIL YOU ARE BREAKING A GOOD WOMAN HERE

Also to Nye Bevan. Thank you for approximately half of my life

CONTENTS

MORANIFESTO: PART TWO

THE FEMINISMS

INTRODUCTION

So, welcome to my second collection of writing. Hello! I embrace you. I am sorry about the smell. I get very sweaty when I write. I don't know why. One day, I will learn how to varnish my armpits, and it will be easier to be my friend again. Until then – I apologise.

I've been a columnist for twenty-three years now. I started when I was seventeen, at *The Times*, when I faxed them a speculative column from the fax machine at the Stars newsagent on Warstones Drive, Wolverhampton.

The Times offered me a job, so I moved down to London, and started writing about what I knew: pop music, TV, film, radio. Life stuff, like, 'What to do in a nightclub' (always work out a dance routine in advance; keep your money in your bra) and 'How to smoke a cigarette in a cool way' (always make sure you put it in your mouth the right way round; the taste of smouldering filter is deeply unpleasant).

Mainly, I just tried to be funny. And I stayed away from anything political – because politics wasn't for seventeen-year-old girls trying to be funny. That was for serious adult men, in suits, who knew people in Parliament, or had been politicians themselves, or wanted to be politicians in the future. Politics was for the political people, and I was not one of them.

Anyway, the years passed and I grew up, and, as one does, I read the newspapers, and I watched the news, and I started to have opinions on politics – this is stupid! That is amazing! Why are we not doing *this?* – but still I didn't write about politics: because I wasn't a Professional Politics Person. I thought that 'the grown-ups' would round on me if I did – that they would read that column and point out that I did not have the education, or knowledge, to have an opinion on these things, and I would be shamed for writing something foolish, or ignorant, or which didn't go into huge details about the Whig government of 1715.

But then, in 2011, I wrote *How to Be a Woman* in a huge, five-month frenzy. I had spent years wanting to write a book about feminism, but had thought it would be the same deal as with politics: that feminism was a job for Professional Feminist People, and that it wasn't something you could rock up to unless you'd been to the right university, joined the right groups, read the right books and learned the right history and terminology. Maybe you'd even need to know about the Whig government of 1715 here, too. I didn't know. It was entirely possible.

However, the arrival of my daughters viscerally over-rode that fear: as they began school, I became so wild with panic that they would, as they started to go out in society, have to deal with all the same crushing, debilitating, time-wasting, unjoyous bullshit I'd had to deal with when I was their age – the same, anxious, enraging, dull deforming of the female spirit – that I wrote the book anyway. I wanted to write something that laid out, all in one place, as much as I was able, why the world is as it is for women, and pass on as many tools as I was able for them to analyse it, and deal with it, while at the same time detailing all the times I'd been a massive knobhead, so they could, maybe, avoid perhaps *half* of all the mistakes I'd made.

And when *How to Be a Woman* took off, in the most unexpected way – despite me not being a Professional Feminist Person – I started to think, 'Maybe there's something to learn here. Maybe you don't need to be the "right" kind of person to write about big things. Maybe *anyone* thoughtful, and making an effort, can contribute to the debate. Maybe there are thousands of us who are not thinking, and not writing, and not talking – just because we think we are the wrong kind of person. So – I *am* going to write about politics, now. Firstly, because I think I should; and secondly, because I'm old enough now not to care if people think I can't. I love getting older. You might lose skin elasticity, but you also lose the amount of fucks you give. It's awesome.

So I rang my editor at *The Times* and told her that I would now like to give up my humorous column in the *Magazine*, and move to the Op-Ed pages – because that's where all the Professional Political People write – and that I would write only serious political pieces from now on. Because you can't write a column for a glossy magazine where, one week, you detail how much you hate printers, and then the next, Syria. That's just not one of the careers on offer.

And she replied, 'You massive idiot. Of *course* you can do both. In fact, you *should* do both. There's a whole section of people who'll never read the Op-Ed pages, because they don't think politics is for them – but they'll read it if they come across it accidentally, in a glossy magazine. Really, it's the *only* place you should write about politics, if you want to reach as many people as possible. I'm going to say it again – you're a massive idiot.'

So, I stayed – and this collection is the result of that conversation.

To my great relief, I didn't have to give up the fun, joyous stuff – and so half of what follows is getting drunk with Benedict Cumberbatch; boggling over the rainy, catastrophic Queen's Jubilee; hangovers; cystitis; and being quite angry about the utter betraying motherfuck properties of printers. It's reviewing documentaries about David Bowie and falling in love with him all over again; wishing I could wear tights all year round; and sharing all my hard-won advice about dealing with people on the 5:2 Diet.

And the other half is about the wider world, which starts to feel far less abstract, and closer, and more pressing, as you get older: Syria, abortion, welfare, rape, the death of Margaret Thatcher, FGM, sex-work, renewable energy, ironic bigotry, boarding schools, refugees, austerity and inequality. The things which shape the outside world – which seem distant, merely 'issues' – but which at any minute can come into your house, or that of those you love, and blow all their plans away. The stuff we think we can escape when we shut the front door – only to find it has come in through the kitchen window and is sitting on the table, waiting for you. Setting fire to your books, and your calendar, and your life.

And as I collected all these pieces together for this book, I started to see that a lot of what I was saying all seemed to … join up a bit. That these things interconnect – of course they do! Everything in the world is interconnected! The primary point of that Kevin Bacon game was to teach us this! – and that my instinct was to start trying to lay these things out in some form of world view, in which I might make suggestions for how I think things might change.

Basically, I thought it would be cowardly not to. After twenty-three years of commenting on things, you're not really just commenting on things any more. You're starting to … suggest alternatives. You're forming a plan. And once you've thought of the word 'Moranifesto' you know what you have to do. Make a cup of tea, roll up a ciggie, put on David Bowie and play that classic working-class game: 'How I would change the world.'

But alongside this blatant attempt at world domination, this book is a snapshot of where we are now, sixteen years into the new century: what Starbucks *really* is (p. 30), what the Olympics can mean (p. 137), why hipsters should be loved (p. 39), how Lena Dunham's *Girls* changed all the rules of television (p. 252), how bacon rules the Western world (p. 95) and why it's a toss-up between the urethra (p. 249), the legs (p. 27) and the face (p. 171) as to which is the most problematic part of a modern woman's body.

I hope you enjoy reading it. I ate a *lot* of cheese writing it – not that I regret this decision at all. If I have any motto, in my later years, it is 'Never regret the cheese'. *Je Ne Regrette Brie-en.*

MORANIFESTO
part one

'Only a crisis – actual or perceived – produces real change. When that crisis occurs, the actions that are taken depend on the ideas that are lying around. That, I believe, is our basic function. To develop alternatives to existing policies, to keep them alive and available until the politically impossible becomes the politically inevitable' – Milton Friedman

Oh my god, a change is coming – can you feel it?

Of course a change must come! All the signs are there. We have wealth inequality that has returned to Victorian times. We have 50 million refugees across the world – the most people in transit since the Second World War ended. Depending on where you stand on climate change – with, on the one side, the 97 per cent of scientists who say it's a certainty, or, on the other, Donald Trump taking advice from his wig, like the deludo chef with the rat under his hat in *Ratatouille* – you can't argue with the fact that we're demonstrably running out of lions, fish, glaciers and sparrows. I'd like to think they've all just popped down the shops to get the papers and some fags, but I suspect they're kind of … extincting.

With industry in terminal decline in Britain – replaced by financial services and banking – the best contribution the average, low-wage citizen can make to the economy is to get in debt. Hence the lack of willingness to deflate housing prices, and the subsequent huge mortgage payments. And the shift to fees for higher education – thus tying young people into long-term loans. The average *non-mortgage* debt of a British citizen is £10,000 – plus interest. And this huge national debt is a key part of our current economic model. We are now an economy largely based on people *buying money*. It's seen as normal. But it is, of course, incredibly risky behaviour – because if interest rates go up, so will the number of people in financial ruin. This seems like a … bad plan.

And then, of course, there's inequality – the frankly mortifying under-representation of the working classes, women, people of colour and the LGBT community in any seat of power – business, government, finance or media. The under-representation of the *majority* of people, in other words.

Things are … unbalanced. There are too many monopolies and bottlenecks. The spread of power – of ideas – is puckered and lumpy. The upward generational rush of social and economic improvement – the hallmark of the twentieth century – has ended: my children and your children, are, by all indices, set to fare worse than my parents, or your parents. If history has taught us anything, we know that, by necessity, a change will have to come.

Because a change is *always* just about to come. One of the delightful delusions we have as a species is that changes only occur very rarely – and when they do, they are seismic, and sudden. In between these seismic changes, everything is still, and peaceful. Old maids cycle to church, and the thwack of cricket bat on ball, etc., etc.

In reality, change is constant. We are a species that is always on the move – all our civilisations were built on the run. There is no walking pace. There is no rest. Change was happening yesterday, and last year, and now, and tomorrow.

You are, infinitesimally, changing things now, by Tweeting, or drinking Fairtrade tea, or booking a flight, or talking to your child about Equal Marriage – or, more likely, listening to your child tell *you* about Equal Marriage, because your children are often far ahead of you. They cannot remember the past, and they see more of the future, because they will be in it for longer than you. That's why they're posting pieces about teenage coders in Ghana on their Facebook pages, or telling you what 'vontouring' is (don't look it up. It's plastic surgery for your vagina. You don't want to know. Just imagine your flaps looking like the Bride of Wildenstein and leave it at that).

So! A change is coming – and there's no change there. As far as humanity is concerned, change is business as usual.

'Revolution Number 2' – the song the Beatles never wrote

I have heard, in the last five years, the word 'revolution' mentioned more times than I did in the preceding twenty. In protest groups, at meetings and, overwhelmingly, online, I have heard people talking about 'revolution' as if it is a coming thing – a necessary thing. Occupy, Syriza, Podemos, the Arab Spring, the near break-up of the Union during the Scottish Referendum – we slip into talk of revolution easily these days. It's where the heat is. When Russell Brand wrote a book called *Revolution*, it sold over half a million copies, and his interview on *Newsnight* was watched by 11 million people – twice the number who regularly watch *EastEnders*. For a man discussing the overthrow of the entire political system, dismantling multinationals and setting up anarchist collectives! Not even the drunkest gambling addict would have put their money on that in 2000.

Personally, I'm thrilled with the current modishness of 'revolution', because I like the word 'revolution'. It's my third favourite, after 'cathedral' and 'shagreen'.

But, I should make clear, I like the word 'revolution' as defined in the *second* entry in the dictionary, and not the first.

The dictionary's first definition of 'revolution' is: 'Rebellion, revolt, insurrection, mutiny, uprising, riot, insurgency, overthrow, seizure of power, regime change, anarchy, disorder.'

Personally, I'm not up for that. The kind of people who are up for mutinies, and riots, tend to be young men – the kind for whom an afternoon of being kettled by 600 Metropolitan policemen before breaking free and wanging a brick through the window of Greggs feels like a life-affirming alternative to sports.

I, however, am a forty-year-old woman with very inferior running abilities and two children. I don't like riots. I don't like anarchy. I've read enough history books to be resoundingly unkeen on extreme politics of either the left *or* the right, breakdowns in society, anarchy, overthrows, seizures of power and disorder. They tend to work out badly for women and children. They tend to work out badly for *everyone*.

My general rule of thumb is that you're always a *little* bit closer to the conditions that led to the outbreak of the Second World War than you think you are – which is why I'm all for political and economic stability, non-tumultuous cultural change, the bins continuing to be being emptied on time, etc., etc.

I like order. I like calm. I like not Googling 'how to get/hide gun cache in case of break-down of society'.

That's why the revolution *I* like is the second dictionary definition: 'Revolution: sea change, metamorphosis, transformation, innovation, regrouping, reorientation.'

Now that's a revolution I can get behind – metamorphosis. Sea change. A revolution that sounds like the moment *The Wizard of Oz* goes from black and white into colour; Cinderella's ball gown appearing around her in a blaze of Fairy Godmother magic. Not upheaval, but an *upgrade*. Even the most entrenched conservative would find it difficult to argue with the idea of a notable upgrade to the way we do things. Capitalism has been the defining political movement of my age – but it's not really gone through a thoughtful, planned improvement in my lifetime.

By way of contrast, I've lived through ten OS upgrades on my Mac – and that's just something I use to buy playsuits from Topshop. com, and piss around on Twitter. Capitalism is, surely, due an upgrade or two. Snow Leopard capitalism. Yosemite capitalism. Isn't that the fundamental point of capitalism, anyway? Of competition and markets? Constant product improvement and more choice? It's kind of weird that, under market-led capitalism, we can get 300 different kinds of latte but only one kind of market-led capitalism, with all the main political parties save the Greens peddling pretty much the same basic model.

It's almost as if the current political system doesn't see itself. It just believes it exists – that it sprang fully formed, via evolution, as the natural way of things. It doesn't see itself as so many others do, as something that was constructed by human beings – fallible, faulty human beings – and so therefore could be changed by human beings. We don't even really have a *name* for this current economic and political system – to call it 'neo-liberal capitalism' is seen as an inherently left-wing labelling; it marks you out as, well, a Marxist. And when you can't even *name* a system, you can't have a conversation about it – which is proven by the general confusion, and feeling of being tongue-tied, in most voters when they discuss how things are, and how they'd like them to change. When you live in a social and economic system that is presented merely as *the* system, you prevent people from naming and inventing new ones.

But we do need to start talking about new systems. This restless feeling – that's what it is.

So, we're due an upgrade. What would this upgrade be? Where will this upgrade come from?

Well, it's us. If we're talking about a basic upgrade of the operating system of the Earth, there's one huge, untapped resource which would allow a light-speed jump in progress – and it's us. *We* are the big, obvious resource of our age.

And we are the key and unique resource of our age – for, in all of history until now, most of our processing power has gone to waste. Unless a brilliant mind was born into the fortunate circumstances of a) being male b) not dying of a terrible disease before the age of three c) being able to afford education and d) being in a social situation – usually predicated by location and wealth – which enabled him to disseminate these ideas, then, without that, all this potential died with its owner.

This, then, is the ultimate argument for the urgency and necessity of equality. For equality isn't some fabulous luxury we treat ourselves to when we're rich enough – the legislation and infrastructure we get round to *after* we secure our economies, or wrangle our foreign policy. Equality isn't humanity's cashmere bed socks. It's not a present we treat ourselves to, like champagne. It's a fundamental necessity, like water.

In the twenty-first century, humanity's greatest resource isn't oil, or titanium, or water, or gold: it's brains. It's people's brains. The reason the more unequal countries are so troubled is, to be brusque, because they are more stupid. They disregard their female population – thereby halving their potential brainpower – and then limit themselves to a problem-solving elite made up of a tiny percentage of the remaining 50 per cent.

And so while we keep these billions of tons of brains offline, we put humanity in an illogically difficult position. By believing some people are naturally superior, we make our species, as a whole, inferior. Weaker. To be frank: stupider.

And this weakness extends into our politics. The 'poli' in politics, the 'demo' in democracy – they both mean 'people', and that's what's currently missing. Us. Despite all the hot talk of revolution, when it comes to voter turnout the problem of apathy is rampant. Even with the highest voter turnout since 1997, over 40 per cent of young voters (18–25) did not vote in the last UK election – arguably the demographic that should be most politically engaged, as the business of politics is inventing the future *they* are going to live in.

And just as huge swathes of the population are missing at the polling booth, so they are in Westminster. Out of 650 constituencies, just 191 are represented by women.

Britain's non-white population is also seriously under-represented – just forty-one MPs to represent 13 per cent of the British population. And when it comes to working-class representation in Westminster, 33 per cent went to private schools (compared to 7 per cent of the population).

Out of 260 new candidates in 2015, forty-seven had previously been 'consultants', twenty-nine barristers and nineteen journalists. Sometimes, on bad days, it does seem that, if you have the right 200 people in your social circle, you've got a roughly 50/50 chance of being the next Prime Minister.

However you look at it, that's not a wide, healthily diverse mix coming into Westminster as fresh blood, and bringing in new conversations and ideas.

And little wonder we have such a small, incestuous slice of the population representing us – for politics has been terribly devalued. These days, if your child announced that they wanted to be a politician most people would react as if they had come down to the breakfast table and said, 'Mother, Father – I've decided to become a massive pervert.'

Our default belief is that politicians are venal, shifty, double-dealing liars, out to serve the interests of their friends and business associates. It's hard for an honourable man, woman or asexual to say that they wish to run for government without instantly being suspected of slight … evil. And that is, to use the scientific phrase, balls. There's no point in us *having* a democracy if we distrust everyone who wants to engage with it officially. If, in the very act of trying to gain power, you lose the trust of the people you wish to represent. That by wanting to stand for something you are presumed to be standing only for yourself.

There, the entire notion of being a public servant – a key tenet of the modern age – fails.

So: the problems are, as it stands, who engages in politics and what they do. That the idea of politics has become threadbare and dirty; the debates clownish and offputtingly pugilistic; the participants limited and lacklustre. The system's borked.

The good news is, we have a billion ways to improve it. Us. For we are the point of democracy. We *are* democracy. We are the conversation. We are the climate. We set the tone – we make the spaces where conversations turn into ideas, which then turn into action. We are the drivers – not just at the polling booth, every five years, but in the choices we make every day in what we buy, what we eat, the language we use, the ideas we share, the comments we make and the connections we make across the world.

In many ways, culture and society are a billion times bigger than politics. The coming of the internet – and the rapid surge towards everyone being connected and being able to talk to each other – means there is a whole other world of power, influence and knowledge operating independently from the conventional old institutions of power, knowledge and influence – Westminster, Holyrood, Stormont, universities, the City, the media – and on a vastly larger scale.

In many ways, social media already *is* the media, and in a way that can only accelerate as the years go on – even the biggest news organisation in the world, the BBC, has only 3,500 employees. Facebook and Twitter, on the other hand, have 1.3 billion between them: 1.3 billion reporters, photographers, hackers, opinion writers. These days, we both receive *and* broadcast. There is no such thing as a passive audience any more. We all wish to have our say – whether our 'say' is a 6,000-word blog entry, or just the simple act of intellectual dissemination and approval that is pressing 'Like', or 'Re-Tweet'. I enjoy bringing Karl Marx into conversations, so I'll just point out that, in this respect, the internet is Marxist: it has seized the means of production – producing news – but *only* because monolithic capitalistic multinational corporations like Google, Facebook and Twitter have enabled it in the first place. There's a pleasingly knotty paradox for the next time you've had three gins.

Look at one of the biggest stories on social media in the last year: racism in the USA. By all accounts, white cops have been beating and shooting black citizens for years – and the reporting of it by mainstream media was cursory and short-lived. Twenty years after the savage beating of Rodney King, these incidents were still being presented on TV and in newspapers as isolated events.

In 2015, however, social media took on this story and made it huge. It set the climate. Advances in technology mean that people have been able to film violent incidents, and finally show the world what is happening. Activists blog, start hashtag campaigns – #blacklivesmatter, #icantbreathe – and even in the simple act of re-Tweeting these stories, the topic has been pushed to the forefront of the news agenda, and stayed there all year. Questions about racism in America are now being asked in a way that has become pressing and urgent. In a recent poll, 53 per cent of Americans said they believed that racism had become worse in the last five years. No. It's just that we're *talking* about racism more. We're finally *seeing* it – in iPhone footage posted to blogs, of white, armed cops pinning down crying fourteen-year-old black teenage girls in bikinis, crying for their mothers; in Eric Garner in a chokehold, saying his last words: 'I can't breathe'.

Many of the things I will be discussing under the heading of politics are, in fact, cultural, social and technological. Society and culture often marches faster, and longer, and harder, than politics. They frequently effect change fastest, and in the coolest way possible.

One of my favourite examples is that of *Doctor Who*. Russell T. Davies convinces the BBC to revive *Doctor Who*, because he loves it. Into the first series he writes in a character, Captain Jack Harkness, who is a hot, charismatic, pan-sexual super-hero. Essentially a Han Solo who'll do it with anyone.

In one episode, he kisses the Doctor, full on the lips. This is a prime-time BBC show – screened at teatime – watched by families. Not only was there not one letter of complaint, but on Monday morning, in my children's playground at school, there were ten-year-old boys fighting to play the role of Captain Jack in their *Doctor Who* games.

Now, that's something that, with the best will in the world, no piece of legislation, or Equalities Minister, could have achieved – making ten-year-old boys think bisexual super-heroes are cool. Not overnight. Not without any arguments. Not done entirely with love, and fuelled with joy, and almost as a by-product of a show that wanted to entertain, dazzle; make you laugh and cry and gasp.

I can draw a fairly straight line between that kiss in *Doctor Who* in 2007 and the passing of the 2013 Marriage (Same Sex Couples) Act in the UK – for what elected representative can vote against human rights for a section of the population that their children, and grandchildren, totally accept?

So much of the groundwork for change is done simply through human creativity, joy and a willingness to consider future and parallel worlds. The BBC made that show, and we watched it, and in a small way – while we were at play, while we were *happy* – the world was changed.

For the first time ever, thanks to the explosion of social media, the world can talk to the world – unmediated. Information known by one person can be shared around the world in less than an hour – as evidenced by WikiLeaks. Voices that previously would never have been heard can lead the debate – as happened in the UK with the Daughters of Eve anti-FGM campaign that led to changes in legislation.

Through the internet of the world, we have, finally, gained a global sentience that was unthinkable even in the era of the satellite phone link-up, or the fax. Someone, observing the Earth from space, would have noticed that, since social media opened up the skies, conversations and introductions and information and networks have lit up the globe with a trillion golden skeins. The whole world is firing up, like a teenage brain – burning neural pathways across the globe, making connections, expanding, leaping. Previous spiritual, or religious, notions of a collective human consciousness now look like simple predictions of the future. We are now in a collective consciousness. That's the ultimate purpose of the internet. Oh my God. I'm going to have a fag.

THE TWENTY-FIRST CENTURY, WHERE WE LIVE

So! Let's get started. *As the philosophers Roxette said, so eloquently, 'Don't bore us – get to the chorus.' Let's begin with …*

… a scientifically- provable, universal truth.

NO ONE WANTS TO GO OUT

We're sitting on the sofa with the kids, watching *You've Been Framed*. I haven't seen the show for years. Coming to it fresh, it seems to be an unspeakable montage of horrific testicular injuries, and unstable toddlers being terrified by massive dogs. All I can see is pain, and fear. It's like some awful illustration of the fragility of human existence. With rewinds. The children are laughing at it, joyously.

'He fell!' Nancy gurgles. 'On his head!'

'What time is it?' my husband asks, staring at the screen.

'Nearly six,' I reply. 'We should start getting ready.'

The babysitter is due – we're both going out tonight. My husband is off to see the KPM Allstars Big Band – a collection of TV theme-tune composers who gig four or five times a year, rolling out all their big hits: *Countdown*, *Grange Hill*, *Dave Allen at Large*, *Channel 4 News*. Apparently, last time they played everyone sang along to the *Channel 4 News* theme, with the spontaneously composed lyrics of 'Channel 4/Channel 4/Channel 4/Channel 4/Channel 4/NEWS!'

I, meanwhile, am going to a gay club in Vauxhall where – if it's anything like the last time I went – I will end up soaked in sweat, dancing to Azealia Banks with a bearded man in a rubber dress, margined on gin.

We have both chosen our nights out to cater exactly to our interests and desires. These nights have been on the calendar for months. They are our rewards for being hard-working employees and parents.

'I don't want to go,' my husband says.

'Neither do I,' I say.

We continue sitting on the sofa.

'I'm really tired,' my husband says, piteously.

'Vauxhall is so far away,' I weep. 'It's practically in France.'

There is a pause. A man falls off a chalet roof and crumples his thoracic vertebrae. The kids scream with laughter.

'The thing is,' I say, 'no one ever wants to go out.'

My husband nods sadly.

'No one ever wants to go out,' I continue. 'At the point when you write down the night out in your calendar, that's the most excited you'll ever be about it. After that, every day that passes, you become a little less enthusiastic about the whole endeavour. This reaches its finite point on the morning of the night out itself, when you wake up to find that the engagement is lying across your face like the body of a dead horse. It is like a warning. A terrible, terrible warning.'

'Why have I put something in my life in the slot where I would usually be having a hot bath, and a bowl of cereal, then watching BBC4?' Pete says, miserably. 'What was I thinking I would achieve? Something better than that? There's *nothing* better than that. I have made a terrible error, vis-à-vis the other side's grass.'

I think back over my social life. One of the most enjoyable drunken nights I've ever had with my friend Grace was both of us admitting we'd spent the whole afternoon wishing the other one would cancel.

'I was sitting at home, going, "She's not had cystitis for ages. That bitch must be due a bout by now." I was praying you'd got it. Not in a bad way,' she clarified, as we ordered more drinks, and stayed out until 3am.

I found her feelings perfectly understandable. Once, a hen-night I was due to go on was cancelled with five hours' notice. I think it might actually be the best phone call of my life. I spent the evening watching reruns of *Come Dine with Me* – chuckling in the way that Wile E. Coyote does when he feels he's got one over on the Roadrunner. I felt like a winner. A social engagement-less winner.

I'm sure that this universal feeling – sleepy 4pm dread over seeing 'the guys' at 8pm – is why adults rely on alcohol. It's not for the booze. We don't really care about the booze. It's for the sugar, instead. We need the calories – for energy. City nights are essentially full of massive, tired, thirty-something bees, drinking shots of boozy sugar, for the rush. Until we get stuck against a window, buzzing, and have to be herded into taxis by bouncers wielding rolled-up newspapers. We are bees. And bees should sleep when it's dark. It's all wrong.

The babysitter arrives, bang on time. I go, wearily, to backcomb my hair. I should never have said yes to this night out.

5.30am. I get into bed – hair standing on end, eyes pointing in different directions. I think my nightie might be on backwards. Pete wakes.

'Good night?' he asks.

'Yes!' I say. I am flying. I have laughed so much I am practically mute with hoarseness. 'We danced in the pouring rain, I've gone deaf, and a gay man pretended to have sex with me while I queued up for my coat. You?'

'They played *Grandstand* three times,' he says, happily. 'We went right down the front and pumped our fists to the brass bits – I *think* non-ironically.'

'I love a great night out,' I say.

'A great night out,' Pete agrees.

I like a binge. I'm a classic binge-drinker – nothing for two weeks then HELLO GIN. I can get through half a kilo of cheese in an evening; I apply my eyeliner using a roller. And when I like a song, it becomes an almost medical problem.

I CAN'T STOP LISTENING TO 'GET LUCKY'

I'm listening to 'Get Lucky' right now. Don't be scared. It's totally safe. I am absolutely capable of both working and listening to 'Get Lucky' without any impairment to my faculties. This is because, for the last three weeks, I've been doing *everything* while listening to 'Get Lucky' – working, parenting, cooking, being drunk. My iTunes informs me I've listened to it 113 times. It's taken over my life. I'd call for help, but it's the happiest I've been since Amy Winehouse's 'Back To Black' came out in 2006. Eventually, I listened to that 427 times. To be sure.

Here is my 'Get Lucky' addiction diary. They said I would need to write a full confessional, before I went to rehab. Apparently it helps, with the 'problem'.

Day I of 'Get Lucky'. 19 April. My husband comes into the kitchen, looking a little bit shocked, and says, 'The new Daft Punk single's been uploaded to YouTube. It sounds like it might be … utterly perfect.'

As he's a rock critic, I'm used to him coming in and making dramatic pronouncements like this over things I subsequently find to be absolute and utter balls. He once said this about a song called 'I'm Considering A Move To Memphis' by the Colorblind James Experience which was so awful, I took it out of the CD player and threw it out of the window. We both watched as a street cleaner then ran it over.

'I'm not sorry about that,' I said, just to make things clear. 'I am not sorry about that *at all*.'

Anyway, he plays me 'Get Lucky' to, initially, a reception of absolute indifference. By the end, however, even I can see it was quite good.

'That's a good rip-off of disco legends Chic,' I say.

'That's because Nile Rodgers from disco legends Chic is playing guitar on it,' he replies.

And that was the first time I listened to 'Get Lucky'.

Day 2 of 'Get Lucky'. I see some friends discussing 'Get Lucky' on Twitter. 'I can't stop playing it,' one says.

'I think it might be perfect,' the other replies.

Prompted by this second, intriguing reference to its 'perfection', I go on Spotify, press play and – THE WHOLE WORLD EXPLODES.

Within seconds, it becomes apparent that the initial listen to 'Get Lucky' acts by way of a massive decoy. Because that's when they *get you*. While you're busily, self-importantly going, 'Meh meh meh it sounds like Chic!' with your stupid music-expert face on, Daft Punk reduce down to the size of nanobots, fly as vapour up your nose, access your nervous system and lay 6,000 tiny, invisible disco-mines right up your spine.

Subsequently, the second – and, indeed, the following million – times you listen to 'Get Lucky', the disco-mines all trigger, one after another, in a white-out chain of hooks, off-beat mis-footings and melody. You've got adrenalin and oxytocin and Nile Rodgers going off all *over* the shop. It's like the 4th of July. You have *never* felt this warm inside.

And the minute it ends, you suddenly feel cold and shaky – like you need to put it back on again *right away*. Or else you'll just shiver and freeze to death, right here, in the kitchen.

Of course, at that point I don't how *many* times I will need to listen to it again, in order to regain my normal body temperature. I thought it might be one of those 'five times in a row and then you're done' jobs. Like 'Milkshake' by Kelis.

Seventeen times later – that is *one hour and eight minutes* of solidly listening to 'Get Lucky' – I realise I am in trouble. I take to Twitter to voice my concern for me.

'I wonder at what point I'll get "Get Lucky" poisoning, and die?' I ask, morosely, while still – of course – chair-dancing to the song at the same time.

Terrifyingly, my timeline instantly turns into some kind of makeshift emergency helpline – full of wide-eyed, sweaty people admitting to being similarly, utterly, disabled by their obsession with 'Get Lucky'.

My friend Robin has a particularly bad case of 'Get Lucky': 'For the first three days after it came out, I sat around in my pants doing amyl to it, over and over,' he admitted. In common with all people discussing their profound powerlessness in the face of 'Get Lucky', he also sounds deliriously happy about this fact.

Day 13 of 'Get Lucky'. So far, I've only heard 'Get Lucky' playing on the tiny speakers of a laptop, or a taxi. Tonight, however, I go to the after-show party for the *Star Trek* premiere, where the DJ 'drops' it, just after midnight.

In my life I have, of course, seen rooms 'go off'. I was, after all, of a generation to be a terrified onlooker in the corner of Acid House, murmuring, 'This is all a bit sweaty. Can't we sit down and have a nice chat, instead?'

Unlike those days, however, this is not a room full of scallies boxed off their minky on wobbly eggs. Instead, it's filled with incredibly famous people, in very expensive outfits, who've just had two drinks. And they go *nuts* when the song comes on – they absolutely *lose* it. It's the first time I've ever seen people properly *cheer* a song. Shouting 'HURRAH!' – literally the word 'HURRAH!' – and dancing in a manner so joyous, it recalls Snoopy capering on the roof of his kennel. Everyone is dancing *at* each other – everyone is as happy as they've ever been in their lives. This is an Olympic level of communal bonding. I'm watching Captain Kirk dancing to 'Get Lucky'. I *am* the legend of the phoenix! I'm going to have nine more drinks! I'm up ALL NIGHT TO GET LUCKY!

Day 14 of 'Get Lucky'. Terrifying hangover. Hot sweats. Play 'Get Lucky', in lieu of codeine. Start to wonder what would happen if you could actually eat 'Get Lucky'. Surely, you would poo out sleek, gleaming disco panthers. Disco panthers, wearing glitterballs as earrings. That is the 'legend' the phoenix was talking about. The pooing out of the disco panthers.

As I float the idea of disco panthers on Twitter, people keep asking me if I've seen the Alan Partridge/Peter Serafinowicz tributes to 'Get Lucky'. I watch them. My hangover instantly deepens – into vicious fear. Yes, these are very funny videos. These are very funny indeed. But when people have to make their own *films* to cope with how obsessed they are with a song, the general impression is of mankind being gradually overwhelmed by a force it cannot control. I begin to wonder, darkly, if society will ever recover from 'Get Lucky'.

Day 21 of 'Get Lucky'. My husband finds me on the internet, researching musicology blogs that rigorously, nerdishly analyse the composition of 'Get Lucky' in order to work out why it's so catchy. I am, of course, listening to 'Get Lucky' as I do this.

'Pete,' I say. 'Do you know why you feel like you have to keep listening to 'Get Lucky'? Apparently it's because it's in a minor key – thus giving the feeling of dissatisfaction and irresolution – and it uses alternating syncopation of bass, guitar, lyric and melody to provide a hook *every 3.75 seconds*! We could *never* have resisted those kinds of stats. NEVER! "Get Lucky" was always going to win!'

Pete looks at me. I'm very pale. I'm twitching as I listen to 'Get Lucky'. During my speech to him I've had to break off a couple of times in order to mouth along to key lyrics – *'Up all night til the sun'*, *'Up all night for good fun'*, and the falsetto bit on *'So let's raise the bar/ And our cups/To the stars'*.

'Cate,' he says. 'This is like 'Back To Black' again. You need to get out of the house. I'm taking you to the park.'

He puts me in the car and we drive towards Regent's Park. He puts on a song that is not 'Get Lucky' – 'No, no, love – it's not called "Not Get Lucky". This is Pentangle.'

Slowly, I start to adjust to life outside of 'Get Lucky'. The sun is out. This song is rather wonderful. I have listened to 'Get Lucky' 113 times in three weeks. That is probably enough, now. I should probably stop.

As we drive down Kentish Town Road, I start to feel the warm afterglow of the song finally leaving my system. Like some brief, incredibly sexually intense affair, me and 'Get Lucky' have now burned out, leaving me, yes, changed forever – but also filled with good memories. I will now move on. I wish 'Get Lucky' nothing but good luck.

As we approach the crossing by Royal College Street, I see, on the right, a girl and her boyfriend, waiting to cross the road. She's dancing on the spot, and singing 'Get Lucky' at him. I can tell this, even from 100 yards away.

Scrambling across Pete with all the urgency of an asphyxia victim, I wind down his window.

'*I'M UP ALL NIGHT TO GET LUCKY!*' I scream at her.

'I'M UP ALL NIGHT TO GET LUCKY!' she screams back at me. We beam at each other, in pure joy. She keeps dancing.

We are as one. We've come too far to give up who we are. We're up all night to get lucky.

BUT! You might be thinking. A catchy pop song is all very well – but where are the politics? When are you doing to do The Serious? And in many ways, that starts now – with tights.

THE LEG SEASON

I read something a couple of weeks ago that put a dent in my normally jaunty stride.

'At the end of April, it's officially NO MORE TIGHTS UNTIL OCTOBER', a fashion column instructed. 'It's time to GET THOSE LEGS OUT, LADIES.'

There then followed a guide for preparing for GETTING YOUR LEGS OUT if you're a LADY – the scrubs, fake tans, leg make-up and pedicures that would prepare one for The Leg Season. A Leg Season that, as a woman, one is supposed to look forward to – as if you were a farmer finally able to let your livestock (legs) out of their winter barns, to gallop freely upon the newly meadowed fields, in the sun. Your time of leg imprisonment is over! This is what your legs have been waiting for! It's a great time to be a lady!

What The Leg Season means in reality, of course, is 'The Women Being Half Naked Until Hallowe'en Season', and I have to say it put me into a terrible gloom. As I pulled on my tights that morning, I said to them, sadly, 'Soon I will say farewell to you until Hallowe'en, when I put on my Mummy Mummy costume (normal outfit, but with a whole loo-roll wrapped round my head), and go Trick or Treating. Oh God! I shall miss you! Don't forget me!'

Perhaps I am a simple, fearful creature, but I love tights. I love putting them on in the morning: placing my legs in a place of safety and warmth (inside the tights) so I don't have to worry about them again for the rest of the day (because they're inside the tights). I like the way the tights prevent me flashing my knickers at people, if the wind blows up my skirt. I like the way they cover my skin, so I don't have to worry about my skin, and I like the way they mean the bottom half of my body isn't completely naked. Is this weird? Is it weird to want clothes on the bottom half of your body?

'Men don't have to worry about this shit,' I thought, sadly counting down the days until I had to GET MY LEGS OUT. 'Imagine if, at a certain time of year, men had to stop wearing trousers for the next five months. If everywhere they went, people were going, 'No more trousers for YOU after next week! LET YOUR SEXY MAN-LEGS OUT! PREP YOUR CALVES! START WORRYING ABOUT FLASHING YOUR BOLLOCKS WHEN YOU SIT DOWN ON A CHAIR, OR CLIMB OVER A FENCE!'

Minute for minute, I would boldly state that legs are the most problematic body part of a woman – which is quite the claim, given that they vie for this honorific with the womb (exploding blood bag of insanity and pain), the breasts (wibbly wobbly magnets for harassment, will regularly hurt for no reason) and the face (oh God, where to start: acne? Blotchiness? Your nose suddenly looking like your granddad's?).

My legs are a problem for me. Due to my genetic inheritance, they have the thin, pale-blue skin of my Celtic peasant forebears – who, incidentally, never had to worry about Naked Leg Season, as they were perpetually up to their withers in rotting potatoes and mud, which is not something any rational person should be jealous of – and yet, I am.

If I shave or wax my legs, I get what I like to refer to as 'Leg Pox' – a horrible rash that takes almost *exactly* the same amount of time to die away as the regrowth of the leg hair takes to come back in. 'Hairy – or blotchy?' Those are my leg choices – save for a two-day window where there is neither hair nor blotch, and they are, without fail, rainy days, where I am wearing jeans anyway.

The way I see it, my legs are essentially an internal organ – they can peaceably get on with their job (jaunty striding) so long as they are kept safe from wind, rain, razors, hot wax and the scrutiny of the human gaze. Really, I might as well be epilating my liver and walking it down Oxford Street for all the good it does my legs, my peace of mind and the pleasure of onlookers to take part in Leg Season. Some women just *cannot* get their legs out. It depresses us too much. You know when women sometimes call in sick, on hot summer days, with 'asthmatic hay fever'? Fifty per cent of them actually have 'asthmatic blotchy-leg fever', instead. They've started hyperventilating, just from looking at their sad, naked, inexplicably purple legs. When the weather turns and they can put some slacks on, they'll be back in the office – guiltily brandishing an untouched inhaler.

Anyway. Yesterday, I had a breakthrough. I suddenly realised what was going on: 'Whoever came up with the idea of "getting your legs out" is a fucking lunatic who just likes getting *their* legs out,' I thought. 'They don't own *my* legs. I've spent twenty summers walking around in 60 denier black M&S tights and a pair of shorts, it was extremely pleasant, and I'm not going to stop now. I'm unionising my legs. ONE IN ALL IN. In tights.'

We will get to the revolution – but I'm seeing this bit as the kind of 'easing-in' part of the book. You know. We're just hanging a bit. Chilling. Chatting. Having a coffee.

THE REAL PURPOSE OF STARBUCKS

This is the true and real story of Starbucks in Britain – 1998 to the present day.

When it first arrived in this country, Starbucks smelled of Seattle's cold Pacific air, and internet start-ups, and the cast of *Friends* – mainly Chandler. Each branch felt like a podule dropped down on the world by the Sexy Future People: 'Yeah, just getting my latte,' we would say to ourselves – thinking it sounded the equivalent of 'Just getting my keys to the CITY OF FUCK YOU, CAVEMEN. I HAVE A SILVER TWENTY-THIRD CENTURY CAPE'.

In 2001, I took my twelve-year-old brother Jimmy to the branch on Clink Street – overlooking the Thames, next to the pirate lines of the *Golden Hind*. It was a time when Starbucks' interior of blond wood floors, burgundy armchairs and grainy black and white pictures of Guatemalan coffee-bean pickers defined that new 'urban luxe' thing.

Down from Wolverhampton for the day, Jimmy was open-mouthed by the room. He'd never been to a restaurant, or hotel, before – he'd never sat in an armchair, or been served a drink.

Sipping his cappuccino, staring out at the cold, hard, oily Thames, he had an onrush of caffeine, and future-vision.

'I'm going to go to Cambridge University,' he said, with sudden resolution. 'Then I'm going to move down to London, and live opposite this Starbucks.'

Reader: he did.

In 2001, Starbucks was inspiring. You wanted one in your town. You yearned to see their logo on the motorway. Their thick white cup in your hand felt comforting. It made you feel carefree, and clever. No one was going to go to a tiny net-curtained café and buy a 50p cup of tea off a nan ever, ever again. Starbucks' roiling green mermaid was our sexy hero muse. She was going to take us into the future.

In 2013, however, it's all changed. No one fancies the Starbucks mermaid any more. In the ten years that have passed, Starbucks has come to mean something very different. It's 'Starfucks' now – enemy of the people, grubby from having paid only £8.6 million in tax over fourteen years of trading in the UK. A PR disaster in a time of austerity. There are protests in their branches – sit-ins with placards and leaflets.

Its tattered image matches its interiors. The armchairs are shabby, the blond floors weary. Somehow, unfailingly, amazingly, every branch has a toilet that is malfunctioning – the heavy orange-scented spray Starbucks use almost, but not quite, covering the pooey with hooey. To walk in is to be spritzed by a miasma of caffeine-triggered toilet troubles and synthetic citrus. And – after ten years of drinking coffee – Britain has discovered the most fatal truth of all: Starbucks coffee is not good. In fact, it's awful. Some acrid wartime siege-brew of burnt acorns and mud. Shamingly, McDonald's do better. Shamingly, one-button machines in petrol stations do better.

So if Starbucks isn't the future any more, what is it? What are these 650 supposedly unprofitable branches spreckled across Britain?

This: in 2013, Starbucks is basically a slightly shabby council facility. Look around one now and it resembles a drop-in centre from 1989. Loitering youths flicking milkshake off their straws at each other. Groups of weary mothers breastfeeding ham-faced babies. Someone who, on closer examination, you realise is probably homeless, trying to be as inconspicuous as possible with the smallest cup, at the tiniest table for one.

Starbucks has turned into our 'third space': more accessible to the community than pubs used to be. Superior to libraries in that they have cake and music. In the centre of town – unlike the dwindling supply of actual drop-in centres, at the rainy end of the bus route. Where else is there to go, on a wet day, if you only have three pounds in your pocket and want to meet a friend? Those independent coffee shops are always so tiny. You feel guilty hogging a table for two hours with your laptop. You cannot let your toddler wander around somewhere with lovely vintage tablecloths dangling. But the beauty of Starbucks is that you feel you can exploit its big, global-chain space a bit. No one ever worried they were taking advantage of a place with 20,366 outlets. Starbucks can take the hit. Starbucks is a bit ... abuseable.

But the main thing about Starbucks, in 2013, is that half-covered toilet smell. Because now 50 per cent of Britain's public toilets have closed – Manchester has a single one left – this is Starbucks' unspoken, primary purpose: they are our new, national public toilets. Who has not spent a pound (black filter coffee – the cheapest one) in order to spend a penny? Who has not – child wailing 'I'm desperate!' – seen a Starbucks at the end of the street and thought, not 'coffee!', but 'cubicle!' Perhaps this was Starbucks' reasoning behind skipping that tax: they are not a coffee chain, now, but a public utility. You can't tax a public utility.

So that is the story of Starbucks in 2013. A business that, were we allowed to go to the toilet in the street, like poodles, might fold within a fortnight.

And all that oppression I was talking about at the beginning? All the minorities who are looked down upon, and belittled? Well, I will come to the defence of all of them. Even the hipsters.

IN DEFENCE OF HIPSTERS

There was a report last week which I looked at for a bit, and went, 'Yeah, yeah – that definitely wins the "Most 2013" report of 2013.'

NBCnews.com ran a story about how animal sanctuaries, from California to New York, are being 'over-run' by pet chickens – 'dumped' when their urban hipster owners 'can't cope' with them any more.

'They're put on Craigslist all the time when they don't lay any more,' said Nation Shelter director Susie Coston. Who was, to be clear, talking about the chickens – not the hipsters.

Mary Britton Clouse, who runs the Chicken Run Rescue in Minneapolis, concurred: 'It's the stupid foodies,' she said, presumably surrounded by sad-looking chickens. 'We're just sick to death of it.'

Now it may be that while you, as a *Times* reader, know perfectly well what 'a chicken' is, you may *not* be totally clear as to what 'a hipster' is. You may be too busy running an international conglomerate, finessing government policy, or writing an angry letter about the call of the cuckoo to the letters page.

Allow me to thumbnail for you. Hipsters are, currently, one of the most reviled sub-species in the Western world. Have you seen one? In all probability, yes. For instance, if you have, recently, seen a young gentleman walking around with a beard that looks like a badger stapled to his chin, wearing a pair of deck shoes in an 'ironic' manner and playing Robin Thicke's 'Blurred Lines' on a tiny ukulele with an expression on his face that says, 'Yes! I'm playing Robin Thicke on a ukulele! Can you handle this level of archness?' – then that was not, as you thought, an attention-seeking lunatic who'd recently seen all his *proper* clothes and shaving gear burned to the ground, in a fire, and was in the throes of a nervous breakdown, but a hipster instead.

This 'Festival Missed Connections' advert – on hipster music online Pitchfork – gives an even more poignantly accurate insight into the working modes of hipsters: 'During Waxahatchee on the Blue Stage you were eating vegan Vietnamese food out of a little container. I was the girl in the overalls with the rainbow bikini top, French braid and braces. Hope to hear from you.'

Perhaps, after reading this, you feel that you, too, are now the kind of person who would – along with the creators of the 'I Hate Hipsters' Tumblr – happily spend half an hour imagining the best way to kill the hipster that has just moved their sit-up-and-beg bicycle, and soon-to-be-abandoned chicken, into your apartment block (maybe dying under a landslide of ironic vintage t-shirts in Beyond Retro – the *ultimate* ironic death).

But! Actually! No! For I would like to speak out on *behalf* of the hipster! I wish to defend them in the cultural kangaroo court they find themselves dragged into. I will answer all charges thus:

1) **'This wearing of second-hand ironic clothing, particularly the t-shirts – this is annoying. A childless mustachioed 26-year-old media studies graduate drinking cocktails out of a jam jar in a pop-up Peruvian diner in Shoreditch, while wearing a "Super Dad" t-shirt? NO! STOP!'** But come on – no one *else* is going to wear that t-shirt. No one *else* has use for it. This is the First World equivalent of you and your favela scavenging for used batteries and bottle tops off a teetering city dump. Ironic hipster t-shirts are the bottom-line reality of the necessity of recycling. Without them we would drown in 'Hurrah for Benjamin's Bar-Mitzvah!' t-shirts, which *we* would be compelled to wear in all seriousness. The system is better this way.

2) **'They keep hens in one-bedroom flats in Hackney. This is both impractical, and done for effect.'** But Lord Byron kept a bear

and an eagle at Cambridge and we think *he's* a total legend. We've got to have a consistent viewpoint on young, drug-addled people keeping pets in unsuitable locations. Otherwise it's just not fair.

3) **'Hipsters ruin all music by claiming that they were into it before you.'** You know what – they probably were. And thank God. After all, *someone* has to go out there and forage for new bands, in horrible clubs, in the middle of nowhere, at 1am, and subsequently make them famous enough for me to simply listen to them on Magic FM in a minicab instead. I'm perfectly happy for hipsters to put in all that vexatious spadework, in exchange for a bit of ZERO FINANCIAL GAIN smugness afterwards. This is the cultural eco-system. Hipsters aerate the rock-Earth. They pollinate Pitchfork. They do … whatever it is that wasps do. Let them carry on. It is Mother Nature's plan.

4) **'I'm sorry, I still want to kill them with a suitably old-fashioned retro-agricultural implement – such as they will have reverently-yet-ironically put on the wall of their local coffee shop. Maybe a thresher, hay baler, or scythe.'** Oh, come now! This makes us sound, frankly, spoiled. How jaded have we become that we cannot enjoy the sight of a young man with a handlebar moustache wearing a Second World War flying helmet and riding a penny-farthing to the Apple Store with a very self-conscious expression? How can we – P.G. Wodehouse fans – love Bertie Wooster, but not a hipster? Let's face it – having a go at hipsters is just basically picking on well-meaning young people trying to be different – as all young people are wont to do. 'Ah,' you reply. 'But I don't really *hate* them. I don't *actually* want them to die. I'm just being a bit sarky and ironic about it, because, to be honest, I'm a bit bored.' Well, if that is the case, my friend, I must inform you that 'being a bit sarky and ironic because you're bored' is a *classic* hipster trope, and suggests you are desperately trying to crush the tiny unicycle-riding hipster inside *you*.

The thing is, if you hang out with hipsters, drinking ironic cocktails – 'Death of a Cucumber Salesman' – from jam jars, you will, eventually, get a hangover.

I AM HUNGOVER AGAIN

Once you have realised that you will never be a reasoned and disciplined drinker, it all gets easier, really.

It's the years where you keep thinking it might be possible to go out, have two glasses of wine over dinner and be safely in bed by 11pm – flossed and serene – that are the hardest. The constant collapse of intentions confuses you. You are discombobulated by the regularity of the chaos. You don't know why it's happening again.

Last time you spoke to yourself in the restaurant it was 9.38pm, and you were in the toilets, going, 'Hey, dude! There we are, in the mirror. I will be honest with us – I feel pretty sober, tbh. The wine seems unexpectedly … thin tonight. I think we might need to have a third glass – just to see this thing off properly. Maximise the potential. Promote the healthful sleep etc. Still totally on for that 10.30pm bus, though, amigo! This isn't one of *those* nights! We remember it's Tuesday! Or Wednesday! Whichever day it is! It is that day!'

Five hours later, and you're standing in the alleyway behind a Spanish bar, smoking a brand of cigarettes you've never seen before, which seem very dry, and which you bought off a passing tramp for a pound. ('Kind sir! Let us come to some manner of agreement of equal benefit to us *both*!')

The last ten minutes have consisted of a rant about Marxism, which jolted – with the jump-cut high-flying magic that alcohol brings – into an equally passionate display of how you can boost the volume levels of the speakers on the iPhone by putting it in your mouth.

You are now triumphantly pointing at your face, issuing muffled cries of 'See! See! LOUD!', while your head transmits a pounding version of 'Now That We've Found Love' by Heavy D and the Boyz.

Your schedule has been far too busy – two bottles of red wine, three gins, a shot of vodka and whatever the hell this is in this glass right now. Fernet-Branca? Aquavit? – to really check in with yourself again, but you do remember seeing yourself, dimly, in the dark window glass, halfway up the stairs, coming back from the toilet.

You only looked yourself in the eye for a moment, mouthing the words, 'Tuesday. It is Tuesday', to which you replied, 'I am going to kill tomorrow for tonight. I will make the beautiful sacrifice.' And then you passed again, and you saw yourself no more.

After, in the morning – in the terrible morning – years ago, you would have panicked. In your twenties, or early thirties, you were shocked fresh that you were always crashing in this same car.

'When will I stop doing this?' you asked yourself, under the shower – washing your hair clean in the way you wish you could wash your lungs.

And you would spend the day berating yourself – making the panicky, sweating promise that last night was, obviously, by way of a wake for drinking. Last night was the night you toasted the toasts – raised the glass for the last time; as you are now, surely, too old to do this any more.

Certainly, looking at your hands – veins raised, and everything of a mauveish hue – they appear to belong to a 200-year-old.

But years later – now – you know there is no ending. You will never learn to have just two glasses, because you don't want to have just two glasses – you don't want to miss a trick; you will ride every tiger that passes by the pub door, until you know them by name, and call them in from the street.

As intimations of the grave occur – the child now up to your shoulder, the wondering horror of remembering something from *twenty-five years ago* – a hangover seems a slight prospect, in comparison. Indeed, it seems kind of necessary.

Because you don't fight these hangovers, now – you don't deny them, or try to wash them away. Instead, you lie perfectly limply in the beast's jaws, until it takes you for a corpse – and finally moves on, around 5pm.

You offer no resistance – you sit squarely in the centre of the thermonuclear sweats, the urine like treacle, the sporadic pulses of self-loathing where you must find a mirror in order to tell yourself, 'Dude, no. You are not an international terrorist', and you let them have their full head. You allow the full horror.

And you say to yourself, 'I am currently in the kiln, being burnished. My enamel is being baked. This is where I become truly powerful, and unafraid. Every one of these I sit through, unblinking, takes me up a level. So that, when Death finally comes, I will just treat him as nothing more than a hangover, too. I will come to him in the doorway in this cheap polyester slip, with this dishevelled hair, and this sausage sandwich, and simply say to him: 'Dude, do you know where I left my purse last night? I think I left it in the cab.'

Until I was eighteen I don't think I'd ever spent more than four hours on my own. There were eight children, two adults and three large, demented Alsatian dogs in our house, and so 'learning how to cope when alone' was a skill I never really had the chance to develop. Not even when on the toilet – where the shower curtain could suddenly and dramatically be pulled back, revealing three children staring at you from a bath full of Matey. Perhaps that explains why I'm traumatised by it now.

I DON'T KNOW WHAT TO DO WHEN I'M ALONE

My husband went away with the kids for the weekend, leaving me to hit a big deadline. After doing my traditional farewell – standing in the doorway wailing 'DON'T GO! I CANNOT TOLERATE THE LONELINESS! DO NOT LEAVE ME OR I WILL DIE, I WILL LITERALLY DIE!' – I went back into the silent, empty old house and turned into someone completely different.

You're different when you're alone. Well, I am. There's a whole other me that lives a whole other life when I'm the only one around. Obviously I smoke in the kitchen, watch *The Antiques Roadshow* ('Mum this is *boring*. It's just a man saying a chair is old') and live on the sofa; slowly building a castle wall of dirty cereal bowls and teacups while wearing a dressing gown that is so repulsively stained and funky that I now fear putting it in the washing machine, lest it make the drum smell forever.

Essentially – as all people on their own are apt to do – I turn into The Dude from *The Big Lebowski*, but without his rigorous sporting lifestyle (bowling while drinking beer, and eating chips).

However, in addition to all my quotidian 'lonely behaviours' there are several other things I do when I'm alone which are a bit more ... specialist. For instance:

1) I listen to Jeff Buckley. I don't know why I feel embarrassed to listen to him when my husband is around – this is a man who has 50,000 records, is insanely open-minded about all music and also had a childhood crush on The Dooleys. He is the last person to find me listening to Jeff Buckley and sneer about it – not least because he has Jeff Buckley records himself.

And yet – if my husband walked into a room where I was playing 'Lover, You Should Have Come Over', I would feel more mortified than if he'd found me, I dunno, taking a 'sexy' selfie, or leaving the comment, 'When will the Pulitzer committee honour this amazing woman?' under one of my articles online. Loving Jeff Buckley is such a … *woman* thing to do, with his beautiful face, and his falsetto voice, and his tragic early death in the Mississippi River. I like to cry when listening to Jeff – cry while watching my reflection in the window and pretending I'm in the video for the song. I also like to pretend I'm Jeff by singing along, and I like to pretend that what I am doing is 'weaving intoxicating modal harmonies' around my own original vocal take – rather than, as is the actual case, semi-hitting random notes in a barrage of unpleasant noise, in an empty house. Whilst crying.

2) Not going out and seeing people. I don't do that when I'm alone – even though that would, obviously, stop me from being alone – because it would mean coming back to an empty house. And on some level I fear that the house – having been utterly empty for the evening – might kind of *seal up* and not let me back in, and I would be reduced to kneeling in front of the letterbox, calling out to the cats to vouch for me. Yes – I am basically worried my house won't love me any more if I leave it. Oh God, that's projection, isn't it? Is the house my mum? I can't work it out. Also, I can't leave the house.

3) I start liking the cats. Normally, my relationship with the cats is, at best, frosty. I find them needy and stupid – after seven years, they still haven't grasped that *not only* will kneading my leg not yield the delicious mother-cat milk which they so obviously desire, *but also*

leads to them being lightly chucked across the room. After *seven years* of flying across the room, they still haven't learned this. *Seven years.* They also keep trying to kind of get *inside my hands* when I'm typing, stand on the stairs stupidly where my foot is about to land and scratch my new chair. I find them utterly vexing.

However, within twenty minutes of my husband and children leaving, I will hunt through the house to find the cats, bring them downstairs and drape them over my shoulders. I dote on them. 'Come over here, little matey!' I'll cry, sitting on the sofa. 'Come and see if you can get the delicious mother-cat milk out of my leg! Scratch away!'

4) I can't sleep. Normally I'm out like a light by 10pm. With my husband away, however, 2am will roll around and I'll still be depressingly wakeful.

I've worked out, with science, what's going on – my husband must emit some kind of soporific miasma, like human valerian, that minutely regulates my body clock, and this is part of the reason I was initially attracted to him.

Still, it is best that I can't sleep – given that I need to be awake to hear the burglars and murderers in the kitchen, making small, weird noises. The number of burglars and murderers who troop through the house when I'm alone is astonishing. Perhaps they all come together, on a minibus. Burglars and murderers don't like being alone, either.

It's war.

PRINTERS ARE EVIL

Look, I'm only going to talk about this if we all promise not to get angry about it. I know most columns about abortion, Israel, freedom of speech, Europe and the prospect of a female Doctor in *Doctor Who* should start like this – but, to be fair, those are all subjects we *could* all agree on if everyone went down the pub, with the conversation chaired by a couple of mums who made it *very* clear that everyone had to be on best behaviour, no shouting, and it all to be finished by 5pm, so they could get back and pop a whites wash on.

This subject, however, has no such possibility of resolve. For it is printers. Printers – the motherbeeping hate units that inspire more loathing than any other invention on Earth. Their evil unreliability is the high water mark by which every other device, past and future, must be measured. To purchase one is an act comparable to purchasing a succubus, demon, or tiny Nazi for £200, plus VAT.

The printer's grasp of evil is perfect – for they prey on your weakest moment, when you need them most. There's a taxi idling outside – all you need to do is print out your train tickets/boarding pass/homework/speech notes. You bought the printer four months ago and you've only used it six times, so pressing 'Print' will mean a joyous printing sound, followed by you running out of the house. Hang on. What. What? WHAT? 'Replace cyan cartridge.' 'Invalid driver.' 'Print is not aligned.' 'Paper jam.'

What are you SAYING to me? What does this MEAN?

'Print is not aligned' – that's just a Situationist slogan about post-internet media, daubed on a wall. It's not telling me what button to press. HOW am I supposed to 'align print'? Do you want me to do a seminar on a 360-joined-up media? Because, so help me God I will – except I can't, because I would need to print out all my notes on it first.

'Invalid driver'? To me, this means 'too drunk to get home, order a taxi'. IT'S NOT TELLING ME WHICH PART OF THE PRINTER TO PUNCH.

'Paper jam.' Okay – I know that one. It's the state wherein a single, non-complex sheet of A4 paper has, by some inexplicable process, been rendered into a solid origami swan of bullshit by your printer. Said swan is now lodged in a part of your printer wholly inaccessible by any of the useless trapdoors, which means you have to grab the swan's tail and yank it from the machine, even as the manual insists this will totally invalidate your warranty. But that doesn't matter! Because you're about to throw the printer out of the window anyway!

The thing is, the more you learn about printers, the more you hate them. You know that infuriating little 'whurdegurdy deee huurrrr dee hurrr' that an ink printer makes for three minutes, on start-up, that makes it sound like a pompous man at the dinner table about to say 'I'm not racist, but …'? That's the printer lavishly squirting ink out, to 'clear the nozzles' – ink which PC World recently calculated costs £2,291 per gallon. That is more expensive than blood, or liquid Ecstasy. This means it's perfectly possible to run a cartridge dry *simply* from turning a printer on and off again – without ever printing a single document. Yes. Things suddenly make more sense now, don't they?

But don't think getting a laser printer would be better – according to an Australian study, the ultra-fine particles they emit cause a health risk equal to passive smoking. Whether from stress or lung cancer, your printer *will* kill you.

In *Game of Thrones*, the unfortunate Ayra has witnessed most of those she loves being slaughtered. Consequently, she now recites a list of those she must now kill, like a prayer: 'Cersei, Joffrey, Walder Frey, The Mountain, Meryn Trant.'

I have an almost identical prayer, except mine goes 'Hewlett-Packard, Canon, Epson, Fujitsu'. One of each of the eleven printers whose last act was to insist 'Wifi not detected', even as I bodily rubbed them against the router, screaming 'LOOK! THERE IT IS! CONNECT!' Or insisted they needed a full cyan cartridge, even though I was printing in black and white – essentially acting like some rock star insisting they want all the blue M&Ms removed from their rider. I threw them all out of the window. All.

How can printers have become so spoiled and demanding? They are the *ultimate* basic bitch item. I have devices in my pocket that will allow me to video-conference someone on a beach in Tasmania – and yet my pampered, toad-like printer, used just six times a year, cannot manage to do something that peasants were handling in the sixteenth century, by using carved pieces of wood. COME ON! I beg *any* half-competent organisation to start making printers. John Lewis, Waitrose – even ISIS, at a push. The world cannot tolerate this much longer. Our spiritual cyan is running dry. We have a paper jam in our souls. PRINT IS NOT ALIGNED.

The thing about being famous is that it's a) absolutely not what you think it will be and b) there are such degrees of fame as to make opposite ends of the spectrum seem like different worlds. At one end – Kate Middleton. At the other – Matt Cardle from The X Factor, *or Cat Bin Lady. My friend once went out with a drum'n'bass DJ who was, as she explained, 'Absolutely legendary – to a very small community'. When pressed as to how small that community was, she screwed her eyes up for a minute, and went, 'Nine'.*

Anyway. I've worked out how famous I am. It is exactly 35 per cent.

THE EXACT AMOUNT OF FAMOUS I AM: 35 PER CENT

Fame is rarely an on/off button: one moment in the darkness of anonymity, the next – in the light of fame. If, of course, you think fame *is* the light – and not, when all is said and done, the real darkness, after all.

But the key thing is that fame is not binary – either/or. Fame is, instead, a dimmer switch with a million increments of notoriety across the scale.

On the dimmer switch of fame, I'm currently – after a solid couple of months of promo for a new book – *Newsnight, The One Show*, intense Q&A with *Good Housekeeping* – at around '35 per cent famous'. I can tell you exactly how famous this is: famous enough to be invited on to the red carpet at the *Glamour* Awards, to pick up a trophy – only to be greeted with 'PALOMA! PALOMA!' from paparazzi who believed I was the similarly badger-haired Paloma Faith. That's exactly how famous I am. To be announced as a winner – while the paps go *'Who?'*

It's only very specific people who ever know who I am: girls who wear eyeliner. Homosexuals into sci-fi. Librarians. Benedict Cumberbatch fans. Dirty, boozy mums. English teachers. Bad-ass

Marxist-feminist nannas. *Times* readers – the ones who don't just get the paper for the Business and Sport.

I have to say, as far as I'm concerned, it's the perfect level, and type, of fame: I can be fairly assured of getting a discount on kale in health food shops, an overdue library book fine waived, or priority service in a gay bar – yet will be left to buy multi-packs of sanitary towels in the Big Tesco, Edmonton, in peace.

In the last month, on a signing tour for my novel *How to Build a Girl*, the kind of people who recognise me have given me: a free cashmere shawl; a necklace with a quote from *Ghostbusters* on it; a bottle of gin; a crocheted vagina; and a postcard from a fourteen-year-old girl saying she wished I was a lesbian. Does it make me feel happy? Obviously, yes: this part of 35 per cent fame is very simple. This bit doesn't feel like 'fame', which you imagine to be hot, and white, and possibly blinding: this is just a warm, mellow 'knowing' – where both parties hold each other's hands and say 'thank you', simultaneously, several times over, and both mean it. Because words are dead until they are read, and a writer without a reader is nothing. And a writer with a reader *and* a cashmere travel wrap is clearly having a very good day indeed.

Sometimes, the signings last two hours, three hours, and a couple of people shake, or cry, when I say 'Hello' – which is understandable given that they have been standing for three hours. And when this happens I am awestruck by just what it is when someone declares themselves 'a fan', and waits three hours to spend two minutes with you: that they have made themselves utterly vulnerable in a way that is oddly brave. They trust you enough to believe you won't make them feel like a dick for waiting in a line, and you are utterly respectful and grateful for the leap of faith they have made. Unless you *are* a dick, you make sure they walk away feeling it was not a stupid thing to have done: you hug, and you kiss, and you tell them that they can do amazing things, too, and that they *must*, and that their hair is beautiful, because it is, and their eyes look like the eyes of revolutionaries, and their shoes are perfect for dancing in, and the dress their mother made them – with its print of Frida Kahlo – makes it clear that they are too good for this town, and that they must run away, and break some hearts, and change the world. And that when they do, you will cheer them on, in the way they have cheered you on – because you know each other now.

Do you know what 35 per cent fame does? Not 100 per cent fame – the raging, uncontrollable furnace in which, say, Amy Winehouse or Michael Jackson lived – but this lovely, manageable torch glow? It basically makes you be a better person. At 35 per cent famous, it's rare you leave the house without someone on Twitter noting they saw you on a bus, or in Pret, or going to see *Boyhood* at the Odeon.

And so you – previously God-less; unschooled in being constantly observed and being judged – finally feel what it's like for your every action to be noted by an omnipresent eye. You start to live in a way that is exaggeratedly good – ostentatiously giving homeless people tenners; helping mums with buggies up stairs – hoping someone will Instagram it, captioned, 'More Moran nobleness! She is such a *humanitarian*!'

But, after a while, you note that constantly pretending to be a decent person, and actually *being* one, are basically the same thing. And that 35 per cent fame has worked for you by way of the warm, positive affirmation that parents give a querulous child. That it makes you calm, and purposeful, in a way you would never have anticipated. That the mask, when it eats into the face, can be – unexpectedly – a serendipitous thing.

The thing is, even if you're a bit famous yourself – cruising around on your 35 per cent, enjoying occasional, modest discounts in second-hand bookshops – you are still liable to be a total arse when around other famous people. It's almost as if you learn nothing, ever.

ALL THE DIFFERENT WAYS I HAVE ANNOYED FAMOUS PEOPLE

Not counting my father's favourite drinking anecdote – that, in 1980, he once nearly knocked over *Midlands Today* presenter Alan Towers on a zebra crossing – the first famous person my family encountered was the writer Helen Cresswell, in 1982.

Author of children's series *The Bagthorpe Saga*, Cresswell came to a literary fair in Wolverhampton to sign copies of her latest book. The whole family queued for an hour to meet her and, when we finally got to the top of the queue, we regretfully explained to her our situation: that, no, we hadn't read any of her books yet – as we were waiting to get them out of the library – and so could she, therefore, just sign a copy of Enid Blyton's *The Faraway Tree* instead?

She – baffled yet courteous – did so. We – ebullient – capered away like joyous chimps. The famous lady (whose books we hadn't read!) had signed a book (that she had nothing to do with!) – and it had only taken all afternoon! Bonus round! GOLD RUN! COWABUNGA! TOUCH THE GLORY OF THE FAMOUS PEOPLE!

In the twenty-nine years that have passed since that incident, my job has involved meeting many, many famous people. Indeed at one point, in my early twenties – during Britpop – I was probably on about twenty famous people a day. I subsequently developed a hacking Fame Cough.

But, in all that time, I have often reflected on how that first brush with a celebrity, back in 1982, so perfectly encapsulated all my reactions to meeting celebrities since. For although I have cycled through many different coping techniques, every single one of them has been persistently, unwaveringly, and *astonishingly* stupid. Thus:

1991–3: Gonna make you love me. I am sixteen years old. I am writing for *Melody Maker*. I am able to do a thing which is both amazing, yet wholly inadvisable for a teenage girl – essentially *ring up* my heroes and request that they be delivered to a pub, for me, so they can fall madly in love with me, and propose marriage.

Other people call this activity 'doing an interview' – but *I* know the truth.

Unfortunately, having had no training in either a) conducting interviews or b) getting people to fall madly in love with me, my technique is: to get very, very drunk, and then talk about myself for the entirety of the interview.

I don't know if you've ever really viscerally wanted to stab yourself in the eyes, hair and chest before then throwing yourself off a cliff – but I can assure you that, if you *do*, then listening back to an hour-long tape of you slurringly telling the Beastie Boys 'the thing about me, right, is that I'm a lover – not a fighter' will absolutely motivate you to do that.

1993–7: Blowing their minds. Doing a palm reading for Björk? Showing Roddy Frame from Aztec Camera the pictures you drew of him when you were thirteen? Crying hysterically in Radiohead's front room 'Because I feel the *ghosts* in your music'? Telling Teenage Fanclub, 'Let's not do an interview – let's just play Scrabble, instead, while I "feel your vibe"'? I've done all of these. I just wanted to … liven the place up a bit. You know. Keep things fresh for promo-jaded celebrities. Out of love. Bad love.

This demented tactic reached its unfortunate climax in 1997, when I was in a limo with Robbie Williams, who had toothache. Instead of painkillers, I insisted he use my herbal remedy instead.

Thirty seconds later we went over an unexpected road bump, and Mr 'Angels' was screaming in agony as I tried to rinse a whole spilt bottle of Clove Oil out of his eye, using half a can of flat Lilt.

1997–2005: Hard-core shunning. Having nearly blinded the most famous man in Britain, I had a rethink about a world where celebrities regularly had to come in contact with me – and came out solidly against it.

'I need to protect famous people from me,' I thought. 'They shouldn't have to put up with this shit. From now on, whenever I'm trapped with a famous person, I will *nobly ignore* them. I will erect an invisible Protective Booth of Respect around them, in my mind.'

This noble eschewing of famouses reached its apogee when I did a radio show with one of my greatest heroes, Radio One DJ John Peel. Three times Peel attempted to make pleasant conversation with me. Three times I *physically* turned away from him – thinking, 'John Peel, the best way I can show you my respect is by not bothering you with my replies. Besides, we've got *plenty* of time to become friends – later.'

Peel died six months later.

2005–present day. 'It's because you're *overwhelmed* by their fame,' my husband counselled me. 'They're just normal! Just do that old trick – imagine them on the toilet.'

And, indeed, this advice really did work like a dream – until the night when, due to a sequence of events too long to explain, I ended up seeing Lady Gaga on the toilet *for real*.

I KNOW. WHAT ARE THE CHANCES?

Since then – your guess is as good as mine. I'm all out of ideas.

I know someone who knows David Bowie, and he told me, once, 'One day, I'll introduce him to you. You can't interview him, or write about it – but you will meet him.'

I've spent a lot of time, in the intervening years, thinking about that. Thinking about the day when I finally meet David Bowie. What do I say? What would I wear? What do you wear to meet the man who's worn everything – purple and red jumpsuit; sharp lemon zoot suit; Jareth the Goblin King's knacker-immortalising leggings? I looked through my entire wardrobe and realised the only thing I could wear to meet David Bowie that wouldn't look like I was copying something he'd already worn – and better – was my shirt that is covered in hundreds of tiny cartoon pictures of David Bowies. What's the etiquette on that? Is it wrong to make Bowie look at little Bowies, all over my tits? Or is it – as I am dangerously close to convincing myself – so wrong it's right?

Either way, there's Bowie all over this book, and the first spoonful is here, discussing a documentary about him, which ran the same week as an amazing documentary on Shakespeare – England's other, beautiful, world-changing, bisexual boy.

TV REVIEW: SHAKESPEARE & DAVID BOWIE – ENGLAND'S BEAUTIFUL BOYS

There is a fairly persuasive argument that the answer to the question 'What is Englishness?' may be 'A nation of people who constantly ask themselves "What is Englishness?"'

Very few things can have been as exhaustively examined by the English as 'Englishness'. It's practically all we do. Drink tea, love dogs, queue patiently, plant herbaceous borders, get off our margins on Friday night, live in a constant state of astonished tetchiness about the weather, knock out superlative homosexuals – and constantly ask ourselves what it means to come from this country. And that's the lot. It's only when you go abroad that you notice other countries do not do this.

The French would think you were insane if you were to ask them, 'What is it to be French?' They would sit there, eating Frenchly, dressed in a French manner, and thinking *à la Française*, and stare at you until you stopped. Likewise the Americans, or the Greeks, or the Indians. They all just ... get on with it.

We, meanwhile, get on with earnestly fretting about whether earnestly fretting is inimitably English or not. Since we stopped tending beehives in the grounds of our abbeys, or stoically resisting Hitler, it's become our national hobby.

In this respect, summer 2012 has been an absolute doozy – the twin-header of the Jubilee and the London Olympics allowing us a double-pop at a slew of broadsheet think pieces that would best be headlined, 'GB – WTF?'

And television has, of course, followed suit. This week – in among *Punk Britannia*, Grayson Perry's series on British taste, and *The Secret History of Our Streets* – there were documentaries on two of the brightest things this country has ever produced: Shakespeare and Ziggy Stardust.

Simon Schama's take on Shakespeare came first. When it comes to history documentaries, there are very few pleasures as great as watching Schama: slithering around draughty castles in his black leather jacket, spreading whispery allegations about Charles I in such a manner as to suggest that the King might just be around the corner, irascibly hidden behind a heavy curtain and likely to behead the titillating Schama – rather than dead these 370 years.

Indeed, Schama's confiding tone is so all-pervading that, on occasion – when his nostrils get particularly flared; perhaps over some perfidious long-gone deed by Cromwell – he morphs into Kenneth Williams narrating *Willo the Wisp*. In a bit where Evil Edna's behaved particularly outrageously towards Mavis Cruet, the fairy.

A two-part series, *Simon Schama's Shakespeare* kicked off with Schama at his best. With so little known about Shakespeare, you would think establishing his patent 'gossipy' tone would be difficult – yet Schama managed it with ease. He made the gossip about the work.

'You can take away cricket, skip the last night of the Proms, even lose the Empire – but if you lose Shakespeare, as far as I'm concerned, there's no England any more,' Schama opened; before opining that this was because 'He gives us England unedited – the cream and the scum. The fleabag hostelries, the chilly cathedrals where sour bishops crack their knuckles and plot. The clapped-out actors and greedy squires … and that's what we want. The dirt and the devilry. He gives us the voices of England.'

Schama's thesis was that Shakespeare had, to all intents and purposes, invented England: 'Shakespeare put Britain on stage before it even really existed,' he claimed. Quoting Jack Cade in *Henry VI, Part II*, with his sweeping cry of 'My mouth shall be the Parliament of England', Schama explained just why it is that 'the rhythm, and the way that we speak' are down to Shakespeare: 'He is the river of our language.'

Shakespeare's great luck was to be born on a fault line – a point in history where socio-political tectonic plates were opening a new space.

In 2012, the burgeoning technology of the internet defines us. Shakespeare, by way of contrast, started writing at the point where the technology of words themselves was in the ascendant: between 1500 and 1659, 30,000 new words were added to the English language. This was when the rules of grammar were being fixed – and this was, in great part, down to Shakespeare himself: his use of grammar, then propagated by the success of his plays.

As Elizabeth I began to lay the foundations of the British Empire, Shakespeare's fresh, plastic, plosive English became as exportable and valuable as woollen cloth, or coal. Back in this country, meanwhile, Shakespeare's big stories – the most exciting games in town – filled the entertainment vacuum that had once been filled by the touring Catholic plays. The Reformation made brilliant business for Shakespeare.

And Shakespeare made brilliant business for Schama. He was in his wide-eyed element doing semi-hysterical potted listings for Shakespeare's works

'He put the onion breath into his Dicks and Georges, and let the middling sort smell it,' Schama said, in the kind of glorious 'WTF?' piece to camera that makes you blink several times. Revelling in the Schama drama, he went on to describe the monarch in *Henry VI* as: 'Insomniac, guilt-ridden, doomed never to enjoy the fruits of his usurped throne – trapped in a Death Star where everyone moans and plots within the steel casing of their dark armour.' Henry VI was, therefore, '*Kill Bill*, in tights'.

As a viewer, *Simon Schama's Shakespeare* scored the double whammy of making you go, 'Well I *never* – do next-door know about all this?' *and* 'This summer, I really must start reading Shakespeare. This stuff sounds excellent.'

On to England's other dazzling boy – David Bowie – who, on Friday, had a whole night to himself, when BBC4 knocked out another one of those *Mojo*-friendly rock archive evenings a person of a certain persuasion finds so very satisfying.

The thing about Bowie is that, whatever the Beatles did (i.e. everything), he did it all better, really. Well, harder, certainly. For although working class, the Beatles were essentially a really good-looking gang. They had the power of a brotherhood. They were straight. And they weren't ginger – albeit dyed – either. They were a pretty easy sell, all things told – what with their girlfriends, and their *yeah yeah yeah*.

Bowie, on the other hand, was alone. A man in a dress, who'd outed himself to *Melody Maker* ('I'm gay, and I always will be.' Obviously he was wrong about that, given that he married Iman, but we all make mistakes. Unless, of course, he misheard when he was introduced to her, and thought she was 'A man'. Then he'd still be quite gay), and who wanted to bring the then-uninvited guest of theatre – dance, choreography, mime, make-up, costume, lies, dazzle, inference, narrative – to rock.

And he wanted to do all this without a band of brothers. Without the shelter of the familial name 'Fromthebeatles'. All on his own. No wonder he invented Ziggy Stardust. 'Oh no love – you're not alone!' He needed him, for company.

David Bowie and the Story of Ziggy Stardust covered Bowie's astonishing eighteen-month raid on pop, from 1971 to 1973, when Bowie broke into the world and – rather than stealing something – heaped up the charts, and the imagination, with treasure, instead: leaving *Hunky Dory* and *The Man Who Sold The World* and *Ziggy Stardust* under the Christmas tree, plus tossing off 'All The Young Dudes' for Mott the Hoople, and producing Lou Reed's *Transformer*, and Iggy & the Stooges' *Raw Power*. A CV which genuinely entitles the bearer to refer to themselves as – per the lyrics to 'Ziggy Stardust' – 'The nazz/With God-given ass'.

Ziggy Stardust was a conflation of Little Richard, British rock'n'roll singer Vince Taylor, the world's post-Sputnik obsession with aliens and a tailors called Ziggy's.

Like Shakespeare before him – who took the history, stories of kings and queens, and reworked them to make the future – Bowie took rock's past and used it to kick off the next four decades of pop.

'The eighties would never have happened without him,' Gary Kemp of Spandau Ballet explained. 'The make-up was where we started. The outfits were where we started. [Lady] Gaga's whole act is Bowie.'

'He wanted to be everything,' Mick Ronson said, of the boy who'd already, at twenty-three, changed his name, written 'Space Oddity', and given Peter Noone 'Oh! You Pretty Things', lyrics inspired by Nietzsche (*'You gotta make way for the homo superior'*).

And Bowie was, at that point, the Homo Superior. Here's Ziggy Stardust's first, legendary appearance on *Top of the Pops* – the one every gay man of a certain age remembers as being the gay equivalent of the Moon landings. In some dandy half-harlequin outfit, his mouth is outrageous. He's all hip bone and cock. The blasted pupil in his brown eye makes it look like he was winking during an explosion. At one point, he casually drapes his arm around guitarist Mick Ronson – in an era of absolute homophobia, he might just as well have been violently taking Ronson over the drum riser. Men did not touch each other like this in 1972.

'I had never seen anything like this in my life,' Elton John – one of the talking heads – said. 'It was so exciting. He commanded the stage. He was so ... sexual.'

And then, almost a year to the day after the *Top of the Pops* appearance – with Ziggy having released three albums, and done two huge world tours – Bowie took the Spiders From Mars to the Hammersmith Odeon, with the intention of announcing the retirement of Ziggy Stardust. He had not told the rest of the band.

When he takes to the stage, a girl at the front of the audience, in a red coat, repeatedly rests the side of her face on stage, gently, instantly and ecstatically, like a cat in love. She clearly believes she is living in the era of Ziggy Stardust, and it will last forever.

But before an encore of 'Rock'n'Roll Suicide', Ziggy Stardust shouts out 'This is the last show we'll ever do!', and dies. David Bowie puts out *Diamond Dogs* the next year – then on to 'Fame', and *Station To Station* and 'Heroes', and *Low* – still astonishing right up until *Let's Dance*, and capable of something as beautiful as 'Absolute Beginners' ('I absolutely love you') even in 1986.

And even with your head still buzzing from Mick Ronson's unlubricated, staccato buzzing on 'Rebel Rebel', you think: 'Moonage Daydream'. That's the kind of title Shakespeare would have come up with.

If being a small bit famous is odd, what is even odder is when what you're famous for is … unusual. You yourself do not feel unusual – indeed, you know your experience is a common one – and yet, where you are, doing what you do, you seem … exotic.

That's what it's like living in London and being a writer – but having been brought up on benefits. When Channel 4 began its new series Benefits Street, *about a street in Birmingham and the residents there – the majority on welfare – it became one of the most talked-about and controversial shows of the decade. And it seemed to me – having lived on a benefits street – that so many commentators just could not, and maybe should not, write about it, because to them these people were … unusual. Exotic. Not real.*

THE REAL, TERRIBLE SHAME OF *BENEFITS STREET*

The weird thing about having started so many columns, speeches and meetings with the sentence 'I was raised on benefits' – it has become by way of an odd catchphrase; my version of 'Nice to see you – to see you, nice!', but a lot less fun – is how rarely, in London, it is met with a cheerful, 'Me too!' I mean, it never happens.

I so rarely experience a rejoining 'Amazing! I was *also* raised on benefits!' or, 'Do you remember those old yellow books – that you had to take to the post office? And how Thursday was the best day of the week – because that's when you got your money? Awww, man – old skool vibez! High fives!'

I'm not trying to be disingenuous here but I genuinely can't remember *anyone* having replied, 'Me, too!' in the last ten years.

Back in the nineties you'd get it a fair bit   interviewing bands from Manchester and Glasgow and Swansea. We'd do our povvo-bonding, over the years they spent signing on – before they got a deal. Being eighteen, getting kicked out of your parents' house and moving into a tiny flat: safe. Thank you, benefits. Thank you, welfare. Thank you, for never letting the sins of the father become the sins of the child. For allowing every generation the potential to start again under its own steam. And then letting that generation – some of the ones I knew, anyway – eventually buy a Rolls-Royce and drive it into a swimming pool.

But in the last ten years, since I've given up music journalism, I've pretty much stopped meeting people in London who come from a background like mine. I've stopped meeting people raised on Incapacity Benefit, Jobseeker's Allowance or Child Benefit.

'Sports and rock'n'roll – they're the only two ways out for the working classes,' as my dad used to always remind me. 'There isn't a third way – unless you win the pools.'

And he was right. In the last decade I've primarily hung out with journalists and writers instead: gone to meetings with TV production companies and department heads at TV companies, met with film people, and done most of my socialising (getting drunk with and kind of falling on top of) comedians, actors and TV presenters. And none of them knew about the cream-coloured books, or 'Thursday'. None of them knew about always feeling judged – as if everything could be taken away, at any moment. None of them knew about the terrible, heart-constricting fear. None of them had been on benefits.

And that's because people who were raised on benefits never really make it all the way to here – to London. To this London – Media London. To the place where the power is. Those giro cheques, and those social circles, don't stretch this far. Those people don't get to commission documentaries, or make dramas, or write columns, or books, about their lives – to speak on *Newsnight*, or tell jokes on *Have I Got News for You*. They do not get to the place with the control of all the stories. They do not get to speak.

You just see them in crowd shots, instead, as a mass – shouting on the terraces, or queuing in the Boxing Day Sales at Next. In film terms, people on benefits would be credited as 'extras' in Britain. They get neither names nor lines. And they certainly never sit in the director's chair.

And, so, to *Benefits Street*, the Channel 4 documentary which has caused the biggest controversy, and ratings surge, since *My Big Fat Gypsy Wedding* – also on Channel 4.

With 57,000 signatures on a petition to withdraw the rest of the series, over 1,000 complaints to OfCom, and Channel 4's head of documentaries hauled on to *Newsnight* and accused of making 'poverty porn', *Benefits Street* has kicked the hornet's nest of Britain's 'underclass' issue.

Many have called *Benefits Street* a straight-up piece of character assassination on benefits claimants. The first episode showed two men called Fungi and Danny involved in various criminal escapades, sound-tracked by some oddly upbeat 'Look at the resourceful peasants!' music. Danny lined a bag with tinfoil, in order to go shoplifting, and ended up getting handcuffed, face down on the pavement, in the middle of the Bull Ring shopping centre.

Fungi, meanwhile, stole magazines from a Premier Inn and sold them – pretending they were *The Big Issue* – before spending the money on lager.

Onscreen, these scenes were accompanied by the repeated flashing of the hashtag #benefitsstreet – as if to remind viewers to Tweet such messages as 'gas these scroungers', 'where do we get guns to kill these wankers?' and 'fuckin burn them' – which they duly and dutifully did. About people who let us not forget – we knew the exact addresses of, and the precise, undefended, flammable flimsiness of their front doors. James Turner Street, Birmingham, B18 4ND.

Many others – primarily those who'd actually *watched* the show – argued to the contrary: that this programme was actually *good* for benefit claimants. That it was, in all truth, a well-balanced piece of documentary-making let down only by its misplaced soundtrack and peerlessly *Mail*-activating title.

On *Benefits Street* – this supposed Hammer of the Scroungers – we saw a real and solid community, with people in and out of each other's houses, feeding each other and entwined in each other's lives in a way you would not see in, say, Hampstead, or in the Cotswolds.

Here was a local entrepreneur called Smoggy, who went door-to-door with a tray, selling cups of washing powder, sugar and tea for 50p – often the biggest unit of cash available to residents.

'I'm thinking, for this street, it should be only 30p, or 20p,' he said after only selling a single cup all morning, and giving away washing powder for free to a resident who'd had her Job Seeker's Allowance stopped, and was living on £30 a week.

'I know what it's like,' he said to her, gently, as he handed it over, without payment.

We also saw a progressive, open-minded community – one that would have shamed a similar street in a far higher wage bracket, and with far better education. On *Benefits Street*, there were thirteen different nationalities, co-existing on limited resources, with little or no friction: uncomprehending Romanians tore open bin bags, and travellers pitched up on the park at the end of the street, but there was little more than grumbling and the odd catty comment. No violence, as they dealt, practically – stoically – with the issues Westminster is paralysed and terrified over. Just sitting on the front step with an extra-long fag, smoking and watching.

And, like some idealised Benetton advert, overdubbed with Birmingham accents, kids of all colours played together on the discarded mattresses in the street – the 'chav trampoline', as we used to call them back in Wolverhampton. Actually, we used to say 'pikey', but you can't say that any more. Even though we were the ones called pikey.

So is *Benefits Street* an unkind piece of snide propaganda against Britain's underclass? Or, in fact, a balanced documentary showing how benefit claimants struggle as the Coalition's austerity measures begin to kick in, and multicultural immigration is left, pretty much, to sort itself out?

What *is Benefits Street*?

Here's the statistic I find most interesting: with 4.3 million viewers, *Benefits Street* rated higher for Channel 4 than any programme they screened in the entirety of 2013. Commentators have boggled over what a 'break-out' hit this is – the coverage it has received, from every section of the media.

But in the UK, 20.3 million families claim benefits: more than four times the 'huge' viewership of *Benefits Street*. Pretty much every commentator who has written about *Benefits Street* has presumed that the viewers are very different from the subjects – that one class is tuning in to watch another, to get an outrage boner over 'poverty porn'.

The reality, of course, is that with 64 per cent of British families claiming benefits, most of the people in this country technically live on a *Benefits Street*. That street is *their* street. They know this stuff – or, at least, some of it. They tussle with the same paperwork. They fret over the same bills. They fear the same Bedroom Tax, and they know 75 per cent of the austerity measures – which touch on their benefits and their lives – have not kicked in yet.

This is not an unexplored world to the people who *watch* these programmes, merely to the people who *make* these programmes, and then write about them. They are presuming *Benefits Street* is as alien a spectacle to the 4.3 million as life for seahorses in the mangrove swamps, or protons in outer space. For millions of those 4.3 million it will simply be what they can see outside their windows, instead.

Media London is unaware of how obvious its unawareness is. To everyone else, it's the most noticeable aspect of all.

So this is the real thing I take from *Benefits Street*. Not the hugeness of the outrage – but the tininess of the cause. Reruns of *Shameless* and CCTV of some muggings on *Crimewatch* aside, this is probably all we will see of benefits claimants on television this year: the people who need to claim benefits to top up below-minimum-wage jobs; people who need to claim housing benefits to top up an overheated private rental sector.

Ninety-nine houses on a single street in Birmingham are now being seen as the prism through which we examine the lives of every person on benefits in Britain – a significance under which any six-part documentary series would buckle and break.

For it's impossible to do it. *Benefits Street* is just that – *Benefits Street*. Just one street. Not *Benefits City*, or *Benefits Britain*.

To show how absurd the weight and analysis lumped on *Benefits Street* is, imagine, for a moment, a putative *Middle Class Street*.

If, on our new *Middle Class Street*, we'd seen three out of ninety-nine lovely Victorian terraces engaged in crime – the same ratio as *Benefits Street* – but the middle-class crimes of tax evasion and expenses fiddling, instead, no one would be lining up to condemn the *entire* middle class. No one would be presuming to be an expert on the middle-class 'lifestyle' – no one would be making statements on the moral degeneracy of the twenty-first-century middle class.

And even if they *were*, middle-class voices have so much access to the media that it would be easily counterweighed by dozens of columns and radio sermons on the subject, from middle-class broadcasters and writers. The middle classes would not be talked about as if they were something that must … *end*. Something to be *cured*. Something which has gone on for far too long, and must be remedied. Something that is only ever a problem.

When the irony is, of course, the working-class benefit fraud costs £1.2 billion annually, while tax evasion – inevitably a middle-class crime – costs £14 billion annually.

Fourteen billion! The fact of it being often repeated does not dim the outrageousness of this figure. The fact is simple: richer people steal more. You cannot trust them. Hide your espresso machines when they come round, fellow peasants, lest they sneak them into their Cath Kidston tote and make their escape in a Prius.

But for now – no. There are no other shows about 64 per cent of this country. There are no shows about the reality of the way this country pays for its low-wage economy, and feverish, demented housing market. There's no touching on the statistics that show a worryingly disproportionate number of people with mental health issues are left with no option but to go on to benefits. There's also nothing about local cooperatives, communal allotments, campaigns to keep local shops and pubs open. There's nothing about these people actually *living*.

The problem with *Benefits Street* was that it wasn't about these people's *lives* – it was about their mere survival. About money, and worry, and deals.

We never saw the interior lives of the subjects – what they read, and dream, and joke about. The adventures they have had, as we have all had adventures – the fanciful ideas they amuse themselves with; their views on politics, culture, sex. All we saw them do was try to keep warm and fed – the concerns, to be blunt, of animals. They were denied nearly every other aspect of being human: joy – creativity – revolution – the sublime.

And so it continues. People who we think of as only caring about being warm, and fed, do not get to write drama serials, or sci-fi cartoons, or jokes for Radio 4. They are not in the line-up on *Question Time*, and they do not get to wear beautiful dresses on the red carpet. They don't get to ask questions, and they are never asked for answers. They are nowhere.

Instead, all they have is *Benefits Street*. Six episodes and ninety-nine houses – this one street – that currently stand for 20.3 million untold stories.

It's not all the shouting about *Benefits Street* that surprises me.

It's all the silence that came from that street before, and that will resume again, long after this media spat has blown over.

It's how weirdly lonely, twenty years in, it is writing about all this stuff.

But still the oddness goes on. Council housing, benefits, underclasses – these subjects always written about as if they are distant, odd, alien things, rather than a substantial number of people's reality.

I'm not a writer who writes in anger. I find anger, in the main, a fairly useless tool to bring to communicating – people, by and large, will simply respond to your emotion with their own anger, and not listen to what you're saying. This is half the discourse on Twitter at any one time – two groups of upset, angry people shouting at each other and not listening at all. Also, anger curbs my appetite as surely as nicotine and, frankly, I don't want to miss out on any lunches.

No – anger is generally useless to me, and so I have only written once in anger in the last twenty years. And that was when the benefits claimant and father of seventeen, Mick Philpott, engaged in the catastrophic act of setting fire to his house, in order to frame his mistress for arson – but accidentally killed six of his children, who were trapped upstairs.

Philpott, a well-known thug, petty criminal and wife-beater, was understandably vilified by the press and public opinion. But much of the coverage focused on the fact he was on benefits and lived in a council house – as if these were somehow spurs to his evil: that without the Welfare State, and council housing, Philpott would never have had the resources to accidentally slaughter his own children.

So, yes. This was written in anger.

MY FATHER RAISED EIGHT CHILDREN ON WELFARE, AND DIDN'T KILL ANY OF US

My father raised eight children on welfare benefits, and didn't kill any of us.

I feel I should say that, this week. I feel I need to firmly point to a large family raised on public handouts who were normal, and gentle, and never set fire to their house during a personal vendetta against a former lover.

It's weird I should have to, of course – but the Philpott trial seems to have made it necessary. The *Daily Mail*'s headline on the case, after the 'guilty' verdict, was 'VILE PRODUCT OF WELFARE UK': a profoundly odd summation of the case to have chosen. When Harold Shipman was convicted of killing over 250 patients, the headline wasn't 'THE DEADLY PROFESSIONAL CLASSES'. Likewise, the headline on Fred West was not a succinct 'EVIL BUILDER' – odd, given that both Shipman and West's professions actively facilitated their crimes, as they visited helpless patients, loaded with poisoned syringes, or buried shattered bodies under the patio.

The Philpotts' crime, on the other hand, was not abetted by Mick Philpott (and only Mick Philpott: his co-accused, Mairead Philpott, worked, as a cleaner, in a hospital) being unemployed and financially reliant on benefits. His crime was *not* facilitated by 'Welfare UK' because – and forgive me for being brutal – Philpott set fire to his house full of children outside normal working hours. This was manslaughter carried out in a sociopath's leisure time, as so much sociopathic manslaughter is.

Was Philpott's preceding day – of idleness, subsidised by taxpayers – a contributing factor to his later crime? How Mick Philpott had spent the day – either working, or not working – cannot logically be said to have a bearing on the terrible things he did that evening. If people who had spent years without employment were more likely to burn six children alive, then every pensioner in Britain would be a ticking time bomb – likewise every stay-at-home mother, and carefree man-about-Mayfair with a private income. Mick Philpott's lifetime on benefits did not make him stupidly, accidentally kill his children.

But it's odd how many people think it did. It's odd how much the Philpott case revealed not about the exceptional, abnormal, unparalleled Mick Philpott – with his two lovers, both taken when lonely teenagers; his brutality; his taste for cheap publicity; his seventeen children; his caravan in the driveway, for sex – but about the people who commented on it, instead. It says a great deal to me that some people looking at this case saw it as, primarily, a failure of the Welfare State. Indeed, not a failure of the Welfare State, but the direct *fault* of the Welfare State.

To be brutal again – forgive me: it has been a brutal week – but how distant and cold is your gaze for *this* to be the thing that makes you burst into speech? This little bit of politics – your hobbyhorse; your repetitive, slightly drunken dinner-party speech, as the port comes out – running next to the pictures of the burned bedroom, and the small, sad window that could not be broken in time?

Mick Philpott had been convicted of stabbing a previous lover twenty-seven times; he beat his mistress, Lisa Willis, with a plank, and then torched a house full of sleeping children, out of spite. How exactly he paid for the knife, the plank and the petrol seem as wildly inconsequential as what he was wearing, or the fact it happened in Derby.

I will be honest with you – when I look at the Philpott case, I, too, see 'the product of welfare UK'. I see 'The State'. I see its mark as assuredly as the *Mail* does. But do you know what 'welfare UK' I see? I see Philpott's surviving children, healthy and well-nourished because benefits fed them, attending school, and with some chance of a future, because the state paid for it.

I see the women's refuge that Lisa Willis was able to go to when she left her abusive partner – paid for by the state. I see a man who was given free legal representation during his manslaughter case – so that everyone in the country knew justice had been done.

I saw that while evil operated in the centre of all this – a terrible, destructive, manipulative man – every innocent around him was helped, and aided, and was never abandoned, and had somewhere to turn, because of 'welfare UK'.

For that is why the Welfare State was created – to undo wrongs, to help the helpless, even as strong men rage to destroy them. Anyone inclined to berate 'welfare UK' should consider, for a moment, what would have happened to that woman, and those children, in Victorian times, before Beveridge and Attlee.

Because if you believe that the slums then were not filled with men exactly like Mick Philpott – but whose children starved, and whose wives stayed, beaten, in the house – and that it is only 'welfare UK' that has now created them, I fear the history my father taught me, during his long, 'idle' days on benefits, was far more comprehensive than yours.

And, of course, being raised in a council house is an increasingly rare thing.

WHAT IS A HOUSE?

What is a house? I knew when I was a child – it was simple. Houses are homes. Like my home – with the orange front door, and the big, bird-filled tree in the back garden, that levitated in song at dawn and at dusk.

It was a council house, on the last road in Wolverhampton – we were those poor people who need social housing. The house backed on to a bleak dairy farm, separated from us only by a wire fence. One winter, the cows got hungry, trampled the fence down and invaded the garden, to eat our grass. My mother chased them away by banging on a pan with a spoon, and the garden was left punctured with hoof marks, in the frost.

The next summer, the council discovered the roof was made of asbestos and replaced it with a shiny new aluminium one. The rain sounded thin and lancing, like pins, when it fell on the new roof. It made inside – with pots of soup and the children playing with their dolls, in front of the three-bar heater – cosy. It was our first place, and our only place: the end of all journeys. The foundation of all things. It was where we kept our things, and where the world kept us. House. Home.

Our estate had been built after the war, in haste – my father took us to the local library and showed us pictures of it being constructed – the steel skeletons being thrown up on meadows, the road being carved out of mud. The post box appearing, on the corner, where it stood, unchanging, for the next forty years.

'This estate was for soldiers, returning from the war,' he explained. 'These were homes for heroes, to raise their families in, and get Britain back to normal. Nothing was too good for the common man.'

I thought often of the heroes using the door handle I used; the hero planting the tree I now climbed in. That houses had been needed – and were built. It was a comforting system. A satisfying thought.

In the 1980s, when the Conservative government put Britain's council housing stock up for sale, my father received a letter – asking us if we wished to buy our house, for £12,000.

'Even if I had the money, I wouldn't do it,' he said. 'There's no moral logic to it. A council house is for someone who would not have a house any other way. If you can afford to *buy* it, you shouldn't be *in* it.'

Our old house – our home – is now worth £100,000. I looked on a property website this morning. Those council tenants that did buy, back in the eighties – half our street – got an astonishing bargain.

I wonder what stories the fathers living there now will tell their children. Do they tell them about the houses being built by the government, for returning heroes?

Or do they – with a slightly crowing air – talk about what a canny investment this house was, instead? Unaware that their riches are just luck – absolute meaningless luck – and that they were simply in the right place, at the right time, and gained a random advantage?

What is a house? It changes, dependent on who is in it. When I lived in that house – that council house – it was an extraordinary gift; part of a merciful plan.

To the people there now – now it's a private property – it's the family's investment. The nest egg, *and* the nest.

What is a house? For it is *not* just a home, now – not that for so many people. As property prices continue their demented rise, a house has become one of three things, depending on your luck, age and financial status: a painful and unattainable dream; a terrifying drain on your resources; or else a fabulous investment.

What is a house? An *investment*. There are a million reasons to be angry with those who precipitated the banking crisis, but here's the biggest, sourest one: they scared people. They scared the middle classes out of stocks, shares, bonds and pensions, and made them put their money into bricks and mortar instead. The asset that will never disappear.

And now we have a property market spiralling upward, heated by a generation of amateur buy-to-let landlords and foreign investors – 75 per cent of new-build housing in London last year was sold to non-residents. If you look at an *A–Z* now, what you are seeing is not rows of homes any more – but rows and rows of investments, instead. Whole towns of acquisitions.

What is a house? It depends who you are. It could be an entry in a ledger book. A piece of luck. A piece of mercy. A burden. A drain. Your financial future. Or news: good news – big news, when the property market booms. Every time house prices rise, we rejoice. But *is* it good news? Not if you're young, or poor – watching the market soar away from you. Not if you are unlucky, and all – all – *all* you need for a house to be is a home.

What is a house? Could it not just be – would it be better if it were – always just a home?

This is a homes-themed section of the book – a symptom of the current economy in Britain, which is reliant on a housing market so febrile and bullish it is starting to warp everything around it. The Coalition's Bedroom Tax policy – denying housing benefit to claimants in housing deemed 'too big' – has, predictably, made things worse. I explained why, while smoking a fag and sighing.

THE BEDROOM TAX IS A TAX ON LOVE

All recent pieces on the Bedroom Tax have noted how, despite increasingly firm/desperate briefing notes from the Coalition, people are still referring to it as 'the Bedroom Tax' rather than by its official title, 'the Spare Room Subsidy'. Opinion pieces unfailingly start with the fact. Pub conversation majors on it.

It's presented as a little rebellion – people refusing to use the official name; using language to vilify it in the same way as we would 'the Poll Tax', or 'the Hun'. However many arsey press releases you put out, you ultimately can't control how people think about, or talk about, your policies! You can't spin a gut reaction. You can't rebrand emotion.

The thing is, every time someone pointedly refers to it as 'the Bedroom Tax', it makes me increasingly melancholic – that this is the *only* rebellion available: a disparaging nickname. A sarcastic inflection; a momentary breaking of the guidelines.

Meanwhile, just three months into the cuts, half of those affected by it are in arrears – an estimated 330,000 households; a quarter in debt for the first time in their lives. The intention of the policy is to encourage people to downsize to smaller properties. But while 180,000 households 'under-occupy' two-bedroom houses, only 85,000 one-bedroom houses are available for them to apply for. The result is that people are trapped in houses they can no longer afford, and with nowhere else to go.

I understand the logic of the Spare Room Subsidy. Affordable housing is in crisis – so bring in market forces to sort it out instead. Cut everyone's housing benefits to the bone – then let their budgets 'sort' the problem out. Economics will quickly and efficiently place these people where they must now be: somewhere cheaper, 10 miles away. Somewhere cheaper, 100 miles away. Or – if the rent arrears fatally capsize you, and even Wonga.com can't help – someone's sofa. A B&B. A hostel. Market forces are very simple: you can't live somewhere you can't afford. You must move until you find somewhere you can. And that is the end of the matter.

It's interesting that the repeated solution to times of economic hardship is that the working classes should become more energised and flexible. That when someone else ballses up the economy, the poorest, most exhausted people should note a banking crisis on the news, cheerfully say, 'I know what I must do for the sake of my country!', pack up their possessions – cheap fags, market-stall jeans, kids, huge telly – and start again, somewhere cheaper. Get on your bike. If you cannot afford to live in Brighton or London then move to Sheffield or Ayrshire and start again.

But there's a fundamental disconnect here. The thing we pride our working classes on is their 'sense of community'. What more is it to be working class than to have a nanna who babysits, an uncle who helps mend your clutch and a mate round the corner who takes your disabled brother to the shops, every week? To be poor is to be connected to others – unions, gangs, big weddings, territory, the endless cast lists of *EastEnders* and *Coronation Street*. It's not simply cultural – although that is important. It is, above all, necessary. When you are not strong, powerful or wealthy enough to sort your problems out on your own – hire help, buy devices, pay repair costs – you must tap into the unpaid, unseen economy of communal goodwill. In the most basic sense, you rely – more than someone in a higher income bracket ever will – on love.

And so every time we bring in a policy that insists that poorer people must uproot from families and friends – unpick their carefully woven lives, their million achingly negotiated arrangements and routines – and resurrect in another town, or county, alone, where there is no love, we take away the most important, most crucial power in poorer people's lives.

This was the obvious phenomenon David Cameron was clumsily, blindly, trying to articulate, with his 'Big Society': the interconnectedness of people's lives. The things that are done without charge. The things that are done for love.

But the thing that Cameron, and the Coalition, didn't understand about 'Big Society' is that things done without charge – those nannas looking after kids; those daughters tending the dying – do, still, require a little money: enough money to keep people where they want, and need, to be. Where market forces would push people is, very often, not where society needs them. The two forces do not often work in each other's interests.

So, in the interests of clarity, I'm not going to take the small emotional victory of calling it 'the Bedroom Tax'. I am, as the Coalition's press releases would wish, going to call it 'the Spare Room Subsidy' – because I think that name encapsulates the fundamental, awful, privileged blindness of the policy. The Coalition thought that these tiny amounts – an average of £12 a week – were subsidies on spare rooms. They were not.

They were subsidies on society itself.

In April 2013, the woman who utterly defined the social climate of my childhood in the 1980s, Margaret Thatcher, died. Many people I knew celebrated. Many others were furious that they did. I tried to explain why, for some people, her death was something they'd waited to mark for a long, long time.

WHY WE CHEERED IN THE STREET WHEN MARGARET THATCHER DIED

It's an odd thing – being told to mourn. Being told to feel sad. Being chided into reverence.

When the news of Margaret Thatcher's death broke, Twitter became – as it always is – the village well: the place of announcement and discussion.

At first, everyone stuck to a very simple 'Margaret Thatcher has died', or 'Baroness Thatcher, RIP', or, 'It has finally happened'. The first communications were the simple reporting of news.

After half an hour or so, people started to talk about their emotional reactions to the news that she was gone. And whenever someone from the left said anything non-reverent – or even joyous – about her passing, several thousand people from the right would be on hand to scold, 'Show some respect!', or 'An 87-year-old woman has died!' or 'Can you not feel some compassion? Can you not act with kindness? Can you not bow you head, just for today?'

And this was interesting, because those who supported Margaret Thatcher appeared not to believe that otherwise reasonable, considerate people could legitimately feel like this. The right could not understand why, even for a day, some on the left could not bow their heads and make a civilised attempt at deference.

But as someone who comes from a council estate, in a town that rioted in the 1980s (Wolverhampton: the McDonald's was left intact.

Even as we rioted, we protected the chips), but now mingles with the elite (I've been snubbed by David Cameron at a garden party: my echelons are 'upper'), I know why those feelings exist. How it is perfectly possible for kind people to not be capable of mourning a death of an old lady. Why your bones can boil against someone who should, ostensibly, be assessed as a hard-working public servant.

As a class jumper, I would say, as a sweeping generalisation, that politics can never mean as much to the professional classes as it does to the working class, or the underclass.

What is the worst – the very worst – government policy can do to you if you have a job in an industry with a strong future, live in a pleasant and well-equipped part of the country, and have enough money to have always thought of shoes as a necessity rather than a luxury? Push the highest rate of tax to 90 per cent, and let the bin men go out on strike. Annoying – but not fatal. If you are generally secure, a government can certainly inconvenience you, make your poorer, or make you angrier – it can be, let's be frank, a massive, incompetent, depressing, maybe even immoral pain in the arse – but *you*, and your family, and your social circle, will survive it. It is unlikely the essential course of your life will be much different under one government than the next, however diverse their ideas.

By way of contrast, what's the worst – the very worst – a government policy can do to you if you're poor – food bank poor? Dependent on the government poor? Well, everything. It can suddenly freeze, drop, or cancel your benefits – leaving you in the panic of unpayable bills, and deciding which meals to skip. It can underfund your schools and hospitals – death in a corridor; no exams passed: no escape route into private hospitals, or tutors, when your purse is full of buttons and old bus tickets. It can let your entire industry die – every skill learned and piece of knowledge earned left useless. It can leave your whole city to 'managed decline', as Geoffrey Howe's recently published suggestion for Liverpool revealed.

You know when middle-class people feel 'absolutely devastated' by the government's policy on the EU? They're not devastated. They're just annoyed.

You know when poor people are 'absolutely devastated' by the government's policy on housing benefit? They *are* absolutely devastated. They're in a hostel, with their children. It's not just words to them. It's the reporting of a fact.

Because if you are in the wrong town, in the wrong job, in the wrong class, the policies of a government can ruin you. And all those around you, too – so that you are all in fear. I don't know if you ever went to a former manufacturing town in the 1980s, but that's how they felt. The sadness and fear was everywhere – it saturated estates like greasy fog. It saturated the people like greasy fog: even now.

Whenever people reminisce about the eighties now, they always mention how the prospect of nuclear annihilation was a palpable thing. We were thoroughly and repeatedly talked through what it would be like to live in a post-nuclear wasteland: the lack of resources, the lack of hope. We were all conversant with what would happen when the wind blows. We knew what waited for us, if diplomacy failed.

As a nine-year-old when *Threads* – with its bomb blast, and melting St Paul's, and evaporating, screaming citizens – was broadcast, I had that hazy, childish thing of half believing, half not believing, that the dropping of the bomb had now happened. In Wolverhampton, it looked like diplomacy *had* failed. So much of what was promised for the apocalypse appeared to have come to us, bar the radiation burns – and, in the 1980s, antibiotic skincare for acne was so in its infancy that, often, one saw a particularly unlucky, gangling, pustule-crippled adolescent who looked like he really might have been the epicentre of the mushroom cloud.

We would drive into town, and my father would start the same, rattled monologue: 'When I was a kid, at this time of the day, all you'd hear was the "tramp, tramp, tramp" of people's feet as they walked to the factories – every bus would be full, the streets would be seething. This town had something to do, and money in its pocket. People used to come here for work, and get it, the same day. Look at it now,' he'd say, as we went right through the centre: boarded-up buildings, buddleia growing out of windows.

'A ghost town. Where have they gone? Where have they all gone?'

We were here to shop, at the cheapest place in town: the big, empty supermarket by the retail market, where someone had thrown up shelves inside what used to be a factory, and piled goods high and sold them cheap. Mice would run from the sacks of rice. Ghosts seemed to live up in the roof, in the tangle of pipes they'd simply painted over, in a sickly, unlikely turquoise.

It was only driving back home that you'd see where 'everyone' was – queuing outside the Job Centre, heads down. The old fellas, like my dad, who'd always thought they'd work jobs wet with sweat, who could only sign their names with an 'X', and who knew they were, in the resettling of the economy, fucked. The younger men, who looked pole-axed by knowing that 2,999,999 people had signed on before them – although part of their discombobulation could have been their jeans, which were still, at the time, worn very tight, and without the mercy of a Lycra mix.

I was, accidentally, in the town centre when the riots happened – when it seemed like every man in the city ran down the main road, screaming, and the police vans boxed us in, and our dad pulled us into a doorway, and pushed us to his chest, under his coat, with the shrill, sour smell of his sweat, as he panicked, and tried to hide us from screaming men under his padded, Burton's anorak.

And then, in times of calm, the attempts at pleasure. We went to West Park – Wolverhampton's green space – once. We were the first people in the park that day. As we walked through the gates, the muddy banks of the lake became animated, and the water began to churn, and there was a chittering sound that made you want to wipe your hands clean over and over and over again. Hundreds and hundreds of rats were fleeing at our approach – they were swimming out to their nests on the island in the middle of the lake, while emitting odd rat screams.

So that's where I grew up. The riots and rats and ghosts and sad, silent queues. It seemed like diplomacy had failed in Wolverhampton, in the 1980s. Like some kind of bomb *had* dropped.

And when an entire city falls – when you live somewhere that feels like the ruins of a civilisation; when your elders tell you, with a look of shock that is still new, that it did not use to be like this: that things were better, that things were pleasant, but not in your lifetime; and you see that they mourn the childhood you are having, and want to cover it up with their big, hard hands – you look, as all ruined, bombed cities must, to your leaders, to see what their reaction is to your unhappiness. You look to see what their solution is.

And the government of the eighties did not come and help. I sound as pathetic as a child when I say this now, but that's how we all felt. It was made clear that governments do not help in these matters – that the spores of private enterprise blow as they may, and that everything else was down to the individual. That is your city that was ruined; it was because not enough citizens were being dynamic, and opening wine bars, or starting up tech firms, or trading on the Stock Exchange. If a city was inferior, it was simply because its people were inferior. We were the problem. We – in Liverpool, and Sunderland, and Glasgow, and in the Welsh Valleys – were just ... wrong. We should have turned into something else, and we hadn't. And, as a consequence, we were disliked by our own government.

I grew up knowing that Margaret Thatcher disapproved of my entire existence: a family of eight children, in a council house, with a union-leader dad: home-educated, bohemian, scared of arguments, immersed in gay culture, with Welsh mining relatives sitting in the front room, talking about their picket lines. We were the kind of people holding people back.

In recent years I've frequently been told that my childhood dislike and fear of Mrs Thatcher was deeply ironic – as I am, in actual fact, a classic child of Thatcher. 'Look at you! Self-made! Working since you were thirteen, from a council estate in Wolverhampton! Pulled up by your bootstraps! A strong woman in a man's world! You are the absolute proof of everything she was saying! Margaret Thatcher made you!'

To which I always reply, very quietly: 'Yes. But look around. How many others like me made it out? How many ascended into the world of boys from Eton and Cambridge and the Home Counties, at ease with walking into big rooms, and making things happen? Where are the other working-class kids from my generation? Because I look around, and I don't see them. The barriers did not come down. Indeed, compared to my father's generation, they appear to have gone back up again.'

So this is where all that anger started – the anger that confused so many, on the announcement of Baroness Thatcher's death. All those people childishly downloading 'Ding, Dong! The Witch Is Dead', or throwing parties to 'celebrate' her passing. Among many commentators, there was bewilderment over the fireworks that were set off, and the champagne – put away in cupboards for so many years, waiting for this day – being drunk. Why would you celebrate a death? The death of someone hard-working, old and confused? It is, surely, unnecessarily crude. It's spiteful.

But for all those who were left behind, to mourn their own towns, the sadness and the fear had turned to sour anger, as it always does. And that is when so many impotent but determined entries were made in diaries. Entries made when a factory closed, or Section 28 was brought in, or a relative came back from a protest, bleeding. Entries made when politics seemed to get very, very personal – in your wage packet, and in your bed. Entries when politics became dangerous, and destructive, in so many towns.

And they will all have been written differently, on different days, in different pens in a thousand different ways, but what they all boiled down to was this: 'I can't do anything else, now, but outlive this. Outlive you. All I can do is outrun you.'

And that is what all the cheap, unworthy, yet ultimately heartfelt celebration was on 8 April. It was the simple astonishment and relief of people – in the Valleys, on the estates, in the hostels and on failed marches – who felt they had, against all their own predictions, survived something.

I was brought up to shout 'CLASS WAR!' at any opportunity – particularly if someone in a Mercedes cut my dad up on a dual carriageway – but I've learned it's more ... complicated than that.

This column was written after Ed Miliband – remember him? – gave a Labour Conference speech where he basically called the Tories dim. And, as I say, it's more complicated than that.

THE RICH ARE BLITHE

So, Ed Miliband's conference speech – which, unusually, abandoned the usual accusations of Tory maliciousness, in favour of a wholly new tactic: calling them divs, instead.

'Have you ever seen a more incompetent, hopeless, out-of-touch, U-turning, pledge-breaking, make-it-up-as-you-go-along, back-of-the-envelope, miserable shower?' Miliband asked, in a speech that frequently looked like it might end – like the 1980s McDonald's advert which it appear to ape – with the line, '... and all wrapped up in a sesame seed buuuuuuuun', but, alas, did not.

Labour's new line seems to be that the Tories are not a cold-hearted bunch of peasant punchers – but an intellectually busted flush, instead. That they're stupid. That's their problem.

However, I'm not sure the best attack is claiming stupidity. There are quite a lot of clever people in this government. I think the Tories' real weakest spot is their ... blitheness, instead.

Blitheness is an odd thing. Blitheness is different from optimism – which is basically a graceful digging-in; a silent vow never to give up. Optimism is a fit soul, committed to outrunning the darkness, however long it takes. Optimism has looked at the alternative – cynicism, resignation, despair – close up, in the eye, and, horrified, stiffened its resolve, and kept up a steady trot, toward the uplands.

Blitheness, on the other hand, is not hard-won. Blitheness is what you are born with – like lanugo. And, like lanugo, blitheness starts to wear off as soon as you rub up against anything abrasive.

Adults, then, who are still blithe have not rubbed up against anything abrasive. Blitheness does not have calluses on its hands; it does not stay awake at night, worrying what the next day's post will bring. Blitheness only ever gets birthday cards in the post; and postcards; and catalogues for candles, cashmere and pinafores. Blitheness is cushioned in the velvet surround of there being enough money to sort nearly every eventuality out.

To people who have often dreamed, in panic, of sealing up their letterbox, so that bad news can never be delivered, David Cameron's speech, a week after Miliband's, came from deep within this swaddling.

Explaining how £10 billion of cuts to the welfare bill would be introduced, Cameron mooted the end of housing benefit to single people under twenty-five.

'If hard-working young people have to live at home while they work and save, why should it be any different for those who don't?' Cameron asked, to wild, blithe applause.

It takes a blithe man to ask this question. Someone for whom 'at home' is Mum and Dad – careworn, but still loving – wryly opening up a bottle of wine when their postgraduate children camp out in the spare room, saving for the deposit for a house.

Sure, there will be arguments outside the bathroom when the hot water runs out; and the awkwardness of having massive adult bodies in the room that once held a toddler never quite goes away. But in a world where the money has disappeared, families must stick together and help each other out. Austerity measures mean feeling cramped; not having much privacy. Cancelling a holiday. Delaying your life plans for a decade.

If you are blithe, it would never occur to you that there are homes that are not a refuge at all. Rather, that 'home' is actually darkness, or a trap, and Mum, or Dad, are not welcoming – but dangerous. It's a blithe man who does not know how much damage can occur before the age of twenty-five behind the family doors. You can be blithe if you've never been in a flat so tiny the place feels like a pan coming to the boil, filled with grease, smoke and sour anxiety. If you'd never been somewhere so small that there *is* nowhere to work, and save.

Optimism is saying, firmly, 'Things will get better.'

Blitheness is saying, easily, 'Things never get that bad in the first place.'

Churchill was, despite his depression, an optimist. Bertie Wooster, in his spats, blithe. Blitheness is telling everyone to tighten their belts – and it never occurring that some people just don't have a belt.

But, of course, who does not love Wooster? For this is the deep irony of the appeal of the Tories – that this Boris-y, Cameron, public school blitheness is one of their biggest appeals.

In times of depression, frustration and despair, who doesn't find their spirits lifted by someone with the sunny, seductive belief that the solution to poverty isn't to spend money – but to save it? Who doesn't find their anxiety relived by these girl-faced, almost nonchalant boys, who exude an air of things being fixable simply by a stiffening of character, and everyone pulling together? These aren't *stupid* beliefs. They have often been the saving of our country. But believing that these are the solutions to *everyone's* problems? That's … blithe.

Ah, the rich. They all come to London, now. London – once a fabulous, slightly tatty, always rakish ale-house for the rackety and odd; but these days an increasingly venal, blanding, ageing money pit, where you cannot work out which is more objectionable: the £40 starter, the £14,000 handbag, or the £44 million house. Sometimes, I walk around it and feel like I'm the last scruffy person here who remembers the old warehouses being turned into clubs, and the new hopeful bands playing in pubs, and the trains delivering down, every day, young people from Manchester, Glasgow, Bristol, Swansea – all coming here to play the place, like a fabulous slot machine.

In 2016 they cannot afford to come here. They stay in their home towns. And that will make their home towns rise up, and eventually overtake London. And now I think I would like to see that. I would like to see London – that I once loved so passionately – quietly smothered by the rise of the west, and the north. London is a bad beast right now. Do not buy a house there, or in the south.

DO NOT BUY A HOUSE IN LONDON, OR THE SOUTH

You cannot escape the madness of sweating property fever in London, and the south.

It's a palpable heat, now. The market is tinder-dry. Everything is starting to smoulder. Some people like the smoke – they get high on it – but most people know this means that, soon, it will all ignite. Don't buy a house now, in London, or the south. You know this, in your guts. I say this back to you, as a friend. You know this 'never-ending bubble' is a tautology – no bubble lasts forever. That's why we call them bubbles. They are all made of mesmeric, rainbowed soap and hot air. Puff. All bubbles are at their biggest before they pop.

As we have no power over the mechanisms of this heat – we do not control interest rates, government lending schemes, or building initiatives – perhaps we should start using the only power we do have at our disposal to quell this roasting: conversation. Use language to cure ourselves of this fever – activate the sprinkler system, to bring the temperature down a degree or two.

When the news talks of 'the rising housing market' – all joyful images of Mr Fredricksen's house being born aloft, in *Up*, to great adventure – we should, insistently, refer to it as 'property inflation' instead. 'Inflation' is one of those sobering words that acts as cold compress to the fevered forehead. Inflation is Calpol. Inflation is sanity. Last week, over dinner, a mathematically inclined friend calculated that, if houses had risen in line with inflation, the average house in 2014 would cost £65,214.29 – not £250,000, as it currently is.

Conversely, if *food* had gone up as much as property has, in the last thirty years, a pint of milk would now cost £10. That's how you should talk about the 'rising housing market' now. This rising housing market that no one in this country can afford, and everyone knows we can't afford. And when the feverish explain that this doesn't matter – because British property is hot on the global market – quietly tot up in your head how many entries there are in Wikipedia for 'global market crash'. And *don't buy a house*. You know this, in your heart. Do not buy a house, in London, or the south.

For this heat is good for no one – for no one, at any time. Even in London, and the south. I drive through Hampstead, and down Bishops Avenue, every day – Bishops Avenue: infamously, the 'Most Expensive Street in Britain'. This is the area where the super-wealthy own houses that have doubled in price in the last ten years – £17 million, £22 million. The streets that should bask the most in the lovely heat of the rising market – if we think heat is, universally, lovely.

But driving down Bishops Avenue, and its neighbouring streets, prompts you to ask, 'What use is heat? What does £22 million actually *mean*?' For this area of London is unloved, unpleasant and semi-abandoned, now. Some houses were bought, you suspect, just for the thrill of buying for £22 million. They have sat empty for a decade – with pigeons flying through the windows and buddleia growing through oak parquet, buckling, wet, in the hallways.

Others, meanwhile, are being 'maximised' – as something worth £22 million is apt to be. There is one street, near Bishops Avenue, where nearly every house is either just built, or being built. A desert of builders' sand, and mixer trucks. Where cranes perpetually bow low, as if genuflecting to money. It is not a place you would enjoy living. These are not homes.

I cannot tell you how bleak and depressing the new, monstrous, finished houses are. Their façades have all the impassive menace of a Doberman Pinscher – staring at you from behind a chain-link fence. So often, when driving past the crews on these sites, I feel like stopping – to defend Britain.

'We do make lovely buildings, you know,' I want to tell them. 'We are capable of it. I could show you the wet slate roofs of Aberystwyth – black and shiny as whale skin – or the imperial magnolia crescents of Regency Bath. You, on the other hand, are being employed to build ossuaries for money to be lived in, at most, for four months a year. No one here loves these.'

Outside the biggest of these houses, there are architects' 'photos' of what the interior will look like. All show swimming pools, sunk below ground: windowless, in black marble. Like the pool inside the mountain in which Gollum gradually turned death-white, and his hands became clawed, and webbed.

These pictures astonish me. For what originally brought the burning Sauron's eye of international capital here? Hampstead Heath – which lies at the end of this street. Where bluestocking octogenarians slide into the Bathing Ponds at dawn – geese skeining overhead – and swim, in the willowed-edged, brown cold. This was a place founded on love.

Meanwhile, in the heated pool-bubble down the road, the pop awaits. Because mankind cannot – will not – sustain in a bubble. Do not buy a house in London, or the south, now. You know this, in your guts.

And this piece is on how property becoming an unobtainable fantasy for most has affected London. You'll be surprised to hear I think it's quite bad.

LONDON IS DYING

I've been having a recurring conversation with friends over the last few months. They've been in an amusingly disparate series of locations – dandy restaurant, rainy park, literary launch, council tip – but always the same thing. We'll be chatting about something, there'll be a pause, and then one of us will go, hesitantly, 'Is it just me, or has London … gone weird?'

Has London gone weird? In many ways, it's hard to say – there are so many Londons: how could you ever speak for them all? The London of the City boy, or the Tory policy wonk, is different from the London of the trans* burlesque dancer in Vauxhall – and different again from a Turkish Muslim running a deli on Green Lanes. There are 7 million Londons – one for each person here – all of us bound together by the free-for-all joy of being able to walk over Waterloo Bridge at sunset; or suddenly catching St Paul's pearling at the end of the street, emitting its long, low bass-note through the City.

But here's the thing: London has never been just a place, but a game, too – a fruit machine in which *you* are the coin you put in, with the prospect of coming up all cherries, or bells. When I was young, London was where you came when you were a hungry, fizzing freak: the kind of person who would be beaten up in Ayrshire, or Dudley, but who could come to London and make money cascade from the machine by writing, acting, singing, coding, opening a club. Maybe not golden coins – but enough brown ones to find a little flat above a shop, ride the bus, eat chips in the street, and suspect, with reasonable evidence, that tomorrow would be better than today.

London was a big waterwheel, with a steady current of the young, odd and determined pouring down the country, and on to its paddles, keeping it turning. We all poured down here. This is where Britain's gravity sent us.

About five years ago, though, this noticeably stopped. Rents become so grotesque that even Britain's hard tilt towards the capital couldn't keep the young people flowing: the gates into London effectively closed, after the 2008 crisis.

And now, in 2013, no one new is being let in, any more – unless, of course, they are oligarchs, or of the bonus class, who may helicopter over the gates, at will. No one I know can afford to move here. The key to the average first flat is made of gold: £404,000. They are locked out.

At first, this wasn't noticeable – London lived off the previous generation of young, odd, poor things for a while. But, now, in the tired autumn a year after the Olympics' hot blood and genius, it has really hit home: the creativity and oddness of London slowly dating and atrophying, as the population trapped within the city gates ages, wearies, and, inevitably, corrodes.

The opening of lavish yet oddly revolting restaurants – for who wants to eat beautiful food surrounded by Rolex-flashing old men, being tolerated by call girls? The return of the kind of grotesque, dumb art created only to flatter super-rich buyers at this year's Frieze. The centre of London being rebuilt in the same black glass and steel that has made the area around Times Square in New York look like a massive, cold, dilated pupil – the face of a dead giant, beginning to rot around the nose, and eye, as everything warm, and mammalian, and gleeful, flees to Brooklyn, and Queens.

And as the population skews to a self-selecting majority of the wealthy and conservative, you see London's subconscious trying to rebalance the culture – in an odd, mutated, dreamlike way. As the *real* poor drain out of the city, the foodstuffs of the poor perversely burgeons – 'street food', sloe gin from dinky salvaged jam jars, burger joints called ever-more-humble things: the Shed, the Shack. Dirty Burger, in Kentish Town, in it's faux-favela corrugated iron lean-to, in an area where the average three-bedroom house costs £1.4 million.

Elsewhere, there's offal, 'forest foraged mushrooms' and rough, hand-turned bread. The increasing Marie Antoinette-ishness of this feels like a communal fever – London punctured with dozens of 'humble' £12 burger dairy cottages while, all around, the rest of the city Versailles itself into sheer mirrored cliffs of glass, steel and endlessly excavated underground swimming pools.

What will happen? What will happen in the end, if London remains closed to the young and new and restless and weird, and becomes merely a place that the global elite invest in houses, in the way that – before 2008 – they more usefully invested in stocks and shares?

Well, it's good news for Britain. A million ideas a week that would, previously, have migrated to London will now remain in their home towns, and make *those* towns glorious instead. As London, glassy-eyed and compulsive, begins to eat its own heart out, Manchester, Birmingham, Bristol, Glasgow, Sheffield, Liverpool, Cardiff and Plymouth will rise again.

And London will simply continue to admire itself, endlessly, in the mirror of the Thames, until, one day, it realises it has dried up completely – and turns back to find the city empty, save for skeletons and bad money.

Frankly, if push came to shove, I wouldn't mind if the rest of London did die, or became so ossified by money and Botox that it simply stopped moving, and was mistaken for a statue. I wouldn't mind if every part of it eventually got bought by a Russian and used as a nick-nack – so long as we save Soho. London's dirty, musky, belly button – the absolute concentrate of the city through the ages. Whenever I don't know where I am at 3am, because I've had one too many peppy snifters, I know where I am really: Soho. Where you always end up, if you're the right sort of bad sort of good person.

THE SHIT-HEEL BUTCHERS OF SOHO

All my life, I've been scared of sticking at skiffle. You know – those stories of people who, when rock'n'roll came along, said, 'Ooh, no – this isn't as good as *skiffle*. A guitar, a washtub bass, a jug and a musical saw – that's *proper* music. Not like this Little Richard fellow, or those Beatles. No – I'm going to stick with skiffle, thank you very much.'

So, no. I don't want to be nostalgic for the sake of it. My default is always to be excited about the new thing – even if, sometimes, welcoming the new thing means discarding the older things, or letting them fade away. Sometimes, you have to burn up a little bit of the past to light up the future. Your sweet memories might have to be used as tinder to make someone *else's* memories. I get that. That's progress. I understand about change. I am not smashing the looms.

But there are times when things are about to change when you must say, 'I think keeping this would be *useful* to us, actually. To change this would be to also change a million other, interconnected things. To change this is to take the heart out of something – the heart of something living – just to sell as meat. This thing, *this* thing needs to stay the same.'

And, so, London. Yes – all the wankers live here. The very worst kind – the kind who actively ruin everything – but London is still also where you'll end up in a room with the ten oddest, brightest, most on-fire people – half of whom will be furiously engaged in trying to stop the wankers previously mentioned – and think, 'London still isn't just a place – it's an idea. Out of this room will come hundreds of small futures.'

But ideas need a place to happen, and they can only happen in certain kinds of places. If you look through the history of culture, you will see that ideas tend to come from attic flats, dingy boozers and nightclubs full of freaks. They come from areas with manky pigeons and tiny button shops, where all the misfits – women, gays, immigrants, shy boys, hot alcoholics and people generally on a mission – can converge.

And this is why there is a campaign to save Soho at the moment – for the Crossrail station is nearing completion, and it seems the moment it opens its barriers it will blow away those hundred tiny streets of Soho – the sticky basements, coffee houses, guitar shops and furtive corners; the boozers with gravy-brown tables, burnished by a million woozily sliding elbows – and replace them all with a new plan: executive flats, and office space, rendered in uniform International Architecture. All glass and steel, with brightly coloured atriums in hot-orange, or unexpected teal.

That's the plan – to monetise Soho. To take its name, known across the world, and use it to sell this new, gutless, hand-sanitiser wankers' farm. To take the Soho out of Soho, and turn it into … Bro-ho. No-ho.

Where is London, if Soho is gone? Once they've seen Buckingham Palace, and the Thames, what are the millions of people who come to London going to see, if the places are gone that the fleeing Huguenots built, and the Italians turned into cheap eating places, and Dylan Thomas drank, and Bob Dylan played, and beatniks and strippers and drag queens rubbed shoulders, as jazz smoked in the basements? How much of historic, eccentric, transgressive London can you replace with well-appointed apartments for foreign investors, before people stop wanting to come here any more?

For that's the dangerous game being played with London's 'development', at the moment – that new, faceless skyline rising up by the Thames; Camden Market's bland, chain-store ruination; the cherry-tree gardens of Hampstead being replaced with hulking, gravel-drived super-mansions.

'I'm going to London.' 'Where is London?' 'I'll be honest – it's not there any more. But I can show you some pictures of what it *used* to look like.'

Where do you go, and what do you do, when you go to Paris, New York, Berlin or Dublin? For you don't just go to a *place* – you travel to see if you can see other times, too: you go to the old parts, the intact parts, to hunt echoes and ghosts. You look for the footsteps and fingerprints of Bowie, Dickens, Gainsbourg, Joyce – the thrill of being able to stand on a doorstep and say, '*This* is the doorstep they would have used. They came here for a reason – and I have, too. Because there is nowhere else like this. This place is a matrix, a melody, a curation – a carefully constructed and unique thing – known across the world – and to change too much of it is for it to cease to exist.'

London cannot be turned into one, uniform SuperTown – apartments and offices, all the same, from Heathrow to Stratford, from Walthamstow to Peckham. Cities need their villages – their tiny sheltered coves, among the otherwise sheer cliff faces of high-rise glass and steel. If Soho goes, then there is truly nothing left in this city that will not be sold. We have become cheap, shit-heel butchers, selling hearts for meat.

Of course, there are lighter, more enjoyable aspects of living in London. Regent's Park Rose Garden; tiny dogs; spotting celebrities getting keys cut in Timpson's. And the 5:2 Diet. For a brief spell in 2013, everyone was on the 5:2 Diet, and I found it very, very amusing.

HOW TO HANDLE OTHER PEOPLE'S 5:2 DIETS

At this point in the summer of 2013 there is nothing most urban Westerners need more than advice on how to cope with a friend, colleague, loved one or fellow lift-user who is on the 5:2 Diet.

For those who don't know what the 5:2 is, it is a diet wherein the dieter eats perfectly normally for five days of the week – then spends the remaining two days on a very restricted diet, of no more than 500 calories for women, and 600 for men. The 5:2 is also referred to as 'intermittent fasting', which gives it a pleasingly religious/medieval air – the subconscious suggestion being that the dieter will end up not only more slender, but also wiser, calmer and closer to God.

Current proponents of the diet are bogglingly varied, and are said to include Benedict Cumberbatch ('It's the only way to slim down into Sherlock'), Sir Mervyn King, Beyoncé and Hugh Fearnley-Whittingstall and the book *The Fast Diet* has now sold over 250,000 copies in the UK. So, yes – the 5:2 is all around you. There is no escape. Indeed, you are almost certainly going to spend some time today with someone who is following it. Here is my advice for you, when that interaction should happen.

1) Establish, as soon as possible – as if it were an emergency – if they are on a 'Fast Day' or not. This is key information you will need to know right up front, before you say or do *anything*. I cannot stress how vital it is that you discover this. Thankfully, it's very easy to find out if someone is on a Fast Day, because anyone on a

Fast Day will tend to say 'I'm on a Fast Day' in a small, tense voice within thirty seconds of meeting you. They will then look at you as if expecting you to respond with something that expresses great sympathy – 'Oh no! A Fast Day! You must be *very very* hungry!' but *also* admiration – 'But, then, eating only 500 calories for a whole day is an amazing thing for you to be doing, Sue! Go *you!*' Bear in mind that even if you *do* give this perfect greeting – rather than the far more likely nonplussed 'Oh' – it's important for you to realise that, ultimately, nothing can go well between you and this Fasting person today. This is someone functioning on 40 per cent of their brain capacity, at best – disabled as they are by extreme hunger and constant thoughts of how much they would like some delicious frangible buttery toast. They hate you because you are a person who *can* have some toast. And if you go so far as to eat some toast in front of them, they will turn away in a poorly suppressed murderous rage, probably to go and stab a picture of you eating some toast, which they are about to draw, in the aching hours of free time unfilled, today, with lovely breakfasts, dinners, lunches and snacks. Although any point in the day with someone Fasting is basically going to be a tense and unpleasant pain in the arse for you, there is a particular danger time:

2) Between 2 and 5pm on a Fast Day is usually the peak of the hunger – and, therefore, the peak of the danger for you. During this spike in hunger, brain capacity appears to drop as low as 9 per cent, and Fasters become actively evil. Like demons. Personally, were I Prime Minister I would make it so people you were talking to on the phone had to say, at the start of the conversation, 'It's 4.30pm and I'm on a Fast Day', and then you could just simply put the phone down before they inexplicably refuse to process your claim, send out an engineer to mend your boiler, or authorise an emergency crew to come and cut you, bleeding, out of the wreckage of your car. NB: In all likelihood, the person who just crashed into your car was someone else on a Fast Day, who'd just driven past a Burger King, and was blind with tears of hunger.

3) Often the rage suddenly turns to sorrow, accompanied by massive physical weakness. You see fully grown women struggling to open a can of Diet Coke; or big men trying to turn stiff door handles before collapsing, shouting, 'My wrists suddenly feel as limp and powerless as Cheestrings. Oh GOD! HELP ME! THINK MY BODY HAS STARTED TO CONSUME ITSELF FROM WITHIN!' Operating a photocopier is beyond these people at this point – you will have to do it for them. You will essentially become one of those Helping Hands monkeys that disabled people have – but for a 38-year-old accountant from Hackney.

4) Smugness. On 'normal days', this: 'I've lost three-quarters of a stone!' they will say, folding fistfuls of chips into their mouths. And you'll be all like, 'Hang on – you only did that because we didn't *kill you* on the days you were behaving like a Roid Rage Colin from *The Secret Garden*! This is *society*'s achievement – not yours!' But they just sit there, being a size 10, not listening.

And you know what drives people on the 5:2 Diet most crazy on their Fast Days? Bacon. They dream bacon dreams, and cry bacon tears. For bacon is the most powerful substance on Earth.

BACON!

I had one of the Big Realisations of my life this week: up there with 'It's okay – *no one* has a clue what they're doing', and 'Put the fez back on the shelf – you will never be the kind of person who can style out a hat.' And it is this: bacon is the single most important thing in the world today.

This is not, you must understand, some ludicrous thesis that popped into my head, which I then worked backwards to try to prove. On the contrary – looking at it now I can see it was a fact that had been startlingly obvious for some time, but which I had simply chosen to ignore: much like Terry and June having had sex, or David Cameron running the actual country my life is in.

It started with Bacon Salt. Some friends of mine heard of Bacon Salt. 'We must get the Bacon Salt!' they shouted. 'We will order the Bacon Salt, from America, and when it gets here – all covered in foreign stamps, in a brown cardboard box that's a slightly and excitingly different brown from the brown of British cardboard boxes – we will have a Bacon Salt Party! Awl-*right*!'

Bacon Salt is, as you have correctly guessed, some salt that tastes like bacon. No calories, no fat, entirely vegetarian and kosher – it is a product which both believes, and makes possible, its mission statement: 'Because everything should taste of bacon.' Mashed potato, chicken sandwich, macaroni cheese – even a cup of tea, I suppose, if you're deeply perverted for bacon. It can all be hogged up in a second. With one shake, everything can taste of smoky pig.

Well, I can't say I wasn't amazed. I *was* amazed. It's almost as if, for the world that has everything – penicillin, Mozart, an ability to leave rubbish on the Moon – we've had to think of increasingly bizarre things to give ourselves on our birthday. We have, finally, almost in desperation, given ourselves the Universal Bacon Facility.

But you know what? That Bacon Salt amazement was a false amazement. I should have held my amaze. Because the next day, tootling around the internet, I found a website that was as if I were falling down a rabbit hole. But a rabbit hole made of bacon. The Bacon Hole.

This website made Bacon Salt seem as nothing. For this was a site that sold pretty much every product you could ever conceive of – but with the implicit understanding that the most important thing about the construction of an item should be that it encompasses bacon. Bacon-scented candles. Bacon vodka. Bacon chocolate. Bacon coffee. Bacon-flavoured toothpicks. Bacon rolling papers. Bacon mints – 'How do you know you don't like it if you haven't tried it?' Bacon-print dresses. The bacon bikini – the 'Bac-ini'. Bacon tattoos. Baconnaise – the mayonnaise/bacon hybrid child the twenty-first century has been waiting for. It even included recipes for Bacon Martinis, meaning that there could now be a third option: shaken, stirred – or crispy.

The website was, and is, a terrifying, telescopic reveal of one species' hog-based insanity. Because, according to a 3,000-word entry on Wikipedia, America – and, ipso facto, the world – is officially in the grips of 'Baconmania'; making bacon the Meatles, I guess. The per-head consumption of bacon has shot up in the States in the last ten years, with Americans embracing bacon as not just a foodstuff, but an entire way of life. 'Bacon IS America!' Salon.com claimed. More cynical hands might suggest that it's less that 'bacon is America' and more because, in an era of endless stupidity, bacon is basically Meat Toast – you can't screw it up. It practically cooks itself if you leave it on a windowsill for ten minutes.

But while America – in the dying days of its global supremacy – loses its mind to bacon, the keener observer may begin to notice how bacon has power and influence stretching over the millennia. Consider, for a moment, the things forbidden by major religions: adultery, incest, murder – and, for nearly 2 billion people, pork. Yeah, well, I think we know what's going on there – the whole 'pork' thing is just a sledgehammer TO BREAK BACON. No one gives that much of a toss about a pork chop – it's bacon that's the will-breaker. It's what always gets the vegetarians.

Clearly aware of the siren call of bacon, a prehistoric organisation of Jewish and Muslim elders – the Grilluminati, perhaps – put in place laws that would stop their people from perishing in a hoggy fug of bacon abuse, rind fatigue and fannying away colossal technological advances on inventing the Bacon Bra. Poor, sweet, stupid Christians, then. For without the fear of eternal damnation, bacon has a clear, unimpeded expressway into our souls. We are helpless in its presence.

As America's current bacon frenzy illustrates, when culture, technology and economy allow Mankind the option of unlimited bacon – for bacon to fill every moment and aspect of its life – Mankind will hit the 'Bacon Me' button like an unhinged mandrill. In David Lynch's *Dune*, when Kyle MacLachlan gnomically insisted, 'The spice is the worm! The worm is the spice!' we can see, now, that both worm and spice were, in fact, bacon. Bacon is the Dark Matter that holds together the universe. *Richard Bacon has just taken over from Simon Mayo on BBC Five Live.*[*] We are stardust. We are bacon.

Anyway, yesterday, my friends finally get their Bacon Salt.

'We're having that Bacon Salt party!' they cried. 'Come over! Bacon Salt all round!'

It was at that moment that a towering disdain for the whole concept of bacon finally overwhelmed me.

'No thanks,' I said. 'I want to live in a multi-flavoured world. I don't want to be the generation that forgets what non-bacon popcorn tastes like. I believe the flavour of bacon should be kept exclusively to the foodstuff, bacon – and not allowed to blot out every other thing,

---

[*] Although, of course, had the station controller known about Baconnaise, the entire daytime schedule could be different.

like some rampant culinary knotweed. I draw a line in the sand, here and now. I reject bacon! IT LOOKS LIKE PRINCE PHILIP'S EARS, FOR GOD'S SAKE.'

And, besides, if you sprinkle smoked paprika on stuff, it does exactly the same thing.

There is nothing I like more than a huge live event on TV – as you will see later in the book, with all my hysterical coverage of the 2012 Olympics and Paralympics.

Of course, the Olympics and Paralympics were inspiring global events celebrating the very best of humanity – lush, panoramic coverage of sweat, pain, endeavour, crushing defeat and glory. Everything you would wish to know about our species was laid out there, for the world to marvel at. A true, notable pinnacle in the world's calendar.

But they're not my favourite events.

I like it when it all goes tits up. Massive failures. Shumbolic botches. Awkward on-air silences. The sound of millions of people rolling their eyes, and sighing. Or else, not failure, but an increasing sense of weirdness and WTF? Think of Michael Jackson's funeral, when the r'n'b star Usher appeared to be trying to open Jackson's casket; or the Royal Wedding of the Duke and Duchess of Cambridge, when TV magician Paul Daniels got into a Twitter fight with Stephen Fry, when Fry announced he was watching darts, instead. That's what fattens my goose. Humanity trying to do something significant, solemn and appropriate – and getting it a bit wrong.

And, so, the weekend of the Queen's Diamond Jubilee. A national holiday, and three days of televised events. All of which went a bit – thank you sweet Baby Jesus – wrong.

THE RAINY JUBILEE – GOD BLESS YOU, MA'AM

On the Saturday of the Jubilee I go on my usual run through north London. It's like an exhaustively planned establishing tracking shot, in a documentary called *The Changing Face of Britain: 2012.*

Down in Finsbury Park – past Wig World, and endless fried chicken shacks – urban Britain is making its nod to the Jubilee. Outside the pubs, drinkers – big men, in shorts – have staked out tables and benches. They exude the quiet, low-level confidence and skill of people who intend to be off their margins by 1pm; then remain that way for all four days of the Bank Holiday. They have an air of purpose usually seen in sheet-metal workers, cutting out car doors; or code crackers, sitting down at desks at Bletchley.

One is wearing a cardboard mask of Prince Harry. Another has one of Pippa Middleton. This weekend, their job is to drink, unceasingly, to Queen and country.

Outside Nando's, there is a double-sided sandwich board. On one side, it says 'PERI PERI CHICKEN'. The 'ER' in 'Peri Peri' has been made to look like the royal insignia. It's quite classy. On the other side, the message – which I feel genuinely speaks for the hearts of all customers – reads, 'Thanks for the days off, Ma'am!'

Five chicken wings are just £5.20.

Running on, north, the road pitches up, the gardens fill with pink roses, and I am in Highgate – the dandy hilltop village enclave of bankers and millionaires. There, the window of the vintage tea shop 'High Tea' is filled with Union Jack cupcakes. The hanging baskets have been fluffed into a Richard Curtis-like vision of English winsomery. The olde-style apothecary has filled its bow-front windows with bunches of lavender and British toiletries.

Yardley's Triple-Milled English Rose Soap is just £7.99.

I turn, and start looping back. A mile away from home, and I return to privet-hedged suburbia. The sky starts lowering. The temperature is dropping. Summer looks like it's being recalled. I run past the red, square Catholic church at the end of our street. There is a funeral in progress – the coffin is being carried out of the hearse, into a crescent of black-shoed mourners. It is draped in a Union Jack flag.

This weekend, even the dead are taking part in the Jubilee.

It starts to rain.

Back home, and the children are getting ready for tomorrow's Jubilee party. Both are wearing the Jubilee crowns they made at school – eight-year-old Nancy's is decorated with a picture she drew of the Queen. The Queen looks quite masculine, and angry. A bit like Bill Oddie, when he sees an adolescent heron caught up in a discarded fishing line.

On Friday – in honour of the Jubilee – the children were excused from wearing their school uniforms, and told to come in 'something red, white or blue', instead.

'All the boys came in Arsenal strips,' Nancy says.

She's making cupcakes. For some reason never quite explained, making cupcakes seems to be a vital part of this Jubilee. As if responding to some manner of embedded race memory, on hearing the words 'Diamond Jubilee' every household in Britain has automatically started dedicatedly creaming gigantic quantities of butter, sugar and eggs. This week, it is an issue of patriotic duty to make small cakes. Our Queen sits on a throne made of sponge and jam.

In the absence of any formal ritual or schedule, such as with Christmas (stockings, massive lunch, *EastEnders*, standing at the bottom of the garden with a fag going 'We're going away for Christmas next year. This is the *last time*'), Britain is carefully improvising its way through this Jubilee, using the props of 1950s tea dresses, bunting, charmingly mismatched china, red lipstick and vintage tablecloths. In many ways, the Queen's Diamond Jubilee is the 'Kirstie Allsopp Home-Made Jubilee'. 'The Cath Kidston Anniversary.'

Studying the origins of jubilees is of no help to our shaky planning – the Ancient Egyptians held the first jubilees for their pharaohs every thirty years, by way of 'renewing' their health and vigour. Their ceremonies consisted of the pharaoh donning a jubilee cape, decorated with the tail of a wild animal, then running a race against a bull. Yeah.

All Egyptian ceremonies would then climax with the high priest incanting prayers to the gods, while holding up the flensed pelvis of an ox.

As the 'ox pelvis bit' seemed to have been vetoed by Gary Barlow – organiser of the Jubilee concert – in favour of Cliff Richard singing 'Congratulations', instead, the British have been largely left on their own to work out how best to pay tribute to the Queen.

Each decision, of course, says more about the celebrant than the Queen herself, or the nature of the monarchy in the twenty-first century. Soft-porn men's magazine *Zoo*, for instance, has issued a 'Diamond

Boobilee' special – 'A right royal collection of the best British boobs!' including 'A free massive poster – sixty-boob salute to the Queen!'

Royal perfumiers Floris, on the other hand, issued the 'Private Collection Perfume', in an antique crystal bottle, hung with a 'delicate gold chain featuring a white diamond', and a hallmarked Royal Arms charm, for £15,000.

For those wishing for something in between tits and diamonds, meanwhile, there is Marmite's limited edition jars, 'Ma'amite' – normal Marmite, but with a thought about the Queen on the jar. So that even breakfast might celebrate the Jubilee.

And, in the meantime, there's cakes. Cakes cakes cakes. Cakes, while we figure out what this Jubilee actually is. Cakes, as a holding operation, while Britain works out just what the Jubilee, and the Queen – and, indeed, being British – all actually consist of.

In the twenty-first century all three remain, essentially, mysterious. If Britain's unofficial motto has become 'Keep Calm & Carry On', its interim Jubilee motto is 'Get Drunk & Make Cakes, Until Further Notice'.

The next day, Sunday, is ten degrees colder than yesterday. It's raining, hard. Summer is unconscious. In London, my kids are dutifully making a three-metre-high pile of cupcakes on the kitchen table – the rain having moved the day's street parties indoors.

I, on the other hand, am now far away, in Hay-on-Wye, at the literary festival. As I eat breakfast, I watch *The Andrew Marr Show*, which has an interview with the Pageant Master, the man who has organised the 1,000-boat-strong Flotilla along the Thames.

He is being asked about the catastrophic weather forecast for the afternoon, which seems to be specifically focused on the Thames, and, micro-specifically, over the 86-year-old Queen's hat.

'I'm hoping the cloud will burn off,' he says, with the 'stay positive!', intense eye contact of someone who, deep down inside, is screaming an endless, silent scream.

'But there's so much zeal and pride,' he continues, 'I'm hoping it will reflect off the river, and bounce on to the people on the riverbank.'

'Good luck with that,' I think. 'Good luck with that plan. Myself, I would have preferred a giant awning.'

The Andrew Marr Show ends, and I've got three hours to kill in Hay. The Jubilee must be out there somewhere, I think. I'm going to walk around the town, and try to find it.

Past the hotel door, the rain is tumultuous – it is coming sideways, and down; but also, interestingly, it is bouncing upwards, from the road, too. The scenes I had fondly imagined – trestle tables, jam jars filled with wildflowers, tipsy nannas, bunting, and cake, obviously – are resoundingly absent. Laburnums drip. Slate roofs shoot rainwater into gutters like a cannonade.

I walk past one house, garlanded with bunting, as the front door opens and a woman pops her head out.

'Perhaps she is about to start preparations for a street party!' I think. 'This is the start of the festivities!'

She puts her hand out, and feels the rain – then scowls and withdraws back into the house. The door slams. This is not the start of the festivities.

I know I have not picked my location well. I am scarcely in a hotbed of fervent monarchism – I'm in a Welsh town that's holding a left-wing literary festival. I go into a teashop, to seek respite from the rain, sit next to a display of silver sugar tongs, and order some Bara brith.

'Are there any Jubilee events happening today?' I ask the waitress, as I drip onto the flagstones. 'To honour our Queen?'

'I don't think so. But I did just see A.C. Grayling!' she replies, cheerfully.

Having eaten the Bara brith – it's some cake! My best contribution to the Jubilee so far – I go back out into the rain, and trail around the shops. In Britain in 2012, consumerism is the barometer of humanity's soul. Have people literally been buying into the Jubilee?

'They were until yesterday,' the man behind the counter in The Green Room says. He's from Birmingham. He has the impossible, non-specific melancholy of all Brummies. 'Bunting. A lot of bunting. But today, I've only sold two car flags.'

'Are there any Jubilee celebrations going on in Hay?' I ask.

'There's something in The Square tomorrow, I think,' he says, mournfully.

'Nothing today?' I ask.

'Isn't one street party enough?' he replies, with a burdened sigh.

I cross the road, to Mr Puzzles Jigsaw World, which incorporates Teddy Bear Wonderland.

'Do you have any Jubilee jigsaws?' I ask. 'Colourful ones, with pictures of the Queen on – from all ages of her reign?'

'There's just one left, yes,' the lady behind the counter says. 'In the window.'

I have to say, I'm surprised. I thought my request was so ludicrously specific that I would get a definite 'no'.

But then, as I stand there – holding the 1,500-piece 'Diamond Jubilee' box in my hand, featuring over thirty different pictures of the Queen, from all decades of her reign – I realise that Mr Puzzles Jigsaw World is a place that sees a great many specific requests. At the counter, a man, accompanied by his daughter, says, 'You've got a llama one here – but would you happen to have any alpaca? She can tell the difference.'

In the hardware store down the road, the Union Jack toilet paper – displayed in the window – has been a runaway best-seller, at £4.20.

'How have you analysed that?' I ask the woman behind the counter. 'Is it an act of fervent monarchist patriotism, to buy Union Jack toilet paper? Or is it just republicans, wiping their bums on the national flag?'

'I don't know,' she admits. 'But our Reverend Charles has told us we mustn't refer to it as "toilet paper" – but "bunting for bums".'

This is Jubilee toilet paper that has been mentioned in a church sermon. God has had to intervene. That's how confused we all are.

Back outside, the side streets are empty. The road is shiny black. Buses pass in waves of splash and surf. I take my iPhone out, to write down a poignant thought about the Queen, and three super-fat raindrops hit the screen so hard that they type the word 'trr'. The weather is beginning to give the impression of sentience. No one will be out celebrating the Jubilee in this filth. Already slightly anxious, a terrible thought suddenly strikes me.

'Oh God,' I think, in sudden panic. 'Is it in my heart? Is the answer to my quest – to find the Jubilee, out here – is that it is actually "in my heart"? Oh God, please don't let the Jubilee be in my heart.'

Ten minutes later, and I realise what an idiot I've been. Of *course* the Jubilee isn't in my heart. That would be ridiculous. The Jubilee is on the *telly* – where all the best things are.

1.30pm, and the BBC's coverage of the Royal Flotilla begins. The BBC have already put an astonishing amount of spadework into the Jubilee. On Friday night I watched Jennie Bond's tribute, which had taken the frankly left-field editorial decision to tell the story of the Queen's sixty-year reign – but solely and only through all her visits to the south west of England.

Stock footage of the sixties showed Britain's cultural explosion: the country taking acid and landing in *Oz*; Technicolor and magnificent in floral minis, floral Minis, and John Lennon's kaleidoscope eyes.

'But things were different down in the south of the country!' Bond's voiceover said, cheerfully.

A lovely auld fella in a cap appeared. 'What us lot were looking forward to,' he said in an intense Cornish burr, 'were the Royal Yacht *Britannia* coming into the harbour at Plymouth. Boy oh boy – what a boat!'

The 1970s, meanwhile, were heralded by the fabulous, drawling decline of the Sex Pistols' 'God Save The Queen' – *'No/Future!/No/Future!'* – accompanied by some footage of the Queen cutting into an enormous piece of cheese, with a sword. I presume she was in Wookey Hole.

The nineties were my favourite decade, however. Over pictures of the troubled marriages of Prince Charles and Prince Andrew, Windsor Castle on fire, and Diana's funeral, Bond's voiceover chirped, 'This was the start of a time of turmoil for the Royal Family. And it was also my start in my tenure as the BBC's Royal Correspondent!'

Because that's how we all remember it. Bond-time.

Back on the Thames, on Sunday, and the BBC's coverage of the Flotilla was off to a worrying start. Settling down on the sofa with a yard of cake – lemon sponge! God bless you, ma'am! – and consulting the *Radio Times*, it became apparent, with increasing panic, that there were no Dimblebys involved in the forthcoming coverage. This was the harbinger of a terrible and dark shadow – darker even than the clouds above Tower Bridge.

I looked down the list of broadcasters the BBC had lined up: Anneka Rice, Sandi Toksvig, Fearne Cotton, Matt Baker and Sophie Raworth. All perfectly fine in their place, on their day – but here? In a five-hour-long live broadcast that was going to consist – it was rapidly becoming apparent – of one thousand, largely nondescript boats, passing *very slowly* past the Wagamama on the South Bank? This was sending boys in to do a man's job. Lambs to the slaughter. Osborne as Chancellor. You just *have* to throw a Dimbleby at this stuff. It's standard.

Almost the first utterance by the BBC's commentator – Paul Dickinson – augured ill. Getting our first shots of the *Spirit of Chartwell* – the 'floating palace' built specifically for the occasion – Dickinson seemed overcome with awe.

'Look at the gilding on the stern of that boat!' he said, excitedly. 'Absolutely *beautiful*!'

On Sky, meanwhile, the perpetually saturnine Eamonn Holmes had a slightly different view.

'It looks rather like a floating Chinese restaurant,' he said, dourly.

On Twitter, the boat did not find favour with footballing maverick Joey Barton. 'Dear Imperialist Nations – stop robbing the world's poor of their resources and start examining the fabric of your rotting societies,' he Tweeted. Barton sounded like a man who had absolutely no cake in his house.

Diminutive magician Paul Daniels saw it very differently, however.

'LONG LIVE OUR AMAZING QUEEN!' he Tweeted – giving the impression of someone currently weeping Eccles cakes and tiny

Battenberg squares, while covered, loyally, in hundreds of first-class stamps.

Before the Jubilee, when I considered what my potential memories of the Flotilla might be, I had imagined a melange of scarlet and gold, billowing sails, leaping dolphins, and foaming, crested waves. Hundreds of eccentric boats teasing their way past Parliament – in some kind of nautical cross between *Wacky Races* and Dunkirk, but in a good way.

In the event, this was not what the Royal Flotilla was like.

Just twenty-four hours later, my memories of it seemed oddly misty. To all intents and purposes, it didn't really happen. There was no 'there', there. For five hours, the television broadcast a sky as grey and cold as the river, with the odd boat slicing, diminutively, left to right, through the centre – like a missed ball in *Pong*. We were just watching live footage of clouds sitting on London – eating the Shard, soaking Tower Bridge.

Aurally, things were just as scopey. Mics failed, choirs were blown away. Boat horns blared, endlessly, in a mournful loop – even as the commentators trailed away into silence. The impression was of some pale grey fever-dream, where you phased in and out of consciousness, but with your mouth full of lemon drizzle cake. For four hours, the BBC essentially spent millions of pounds broadcasting the inside of a cloud.

Whenever something *did* happen, however, it was often so surreal that you longed for a return to the mist. Everyone's idea of what 'interesting' or 'spectacular' consisted of appeared to come from a different age: definitely one before the internet, CGI, Ecstasy or rock'n'roll, and possibly before universal suffrage.

The *Spirit of Chartwell* sailed past the Sea Containers building, which had been covered with a massive 100m x 70m black and white photograph of the Royal Family on the balcony at Buckingham Palace, during the Silver Jubilee.

'I hope that was a nice surprise for the Queen's party!' Dickinson said.

I'm sure it *was* – it depicted Princess Anne standing next to her ex-husband. Awkward.

'It's the largest photo *ever* of the Royal Family,' Dickinson said, firmly – like a man convinced people at home might be going, 'Balls! I once saw a *much* bigger picture of Princess Michael, at Hampton Court Palace!'

We then cut to an extreme close-up of *Countryfile* presenter Ben Fogle, who was in the midst of the Flotilla, energetically rowing in a tiny skiff, alongside *Blue Peter* presenter Helen Skelton. However, it was a bad time to come to Fogle as he was, at that very second, passing the Royal Boat, and had important work to do.

'Three cheers for Her Majesty!' Fogle yelled, dementedly, mic distorting, going all the way to eleven with his poshness, and thrusting his oar into the sky. 'Hip hip – HOORAY! Hip hip – HOORAY!'

The camera waited for him to start presenting – but he simply shouted 'HOORAY!' again, while beaming at Her Majesty. His priorities were clear: loyalty to Her Majesty first; broadcasting for the BBC a poor second.

Things were equally odd over on 'the world's biggest floating belfry', where the living embodiment of 'jazz-hands', John Barrowman, had committed to spending the next three hours 'ringing a peal with Dickon Love and his guys'.

Observing Barrowman in the rather brutal-looking vessel – it was simply a massive floating box, with eight gigantic bells in it – he did look rather like someone willingly walking into a massive floating torture chamber.

'This is what it is to be British!' he shouted, in his American accent.

Over on the Millennium Bridge, and Anneka Rice was presenting a light-hearted strand – artists painting their views of the big day. However, the rain was so pounding that some of the paintings had literally dissolved. One artist – in desperation – had covered his picture with a cloth, to preserve it.

'Show us what you've done!' Rice urged.

As he removed the cloth, we realised it had got stuck to the canvas with rain – and the whole painting, in perfect reverse, was now printed to its underside, having lifted off completely. He held the sodden, flapping, paint-stained cloth to camera. By now, the wind was so high that the bunting was making desperate 'dapdapdapdap' sounds.

'I love it!' Rice shouted, over the noise. 'It's so ... Monet! It would be easier without the rain, to be honest – but we soldier on!'

John Sergeant simply didn't care. Positioned on Westminster Bridge, he looked like a man who'd spent the last hour on the phone to his agent, shouting, 'Balls to this, Paul! There's shit-all going on down here, and I've just spent twenty minutes padding with Richard E. Grant about whether he's wearing Union Jack underpants or not. You can whistle for your commission on this pile of fuck.'

Having only been thrown to twice in four hours, Sergeant's last link was an act of profound nihilism, delivered with parodic Light Entertainment cheerfulness.

'I have to say, we'll probably see more of the day's events when we get home, on the television!' he said, with hateful brightness. 'We've all been cheering the pictures on the big TV screens down here. Literally any excuse to cheer! Come on!'

He addressed the gathered, sodden crowd with a wild eye.

'Come on!' he repeated. 'Hurrah! Hurrah! It's just a simple, straightforward celebration! HURRAH!'

Back in the studio, there was a similar, terrible faux-brightness. *The One Show*'s Matt Baker seemed particularly, sparklingly supercilious. He had the same air that he did when he asked David Cameron, disingenuously, 'How do you sleep at night?'

Every time he said 'It's an astonishing day' to one of his guests, his eye telegraphed that he was finishing the sentence in his head with '... if you're *simple*.'

At one point, he looked straight down the barrel of the camera with a fixed grin, and asked us, directly, 'What do you think of the event so far?'

The *Spirit of Chartwell* passed a group of people doing semaphore.

'It's not just people waving flags!' Baker said, as if addressing a child. 'It all means something to the people who understand it. I should think it probably means something to the Duke of Edinburgh.'

However, the distress of Baker, Sergeant, Rice *et al.* was nothing compared to the BBC's main guy that day – the unseen Paul Dickinson, taking the Dimbleby Chair, and commentating over this scene of hypothermiating, rain-lashed pageantry.

Over the course of four hours in which – to borrow Spike Milligan's description of the Second World War, 'Nothing happened! But it happened suddenly' – Dickinson slowly fell prey to Partridge Fever: that unfortunate state of affairs whereby a broadcaster has to pad for so long, with so little, that they lose all sense of normal human perspective and humour, and start sounding like Alan Partridge.

The *Spirit of Chartwell* was not just the royal boat – but 'a precious boat, with a precious cargo'.

A shot of twenty rowboats was 'certainly a Canaletto moment – all powered by the human shoulders, back, arms and legs'.

Another boat passed by. 'I've got a feeling that, in that boat, are some survivors of cancer,' Dickinson said, without any further qualification.

After a while, Dickinson gave the impression that he'd actually stopped looking at the footage that was coming in. A Fire Rescue boat sped by – firing its water cannons at the crowd. Onboard, the firemen – being firemen – had positioned the cannons at pelvis height, for maximum lolz.

'A Fire Rescue boat there, celebrating in its own, special way,' Dickinson said, unheeding. Minutes later, he was summing up the day as, 'One of those occasions where you really have to be there to soak up the atmosphere. It really is electric.'

This over footage of a small child with its head slumped on some railings, in the rain.

My favourite moment, however, came when Tower Bridge opened up, to let the Flotilla through: 'An extraordinary machine, lifting an extraordinary road into the sky,' Dickinson said – unconscious that the rest of the country ended this sentence for him with a hearty 'Ah-HA!'

For indeed, on Twitter, the coverage was not going down well. Stephen Fry spoke for the nation when he Tweeted, 'This is mind-numbingly tedious. I just expected better of the BBC.'

Anyone who knew their Twitter history would not have been surprised when, minutes later, diminutive magician Paul Daniels Tweeted a furious reply. Daniels and Fry have been locked in mortal enmity since – during last year's Royal Wedding – Fry started Tweeting about a darts match, being broadcast concurrently.

'WHO CARES?????' Daniels had Tweeted him, furiously, before forming an unlikely online alliance with eighties puppet Roland Rat ('I can't believe this guy is so cynical! Off with his head').

When it came, now, to the Jubilee, Daniels clearly wanted to head Fry's rampant republicanism off early.

'It's a bloody sight better than football, darts, snooker …' Daniels told Fry, firmly.

And in this, Daniels had an ally in Dickinson.

'They say the Queen's seen everything before – but she won't have seen something like this!' he claimed, as nine people in anoraks sailed a barge past her.

And, indeed, the world had not seen anything like it before. And the world was confused. On that night's *Daily Show*, America's voice of sexy liberal reason, Jon Stewart, watched footage of the Flotilla – the Queen, unsmiling, in the downpour, staring at a succession of barges and tugs – with increasing confusion and astonishment.

'Is this the British equivalent of a Monster Truck show?' he asked, eventually.

No, Jon Stewart, you wanted to say. This is our Jubilee. This is what we do. Somehow, being British is all tied up in ruined watercolours, and floating belfries, and the sight of a BBC cameraman having to clean his rain-splashed lens off with a tissue with a quiet 'squick squick squick squick' sound. This is how we roll.

Have some cake. It helps.

Monday, and the Jubilee Concert. While there may have been national doubt about the meaning, and effectiveness, of the Flotilla, there were no such doubts about the concert. Putting on a themed concert, full of megastars playing no more than three songs each, is one of our great national talents – along with producing flamboyant homosexuals and great cheeses. We invented Live Aid! How difficult could this be?

Where Live Aid was organised by Bob Geldof, with the intention of aiding the starving, the Jubilee Concert was organised by Gary Barlow, with the intention of making Her Majesty tap her foot a little. And if – as a consequence of this concert going magnificently – Barlow should seem like a right and fitting person to subsequently get a MASSIVE knighthood, would that be such a bad thing? Would it? Does 'Sir Gary Barlow' seem like such an unlikely invention? Does it?

After all, it wasn't just the concert Barlow had put on for Her Majesty. For currently at Number One is the song Barlow wrote for the Jubilee, 'Sing', which was accompanied by an hour-long BBC documentary on Barlow's 'mission' to include subjects from across the Commonwealth in its making: the African Children's Choir, Slum Drummers from Kenya, Jamaica's Jolly Boys and Aboriginal guitarist Gurrumul, all contributing a rich global heritage to make 'Sing' sound exactly like a classic mid-paced Gary Barlow number.

The main difference between Live Aid and the Jubilee Concert was that, while Live Aid began with Status Quo and 'Rockin' All Over The World', the Jubilee Concert began with a statement from Huw Edwards, about the Duke of Edinburgh's bladder infection: 'So, sadly, he will not be joining the Queen tonight,' Edwards said, solemnly, in the very antithesis of screaming 'LONDON! ARE YOU READY TO ROCK?'

Over the next three hours, it became quietly apparent that, when it comes down to it, pop music is just *better* than some boats. Barlow gave the cake-eating audience what it wanted – Robbie Williams doing 'Let Me Entertain You', Sir Elton John doing 'Crocodile Rock'; but, also, what it didn't know it wanted – most notably with Grace Jones, stalking on to the stage in what appeared to be Intergalactic Sex Armour, and hula-hooping, imperiously, throughout 'Slave To The Rhythm'.

There was a slightly awkward moment when Annie Lennox appeared onstage, blonde, and wearing a pair of wings, and the actor Rufus Jones Tweeted 'DIANA!!!!!' – but in all – as has so often happened – Britain's ability to knock out great pop stars covered up for its awkward inability to know what to do with its heritage any more without seeming slightly embarrassed.

At the end of the performance – after Madness turning Buckingham Palace into a terraced street for 'Our House', and McCartney's 'Live and Let Die' – the Queen came onstage, escorted by Barlow.

Gary had his most solemn 'I'm with the Queen' face on. He looked so knightable. He looked like he'd momentarily considered pretending to drop a pound, and kneeling, to pick it up – just to give her the idea.

As the Queen gave a small wave, to thank everyone for coming, Twitter was still churning away at an incident that had happened earlier in the evening. Joining Stevie Wonder onstage, will.i.am from the Black Eyed Peas had shouted, 'Happy birthday Your Highness!', before launching into Wonder's 'Happy Birthday'.

Twitter had exploded with Yank-bashing righteousness – how *embarrassing* that an American should have mistaken a sixtieth Jubilee for a sixtieth birthday! How brash! How gum-chewing! How ridiculous that we had worried about what the Jubilee 'is' – for, however much we didn't know what a jubilee is, at least we get it that *little* bit more than the Americans, tsk.

But then, as the credits on the Jubilee Concert rolled, someone Tweeted that, actually, having Googled it, today *was* the Queen's birthday, after all.

This meant that the big fact we could take from the entire Jubilee weekend – boats, fireworks, street parties and McCartney – was that will.i.am from the Black Eyed Peas is a far better subject than every single other person in Britain. And that, if you eat cake for four days straight, you will become very, very nauseous.

If we are to talk of the things that not only make us proud to be British, but define us, I could make a very good fist of arguing that, of equal importance to our Queen, cakes, Anneka Rice in the rain and Prince Philip's cystitis, are Ant & Dec. When their Saturday Night Takeaway *returned to ITV1, I became quite emotional while reviewing it. I love those boys. I LOVE THEM.*

TV REVIEW: ANT & DEC & ME

Look, I watch all your cool, dark comedies – your *Thick of It* and your *Peep Show* and your *Louie* – and I love them. I've done them all on repeat – basking in lines as light and thin and sharp as Japanese knives. A good sitcom is, I believe, the greatest achievement possible for man, this side of a moonshot. I love these men sitting down and fusing their possibly poisonous characters and plots and dialogue together, with all the genius precision of electricians working on CERN.

But you know what? Minute by minute, taking my whole life into account, I don't think anything's ever made me laugh as much as Ant & Dec have.

Ten minutes into the newly returned *Ant & Dec's Saturday Night Takeaway* and I'm quacking away like an amyl duck: every laugh I'm having doubled because my kids are killing themselves laughing, too, and there's something about a genuinely family-friendly show that inspires euphoria.

The kids are getting *all* of these jokes! But, at the same time, as an adult, I'm getting the bonus round of Ant & Dec's slightly-too-long glances to camera. They exude a borderline filthy naughtiness, without ever actually manifesting it. Their entire career, from *SM:TV* onwards, has been getting the viewer to gasp, 'Oh my God, I can't believe they just did that!' – before realising that, actually, they hadn't done anything at all. They just looked like they were *thinking* about doing it. And that's something you can't learn to do. You either have that ability to calibrate the watershed, down to the last millimetre, in your bones, or you don't.

So, the return of *Takeaway*. *Takeaway* was taken away in 2009, in some scandal – viewers were using premium-rate phone lines, long after a winner had been chosen: nothing to do with Ant & Dec, but enough to have the show removed for a four-year-long brand decontamination, *Silkwood*-style. At the time, they thought their careers were over.

'Completely, absolutely,' Dec had confessed, in a recent *Guardian* interview. 'It was the worst time ever. Ever.'

On top of this, the day before *Takeaway* returned, the *Mirror* had splashed with one of the all-time classic tabloid front pages: ANT & DEC: WE'VE TAKEN DRUGS & ANT VOTED TORY. (Ant only voted for the Conservatives once, at the last election: 'I haven't told my family yet', and the drugs – 'years ago' – aren't specified.)

By all accounts, the hosts should look a little rattled.

But they arrive on the stage – Dec skidding on, Ant a little more composed – looking as joyous as two men who've just had the first pint of the weekend put in their hands.

'Can I just say how absolutely chuffed we are to be back on your Saturday night?' Ant says, and that's it – everything dealt with. It's the confidence of knowing you've got a great show on your hands: a show they conceived, and produced.

Within minutes, they're into the first bit, which involves having taken all the audience's Twitter names, before reading out their sundry Tweets. No one's ever done this before on a TV show, so it feels fresh – but it's also unusually warm for a prime-time show, too. No one ever gets humiliated on an Ant & Dec show – the humour never tips over into that most horrible of developments: sour, pin-pupilled, twenty-first-century 'bants'. It feels pleasingly retro to have Saturday night given over to something good-hearted again – recently, this slot has been home to the weeping rejections and sniggering Bedlam-visits of *The X Factor* and *Britain's Got Talent*, where people are treated like factory-farmed pigs being herded through mazes, for the edification of the viewer.

On *Takeaway*, however, the people are treated as wonky joys. When they take the Twitter segment on a step further – a girl called Sarah from Barry, Wales, is a prodigious, dramatic Tweeter – it continues to be filtered through the always trustworthy motivation of 'silly'. They take her Tweet of 'Lost a homemade shortbread earlier #fuming. Get a teaspoon. Fish it out' and incorporate it into the script of *Emmerdale* and film it.

'Big boobs don't count if you're fat. This is how you comfort me when I lose weight. #classic' is delivered as a breaking news item by John Stapleton on *Daybreak*, while a supergroup composed of 911 and 5ive sing the rest of her Tweets as wildly histrionic ballads.

It's an enormous amount of effort – a week, easily, of organisation, research, celebrity wrangling and filming. Five times the effort of a comparable five minutes of *The X Factor* – for something that eventually comes across as light and appealing as Butterscotch Angel Delight, and where *no one* is the butt of the joke. My whole family hoots laughing throughout.

Similarly Fair Trade laughs come with the segment 'I'm a Celebrity – Get Out of My Ear!', where a celebrity is put in a situation and told what to say, via an earpiece, by Ant & Dec. Usually, I can't watch these kind of things – they're about the agony of confusion, and humans making other humans feel like dicks, and I literally have to leave the room until they finish.

But this one – with Louis Walsh – does the gentlemanly thing of, again, treasuring 'silly' above all else.

Walsh invites a succession of decorators to 'his' house, and shows them around.

'Say to him, "Guess how Irish I am, out of ten",' Ant orders him. Walsh does so.

'Ten?' the decorator says.

'No. Seven and a half,' Walsh replies, at Ant's insistence. Walsh is instructed to show the decorators 'my favourite room' – when he opens the door, it's empty save a chair, and 200 posters of Louis Walsh.

'Let me explain this room,' Dec prompts Walsh. Walsh repeats the line.

'Go on then,' Ant says, turning off the mic for a minute, and laying his head down on the table, weak with hysteria, as Walsh manfully represses his own hysteria and the decorator suppresses his.

At the end of this segment, back in the studio, we see the decorators have been invited into the audience tonight, and are greeted by Ant & Dec – another little humanity nod you'd never get off Cowell, who looks like he now routinely, unironically, refers to most people he meets as 'another drone from Sector B', Mr Burns-style.

You know what – I could quack on for days why I love *Saturday Night Takeaway*. The *Apprentice* spoof that had a load of kids auditioning to be the new Little Ant & Dec wheeling into the boardroom on Trunkis. Louis Walsh being made to pick up a banana, and pretend to talk to Danni Minogue on it. Robbie Williams looking palpably happy to be on the show. The quiet skill involved in one shot that involved Ant & Dec walking through three locations, doing two short interviews, an audience interaction and a throw to VT – all with the same glee with which two kids would run into a playground and have a quick go on each thing in turn.

I will admit now that I am writing this whole thing with a virus and a temperature of 101, and am increasingly having a distant relationship with reality – so you must ignore the fact that I genuinely finish this with tears running down my face, repressing the urge to type 'Ant & Dec are the one true source of light in the universe. It is in their gift to prompt photosynthesis. They make me photosynthesise. Is it Saturday again yet? I want to live in Saturday for ever.'

More Saturday night TV – this time, BBC1's The Voice, *and my obsession with the legend and force of nature, Sir Tom Jones.*

TV REVIEW: TOM JONES – A VOICE STRAIGHT FROM THE GONADS

'Do you realise – you just opened the biggest show on TV right now?' Holly Willoughby asked Joelle Moses, the first contestant on Saturday's live round of *The Voice*. 'How does it *feel*?'

As anyone would, Joelle struggled to reply to this question. 'Argle rargle mazin; can't believe I'm here time of my life mazin,' she managed, as Holly beamed at the camera.

To be fair, it wasn't a question that had ever been asked to get a reply, anyway. The question existed simply for Holly to say, on behalf of the whole production team of *The Voice*, the phrase 'The biggest show on TV right now!'

Six weeks into its run, and *The Voice* is, on aggregate, the biggest show on TV right now – triumphing in the ratings every week, save one, over *Britain's Got Talent* on ITV1. *The Voice* vs *Britain's Got Talent* has become one of those amusing showbiz niggles – like Blur vs Oasis, Cheryl Cole vs Nadine Coyle, North Korea vs South Korea – that the press enjoys so much. There have even been guerrilla-style tactics deployed between the two camps: two weeks ago, *The Voice* 'accidentally' overran by three minutes, delaying *Britain's Got Talent*'s audience from seeing the start of the show, and shaving 4 million off their viewing figures.

'Shows often overrun by a few minutes,' the BBC said – clearly before rolling around on the floor, laughing hysterically and waving their legs in the air, like a horse.

I love it when inter-show rivalries spring up like this. First of all, it allows a load of people in offices in Soho and White City to act like they're in some Darth Vader vs the Rebel Alliance scenario – friending people on the rival production's Facebook accounts, and trying to derive tactics from their status updates; running into offices shouting 'Someone's just seen Jessie J's wig for Saturday night. That show is DEAD, man. DEAD!'

And secondly – and very specifically – it's never not funny when things go wrong for Simon Cowell. As Cowell's whole shtick is 'Go hard, or go home', having a show that's having to tussle for success is a crippling blow to his self-image. It's like the Wizard of Oz having to move into a bungalow; or Kim Jong-un having to pump up the tyres of his own trike. I'm prepared to bet Cowell has 'I Never Come Second' inscribed in swirly gold leaf over his bed. Consequently, all this must be *killing* him.

However. All this ratings success would suggest that *The Voice* is a superior show to *Britain's Got Talent* – something which is, most assuredly, not the case. *The Voice*'s initial promise – that it would be 'the nice' talent show – is hobbling it quite badly. With the live rounds now underway, *The Voice*'s determination to be positive at all times – no matter what the circumstances – is pushing viewers' credulity to breaking point.

As the nervous, inexperienced contestants gave a series of performances hobbled by pitching errors, tuning issues and the straight-out 'making of bad honking sounds', the judges had to pretend they were *all* amazing – come what may. As a consequence, Twitter was ablaze with viewers shouting 'WHAAAAT?' after each successively more awful performance was declared to be 'Out of this world', '110 per cent', or 'Game-changing' by judges who appeared to be either lying, deaf or mad.

In the most notable case, one couple did Fleetwood Mac so badly they actually started to warp time and causality. With each 'SKRAK!' and 'URGK!' sound, it was as if the *real* Fleetwood Mac started to fade – like the photo of Michael J. Fox and his sister in *Back to the Future*. By the end of their performance, Fleetwood Mac's name had changed to Fleetwood Whack, and their follow up to *Rumours* was not called *Tusk*, but 'Tsk'.

Everyone watching *The Voice* has a favourite judge. While I would most like to go down the pub with Jessie J, and her amazingly shiny hair – I just want to touch it. It is like oil, or glass. Would I even feel it? Perhaps no human hand can sense a shininess this immense – my favourite judge to *watch* is Tom Jones.

Now seventy-one, Jones is unlike anything we see on television these days. Let's face it – Jones has *always* been unlike anything we see on TV. This was a man so alpha, even Elvis Presley deferred to him, let us not forget. And we really cannot forget. For Jones mentions 'my friend Elvis' every week.

His Zeus-like ur-Mandom became particularly apparent last Saturday when the judges took it upon themselves to perform a four-way on U2's 'Beautiful Day', to open the show. First up, will.i.am's performance was oddly discreet, and muffled – he sang like he was on his mobile, trying to make an appointment with a 'specialist' clinic without anyone else on a crowded bus overhearing the details.

Danny from The Script, meanwhile, came on second, and treated it like the best evening in Lucky Voice ever – turning in a 100 per cent 'going for it' impersonation of Bono, down to sliding on his knees towards the camera while grimacing, like Bono does in the video to 'Mysterious Ways'.

Then, the advent of The Master. Tom Jones appeared at the back of the stage, and gave out a primal bellow – in much the manner of Godzilla, when he sights Tokyo for the first time, and begins 'the stomping'. It was a noise that appeared to have started before the beginning of time, and that would go on to outlive everything there is to come – including background radiation, and Duran Duran. For when Jones sings, it is not, technically, singing at all – but a primal energy-ray, from deep within his gonads, expressing his wish to have sex with every woman on the Earth. It is a sound that is meant to make all other men on this planet hide in cupboards – their testicles withdrawn up inside them, from fear – while their womenfolk take off their clothes and run towards Jones, shouting, 'I'm ready!'

As a consequence of this unstoppable, unending testicularity, the 'Tom Jones Reaction Shot' is the second-most reliable trope of *The Voice*. Jones Reaction Shots are as unvaried as they are powerful. In the audition stages – when the judges could not see auditionees until they turned their chairs around – Jones's reaction on sighting a young lady was, without exception, a slow, hungry grin that could be clearly and unambiguously captioned 'I would like to fuck her'.

Or – for contestants over a certain age, whom he may have met, back in the day – the slightly more quizzical 'Hang on – *have* I fucked her?'

Now Jones has met all the contestants, his reaction shot while watching their performances has changed slightly. As each female of the species takes to the stage, any cutaway shot of Tom could be captioned 'I would *still* like to fuck her'.

There is something enormously comforting in this unwavering, unambiguous communiqué from Jones's testes to 9.9 million viewers, every Saturday and Sunday night.

Okay – while we're on heroes, let's go back to Bowie. Oh! How I love you, David Bowie! Even though, the first time I knew of you was as Jareth, the Goblin King in Labyrinth, *and so I had a bit of a shock when I found out you'd done 'Rebel Rebel' AS WELL. It was like finding out Kermit used to be in the Beatles. Which actually, if I think about it, is the fan-fic project I would like to work on next.*

TV REVIEW: IMAGINE IF YOU DIDN'T LOVE DAVID BOWIE

Imagine if you didn't like David Bowie. Wouldn't that be weird? Not to love David Bowie. Not to love David Bowie – one eye blasted, hair dyed ginger in the sink, gaying it up with Mick Ronson on *Top of the Pops* for 'Starman'.

Not to love David Bowie – pale like bone; voice like ice breaking – singing 'Heroes' in Berlin: the sound of mankind giving itself a standing ovation.

Not to love Bowie – stalking towards the microphone during the intro of 'Let's Dance' – looking as sharp as any human's ever looked; an albino leopard whispering, 'You know what? In three years, I'm going to play Jareth the Goblin King in *Labyrinth*, in an outfit so tight my knackers look like two badgers having a fight down my trousers – and I'm going to be fucking bad-ass in that, too.'

People who don't love David Bowie? I don't even know what such a person would look like. Perhaps the person in Edvard Munch's *The Scream*.

On Saturday night, then, every person of reasonable mind in Britain watched BBC Two's *Five Years* – a feature-length documentary on David Bowie, made up of 'Unseen out-takes and unused footage', telling the story of five key years in Bowie's life – '71–72, '74–75, '76–77, '79–80 and '82–83.

Chronological and prompt, we started in '71, where Bowie had spent nearly a decade studying mime, acting, writing songs, walking around London in a dress, being a 'thing' – trying to work out which one of the things will make David Bowie big.

Nineteen seventy-one is the year he realises he never had to choose: the point of David Bowie is that he will do *all* of these things – and *that* is the big thing. What will free him up is realising that, for him, it's actually easier to create something dazzlingly, grindingly, blastingly new – to take pop to the Kabuki theatres of Japan, the German avante-garde, into space – than it is to try and just be some kind of redux Anthony Newley. He's not going to fit in *anywhere* – he's going to terraform a whole new world, and take pop with him.

One of the first people he tries to explain this to is Andy Warhol – and Warhol's having none of it. In black and white footage you can't quite believe you're seeing, in '71, in New York, Bowie and Warhol have a stand-off, on camera.

Warhol is trying to direct Bowie in a film he's making – Bowie tries to direct him back. In the end, because it's his film, Warhol shuts Bowie down. Bowie retaliates by filing a take where he mimes how he feels about this: ripping open his guts, spilling his entrails on the floor, and then pulling out his still-beating heart and throwing it up into the sky. Man, these are the pop-cultural moments I live for – David Bowie bitching off Andy Warhol with an angry mime. When the gays take over the world, all wars will be conducted like this.

But fuck Warhol – it's '71–72. Bowie's not messing around. He's got other fish to fry. He's back to the UK for Ziggy Stardust, *Hunky Dory*, 'Moonage Daydream'.

Rick Wakeman – rubicund, crumpled; a keyboard Falstaff – appears, telling us about playing piano on 'Life On Mars'. How absolutely illogical and astonishing the chord sequence is – on both *'But the film is a saddening bore'* and *'Sailors! Fighting in the dancehall'*, the song goes somewhere no one else on Earth would ever take it: a violent, swooningly vertical take-off into genius.

'It really is a piano player's dream,' Wakeman says – newly agape at how confounding it is. He stares down at his hands. 'I must go home and learn it.'

More footage, all previously unseen – Bowie in lapis lazuli trousers with his tits out, singing 'Queen Bitch' – *'Oh, God! I could do better than that!'* Lots of shots of him putting make-up on, going crackers on the Rimmel as you murmur, 'Rewind on the blusher, love.' He kills Ziggy at the end of '73. His scale is vast, fast – how is he doing this while being so utterly off his tits?

'He even ate breakfast like a superstar,' Woody Woodmansey, the Spiders from Mars drummer, recalled, which is quite a commitment if Bowie was eating, say, Shredded Wheat, or kippers.

'74–75: 'David Bowie was never meant to be. He's like a Lego kit. There is no definitive David Bowie.'

This new Bowie, six months later, is pale, cadaver-like – so thin his teeth look fat. He doesn't look like he's eating breakfast like a superstar any more. He doesn't look like he's eating breakfast at all. You've never seen anyone look more ill on cocaine. It practically crystallises on his skin, like salt on salt fish.

'He was the whitest man I'd ever seen,' his new guitarist, Carlos Alomar, says. 'I'm not talking pink-white. I'm talking translucent. I said, "You look like shit. You need food. You need to come to my house."'

But Bowie's driven – 'I was tumbling over myself with ideas.' These are his soul years: the heart is warm, even though his face is frozen. 'Young Americans', 'Fame', 'Golden Years'. He appears on *The Dick Cavett Show*, coked to the gills – sniffing constantly. At one point, you can see a sniff dislodges an old nugget from his nose – it hits the back of his throat, and you can see him register the acrid blast, before chewing on it. He has a cane, with which he traces patterns on the ground.

'What are you drawing?' Cavett asks, clearly scared of Bowie. Bowie is so blasted he can't even look him in the eye. Don't look on the carpet. I drew something awful on it.

Cracked Actor, The Man Who Fell to Earth: 'I knew Bowie had serious problems at the time – I just told him to put his clothes on and walk right through it,' director Nicolas Roeg says. Have I said before how amazing all the footage is? Bowie being interviewed by Russell Harty, and Harty getting the song titles wrong: 'Your new song, "Golden Tears".'

'"Golden Years",' Bowie corrects – a face on a wooden-cased TV screen on a table on Harty's show, with a poor transatlantic connection.

Bowie ends up introducing the song himself, in his cut-glass voice. Los Angeles is not good for him.

'People took so much coke they couldn't talk. They'd just ... whistle.'

'76–77. LA exited. Berlin. Bowie stripped down in jeans, riding around on a bicycle. The cold, clean air of Brian Eno's production – the introduction of new instruments, and Robert Fripp's high, spiralling, exposed-wires solo on 'Heroes'. Co-producer Tony Visconti calls Bowie and Eno – he has a new toy for the studio, called a Harmonizer.

'What does it do?' Bowie asks.

'It fucks with the fabric of time,' Visconti replies. They book him on to the next flight, and make *Low* – a new reset button for pop. Half instrumental, pistons hissing on 'Sound And Vision'. Always crashing in the same car.

'79–80. Bowie on *The Kenny Everett Video Show* in extreme close-up, still with his Steve Buscemi teeth, looking astonishingly beautiful, playing 'Ashes To Ashes' and pretending to be scared. Or perhaps he is scared? You still can't tell when Bowie's being Bowie – or *Bowie*. It's endlessly beguiling. If you were never actually in love with him before you see this clip, you will be afterwards. Still only thirty-three, and he's regenerated ten times, all alone: no George, John or Ringo to hang out with. His only bandmates are his massive genitals, which in these trousers seem even bigger than before: as if a small Shetland pony were living in his knickers. Maybe one was. Hot tramp! I love you so.

It ends with '82–83 – Bowie on the Serious Moonlight Tour, where he comes onstage and attacks 'Let's Dance' like a matador putting a sword right through a bull's heart. How did Andy Warhol not think this would work? Couldn't he see all of this even then, in Bowie's blasted pupil?

'71–72, '74–75, '76–77, '79–80 and '82–83. The date stamp for the invention of much of modern pop culture. Duran Duran, Madonna, Lady Gaga, Beyoncé, Daft Punk – whenever pop is ambitious, whenever pop is odd, whenever pop dresses up, whenever pop looks like nothing you've seen before, it is using tools and a framework largely built by one man from Bromley with tombstone teeth, and his name borrowed from a fixed-blade fighting knife. Did I say I love David Bowie? I love David Bowie. I loved this hour and a half with David Bowie.

My sister works in a perfume shop in Brighton, where they stock the perfume David Bowie wears. 'Do you want to know what David Bowie smells like?' she asked us – opening the bottle. It smelled of pineapple, and smooth platinum, and quietly purring through New York, in summer, in an air-conditioned car, if your heart was made of emeralds. We sprayed ourselves with the smell of David Bowie, and walked around town, drunk, pretending to be David Bowie, which is an excellent and cheap hobby for the young to engage in, and one I can thoroughly recommend.

I have forty-seven perfume bottles in my bedroom, and every plant I grow in my garden must be scented. Even the trees, with their oozing amber sap, which you can cover your fingertips with, and inhale. I love how scent can overwhelm you. It can make you utterly, brilliantly dumb. I like to be completely undone by it. Crushed. Made small.

THE SMELLS OF YOUR CHILDHOOD

There was a conversation on Twitter a couple of weeks ago – started by a writer called @mooseallain. You know – from the Hertfordshire Mooseallains – about what smells reminded people of their childhood.

Some were beautiful: 'My mother's perfume – when I smelled it, I knew everything would be all right.' 'The smell of moss and wood when you're climbing trees.' 'Erinmore, and Old Holborn tobacco smoke – in sweet blue folds, through the living room.'

Others were so specific, small and true they were like tiny plays: 'Pencil shavings at the bottom of a school bag.' 'Savlon on skinned knees.' 'The smell of sweat, released by the heat of the iron on my dad's work shirts.'

And some were just like a shopping list of a child's life, in 1986: 'Matey bubble bath, Pears soap, calamine lotion and my dad's Old Spice cologne' one read: everything an eight-year-old would encounter, in one tiny bathroom cabinet.

The idea was a beautiful way to while away an afternoon, and the whole collection is now on Storify – a catalogue of smells that children were intoxicated and overwhelmed by in the 1960s, 1970s and 1980s. Cola-cubes. Their dad's leather gloves. Chips. Plasticine. A newly opened packet of Panini stickers. Privet. Vimto, in a glass, on a pub table. The wooden seat of a swing, heating up in the sun.

Who doesn't want to think of the smells of their childhood? Childhood – when you have five senses working overtime, and your memory is just a big, white bag, waiting to be filled. And it stays filled: what adult now does not still essentially *freak out* over mown spring grass, or autumn bonfires; rotting seaweed, or the blind, white, echoing smell of first snow?

These smells smell just the same as they did the first time around: they never change, they never fade. They are a note that plays over and over in your life. They are the quickest route back to being just three feet tall – overwhelmed, in love with, or awestruck by, the world.

Were there fewer smells, back then – or more? I cannot tell. Sometimes, it feels like my childhood world was made entirely of coal tar. Coal tar in the creosoted fences, covered in tiny spiders. Coal tar in the thick, medicine-y syrup of Vosene, and coal tar in coal tar soap. Coal tar in the tarmac being poured, black, on to the road: my mother and me the only ones who liked the smell – *loved* the smell – pausing at roadworks and sniffing it, lasciviously, as the rest of the family walked on, pretending to choke. Coal tar fills your lungs, and your head: it's the smell of things getting done, being mended, being cleaned. It's the smell of working-class estates in the 1970s and 1980s.

There were other smells, of course: the packed lunchbox smell, of plastic, bread, crisps, an apple starting to ferment. The tin of Roses being opened on Christmas Eve – half chocolate, half squeaky, jewel-coloured cellophane. Heinz tinned ravioli being heated on a gas hob, in a caravan, at dusk – door open to the Welsh mountains outside, and the rushing black river at the bottom of the valley. Kids running barefoot back through long grass, in the almost-dark, to eat the hot, orange, tin-flavoured squares.

The very specific smell of 1988 – the year my parents bred Alsatian puppies. Puppies, mixed in with Jeyes Fluid – another coal tar smell! – and shit.

We kept the puppies in the old coal hole and, every time we opened the hatch, the ground would suddenly disappear beneath an ankle-high wave of tiny bodies, hysterical with wagging, and barks so small, the sound was bark bark bark. And they would lick your face, with their tiny milky new-earth-smell tongues, and you would think, 'This is the newest and most alive thing on Earth', and you would squash them a bit, between the palms of your hands, because you were so excited.

I'd far rather think of the happiness of childhood smells than the sadness. Because the simple fact is, there are things that you loved as a child you will never smell again – and that will make your heart ache if you dwell on it. People you knew – your nan, your granddad, the soft-lapped auntie who died – you will never breathe them in again; that unique mixture of their perfume and habits and bone. Not even the richest man in the world can recreate what it's like to have his face pressed near to those who have gone, and to inhale. The absence of a scent can make you tearful with longing – or, on the other hand, just ruin a summer.

The year my father sheared all our lilac trees down to three feet high – 'To *invigorate* them!' he said – they did not become invigorated, after all.

Every other summer, we had lived surrounded by their wild, drunk, intoxicating froth – it filled the house like light, birdsong and magic – but this year, they sat – squat and sulky as a bathed dog – and steadfastly refused to bloom. The air remained plain, and undrunk. The house felt dark, and silent. And it was not summer, without the smell of lilac. It was not summer at all, that year.

I went to New York with my sister, and we took a bus. And it turned out to be the most New York thing ever.

THE UNHAPPY BUS TOUR GUIDE, NEW YORK

He sits at the front of the bus – New York-Italian, dishevelled, looking fifty in the eye and not liking it. Like Al Pacino in a cheap anorak. Al Pac-a-Mac-ino.

He's holding a microphone in his hand, and sighing heavily. He is our tour guide on this open-topped bus ride around Manhattan, $27.

'I gotta tell you, sweetheart – I'm only going to be operating on a third of my usual powers today,' he says, pausing by my seat. He has taken a shine to me and my sister. We have no idea why. 'This crowd here – they're not gonna get it. They're not gonna get *it*, London.'

His tired hand gesture takes in the big Pakistani family, a couple from Austria, a woman in a burka, a couple from St Lucia. A single, prim-looking Korean woman.

He sighs. 'I can tell. It's gonna be a waste. Today, London, I'm dialling in Roberto Baddacelli.'

He is Roberto Baddacelli. He might be the worst tour guide in Manhattan.

Generally, I am a fan of the 'bad tour guide' genre. We once had a tour guide in Athens who began his walk around the Parthenon with 'I hate the English. *Hate* the English' – a bold statement even when uttered to a large, internationally mixed crowd; but twice as exciting given that he was speaking to a group that consisted of only me and my husband, who are English.

But Baddacelli might be even better than him.

'The picture's THERE! The picture's THERE!' he shouts, as we go past the Flatiron Building. 'LEFT LEFT LEFT TAKE IT NOW!

ST LUCIA, TAKE YOUR PICTURE! LONDON! TAKE YOUR PICTURE! NOW! JESUS CHRIST!'

Apparently, I am 'London'. He tells a joke. It's about Hitler. The couple from Austria don't look happy. And they haven't even seen the storm yet. As we go across the Brooklyn Bridge, the Manhattan skyline is wearing a massive bouff of black cloud, cracked with lightning. Baddacelli looks personally angry about that weather.

'Everybody, everybody – thanks very much for hauling me out here during a thunderstorm. I really appreciate it,' he says.

The woman from Pakistan is worried. She has three children.

'What will happen?' she asks, in pieced-together English.

'We're in a tin can going over the Brooklyn Bridge – what do you *think* will happen, Pakistan? PULL OVER!'

He bangs on the side of the bus, to alert the driver.

'I know a guy who got KILLED this way. STRUCK BY LIGHTNING!' he tells the bus – just as the sky cracks open and everyone is instantly, violently soaked. In less than three minutes, the floor is four inches deep in water. This is monsoon.

Baddacelli climbs down the central aisle passing out yellow plastic rain ponchos – trying to keep his shoes out of the water by climbing on the edges of the seats. As he passes us, he goes, 'Jesus *Christ*, London. Jesus *Christ*.'

We disembark in Chinatown, and stand under scaffolding for half an hour, watching the lightning lance the sky. It passes slowly. By the time it's safe to get back on the bus, it's gone 9pm. The bus starts up.

'We're off-route now,' Roberto shouts into the microphone, against the gale. 'OFF ROUTE. Because of the storm. So – who wants to go to Ground Zero?'

I'm pretty sure none of these cold, wet, late people want to go to Ground Zero – site of the twenty-first century's worst peacetime atrocity. But the thing is about a bus full of people swathed head to toe in yellow-hooded rain ponchos is that it is unlikely you will be able to take an accurate reading of their mood when asked a question in a language they don't understand.

We circle Ground Zero, at 10pm, in the rain.

'THAT'S THE PICTURE THAT'S THE PICTURE! ON THE LEFT! ON THE LEFT, AUSTRIA!' he says. 'That was just an EMPTY SOCKET IN THE GROUND ten years ago. The whole of this block was on FIRE. It BURNED, God rest their souls.'

He notes the mood is sombre, and tries to lighten it.

'Hey! You know what I drink since they killed Osama Bin Laden? You know what I drink? Two shots and a splash! TWO SHOTS AND A SPLASH! Get it? Get it, London?'

We're going through Downtown now – building after building of sheer, vertical black glass. This part of Manhattan is like a money tunnel; a funnel of souls towards Macy's. This is Gotham.

'This is where I was born,' Roberto says, sitting at the back of the bus. After no one laughed at his joke, he suddenly looked defeated. He holds the microphone in the same way someone suicidal toys with a gun.

'This used to be *all* red-brick walk-ups. That was *real* New York. This new stuff, it just looks – morbid. Like some gloomy Tim Burton movie. I miss the brick walk-ups.'

The bus reaches its stop. A line of yellow-caped passengers exit the bus, shivering. Baddacelli sits at the back of the bus, not moving.

As we walk past, he says: 'I just miss the brick walk-ups, England.'

In America, The Apprentice *has the monumental ass-hat Donald Trump as the 'Boss'. Ah, Donald Trump – a man so consistently, astonishingly appalling that it kind of makes sense he's running for President. Ass-hattery on that scale kind of* would *demand expanding on to a global platform. Why confine yourself to saying dumb things to a purely American audience when you could be saying these things to the UN? In a way, I admire his drive. I'm sure it's a very long and opulent drive. I'm sure it's covered in the most expensive and non-Fair Trade gravel available. Possibly it's pulverised chunks of art, or the Moon. That's the kind of gravel Donald would like best. The gravel that fucks things up for everyone else.*

In the UK, however, fans of the UK Apprentice *have to make do with our 'Boss' being Lord Alan Sugar – a second-rung millionaire who has the additional, amusing attribute of looking like a small and angry bear. I love* The Apprentice. *I have learned nearly everything I know about capitalism from it.*

TV REVIEW: *THE APPRENTICE* – THE ECONOMY RESTS ON THESE CASH-MADDENED CLOWNS

As Season Nine of *The Apprentice* began on Tuesday with Prokofiev's 'Theme From The Apprentice' (this joke remains the copyright of film composer David Arnold, Twitter, 2011), a rather melancholy thought occurred: in 2013, the whole deal with *The Apprentice* has changed.

When *The Apprentice* started, back in 2005, it was simple: in this show, the BBC were serving us up a massive Ass-Hat Pie. A buffet of twattery. Fourteen lovingly chosen hand pumps – displayed in all their tool-like glory, over an entire series devoted to fully exploiting their nobbishness, for the purposes of national, communal ridicule.

For, back then, what more innocent pursuit could there be than a country uniting in derision against a load of wannabe business executives? A tranche of dingleberries who wanted nothing more than a pleather suitcase, a hands-free mobile headset and the chance to work under Grumpy Little Business Bear Sir Alan? These preening proto-honchos were our enemy.

'Pooh and fie!' the nation could mock. 'Look at these soulless corporate shills! Repeatedly humiliating themselves on national television – for nothing more glorious than the eventual chance of sliding through an eggy liquidation of two tech start-ups in Ayrshire. Is this the sum total of their dreaming? Is this the secret need in their heart? Look at them screwing each other over, like glass-eyed weasels. Indeed, screwing *us* over like glass-eyed weasels – because, of course, when they say "I will do *anything* to get ahead in business. I will sell anything to anyone", *we* are the "anyone" they're selling the "anything" to.

This, ultimately, is the face of Horsemeat Burgers Ltd, and DeathTripPrivateHospices-R-Us. This is business – the serious, crucial fulfilment of the needs of a society – depicted as nothing more than a big game for preening cocks. This is a programme where people boast about screwing over the consumer – in front of an audience of 10 million consumers! These are the people *destroying* society. I will be *glad* when Sir Alan makes them sell dinner gongs and Fraggles in Petticoat Lane Market, in the sleet, then reduces them to tears in the boardroom. GLAD.

Katie Hopkins – terrifying iceberg-eyed bitch-cyborg, now turned rent-an-outrage right-wing commentator on late-night shows. Tre Thingy. Stuart 'The Brand' Baggs ('I'm not a one-trick pony. I'm a whole field of ponies – and they're all running towards this job'). Ah, the pleasure of throwing peanuts in your mouth while laughing at these cash-maddened clowns. The pleasure.

But, of course, in the teeth of a second recession this has all changed. It's a massive flip-reverse. Because now, in 2013, the truth is, we *need* these cash-maddened clowns. With the public sector stripped back, thrusting young entrepreneurs are apparently the very people who are going to save us from collapsing into the looming Depression. Private enterprise is the cavalry we've been told to wait for. There is no Plan B.

Basically – and I don't wish to overly alarm you, yet I'm also not exaggerating that much – George Osborne has built his entire economic strategy around the winner of this year's *Apprentice*. Whoever Lord Sugar hires is going to become our new insect overlord. Let's hope there's some brilliant, reasoned, genuinely inspiring people in the starting line-up! Let's all really hope that, guys!

'I take my inspiration from Napoleon. I'm here to conquer,' Zeeshaan Shah said, thirty seconds into the first episode. Napoleon. Great. The man who poisoned his own soldiers when they contracted bubonic plague during the Egyptian campaign. Can't wait to see Shah negotiate someone's maternity leave in Personnel.

Next up was Miles: 'I'm prepared to fight to the *death* to become Lord Sugar's business partner,' he said – a demented level of commitment to show to a project that's just, essentially, work experience, with elements of *The Generation Game* (sausage-making, directing a pretend advert for dog food) thrown in, to jazz it up for BBC1. On top of this, of course, it was also a pretty inadvisable pre-admission to murder. Dunno how much acumen and strategy you're showing off there, Miles, tbh.

'I have the energy of a Duracell bunny, the sex appeal of Jessica Rabbit, and a brain like … Einstein,' Luisa claimed. Personally, I was quite saddened by the premature collapse of her rabbit metaphor. I would have ridden it right to the end, with 'And a brain like … Bugs Bunny.' Bugs was pretty smart. He knew exactly what he was doing with Elmer Fudd. Fudd always failed.

The first week's task was to flog a load of random imported stuff – Union Jack mugs, cat litter, loo rolls, leather jacket with polyester linings ('We'll call that "silky-touch"') – that was waiting in containers, down in Tilbury Docks.

'I've lived in London my whole life – but I've never gone down the docks before,' Jason admitted, perhaps not quite realising the inference of what he was saying.

As always, the first week was Girls vs Boys, with the girls' team naming themselves 'Endeavour'. Jaz stepped up as leader of Endeavour.

Jaz was clearly proud of her 'people skills' – something which, for her, centred predominantly around talking to people while maintaining terrifying levels of 'inspiring eye-contact'.

'There's an element of patronising us,' Suzy, a fellow Endeavourite, said. 'But, then, she *is* a teacher.' Which, of course, ironically enough, is a very patronising thing to say.

Over on the boys' team, meanwhile, the team bonding wasn't going so well. Having offloaded thirty-five 'lucky' Chinese cats, Alex yelped, joyously, 'Let's do a high-five!'

'Really?' Neil said, sourly, walking away.

If there's anything sadder than watching a putative captain of industry left with a dangling, unreciprocated high-five, I've yet to see it this year. Alex looked like he was trying to hail a cab to somewhere quiet, where he could cry and wank for the rest of the afternoon.

With a van full of goods left to sell – 'We're not going to be able to sell forty-one bags of cat litter to one person,' Neil said – fatally forgetting Aslan – the boys' team began to panic.

'We didn't set out on the wrong foot – we set out on no foot at all,' Jason fretted.

On the basis of episode one, for those eager to place early bets on just who will claim the coveted '*Apprentice* Ass-Hat Crown', posho Jason is definitely one to watch.

Twenty-nine years old, Jason has never been 'formally employed' – choosing to become, instead, an amateur 'historian' and student of Greek mythology.

'I'm hoping to live up to my mythological namesake,' Jason said, in a manner so delicate one instantly feared for him in any task that involved 'talking to other human beings', 'moving outside buildings', or 'lifting up anything heavier than a puffin'.

Not that his lack of experience bothered him: 'My intelligence is like a machete in the jungle,' he explained. 'It's just going to take one swipe, and I'm through.'

Alas – Jason found his first swing of the Think Machete vastly hindered by Alex, from Wales. Alex has a truly mesmeric face – one which tells a story. The story it tells is of a close friend of Alex's who works in a beauty salon and who likes, in times of boredom, to experiment with Alex's face. As a consequence of what I imagine was a particularly rainy Tuesday in the Valleys, Alex's eyebrows are now the first 'diamond-shaped' ones I have ever seen on a man.

'Do people ever say you remind them of anyone?' Liam asked Alex, curiously.

'Freddie Mercury,' Alex replied.

'Not ... Dracula?' Liam rejoined.

The trailer for next week's episode shows an argument between Alex and Jason that ends with Alex snapping, 'Jason, will you be quiet, you silly shit.'

I wonder what the IMF are making of it all. Britain's economic future. Hopefully George Osborne's making them watch it on iPlayer.

We are about to enter the Olympics section of the book now, so you might want to pop your Lycra shorts on and start warming up on the side of the track. It's gonna be a sprint and a marathon! And a 4x4 freestyle swimming relay! And the mother of all opening ceremonies!

The Olympics affected me deeply and on many levels – and not just because it gave me the excuse to skive off work for nearly a month, eating crisps and watching equestrian events. As the following columns detail, before the Olympics started we all thought they would be a failure. If the terrorists didn't use it to stage worldwide carnage, then the British ability to be quietly disappointing would surely see the whole thing just … fizzle out, in a limp prft. In the months before they began, anyone living in London regarded the approach of the Olympics with dread. Public transport would grind to a halt. It would rain. The world would laugh at us. When called upon to put on a true, life-changing spectacle, we would make do – as is so often the case – with something dull, safe and digested through the guts of a million, lowest-common-denominator committees. Doomed to tiny-ness, or over-commercialisation, or disappointment, or rain.

But then it started – started with that astonishing, febrile, kinetic, cloud-burst Opening Ceremony, which kind of … reinvented Britain.

I watched the Opening Ceremony in a hotel room in New York, with my sister, drinking the minibar dry, and at the point the Queen parachuted into the Olympic Stadium we become so crazed and overwhelmed with excitement and pride and red wine that we both took off our shoes and threw them at the screen, screaming 'YES! THAT'S HOW YOU DO IT!'

When we went down to the bar, later – for who stops drinking red wine simply because the minibar has run out? – the people in the bar heard our accents and bought us endless free drinks, because they, too, had been watching the Opening Ceremony on the bar's TV, and wanted to celebrate how brilliant Britain was.

I ended up sitting on the kerb at 4am smoking cigarettes with a gay man, whose partner was being driven insane with worry about his health insurance, as he'd recently discovered he was HIV positive. I told him all about the NHS – whose foundation we'd seen re-enacted, just three hours ago, in a global event featuring Mary Poppins floating from the sky, and a hundred children in beds, being tended by NHS nurses in beautiful boots. I told him how he and his partner would not have to worry about a penny of their treatment in the UK – just as I had not had to worry about the cost of giving birth to my daughter, and my friend had not had to worry after being diagnosed schizophrenic.

'It sounds like ... heaven,' he said. And we stared up at the mad, fierce beauty of Manhattan at 4am, and I thought of tiny, rainy, Welfare Britain, and I wept.

I find it fitting – given that earlier in the book I talked about all the woe, status obsession and social sclerosis modern London is afflicted with – that this starts with a piece talking about just how beautiful London can still be, on a good day.

EVERYONE FANCIES BRITAIN RIGHT NOW

God, London looks sexy. Everyone fancies us right now. That's just a fact – you can see it in the world's eyes, when they say 'London'. They want to walk down the Thames with us and touch us on the parks; get drunk, say, 'Christ, you're so hot right now' and kiss our BT Tower.

Three days after the Games opened, there was a picture of the gigantic Olympic Rings, hanging from Tower Bridge. And then there, at the bottom, completing a new, third row, was the Moon – the full Moon, having just risen over the City. And that was the Moon loving us, too: his big old face longing and looming over Docklands, saying, 'I love you, London. In London, the love between a Moon and a city would not be seen as transgressive. We could live together, in a flat above a coffee shop in Hackney. Next door to some gays. We'd all be happy.'

It's been top-shelf Old Smoke pornography for the last two weeks. In the Equestrian events, in Greenwich Park, they provocatively raked the slopes, so you could see the whole London skyline as the competitors came down the final hill. A flash of white urban thigh – cupola, steeple,

Eye – among the arboreal petticoat froth. Those soft grey domes by the river; the lush triangles of park in London's tight middle. This city's been a dirty bitch, all right. It's totally been coming on to everyone. And every night, in those broadcasts of gold-rose sunsets over the Olympic Park – upturned star-bowl over the meadow, and the Velodrome – a billion viewers across the world have sighed. They want to do it to us, all night long.

Of course, it's not just London. It's all of Britain, really. London 2012 has made the whole world want a bit of Britain – Weymouth Bay, Box Hill, Glastonbury Tor. Able to casually throw a princess, or a Beatle, into the audience shots. But the world does not, perhaps, want us quite as much as we newly want a bit of ourselves.

Lest we forget, this time last year Britain was on fire. Croydon was burned to the ground so that kids could loot mismatched trainers and massive bags of rice – which seemed harsh, even for Croydon.

Twelve months later, and a mere £9 billion celebration of human excellence has changed everything. We are amazing. We are stardust. We are golden. We will never do anything bad, or destructive, again. We will simply run and jump and row and hurl shot-puts forever, while listening to 'Heroes', screaming Mo Farrah over the finish line. We've done the kind of crying that does you good: like a fruit-acid peel on a bit of dry-skin cynicism you didn't even notice you had.

After half a century of worrying what Britain 'is' now, the answer appears to paraphrase Obi Wan Kenobi: by striking down our Empire, we have become far more powerful than we could ever know.

For everyone's got a grudge against a superpower. Superpowers become super by screwing other people over. By way of contrast, everyone's gonna love a small, rainy, merry, brainy island filled with dancing nurses, massive geeks, rock'n'roll, and a queen that jumps out of a helicopter. One secure enough to simply let all its territories go. For the last two weeks, we were shown what it would be like to evolve into a newer country still: Greatest Britain. The Okay. Not titanic, or muscular – but moral, and clever, and free.

Who would have thought a massive investment of public money into a glorious scheme would make things so much better? Apart from Roosevelt, that time, in that Depression. So *this* is what spending money on people, and ideas, feels like. It feels far sexier than that time we bailed out the banks; or cut the higher rate of tax. How did we feel then? A bit uptight, and self-righteous. How do we feel now? We don't have time to tell you. We're too busy going, 'What has happened to this country this month? This is amazing.'

'Patriotism' is just the medical word for fancying your country. Although I would always have flirted with that old Britain – all Beefeaters reading Shakespeare, while Dickens and Nelson play cricket – *this* Opening Ceremony, Games-hosting Britain is the one I'd run away from home with. The one where Dizzee Rascal plays 'Bonkers' in front of Isambard Kingdom Brunel, Tim Berners-Lee types 'This is for everyone' as the *Brookside* lesbians kiss, and London feels like the street party that never quite materialised for the Jubilee – a 26-mile-wide trestle table loaded with champagne, and athletes, and a calm, non-apologetic, unexpected pride.

For London is where you feel the Olympics hardest. Everywhere you go there are pink-tabarded 'Games Makers' pointing at things. Ostensibly, they are pointing the way – to the Olympic Park, to the volleyball – but, really, they are just pointing at London. At the joy. At the sunsets. At the hotness.

Everyone fancies us, during London 2012.

And so to the actual Games themselves. I am, as so many are, 'sport-curious'. Most of the time – nah. But every so often, a global event catches my eyes, and I ... dabble.

TV REVIEW: I HAVE OLYMPIC FEVER

So the order is: 1) gymnastics 2) running 3) jumping 4) horses 5) swimming 6) bikes, aka, the Glory of Our Mod Overlord, the Wiggins. They're the best ones. They're the best Olympic sports. Meanwhile the rubbish ones are: 1) ping-pong 2) fighting 3) boats 4) guns 5) hockey. I mean, ping-pong? At the Olympics? Are you serious? That's just something you do on holiday, when you find your rental cottage has a fold-up ping-pong table in an outhouse. I'll be honest – watching the Olympics' ping-pong tournament this year is the first time I've ever seen anyone play the game without a massive glass of red wine in one hand and a four-year-old asleep under the table: 'Leave him there – it's a holiday. Just chuck a coat over him, to keep him warm.' Ping-pong is what you do if you're in Wales and the telly has S4C, instead of Channel 4, and you can't watch reruns of *24 Hours in A&E*.

But then, of course, it can all change in an instant. On Wednesday afternoon, suddenly, it was all about boats – boats was suddenly amazing. As the British women's coxless pair hauled towards the finishing line – biceps like high-tension wire – boats looked glorious. Boats was one of the best Olympic moments ever. Boats was the whole point of the Olympics.

'COUNT THE STROKES!' the commentator yelled, hoarsely, as Helen and Heather pulled 15ft in front of the pack. 'COUNT THE STROKES!'

I was on the sofa, fist stuffed in my mouth, hardly breathing. In under a minute, Britain might win its first gold of the Games – and it would be two young women who did it. Two amateurs on Eton Dorney Lake, synced and sweating, rowing ahead of the whole world;

rowing out of their skin. So alone, out on the grey water – save an entire country screaming them on. Thirty thousand people on the banks were on their feet. The roar was deep but rising, like machinery going out of control.

'THEY'RE TWENTY STROKES FROM THE FINISHING LINE! THEY'RE MAKING HISTORY HERE! HELEN AND HEATHER, WE STAND AND SALUTE YOU – FOR THE COUNTRY. FOR THE MEDAL. FOR THE GOLD.'

Written down, it looks a trifle hysterical, but at the time I remember thinking he was severely underplaying the event. I think I thought him robot-hearted.

As they shot over the finishing line, Heather crumpled backwards into Helen's lap: done. They had done the thing, the very thing. The top of the mountain, the unbeatable fact. That night, Tower Bridge and the London Eye would be lit up gold to celebrate Britain's first gold medal. They were painting London gold.

'The legal high that is an Olympic gold medal,' Steve Redgrave sighed, nostalgically, as 30,000 people in the crowd screamed themselves hoarse. 'It is a high for all of us.'

Five minutes later, Helen and Heather held a tiny posy each, watching the Union flag being raised. Their feet were bare, and they had gold on their chest.

And boats was brilliant. Boats was the very best.

This has been the greatest Olympics ever. Ever. Just like every new baby is the best baby ever, and every new spring triumphs over the last, all Olympics are the best, ever.

Like Batman in the Batcave, in front of his hundreds of screens, tracking Gotham City, I have tried to watch all of it, literally all of it. I don't want to miss a thing. Many, many times I have wished for eight eyes, like a spider.

Equestrian, where, due to the whimsical design of the course, a princess jumped over the moon. Swimming, where a girl-child from China broke a world record and went home with a gold in each hand. Hamadou Djibo Issaka entering the men's single sculls – despite coming from a land-locked sub-Saharan nation and only having taken up rowing three months ago.

'You can do it!' the announcer bellowed, as Issaka approached the finish line, a minute and thirty-nine seconds behind everyone else. He was representing the generic state of Underdogistan, or Pluckyloseropia. 'You can do it!'

Even though the stadiums are so large, and the marathons so long, and the audiences in the billions, it's all still, in the end, about watching the look in someone's eyes. That sixteen-year-old girl from Lithuania who looked like she would explode when she won 100m breaststroke – like she thought she was just high on chlorine and would wake up any minute to find herself back in her bunk bed with her teddy bear, medal-less. Or the 200m butterfly gold-winner Chad le Clos's dad, bellowing, 'Look at my boy! Look at my boy!' at presenter Clare Balding. 'I can't believe how handsome he is!' Arms flailing wide as he burst with pride.

Many would have it that the Olympics is a monolithic event that touches down and occupies a city, like some corporate, muscled parasite – like the alien ships in *War of the Worlds*. But the BBC's coverage took its lead from the Opening Ceremony, and its apposite quote from Tim Berners-Lee, the man who gave away the internet for free: 'This is for everyone.' Their coverage was proper, quotidian, John Lewis-style quality-for-all, for mere pennies.

Having screwed up the Jubilee coverage by being – and I'm generalising here – quite thick and simpering, its Olympics coverage is supremely on the nail. Clare Balding is the Queen of these Olympics: so super-briefed she can pick out athletes' relatives in the crowd (and not just easy shit, like Prince William and Prince Harry or Zara Phillips – like, normals, from Ukraine), but also infused with the kind of joyous, informal enthusiasm you'd want from someone taking you by the hand around the biggest sporting event on Earth. And she's not put off by its size or the pressure of keeping the BBC 'respectable', either: she was the first to ask questions about Ye Shiwen's startling, record-breaking swim. That's what presenters should do – ask questions.

Because we're all at home on the sofa, screaming 'WTF? Did someone just shoot that kid out of a CANNON?', and need answers.

Gymnastics is the best, though, isn't it? I mean, it just is. Apart from the things with Usain Bolt in. I guess it's because it feels like there's a creativity and self-expression you don't get in, I dunno, badminton or something. It straddles the divide between 'sport' and 'art'. Those floor routines, where girls fly through the air like *The Matrix*. The American women's team of 2012 were berserk – a series of perfectly geometric explosions that looked like CGI, or magic. Alexandra Raisman had a trademark thing where, every time she landed after a diagonal flick-flack-flick-flack-corkscrew from one corner to the other, she'd bounce back up into the air again – into huge, mid-air splits. Like she naturally flew at all times, but had to make the occasional concession to the ground. In slow motion her routine was everything, all at once, at perfect angles, like watching someone pull out every item on a penknife and then snap them back in simultaneously.

Then there's the men's rings, where men self-crucify: arms at 90°, in a perfect 'T' of excruciating pain. Ropes as still as if they were made of wood, or steel; faces as impassive as El Greco's impaled, sexy St Sebastian.

It wasn't all glory in the gymnastics, though. The French men's team suffered a nationally shaming style-fail: whoever had designed their outfits had patterned the tops so that the men looked like they were wearing a massive pair of spectacles framing their man-breasts. It looked like a bizarre French tribute to Woody Allen.

The Russian gymnastics team, meanwhile, had red hoodies with 'RUSSIA' written across the chest. When they unzipped them, the tops underneath had 'RUSSIA' written in exactly the same place – like Russian dolls! Amazing nationally thematic gear.

Of course, it's always difficult watching the competitors who come from repressive countries. Obviously, I am 'Team GB'. Indeed, I'm so 'Team GB' I shout 'COME ON, TIM!' at the television at ALL our competitors – like we used to at Tim Henman at Wimbledon, five years go. It's an old British tradition I want to keep alive.

But when someone pops up from Saudi Arabia or China, say, there's always that slight worry that, if they lose to a plucky Brit, they'll go home and be shot, or sent to a gulag. After losing every game in the 2010 World Cup, the North Korean football manager was accused of 'losing the country's trust' and was sentenced to hard labour. However 'Team GB' I am, I don't want that. So I've had to pioneer a kind of lefty liberal pink cheering: 'COME ON, BETH TWEDDLE! STUFF IT UP THEM! SMASH THEM! TONK THESE BITCHES! My thoughts are also with those facing persecution in their home countries.'

And there are more down-to-earth dangers with being an Olympic competitor. Michael Jung of Germany won the equestrian individual eventing in trousers so tight I found myself murmuring, 'Is that an iPhone in your pocket or are you just pleased to see me?' as he waited for his gold medal – before realising that, actually, it was an iPhone. You could see the corners and everything.

It seemed an odd place to keep it, though. I'm pretty sure it would have insurance issues. They got arsey with me when I put my iPhone in my bra that time at a nightclub and it got water damage from tit-sweat. And that's much more plausible than, 'I smashed it against a horse with my pelvis as I was winning gold at the Olympics.'

*And, of course, the 2012 Olympics carried on being extraordinary –
because, for the first time ever, British television broadcast the entirety of
the Paralympics when they were held the following week.*

*If you believe – as I do – that a vital part of the march to equality
is simply giving marginalised people time and exposure while being
totally shit hot and sexy at something, Channel 4's broadcasting of the
Paralympics was one of the most significant decisions of the last ten years.
Overnight, the representation of disabled people went from 'Those guys
you only ever see on the news protesting about a cut in their benefits' to
'Those guys you see on a worldwide stage, running their hearts out and
winning gold medals, as millions scream them on.'*

*It left a real legacy, too (see below for a terrible joke about 'legacy') –
the spin-off show,* The Last Leg, *hosted by comedians with disabilities, was
commissioned to run as a stand-alone series when the Paralympics ended,
and continues to be one of the edgiest, most compassionate and lolz-y shows
on UK TV. It's amazing what a difference a week can make, when you
try something different. When you give people some space.*

TV REVIEW: THE PARALYMPICS – LIKE THE OLYMPICS, BUT BACKWARDS AND ON WHEELS

And, so, the Paralympics – *Use Your Illusion II* to the Olympics' *Use
Your Illusion I*; *Superman 2* to their *Superman*. We loved the first
one so much, there just had to be another one. Let's face it – if,
halfway through, they'd announced a third global sporting event –
Childlympics, maybe; or Nanlympics. Even Catlympics we'd've been
all over that, too. We're in the rhythm of the whole thing now. Sag off
work as much as possible, ignore all world news in favour of sporting
glory, spend a lot of time on YouTube going, 'Christ, look at this
man's thighs. Look at them! They're like two BEASTS in Lycra. Like

two leg LIONS, pumping in tandem. Gngngnk. Imagine him coming at you. Holy moly, I've come over all previous.'

Although there was some culture shock switching from the BBC's imperial coverage to Channel 4's – adverts! What? How *uncouth*. People shilling in the middle of a sporting tournament? It's little better than having some chugger coming at you in a church, waving an empty bucket, screaming 'GIVE US A PAHND!' – the presence of Clare Balding soon smoothed it away again.

Oh, Clare! Clare Balding! With your combination of head-girl sport-swottiness, and air of being excellent company for a night on the gins, you have been the cherry on the London 2012 cake – first on the BBC, and then Channel 4. How sorry I feel for other countries – such as Canada, and Greece – who did not have you as their anchor. I'd like to think those countries had an equivalent of Clare Balding, but I suspect they do not: only we have a former Queen's jockey who, as we learned last week, invented the Mobot. That's one we've got to be proud of.

Only Britain had Eddie Izzard, too: presenting medals after Friday's Men's 800m T54 event, and handing David Weir his gold – nails carefully lacquered with red nail varnish. A multilingual transvestite comedian who himself ran forty-three marathons concurrently, for charity, with no previous training. They didn't have guys like that handing out the gongs in Beijing.

China also, notably, didn't have armed services like ours: Friday was also the day that servicemen and women from the Navy – on security duty in the stadium – led the 80,000-strong audience in the dance routine to that infamous gay anthem 'In The Navy'.

'What's happening to this country?' my husband asked, as we stared at another day's headlines about the people formerly known as 'cripples' and 'spazzes' being lined up for the New Year honours list, and making their countries proud.

'It's like this country's spent the last fifty years inadvertently being fed some Miserable Uptight Curmudgeon pills, and they've finally worn off. Perhaps they were putting it in the reservoirs, and all the early summer rain diluted it. It's brilliant. This is what the Second

Summer of Love would have been like if it had affected everyone – instead of just 258 E'd-up nutters in Chorley.'

The Closing Ceremony on Sunday, then, allowed the nation to gather for one last time to stare upon the wonders of a London possessed by the Olympics – a city as radically and magically transformed as if it had suddenly been designated a major Dragon Port, and massive beasts were regularly banking over Regent's Park, gliding over the Thames, to finally dock, via long silver chains, on Tower Bridge.

As night rolled in, and the BT Tower flashed red, white and blue and scrolled the message, 'Take a bow, London', you wondered: how *will* they end it all with enough pomp and finality for us to accept it's over?

But they did – and they did it the same way the Opening Ceremony of the Olympics kicked everything off in an instantly reconfiguring white-light bang: by just stealing a ton of its licks off the Glastonbury Festival, with all its mad, brilliant sorcery.

As a convoy of fantastical steampunk vehicles entered the stadium – a gigantic fish on wheels; a pirate ship; a rusting horse – Glastonbury-goers might have been minded of District 9: the far-flung fields of the festival where these vehicles can usually be found wheeling around at night, belching fire and freaking out dozens of people who are off their tits. That these renegade areas of a rock festival – run by travellers, enjoyed by the sodden – were being brought into the Paralympic Stadium, in front of a worldwide audience of millions, gave the Closing Ceremony an immediate and enjoyable air of wonky, fuck-you loucheness.

But that wonky, louche, steampunk theme was apt – as presenter Ade Adepitan pointed out later, 'So many athletes customise their equipment, making them functional for the needs they have.'

These are sportsmen and women who have to take a welding torch to their wheelchairs, to fit it exactly to their torsos; sand and hammer prosthetic legs and blades. These are people who learned to run – then lost their legs, and had to learn to run *again*. Anything we venerate an Olympian for, we find fourfold in a Paralympian, because these people holding gold medals have been blown up, rebuilt. Or delivered by doctors who stumbled over the words, 'I'm afraid your baby has some problems ... but these days, the prognosis is very good ... '

These are people who have a different relationship with science, machines and vehicles. As a mass of performers came into the stadium wielding blowtorches, and burned crop circles and fractal patterns into the ground, tattooing the turf, it mirrored the many tattoos we saw on the Paralympians' bodies. Another way of reclaiming your body from the things it's had to endure – a needle used in celebration, rather than necessity, when in pain.

In this manner, Coldplay were a brilliant booking as the night's only band. Although the focus of much contrarian hipster disdain – they are subject to the same sniffiness as fellow earnest stadium-fillers U2 used to be – I truly believe that, in my lifetime, it will be acceptable for people to admit they love Coldplay. They're a band that wear their hearts on their sleeves so guilelessly they essentially have ventricle cuffs: the whole bowl splashed with neon pinks, blue and aquamarines as they choired through the ceaselessly pretty 'Strawberry Swing' with the Paraorchestra. Trumpeter Clarence Adoo – paralysed below the shoulders in a car crash – played the trumpet by blowing through a straw on to an electrical sensory pad. Later on in the set, 'The Scientist' had the line *Questions of science/Science and progress/Will not sing as loud as my heart*. It was as good a description as any of what we were watching.

As dancers holding bunches of giant light bulbs floated into the sky, below them a floor full of paraplegic kids freaked out to the sky-punching bit in 'Paradise', and I wondered what the legacies of these Games will be. One of them is an actual, literal 'legacy' – in that huge swathes of the population now fancy people who've got no legs. As the Closing Ceremony woozed into flashback montage, Twitter filled with lustful discussions of its favourite PILFs. Is it social progress to want to shag the arse off Paralympians? In a world where a teenage kid would previously only have had Daniel Day-Lewis in *My Left Foot* and Long John Silver to look up to, probably yes. It's progress, also, for a society to acknowledge how nothing is won easily in the Paralympics – each gold here was paid for five times over and above any gold won in the

Olympics, and the athletes were respected accordingly. For if we love Usain Bolt for his guileless, effortless dancing over the finish line, how much more do we love Richard Whitehead scything down the final straight of the Men's 200m T42, legs like piston-powered scissors? Or Ellie Simmonds – the smallest thing in the pool, literally less than everyone else, smashing through the water like a fist?

But the big thing about London 2012, in the final analysis, wasn't all the superlative stuff – architecturally wondrous Velodromes, 295 new World Records, cannons shooting glitter into the skies. It was what it made *normal*, instead. For a month, having no legs was normal. Smiling on the Tube was normal. Seeing hefty women throwing shotputs was normal. Having a Mod cyclist as a national hero was normal. Having lavish opening and closing ceremonies based on the culture and heritage of the working classes, the civil rights movement, the travellers, pioneering homosexuals and the counter-culture was normal. Having your kids eschew their Wii to run out in the street and 'play' Paralympics with their friends was normal. Kids spent this summer pretending that they had no legs, or only one arm, because it made them feel *heroic*. My God.

Being hopeful, and unexpectedly excited, about being a human was normal.

It seemed to wake a muscle memory of what Britain was once – able to pull off magnificent acts of planning and construction, able to meet the focus of the world's gaze with grand innovations, and febrile theatre – but, this time around, without all the baggage of Empire and conquest.

At the time of the introduction of the NHS, a US diplomat sneered, 'Britain has given away its Empire in exchange for free teeth and orange juice' – obviously oblivious to the fact that that sounds totally awesome.

With London 2012, it felt like Britain had again given away its Empire – in exchange for these Olympics and Paralympics where men ran on swords, women flew, and the whole month was on fire with wonder.

MORANIFESTO
part two

So, as discussed in Moranifesto: Part One – in a bold opener for a book that is basically a collection of columns about London property prices and Ant & Dec – we know a change is coming. That the change is the possibility of upgrading ourselves – as both voters, and citizens – now that we are connected by the internet of the world. Now that we can finally begin to unite as a collective conscious entity, and, you know, chat to each other.

But the internet of the world is a very young invention, and often makes mistakes. We have seen, a thousand times over, how it can run after the wrong enemies – Jon Ronson's book *So You've Been Publicly Shamed* brilliantly highlights people who said something foolish, or were simply misunderstood, and subsequently had their lives utterly ruined.

And – if that wasn't bad enough – how the firestorm of social media outrage can then rage on: for once news of these hapless Twitter victims' ruination made it into the media, the 'whistle-blowers' who'd first highlighted the story then had *their* lives ruined: being fired from their jobs, or socially ostracised, for being the ones that instigated the fury.

If the internet of the world – social media – really *is* the awakening of a global consciousness – us all becoming one, gigantic, brain – then it is little wonder that this birth of a 7-billion-part 'us' is, sometimes, terrifying. Like some bewildered Frankenstein's monster, waking up on the slab and lashing out – not knowing the power of its new arms and legs.

In order that this fabulous, awe-inspiring beast do no harm, we need to establish some rules for global communication and activism, so that the same mistakes are not made over and over again. So that going online doesn't, some days, feel like walking into a zoo that's been set on fire, with penguins attacking lions, gnus trampling on hippos, and a couple of unhappy llamas in the corner, crying, 'I just wanted to show everyone a picture of my lunch! I am excited about avocados! I do not like all this anger! I am going to hide under my table!'

It's all about *how* you say it

'Fate doesn't hang on a wrong or right choice/
Fortune depends on the tone of your voice.'
'Songs of Love', The Divine Comedy

As citizens, so much of our political conversation – perhaps the majority of it – happens on social media these days. And so I present to you, what is, essentially *A Guide to Discussing Change on the Internet* without being burned to death, looking like a dick, offending anyone, or getting in the way of a possible brilliant, bright future for humanity – just because *you* are peevish after missing out on an Anne of Green Gables mug, mint condition, on eBay.

There are several key things to remember about social media. The first is to bear in mind how young it is. If social media *is* the long-awaited birth of a collective consciousness, it is now essentially in its toddler phase. It's still very young. It tends to sudden rages. It repeats itself a lot. It uses the wrong words. It can be easily distracted by a picture of a cat, or a snack. It flings a *lot* of poo around.

As the years go by, social media will grow up and be capable of much more nuanced conversation – the ability to see both sides of a story, and not to suddenly grow so furious that everything erupts into a massive tantrum. I have no doubt that Twitter will soon be replaced by something with an entirely different atmosphere – where the rat-tat-tat, adrenalised bullet-delivery of Tweets will be replaced by something far more relaxed and discursive.

But for now, remember: you're dealing with a very young, fractious beast that, quite often, clearly needs to be put down for a nap. Don't take its tantrums too seriously. It has a long way to go, is learning a lot every day, and might have just wet itself and want its snuggle-bear.

The second thing to bear in mind is the study that suggested the level of social inhibition on social media equates, roughly, to having drunk two pints of beer. Freed from our physical bodies, and eye contact, we become slightly … intoxicated. We are drunk on wifi.

So whenever you log on, do so in the knowledge you are essentially walking into a bar or pub at nine o'clock on a Friday night. There's a lot of people out to a) either get laid or b) start a fight. People are horny, or lairy. Or both. Your statements are liable to be misconstrued. Sarcasm, or irony, is often not detected – with fatal results. People will overshare. People will suddenly bond with you, intensely. And, if you're a woman, someone is probably going to show you their penis at some point. That is inevitable.

Ah, social media. Pissed children in a bar. I love you so.

So, with these caveats in mind, let's stroll through a couple of handy guidelines for the online citizen, keen to do their bit to change the world by typing out their hopes and dreams on the internet, and launching them out there, in front of a billion eyes.

1) Your tone is key. I've sat through ten years of online debates, and the one thing I can tell you as a fact is that, if you communicate in anger, 90 per cent of the response you will get in return will be just … more anger. Directed at *you*.

It doesn't matter if what you are saying is true, factual or reasonable – because the majority of people will *not* be reading what you actually said. They're just going to see the emotional pitch of your communiqué, and reply in kind, instead.

I've seen so many potentially amazing debates go nowhere, because the person starting the debate was rightfully angry – but their tone seemingly worked as a dog whistle to attract a massive online fight. There were a couple of years when online feminism was basically a bunch of hurt, angry women – women who should have been on the same side – communicating with each other only in fury, and creating only fury in return. Every brilliant, bright, right thing they said was ignored.

When you make an initial post, remember this vital thing: you set the tone, and people will reply in kind. If a conversation starts angry, it will almost certainly continue angry, and end up apoplectic, with people shouting, 'I RESIGN FROM THE INTERNET', 'EVERYONE GET BENT' or 'YOUR MUM,' to the benefit of literally no one at all.

There really is no more urgent place to be relaxed and polite than the internet. It's a basic survival necessity. If you are to be an effective radical, you must be a *polite* radical – which is, of course, the *best* kind of radical. And if you can be gently humorous, you are doing the whole world a favour. Nothing unclenches the angrily clamped-together buttocks of social media in the middle of an outrage firestorm more than someone essentially taking on the posture of The Fonz, and going, 'Heyyyyy – wassup?'

The key to all this is to remember that anger is, usually, just fear, brought to the boil. And people can hear the fear under your anger and, as they would in the playground, they respond to it. They basically go 'RAH RAH NAH NAH NAH' in your face, when they detect it. They give you internet wedgies. Avoid internet wedgies.

Remember: internet anger is like your savings account. You only want to break into it in extreme emergencies.

2) Dismissing people who aren't perfect. Social media has a current, unpleasant hobby: waiting for someone to come along who appears to have captured a mood, or identified a problem, or done something laudable, or progressive – then frantically digging in their past to find a mistake they might previously have made, in order to try and totally devalue the good thing they have just done.

I understand where this desire comes from: it's a fear of being let down. We've been let down by a million heroes, at some point – and so, now, in order not to look like fresh-off-the-train rubes, we race to be the first person to unmask this new messiah, before we are, inevitably, disappointed by them, at some point in the future.

There is a virtual industry, at the moment, in people mining the pasts of the newly prominent to find an ill-advised Tweet from 2007, a Facebook update where they used a 'bad' phrase, or an early stand-up skit where they appeared to say something bad about, say, Mexicans – unless you watch to the *end* of the clip and realise they're doing it in the guise of a dumb character.

But part of being a grown-up is to always have the balls to believe. Cynicism is like an armour – it will, initially, protect you. But you cannot grow in armour, you cannot dance in armour. Cynicism restricts our growth. Cynicism is, in the end, an act of weakness. We must always have the cojones to be optimistic. To trust people. To forgive them their mistakes, if we feel like they are trying to be better people; that they are trying to learn.

3) Getting in the way. Every year, I get some dog tags made up, with my new, annual mottoes. Last year's was 'Always ride out as if meeting your nemesis' – i.e. a reminder to always leave the house with your hair looking big, lest you bump into an ex-boyfriend.

This year's is the more succinct 'Don't get in the way'.

You know how it goes. Some people are discussing something – posting links, proffering ideas – and then some third party will rock up and say – often smugly, I regret to say – 'What about *blah*!' – mentioning some completely tangential but controversial side issue that invariably attract a whole host of controversy-hungry arguers who will then pile into the conversation, arguing among themselves.

The original posters spend an hour or two fending off the increasingly hysterical whirlpool of demands being thrown at them – before finally logging off, exhausted, and leaving the original debate to die.

The kind of people who parachute into other people's debates want, essentially, attention. They are acting as if the only way to draw attention to the causes they are passionate about is to piggyback them on to the cause *you* are being passionate about.

While this passion is laudable, and useful, it is also oddly old-fashioned – a hangover from a time when there was limited space for debating topics. That might have been true in 1600, when you might have to battle a fellow peasant for control of their woodblock printing press in order to disseminate your idea.

But it's 2016! The internet is a literally limitless space! Be passionate about your passion in *your* passion area – do not try to infiltrate *my* passion area! It is one of the key hindrances to things getting done on the internet – loading down one conversational donkey with a million other conversations, until its back breaks, and a whole area of conversation is avoided, because it smells of dead donkey. Don't piggyback on to someone else's mission, man. Have the balls to start your own. Spiderman never rocked up at Batman's house when he was in the middle of battling The Joker, and said, 'Dude – you've got to go and sort out the Green Goblin, man! He's seriously fucking my shit up!'

You're Spiderman. *You* go and sort out the Green Goblin. Leave Batman to sort out The Joker in peace.

One of the key drivers of the 'Getting in the way' crew is the feeling that if someone is talking/campaigning about something, they must talk/campaign about *everything*. The subconscious belief being that, at some point, someone will come along – some Campaign Jesus – and he will solve *everything*. He will compile a complete and perfect manifesto with solutions to everything, and until that person comes along, everyone – and everything – is, essentially, useless.

This fundamentally misunderstands several things – the key one being just how likely this is to happen. (Zero per cent. This is 0 per cent likely to happen. Even if we look at the most inspiring and astonishing people to ever come along – Gandhi, Mandela, Sir Alex Ferguson – they didn't do *everything*. They had a couple of areas in which they were incredibly visionary, powerful and determined – decolonisation of India, the end of apartheid, winning the Treble – but they weren't *also* tackling FGM, climate change, sex-trafficking and the World Cup. They specialised.)

All the answers will *never* come in one person. The future is a communal effort – like a patchwork quilt. Everyone interested in forming our society takes a square each – a square they have chosen according to their interests, knowledge and ability – and sews it, and then we join them together to make a fabulous quilt. That's how things get done.

Essentially waiting for some perfect mummy or daddy to come along and do everything in one go is a terrible psychic hangover from feudalism, the patriarchy, or just watching too many episodes of *24*. In real life, maverick loners tend not to change the world. What *you're* looking for is a lovely collective of specialists, all tending their patches with love, instead.

When you get accosted by someone going, 'You cannot talk about BLAH unless you also talk about BLAH,' the best response is, '*I* know – you do BLAH and I'll do BLAH, and then the world will be *twice* as improved! Thanks for volunteering! Amazing! Check in with me every couple of weeks – let me know how BLAH is going! I can't believe you're doing this! You're a total mensch! On behalf of the rest of the world – *thank you*!!!!'

4) Dismissing people as 'champagne socialists'. You know how this goes. Bono, or Russell Brand, or Emma Thompson, or Charlotte Church, speak out in defence of welfare, or the working poor, and are immediately derided as 'champagne socialists' by the professionally snide.

The denouncing of champagne socialists always follows a strict format – mentioning the price of the house the champagne socialist lives in, their income/net worth, whether or not they went to public school, if their children do, and accompanying it with a picture of the champagne socialist either a) dressed up to the nines on a red carpet (how can they attend a movie premiere *when the poor cannot attend a movie premiere*!) or looking angry and shouting at a demonstration (this person is *crazed with socialism*! Look at them *snarl*! Socialism is the *ultimate Bitchy Resting Face*! You will need Botox now, for sure!).

The demented logic seems to be as follows: that you cannot stand up for the poor unless you are poor yourself. That if you have managed to accrue any wealth and security, unless you have subsequently given away every penny of it to charities for the poor, you are a hypocrite to speak about the poor. Only the poor can speak about, and for, the poor. Poverty is only the concern of the poor. Other people must not comment on the poor. Poor people's business is strictly for the poor. So, if you are a real socialist, you must yourself stay poor forever.

Of course, there are several, very obvious, logical flaws in this argument. The first is a fundamental misunderstanding of socialism.

There are many misunderstandings about what a socialist is: primarily that it's someone who wears a donkey jacket and lives by a brazier, possibly in 1979, and listens only to Billy Bragg.

Well, I know loads of socialists like this, and they're ace. They get shit done. But that's not socialism. That's *people*. People who like old coats and Billy Bragg.

Socialism is just a single, simple sentence: the belief that the necessities for the functioning of a society should be provided without profit. It's such a lovely and simple idea that I want to say it again: the belief that the necessities for the functioning of a society should be provided without profit.

So that's health, education, welfare, transport, the emergency services, the prison service and the justice system, paid for by taxation, and available to everyone, regardless of wealth. No paying Serco millions for running overcrowded jails. No G4S – the guys who fucked up the Olympics – still being paid by the government, despite being investigated by the serious fraud office for massively overcharging. 'The necessities for the functioning of a society should be provided without profit.' That's socialism.

As you can see from that description, there's nothing in socialism that prevents Charlotte Church from living in a nice house, walking a red carpet and, after paying her taxes, earning millions a year. If she were a champagne *anarchic communist* – who believed that all property is theft, and that money should be abolished – *then* she would be a hypocrite. Anarchic communists don't believe in individuals working to accrue wealth, living in a nice house and wearing faintly impractical shoes. Champagne anarchic communists would, indeed, be ripe for pillory. I think we can agree that champagne anarchic communists – all twelve of them – are hypocritical bastards.

Champagne socialists, on the other hand, are people who could personally pay for an Open Return Standard ticket to Manchester that costs £329 since privatisation – but recognise that other people *can't*, and are suggesting that, maybe, society would function better if rail travel were cheaper, so everyone could use it.

What people who denounce champagne socialists are doing is, essentially, trying to shame people who have empathy. Now, that's a bad day down the opinion mines in anyone's book.

Russell Brand might have got many things wrong in these early years of his flowering political awareness, but one thing he said was bang on the money: 'When I was poor and I complained about inequality, people said I was bitter. Now I'm rich and I complain about inequality, they say I'm a hypocrite. I'm beginning to think they just don't want inequality on the agenda.'

5) Dismissing people as 'Tory scum'/'Posh bastards'. Equal in nobbishness to dismissing someone as a 'champagne socialist'/'bleeding heart liberal pinko' is to dismiss someone as 'Tory scum'.

It's taken me a long time to come to this realisation. When I was nine, my father gave me a brief, concise lecture on politics.

'If you ever come home and tell me you voted Tory,' he said, lying on the driveway, dragging on a ciggy as he dropped the clutch out of the car, 'you'll be sailing out of the front door with my boot-print on your arse. In this house, we vote *Labour*.'

He then dropped something heavy on his leg, and swore so magnificently that my mother came and ushered me inside again.

As someone raised in what was, essentially, a hovel, by a miner and a munitions worker, in an era before the Welfare State – 'I've seen rats so big you could *ride them like a horse*' – he'd become a Trade Union rep by the age of twenty-four, disabled by thirty, and was fairly blunt about bringing up eight children on Disability Benefit in the age of Margaret Thatcher.

'They're all cunts,' he explained, over breakfast.

'Kids – put your fingers in your ears,' Mum said.

'Total cunts,' he continued. 'Thatcher would take the bread out of your hands if she could.'

Richie – then four – pushed his entire slice of toast into his mouth.

'Don't think it's safe in your mouth, kidder,' Dad said, sprinkling pickle-vinegar on his fried egg. 'She'll send the fucking police round, they'll push you over, say it was an accident, take it out of your gob and wave your fucking breakfast around like it's a scalp. Vote Labour,' he concluded.

Very, very often, he would conclude a speech with 'Vote Labour'.

'Dad, I need £5 to buy some sandals.'

'Eh? Wellie boots not good enough for you?'

'It's August. I'm sweaty. I can't ride my bike in them.'

'Tell Thatcher, not me. Vote Labour.'

'Dad – I'm in love with Gilbert Blythe from *Anne of Green Gables*.'

'Nice one, nice one. Vote Labour.'

'Dad, I'm locked in the toilet.'

'Vote Labour.'

So imagine my surprise when, as a teenager, I went out into the world and met people who voted Conservative, and found out a lot of them were … lovely. Just lovely. Kind, considerate, intelligent people. Jewish intellectuals; immigrants who ran businesses; boyfriends of friends who sat up all night drinking gin, and talking about their favourite psyche records, until their friends cornered me in the toilet and said, 'You'd never guess *he was a Tory*, would you?' in disbelieving tones.

Similarly, posh people. As feral scum from a council estate, my definition of 'posh' is fairly broad – essentially, I would consider anyone who had both their own bed, not shared with a sibling, *and* a bedside lamp to have parents who'd 'done all right for themselves'. I was brought up to believe all posh people were evil, too.

'They're raised being told they're born to rule,' my dad said, Artexing the ceiling in bold swirls while puffing on a ciggy. 'That's what you pay for, with a private education. Being raised to believe you are born to rule. They'll always see you as a peasant, love. Their natural role is telling us what to do. We're the malleable masses. The lumpen proletariat. Lions led by fucking donkeys.'

He then got some Artex in his eye, and had to go and wash it out with milk while screaming.

But, again, when I went out into the world, and started meeting posh people, I found out *they* weren't evil, either. They are *not* trying to crush the working classes. They are *not* calculatingly trying to strip us of dignity, and opportunity.

What they are, instead, – which, to be honest, is almost as fatal – is blithe (see page 80, The Rich Are Blithe).

6) Shaming idealism. Many, many times in my life I have not said/ Tweeted/written what I really believe, politically, because I was worried about being shamed as 'an idealist'. This is not something I am proud of – but it's something I have done out of expediency, because I have seen, a million times, how saying something idealistic is used to attack your fundamental standing, credibility and status. Indeed, as a politically progressive feminist, I can't work out if it's worse to be called 'Utopian', or 'fat'. They probably tie.

Saying something that seems *currently* impractical is like a small media suicide – you are seen as foolish. Stupid. Unfit to engage in the topic.

But the ultimate pragmatism is to quietly note that idealism has won, time after time, in the last hundred years. Idealism has the upper hand. Idealism has some hot statistics. Idealism invented and fuelled the Civil Rights Movement, votes for women, the change in rape laws, Equal Marriage, the internet, IVF, organ transplants, the end of apartheid, independence in India, the Hadron collider, *Hairspray* the musical, and my recent, brilliant loft conversion. Every reality we have now started with a seedcorn of idealism, and impossibility; visions have to coalesce somewhere.

If we are too afraid to state our dreams – to even begin to sketch out possible futures – then we have begun to disinvent the greatest facility humans have: to invent better. To lie on our backs, staring up at the Moon, and say, 'One day, a man will walk there. And, maybe, open a roller-disco lounge. That would be awesome.'

7) Dismissing an entire idea because some people took advantage of it. You know how this one goes – a story is published about someone with seventeen children who's living on welfare, and 'getting' £38,000 a year, and the piece goes on to discuss the total welfare bill, before concluding that, because the system is being 'abused', welfare should be curtailed, or abolished.

The thing is, if we talked about abolishing everything that was abused, then where would we stop? We would have abolished the Houses of Parliament during the expenses scandal, and the Catholic Church when the paedophile priests story broke. Likewise schools – given the amount of abuse that has happened there, both state and private.

We'd be talking about abolishing marriage – because women are abused, and raped, in relationships. Likewise parenthood, given the numbers of parents who abuse their children.

The simple truth is, people will abuse any system. There's a proportion of humanity that will *always* play the system – whatever it is. That's what humans do. We're just monkeys, looking for a stick to poke in a hole to get ants. Or monkeys who will steal someone else's stick, and ants.

The question is: is the fundamental concept that is being abused good? Right? Moral?

You don't just *give in* when people abuse a system. Instead, you make the system *better*. Anyone wanting to give up a perfectly decent idea – indeed, a necessary, moral and transformative one – because someone *else* took advantage of it is basically saying, 'I am too lazy to do all the admin to improve this. I'm baulking at paperwork. I am eschewing management change in favour of SETTING FIRE TO EVERYTHING AND RUNNING AWAY.'

We must never listen to anyone who confuses 'an idea' with 'how that idea was predictably abused by a tiny percentage of the population'.

So there we go. A brief guide to making sure you are a fully clued-up internet political ninja – helping shape the ideas, and tone, of your society; working as a conduit for good ideas, and not perverting them, or getting in their way. Educating yourself into being the third most glorious thing on Earth, after 'mid-September sunshine' and 'David Bowie': an informed and motivated voter.

THE FEMINISMS

You know what I'm like with 'the ladies' – I'm all 'equality' this and 'humanity' that and 'stop with the raping, for God's sake stop with all the – sometimes literal – motherfucking raping' the other.

It's amazing to me that it's still considered a notable, commendable trait – 'Oh, she's a well-known feminist' – in a woman, or a girl, or a man, or a boy. That that is the unusual thing. Really, it should be the reverse. Rather than what seems like a minority having to spend time, energy, brain and heart explaining why they're 'into' equality, the majority should be explaining why they're not. *You* put the time into explaining *why – in a world where every concept of justice, wisdom, progress and rightness is a human invention – we still prefer the human concept of 'some people being inferior to others' over 'this is a vast, inky, cold, empty universe, and in it, we are the only humans that exist, all sharing a tiny milky green/blue world, and faced with a multitude of problems, and an infinite capacity for joy, and should therefore try and stick together and accord each other some respect'.*

When I wrote How to Be a Woman *I thought – given that it was 320 pages – that I'd kind of* done *all the feminism. As the years went by, however, feminism was a topic I returned to time and time again in my columns. I am still trying to work out how to be a woman. I think we all are. There's still a lot of ass-hattery out there. Thankfully, however, there's also a lot of women. I reckon, if we all got together in one particularly large bar, we could probably sort it all out before the Sambuca shots started – allowing breaks to nip outside, for fags.*

Anyway, let us start with silliness. The first piece in 'The Feminisms' is about my most regular political statement:

MY MUPPET FACE

In both my written correspondence from readers of *The Times,* and in the online comments on the website, there are three observations I receive on a reassuringly regular basis.

The first is, 'When oh when will Ms Moran stop harping on about her "Poor me" working-class background?' (When the revolution comes! Amiright, comrades?)

The second is, 'I have documents which prove beyond doubt that the Queen is a lizard-Jew' (in the interests of politeness I've tried to stay opened-minded here, guys, but have to say – I might be 'out' on this one).

As for the third recurrent complaint, I document a selection of them, faithfully, here: 'Ms *Moron* – why do you persistently allow yourself to be photographed pulling faces? Grimacing adds nothing. On the rare occasions I've seen you straight-faced, your features have looked … perfectly adequate.' 'Any chance we could see what you look like when you're not desperately gurning?' 'My dear, your "whacky young me" persona was grating at the age of twenty-three – now pushing thirty-nine, you look like someone's drunk mother, having a stroke. Stop it. It is profoundly unattractive. Why do you persist in it?'

Well, I am glad you asked! For you see, to the untrained eye, it may very well appear as if I *do* spend most of my photoshoots pulling a 'silly' face, in which I look like a lollygagger, halfwit, or clown.

In actuality, however, this is my *cleverest* face. My *brainiest* face. That bog-eyed rictus – which appears to be little more than a homage to the standard expression of, say, Rod Hull, of *Rod Hull & Emu* fame, on posters for pantomimes in the late 1980s – is, in actuality, a devastatingly realised piece of cultural critique. It is one of my most political statements. It's where I am being the change I would wish to see.

You see, something happens to a woman like me when they have a picture taken while trying to look calm, attractive and authoritative: they lose. This isn't a blame issue. The simple fact is that my genetic legacy does not look good 'in repose' – doing that calm, emotionless expression women are supposed to do when having their picture taken for a magazine or newspaper.

If you want to do a 'serenely impassive' face, you have to have the kind of cheekbones you can hang your coat – and, indeed, metaphorically, your entire *life* – off. People like that look *fine* when they stay still. They look good *asleep*. They'll look good *dead*. Indeed, if they have an open-casket funeral, they'll probably still be able to pull someone by the end of the ceremony. Hot people be hot.

I, by way of contrast, have a fleshy, Irish peasant's face – half potato, half thumb. I know, from decades of experience, that if I'm not moving this facial shit around as much as possible – essentially juggling my features, possibly as they're on fire, almost certainly while screaming – my default look is 'sullen maid-of-all-work being forced to resentfully scrub out the dunny, on her half-day'.

And I do not wish to represent myself this way – only in dour bone, and podge. No. I want to *work* my face. I want to project how I feel on the inside: like a Muppet being fired out of a cannon into a large pie. On Christmas Day. I want to look alive.

This is why I 'pull' those faces. Faces that are, in actuality, just what I look like, all day – rather than the *real* 'pulled' faces – studiedly sultry, or lofty – of most photos.

As unlikely as it seems, it is my *intent* to look like a scruffy 39-year-old Muppet, or a clown – because I would rather cut off my head than try to look attractive in a photo. I don't want to enter that competition – for that's what it is, when a woman dresses, and poses, like that. She gets rated. Rated against all the other women posing like that, and doing those things with her face. Pitched against Merle Oberon and Carol Vorderman, and thingy from the Kardashians.

I, on the other hand, want to be in a different category altogether – the category with Rik Mayall, and Daffy Duck, and Bill Murray in it. Where you look at *their* faces, and it doesn't occur to you to comment on their jowls, or their wrinkles, or their animated yellow bill. You don't think, 'Oh, they're fatter than last month', or 'They think they're *it*' or 'Bad choice of yellow dungarees'. You just think, 'They look like they're having fun.'

And that's all I want to look like. Like I'm having fun. And that I would help you carry your buggy up a flight of stairs, if you needed it.

I'm not trying to project some sexy authoritativeness *at* the world. I am being amused *by* the world, instead. I'm not *transmitting*. I'm *receiving*.

So, yes. To everyone who has ever written to me about my 'silly' face, I want you to know that this is actually my *best* face, and I wrote this *entire column* looking like Les Dawson.

Because I want to. Because it makes me happy.

In September 2015 there was a brief flap about a human rights lawyer, Charlotte Proudman, who 'perv-shamed' an older colleague, Alexander Carter-Silk, who contacted her through LinkedIn to compliment her on her 'stunning' picture.

Aside from reconfirming every suspicion I've ever had about LinkedIn – that it's just a facility whereby you end up exposing yourself to endless hassle; even more hassle than their constant frigging needy emails to join them – it was also dispiriting to see how Proudman's actions were greeted. She was – and this is, sadly, the common story for any woman who pokes her head above the parapet – bombarded with misogynist comments about her appearance, her motives and her career. She was called a 'Feminazi' – A NAZI! – had her social media accounts published in an attempt to shame her, along with all the usual halfwits threatening to find out where she lived and kill her.

I would like to say I was amazed by the reaction – but then, I've seen it happen so many times, I could have told her in advance exactly what would occur. I think she is brave, brilliant and right for what she did – trying to make men realise that it's not just 'giving a compliment'. It's part of a wider problem. It's because there are two things men just don't understand about women.

THE TWO THINGS MEN NEED TO UNDERSTAND ABOUT WOMEN

It is the eternal cry of men: 'I don't understand women!' Women are mysterious to men: they do not understand why we take so long to dress; the number of shoes we need; the way we can suddenly lose all confidence. Our excitement about tiny things – tiny cups and saucers, tiny monkeys, tiny ribbons. A tiny ring.

But those really are the tiny things that you don't understand. It doesn't matter if you never understand those things at all.

Here are the two big things that men truly don't understand about women. The two things that, if you knew them – if you truly understood – would change the way you act, and raise your sons to act, overnight.

The first is: we're scared of you.

Not all of you. Probably not most of you. We feel safe with our fathers – unless we have been unlucky; and our husbands – unless we have been unlucky; and our friends and brothers – unless, again, we have been unlucky.

But we are scared. Of what you can do.

Try to imagine, for a moment, what it's like to live on a planet where half the people on it are just ... bigger than you. We are smaller, and softer, and we cannot run as fast as men. We know you can grab us, and we would struggle to get away. We know if you hit us, we'll go down. We know if you decide to kill us, there's not much we can do.

Every time the murder of a woman is reported on the news, we hear the detail – 'Traces of skin were found under her fingernails, denoting a struggle' – and we know ... that's all we can do. Scratch. We think about that more than we would ever admit to you. We don't want to sound insecure, or morbid, around you. We just walk down any dark street with our keys between our fingers, going, 'Please, not tonight. Let me get to my door tonight.'

Here's comedian Louis C.K.'s routine on women and men: 'Globally and historically, men are the number one cause of injury and mayhem to women. By comparison, do you know what men's number one threat is? Heart disease. Guys, if you want to know how brave a woman is every time she says yes to going on a date, try to imagine that you could only date a half-bear, half-lion. "Oh – I hope this one's nice!" That's being a woman.'

Sometimes, when you think about the stats on sexual assault – 90 per cent of women know their attackers; one in five women are attacked – it feels like a fact too awful to be acknowledged. One in five, man. If those were your odds on the lottery, you'd already have pre-emptively bought the Porsche. One in five means you often look round a room of your girlfriends and think, 'Which one of us will it be?'

If your teenage daughters are in the room – with their big, smiling faces and their awkward, beautiful, perfect trust in the world – you feel so panicked you go into the kitchen and hold on to the sink.

There you are. Scared again. But you don't go on about it to the men you know – because that would be morbid. So men don't know how scared we are. That's the first big thing you don't know about us. How scared we are.

The second big thing you don't know about us is, we're exhausted. So, so exhausted. We have less money than you – the pay gap, illegal since 1970 yet still, astonishingly, here, means we effectively work for free for fifty-seven days of the year. That's exhausting. We must have babies, quickly, before our eggs die, but while we also work – that's exhausting.

And since we were teenage girls – since the moment we went, mortified, to buy that first bra, and left the safe, unisex world of childhood to become 'a woman' – we've been judged and commented on. Catcalls in the streets; relatives saying we're too fat or too thin. Comments in year books or on Facebook; hairdressers saying, 'You have a mannish jaw.' 'Uncles' at weddings, and bosses at parties, and friends of friends, rating you to your face – saying if they 'would' or 'wouldn't', scoring you out of ten, as if you're a gadget for sale on Amazon, or livestock at a fayre.

People touching you, evaluating and owning you – until you find yourself saying, almost as a recurring mantra, in your head, 'Fuck off! Stop talking about me! Fuck off, and stop being the voice in my head! Stop telling me you have decided my worth.'

And, so, yes. Yes, I do understand why human rights lawyer Charlotte Proudman 'perv-shamed' an older, senior lawyer – Alexander Carter-Silk – when he contacted her on LinkedIn and told her her picture was 'stunning'.

In the furore that followed, he – and a million other commentators afterwards – seemed confused by Proudman's reaction. It was just flirtation! It was just an appreciative comment! This is what men and women do!

But men do it without knowing we're scared and we're tired. So very, very tired.

The thing is, when practically the whole world needs to be changed, we get a bit … impatient when it doesn't.

WOMEN KEEP FUCKING THINGS UP

Do you know what the problem with feminism is, in 2016? Sadly, it's the feminists. Time and time again, those women just keep … screwing it up.

Sheryl Sandberg, previously chief of staff at the US Treasury, is now second in command at Facebook, and is regularly voted one of *Time*'s '100 Most Powerful People in the World'.

But this year, when she published her book *Lean In* – encouraging more women to take up positions of high power in business – she targeted an audience who are already well-educated, wholly neglecting to address such issues as childcare, and housework, which hold back so many other, less privileged women. Ultimately, she screwed it up.

Twenty-seven-year-old Lena Dunham, meanwhile, writes, directs, produces and stars in one of the most talked-about shows of the last ten years – HBO's *Girls*. She tackles abortion, STDs, pornography, masochism and her generation's parlous reversal of fortune. Her grasp of the moment is equal with Tom Wolfe's.

But as the first series of *Girls* began to air, it became sadly apparent that Dunham hadn't included a single non-white character in the show. 'They should call it *White Girls*,' was the common pay-off to angry pieces about it. Dunham screwed up.

And then what about Beyoncé? Another woman who does that rare thing – of openly describing herself as a feminist – Beyoncé has an all-female band, manages herself, writes rogue suffragette anthems like 'Independent Women', 'Single Ladies' and 'Run The World (Girls)', and has famously made having a big, fantastic arse and thighs *aspirational*.

But then she got married to Sean Carter, aka Jay-Z, and named her current world tour The Mrs Carter Tour. Women have campaigned for *decades* for the right to keep their own names – and then this sexy chick gets stuck for a title for her tour, and puts back women's rights by thirty years. Yeah, thanks, Mrs Norman Maine.

Indeed, thanks to all the 'feminists' out there who keep *screwing it up*. Because every time you make some error, or miss something out, you're making feminism look foolish.

That's the presumption, anyway. I've lost count of the pieces I've read in the last six months or so, bewailing previously loved feminist icons who've done something that has supposedly caused an immovable stain on themselves and their movement. Whenever I read about Sheryl Sandberg, or Lena Dunham, or Beyoncé, the core complaint seems to be: why haven't these women done *everything*? Why haven't they addressed *all* the problems women face? To put it in the most succinct terms possible: why haven't these women been able to simply and inclusively address the concerns of every one of the 3.3 billion women on Earth?

But, of course, if the infallible guide for being able to detect the presence of sexism is 'Are the men doing this?', as we can see, the men are resolutely not expecting one single dude to rock up and solve all the problems of every *man* on Earth. You know – the men are happy when Jeremy Clarkson merely tells them if he thinks a car is 'gay' or not. Men didn't stand at the bottom of Mount Everest, arms folded, waiting for Edmund Hillary to come down, then greet him with, 'Yeah, nice one, Hillary – but when are you gonna invent the internet?'

But this is what we do – time and time again – with our female pioneers. Understandably over-invested in any woman who *does* begin to succeed, we load a million hot, desperate expectations on to them, then enter a weird world where we become immensely peevish at a thousand things they *haven't* done – energetically attacking wholly phantom, imaginary wrongs – rather than taking a moment to be joyful over the stuff that, against all the odds, they actually *did* do. Imperfect but useful achievements which, even as we sigh over their failings, will inevitably be inspiring others to follow in their wake, with *their* specific quests.

You know what – it really is okay if a woman comes along and does just a *little* bit of pioneering. Encourage childless university graduates to run global companies! Write brutally honest sitcoms about self-obsessed girls! Stand on stage in front of 250,000 people making them sing, *'All the women who are independent/Throw your hands up at me'*! Because, let's face it – no one else is doing that. These are still hardly overcrowded arenas of activity.

We're all working on a massive patchwork quilt called 'A Better Future' here – anyone can pull up a chair and have a go. The only rule of Feminism Quilt Club is that we don't expect one woman to sew the entire damn thing herself, while bitching about her to her face. Oh and crisps. You have to bring crisps.

I would like to say this useful thing, in 2016: if we're waiting for some kind of Feminist Megatron to appear – who will solve all our problems – we will be waiting another 100,000 years. Personally, I don't have that long. I'm happy to make feminism a team sport.

Ironically, sometimes, one of the things that makes it hardest to be a woman is feminism. That's just how it is. Nothing is perfect all the time.

I PROPOSE NOT HAVING OPINIONS ON WOMEN FOR, SAY, FIVE YEARS

As one of north London's top fifteen humorous feminists, I am often asked for my opinion of women who have been in the news.

In the last few months, for instance, there has been Marissa Mayer – the first pregnant woman to be hired as the CEO of a Fortune 500 company. Brave, oestrogen-high pioneer? Or hopeless bun-ovened deludo? Anne-Marie Slaughter wrote a highly publicised article in *The Atlantic* stating that women can't 'have it all', and should stop pretending they can. Had she called it like it really is? Or is she a batshit harpy who couldn't hack it herself and is now engaging in a gigantic bout of post-facto projection on to the rest of womankind? E.L. James became a millionaire almost overnight, as her S&M trilogy, *Fifty Shades*, turned every bookshop window grey and porny. Has she enabled women to finally discuss their sexuality openly? Or merely reinforced patriarchal stereotypes about submissive female sexuality?

And what about Louise Mensch? First the facelift controversy, then bailing out of the Murdoch select committee for the school run, before, finally, resigning as MP for Corby in order to relocate to New York with her family. What does it all *mean*? How is this going to affect the future of women in British politics? Are CERN going to issue any conclusions on the significance of what Louise Mensch, 41, has done?

To save you all time, I can tell you now, no one actually knows the answer to any of these questions – but they spent the summer debating the hell out of them on *Newsnight*, and in the *Daily Mail*. They totally opinionised that stuff.

For, currently, every time a woman in the public eye does something, she doesn't do it just for, and as, herself. She does it on behalf of 3.3 billion other women, too. She is seen to represent her entire gender – a putative Team 'The Birds' – in a way men just aren't. When a bloke screws up, he's just some bloke screwing up. When a woman makes a hash of it, however, she's a cultural signifier, and basis for a million polarised debates. Every famous woman is someone we have to have an opinion on: Lady Gaga, Rebekah Brooks, Naomi Wolf, Rihanna, Mitt Romney's wife. You must be either for or against them. Your stance on them is a telling indicator of your world view.

Over the summer I came to a decision. I decided this was working out quite badly for the women, all things told. That given, I would like to propose the following:

1) We need to stop referring to things as 'female dilemmas', 'women's problems' or 'thorny subjects for feminism'. If there's something which is making life difficult for women, then this is something that is, most assuredly, making it difficult for everyone else in the world, too. Women don't live on a separate continent – Birdtopia – communicating only sporadically with the menfolk by email. If 52 per cent of the potential brain power in the world is being hindered by something – like lack of childcare, or creepy, WTF? debates on rape and contraception – it behoves this small planet for everyone to jump on it and sort it out as quickly as possible. Basically, this is an emergency. We don't have time for another 100,000 years of women feeling sad about their arses, and being held back at work by some swaggering misogynist pinhead called Simon, when there's polar bears to save and cancer to cure.

My second suggestion is, perhaps, more radical. It is:

2) We need a temporary cessation in people having any opinions about any women, ever. I propose a, say, five-year moratorium on having opinions about women, in order to let one generation of girls get from one side of puberty to the other without growing up in a climate where women are constantly being scolded, chivvied,

harassed, or subjected to thunderous opinion columns concluding that, yet again, some woman in the public eye has overreached herself and should wind her neck in.

I offer this last suggestion as some kind of light-hearted, bagsy-no-returns experiment to see if this might benefit the future of the human race or not. Obviously, this 'not having an opinion on women' thing wouldn't be total. I propose that, in an *emergency*, we might write about something that women are doing: if a prominent female politician turned into some manner of malign she-werewolf, and sold her children to Nazis, say, we could legitimately opinionise on that. But on nearly every other matter concerning a newsworthy woman, I suggest one of the following range of reactions: 'That doesn't seem to be any of my business, to be honest.' 'I feel wholly neutral about what this woman has done.' 'Hmmmm – I don't know all the facts here, so I'm suspending my judgement.' 'I reckon she should just get on with it. Good luck!', or, just the classic: 'Whatever.'

And then, of course, my second-most regular political act is an inadvertent one: it is the continuing of my monthly unpleasantness.

A WOMAN'S MONTHLY FAULTINESS

Gentle, sweet readers of *The Times,* this week it is my sad duty to inform you that this column is to be on the topic of an immense beastliness – one I can still scarcely bring myself to mention, even now, after the application of a patent draught for fortifying the nerves. And it is – and Lord forgive me! – this: the circumstance of a woman's monthly faultiness.

Well, I know that I have already lost half of you – to the sanctuary of the library, and a soothing pipe full of best Black Cherry Twist, muttering darkly about the utter unpleasantness of the female sex.

And as for all the *men* – well, I imagine them to have simply bolted out of the back door, and to be pouring across the moors in unhappy packs, crying, 'ARGH noooooooooo NOT THE GROO!'

For it is, is it not, a perfect storm of a subject – one which women find vaguely shaming, and which men are confused and horrified by. Even as a strident, forthright and notoriously 'over-sharey' rogue suffragette, I struggle to use the words associated with the topic. They are all, without exception, vile. I can't say them. I do not wish them to exist in a canon of language that has, by contrast, words as beautiful as 'coracle,' 'iodine', 'mimosa', 'uxorious' and 'zoo'. Indeed, for the purposes of this article, from now on I will be referring to both the event, and its associated substances, with a series of euphemisms guaranteed to be soothing to everyone reading them. I'm not going to say 'menstruation' *once.*

When Paul McCartney's Magic Fairy Potion first waltzes into your life – almost invariably at some drearily disadvantageous time, such as 'while on a rollercoaster', or 'in a bridesmaid's dress, surrounded by sharks' – as a woman, you know one thing, instantly: this is the biggest secret ever. Like some kind of CIA operative, you have now been summoned to the toughest mission of your life: to spend the next three decades hiding every aspect of 'The bit in *The Wizard of Oz* where it goes from black and white into colour'. Go! Go, scared thirteen-year-old girl! Good luck with this task!

Because you really do have to keep it utterly mysterious and hidden. Despite the astonishing amount of effort 52 per cent of the world puts into this repetitive – yet, excitingly, also painful, mortifying and expensive – chore, popular culture will make no comforting, relaxing, casual references to it. You will never put on *EastEnders* and see Roxy in the caff with Dot sighing, 'I'm not opening the Vic tonight – I'm on Mother Nature's Enforced Kit-Kat Break.'

In *Doctor Who*, the Doctor's female assistants never make a crucial, instant bond with an otherwise hostile female alien by lending her one of God's Special Blue-Tailed Mice at a time of urgent need.

Even in places where you would think it was utterly necessary and specific to be frank about the matter – such as washing-powder commercials – one merely sees a blue stain and is left to figure things out for oneself. 'Bold is for … royals?'

And this is bizarre – because popular culture, as a whole, is pretty blasé about all *other* human viscera. In modern comedy films, anything goes – *American Pie* is about a man who has sex with a pie; *Ted* has a party-crashing sex-worker use the floor as a toilet; and *There's Something About Mary* is a film almost wholly based on an idea as slight as it is bizarre: that 36-year-old Cameron Diaz might not know what human ejaculate looks like, and would subsequently and innocently put it on her head, believing it to be hair gel. (Note to scriptwriters: grown women being able to rapidly and correctly recognise ejaculate is a necessary survival skill we master by the age of sixteen, tops. We like to be able to identify and keep an eye on the movement of that stuff. It's often 'quite consequent-y' for us.)

All *other* manifestations of blood are fine, of course: approaching my forties, I couldn't begin to calculate the millions of gallons of blood I've seen from shot men's heads exploding like melons, or people's severed legs issuing parabolas of spurting gore. You can apply that stuff by the tanker-full. Splash it all over! Go nuts! That's the good movie blood!

And yet the small, peaceful, inevitable and – even though I may be in a minority here – frequently amusing arrival of a woman's *Great British Bake Off Christmas Special* is never witnessed on screen. Not a drop, nor a smudge, nor an horrific accidental trashing of hotel sheets that necessitates Lara Croft stuffing them all into a massive, scavenged Tesco Bag for Life, hiding it up her jumper, and dumping it in a bin at Victoria Station – only to be erroneously arrested as a bomb suspect, and buggering up her entire adventure.

What is the sole cinematic exception to this? *Carrie*. Just one huge, horrific celluloid visitation to Café Rouge – then nothing for the next twenty-seven years.

And, as all women will know, that is one hell of an alarming cycle. It probably means, underneath it all, something quite bad's happening.

We live now in a glorious age which we might term 'Post Frozen'. Frozen – the feminist Disney movie where the idiot sexy prince turns out to be a betraying motherfuck, and the whole plot revolves around, instead, the love of two sisters. It is Elsa who gives 'true love's kiss' to her sister, Anna – not a boy. Boys may come and boys may go, Frozen told its millions of young, female fans, but your brilliant, idiot, annoying, amazing sister – she's there for life.

Indeed, it is a measure of Frozen's revolutionary femme-friendliness that it is the male characters who feel slapdash and two-dimensional – not, as is more usual, the female. The bloke with the reindeer is clearly Han Solo, the reindeer's Chewie, and the snowman is totally Jar Jar Binks made of slush. I'm sure they intended to go back and flesh them out a bit more, but then got the demo of 'Let It Go', spent three months screaming it out at the top of their lungs, and forgot. And I understand that. It is one hell of a song – although the best version is titled 'Let One Go', and is about breaking wind – 'Let one go, let one go/Can't hold it in any more/Let it go let it go/ Just push and give it what for/I don't care what they say!/The smell never bothered me anyway' – and which I still find incredibly amusing.

I am forty.

Anyway, very much John the Baptist to Frozen's Jesus was Brave – the also-feminist Disney film from 2012 that was just as ballsy as Frozen, but lacked that vital billion-selling power-ballad. I loved Brave. But, after it was released, there was one problem … Disney tried to make their Brave merchandise sexy.

Happily, in the end – after a massive worldwide protest – Disney recanted, and de-sexinessed their gear. It was a salutary lesson in how just standing up and saying 'STOP BEING WEIRD, THE PATRIARCHY!' can work quickly and effectively to make the world a happier, less dementedly shag-based place.

STOP MAKING EVERYTHING SEXY

I'm going to say this very calmly, and very quietly – but if people don't stop trying to make everything sexy, I will burn this planet to the ground. I will watch it burn to fine black ash, so help me God.

Last week, Disney announced the thirteenth Disney Princess to be welcomed into the canon, alongside Snow White, Cinderella and the Little Mermaid. It is Merida, heroine of their 2012 film *Brave*.

In *Brave*, Merida is a round-faced teenage rebel with a slight overbite, who can split any man's wishbone from 500 yards with her bow and arrow. She's a massive bad-ass. When her father holds an archery contest – the winner of which will marry her – she storms the competition, announces, 'I shall shoot for my *own* hand,' and beats them all, winning her freedom.

Watching the film in the cinema, in the dark, with my daughters – twelve and ten – I was able to loll back in my chair and say, 'Fill your boots, girls! Spoon this film up like good pie! This is the first Disney heroine ever not to have massive knockers, a twelve-inch waist and the kind of mouth that could suck a potato up a straw. Well done, Disney! Well done for finally entering the twenty-first century!'

But not so fast, me! Because when Disney brought Merida into their 'Official Princesses' franchise last week, Merida had … changed. A new picture of her showed her with a jacked-in waist, bigger tits, a lower-cut top and a load of eyeliner. On top of this, Merida was no longer holding her bow and arrow – the source of her legendosity – and was, instead, standing with her hands on her hips, in the internationally recognised pose of 'I am a bit of a vapid pain in the arse now'.

The outcry was instant. Merida's creator, Brenda Chapman, said to Disney, 'You are sending a message to girls that the original, realistic version of Merida is inferior … little girls are subconsciously soaking in the sexy "come hither" look and skinny aspect of the new version. It's horrible!'

Now look. It's not as if I'm a prude – God knows I'm not that. I like a rattle around the down-belows as much as the next person. If the buffet has a big plate of sex, I'll have some, thank you very much – *and* I'll come back for seconds.

But this obsession with having sexiness *everywhere* is becoming, frankly, demented. Currently, twenty-first-century culture feels like a massive groin on a pair of roller skates, caroming insanely off the walls. I feel like saying, 'Where is this all going? Are you going to end up recasting the Statue of Liberty so she's standing on Freedom Island in a tankini?' but I'm worried the mad fuckers might see this and actually do it. That's the *real* last scene in *Planet of the Apes*. Lady Liberty in stripper heels, with her nims out.

Because, let's be clear, the last place – the very last place – you need sexiness is in a Disney Princess franchise. Have you ever *watched* what kids do when the Prince and Princess finally kiss in a Disney movie? They cover their eyes up and go, 'UGH DISGUSTING.' *Billions* of kids, over seven decades, shouting, 'MUM HAVE THEY STOPPED YET?' None of them have EVER watched it.

And that's because children have slightly less use for characters with 'massive sexual allure' than they do for 'a handsome eighteenth-century barometer'. If you replaced every single one of these sexy ladies with a cute dog wearing a hat that could say 'sausages' and farted a lot, then you would, finally, be giving the kids what they truly desire in a movie.

This non-sexy, non-married, galloping, bow-shooting Merida coined Disney $555 million box office *in the first year*. She proved that little girls want these kinds of heroes on their screen. But despite her success, some ass-hat insisted that she just … had to get sexy anyway. No reason. They just … like to do the sexy. It's just what happens next, to girls.

Listen: Merida wasn't *for* you, you bloodless, cash-counting idiots. She was for every ten-year-old girl who hates itchy dresses and kissing, and just wanted to carry on being themselves for a bit longer. You can't put a price on a girl being able to watch a big Disney movie that says that's an okay thing.

Do you know what I'd like? I'd like to sing a sad ballad about all of this – sing a song about my unhappiness, and frustration. And, as I sang, an army of shy, adorable children would gather around me, and they would sing, too.

And as the song shifted up into a determined, major key, we would march on to the offices of Disney chief executive Roger Iger and shout, 'PUT THE SEXINESS AWAY, YOU BORDERLINE PERVERT!'

And he would! Because the one thing Disney taught me is that if you believe – if you really believe! If you really believe in magic – you can change anything!

As every woman will be hauntingly aware, 'the sexiness' is everywhere. Even if you go somewhere pointedly dedicated to breaking down all the norms of society for a weekend – e.g. a festival – a lady still got to look hot. Well, I'm not having that. That can fuck off.

MY LADY FESTIVAL ADVICE

Ladies, I cannot stress enough how nearly everything you have ever read on going to a festival is wrong. Bafflingly, borderline evilly wrong.

The festival briefing men get is to basically prepare themselves for a massive, messy stag party in the countryside – bidden to concern themselves with nothing more than tying a novelty balloon to their tent ('Use two pink ones – then walk towards the floating boobies!'); and smuggling their own body weight in Kestrel on to the site using a false leg, or maybe a pretend baby in a pram.

Women, on the other hand, are instructed in the ways of festival-going as if it were an exhausting, high-maintenance cross between *America's Next Top Model*, a spa break, a Facebook update competition and the worst episode of *Sex and the City* ever: a constant cavalcade of hot outfits, holistic pamperment, memory-making and wild, abandoned sex, all of which will leave you a minimum of £600 lighter before you've even *thought* about finding the henna tattoo stall, and having the Japanese symbol for 'Gullible lady newbie' temporarily dyed on to your ankle.

I'm here to tell you now: sod all of that. Sod all of that into a big jester's hat and wang it into the latrines. I've been going to festivals every year since 1992, and I can tell you one thing: if you're basing *your* festival-going experience on a picture in the *Daily Mail* of Kate Moss at Glastonbury, you're going to be terribly, terribly ill prepared for the reality. In fact, yes – let's start my list of things you need to ignore with:

l) Hot pants. Don't wear hot pants. Hot pants might be fine in a club-like environment, indoors – but you're OUTDOORS now. In heat, your British upper thighs – unaccustomed to the sun – will essentially turn into two hog roasts, making crackling in the sun. In all other weathers, meanwhile, they will freeze. Sit on a rustic wooden bench, and you'll be picking splinters out of your buttocks for the rest of the weekend. And, of course, on grass, ants will form an orderly queue, march right up inside you, and make nests. For ladies, nature contains much to fear.

Indeed, as a general rule of thumb, don't wear *anything* Kate Moss wears at festivals. *Don't* wear an ethnic-y poncho – the tassles will dangle in your goat curry, you'll greatly rue not having access to your arms – traditionally, quite useful – and, if it gets too hot, the extreme 'non-fold-downableness' of a blanket poncho will become apparent as it utterly fails to fit into your rucksack.

Similarly, Moss likes to rock a suede boot at a festival. But then, Moss has never had to sit, crying, scrubbing three inches of encrusted clay off a suede bootie, a week after a festival, using a toothbrush. Moss has been seen wearing 'all-in-one' playsuits – but then Moss has access to a heated, backstage Winnebago toilet. You, on the other hand, do not: meaning that *your* trip to the toilet, wearing a playsuit, will involve you, drunk, in a pitch-dark Portaloo at 4am, stripping naked to the waist, with everything in your now upside-down pockets falling on to the floor.

As an added bonus, it's more than likely that the sleeves of your playsuit will then dangle down the toilet, and 'usefully' absorb everything they come into contact with. Mmmm, poo-sleeves.

I will be honest with you: I have seen performance artists at Glastonbury walking around dressed as giant sausages, and their outfits were infinitely more suitable than anything Kate Moss, God bless her, wears. You want to rock up with: four pairs of tights, three t-shirts, wellies, shorts, a fleece and the most waterproof anorak known to man. If you want to be *really* luxurious, get a bum bag off eBay to keep your fags in, and get one of those necklaces that doubles up as a bottle opener. There you go! You've got that 'festival look'! AND it's not going to lead to you going to Casualty with exposure/heat exhaustion.

While we're on the subject of clothing, may I just add: straw hats in the shape of a Stetson. You can't wear these any more. They make you look like Meg Mathews in 1996. It's better that you know this brutal truth in advance, rather than realise when the pictures go up on Instagram, hash-tagged #wonderwall #sheselectric #wheresnoel.

2) **Sex.** There's a general myth about festivals that they are a hotbed of licentiousness and filth – that, as a modern woman, you will be on the lookout for hot young rock fans to take by hand and tumble, while Mumford & Sons bang away on their banjos – and that you'll return, on Monday morning, in a loved-up haze of booty texts.

Again, I'm here to tell you that this is a severe disservice to the truth. Very little sex goes on at festivals, for the same reason that very little sex went on when you shared a bedroom with your siblings. BECAUSE YOU ARE IN A TENT WITH OTHER PEOPLE. SURROUNDED BY OTHER PEOPLE. A TENT ISN'T EVEN A BUILDING – IT'S BASICALLY A MASSIVE CARRIER BAG 100,000 PEOPLE ARE PRETENDING IS HABITABLE FOR THE WEEKEND. Would you have sex in a bag with loads of people watching/listening? No. Of course not. You are not John Lennon and Yoko Ono. So don't have sex in a tent at a festival. If you *must* have sex, go and find the Circus Field, get right in the middle of the ring and pretend it's performance art. Ironically, you'll have more privacy.

Additionally, women: remember to fear cystitis. Fear cystitis a lot. Although a massive fan of sexual intercourse, I would never do anything that would increase my chances of a urinary tract infection in an environment where going to the toilet is an hour-long commitment, minimum. Do you want to gamble on the robustness of your urethra this weekend, of all weekends? I say: give it a swerve. Have chips, instead. It's a perfectly serviceable alternative.

3) **Alcohol.** No matter if you usually prefer cocktails, ice-cold Gavi or gin – when at a festival, women must immediately become more 'real', and select the kind of alcohol that would be favoured by a ruddy-cheeked nineteenth-century peasant, instead. For this weekend, ladies are supposed to booze on PINTS as lady festival booze.

Again, this is terrible advice. As mentioned many times before, you are temporarily in an environment where it's easier to get a 'functioning' wizard's hat than it is to go to the toilet. If you're boozing, you want maximum impact for minimum liquid.

My personal, well-tested tactic is to purchase the cheapest bottle of spirits known to man – something genuinely nasty, brewed in Lithuania and available only in petrol stations – and to decant a tot into every beverage I have. Brandy, or rum, are the most effective – warming, festive, equally at home in coffee and Coke, and, *in extremis*, the really abrasive stuff is capable of being sloshed over your campfire as a makeshift firelighter, to ward off White Walkers, and/or hammered Glaswegians who keep asking if they can 'borrow a woman for the night'.

4) **'Making your campsite cosy.'** The word 'glamping' has a lot to answer for. When I first started going to festivals – Reading 1992. Nirvana, in three inches of mud – it was a genuine option to just … sleep in a hedge.

'You camping?'

'Nah – just … sleeping in a hedge,' people would say. 'Or on some ground. Might treat myself to a bin bag. It's my birthday.'

By way of contrast, nowadays women are instructed to think of their tents as 'a home from home: why not decorate it with lanterns, ethnic rugs, and bunting?'

I'll tell you why: BECAUSE THIS IS ROCK'N'ROLL VALHALLA, NOT FUCKING *CHANGING ROOMS*. Whatever the most foolish is that you've ever felt in your life, you're gonna feel it 900 times more when the hard rain starts to fall, emergency services start evacuating people from your field in dinghies, and the one carrying Florence & The Machine gets snagged on your

25 yards of Cath Kidston bunting, and takes Florence's head off, like a rerun of that thing that happened to Jayne Mansfield.

5) **Memories.** You're going to fill Facebook with shots of all the incredible things that happen – fantastic pictures of you all dancing, cheering and making friends with new people! That 240-shot folder marked 'Glastonbury 2013' is going to be AWESOME.

Not it's not. You ain't shooting *nothing*. For 98 per cent of the time you're there it's either going to be pitch dark or pissing it down, and/or you'll be drunk and/or dancing, possibly *on* your phone, which you have unwittingly dropped and won't realise until tomorrow morning.

Let me tell you now, to relieve the pressure. You will take a sum total of four pictures during the entire weekend: one on the coach on the way there, of everyone looking wildly overexcited and doing a 'thumbs-up'; one of everyone having their first fag after they've put the tent up – which you will caption 'WELCOME TO GLASTONBURY – THE MADNESS BEGINS' and immediately Tweet; an accidental shot of your own leg at 4am, as you use your iPhone as a torch to pick your way through the campsite without garrotting your own legs on tent strings; and a picture of you and all your mates pulling into your first service station on Monday morning, shell-shocked, and endearingly overexcited about using a proper toilet for the first time in four days.

Festivals are like dreams. You can't photograph them – they just happen to you, and then you bore everyone afterwards, telling them all about it:

'And then we found this man dressed as a *sailor* selling *nitrous balloons*, and all the shattered beer glasses looked like *diamonds* in the sunrise!'

'Shelley – I need those accounts now, please.'

6) **Audience behaviour.** 'The queen of any festival is the one wearing a tiny vest-top, sitting on her boyfriend's shoulders, and screaming along to the headliners, while punching the air in glee.'

Word to the wise here: literally everyone will hate you if you do this. *Everyone*. Hating you. So, so much. The people standing directly behind you, who can't now see. Your heavier female friends, who dislike the way you're flaunting your thighs in those shorts. Your boyfriend, whose spine is gradually compacting down into a single, solid, throbbing vertebra of pain. The band, who – when you get flashed up on to the big screen – can now see that you don't know the lyrics, and are just going *'So I bet that you look good on the dancefloor/Mrah bwah flah tah on romance, door.'*

Simply – never do this. Ever. It's the biggest dick move available to women at a festival. Stay on the fucking floor, like everyone else, love.

Interesting fact: any woman you see sitting on a man's shoulders at a festival is in a relationship that is no more than eighteen months old, tops. Once you have passed the hectic, carnal insanity of the first year, men stop offering to lift lovers on to their shoulders, as a) they don't need to impress any more and b) they are worried that, from up there, you'll see his burgeoning bald spot.

7) **'Chilling out.'** 'It's not all alcohol and moshing! Most festivals now have a "chill out" area – where you can get reflexology, Reiki healing, facials, head massages and yoga lessons!'

Let me put this on the line: anyone who goes to a rock festival for a foot massage is demented. It's just not the appropriate action for the environment. You might just as well take the Argos catalogue and lie in front of the Pyramid Stage, picking out lampshades and nick-nacks for the front room. HELLO? You're at a ROCK FESTIVAL. You don't need 'pampering' from a Reiki healer – you're being 'pampered' with IMMENSE BASS, and a gigantic burrito at 5am. Ladies – this is neither the time nor the place to get the dry skin on your heels planed off by someone wearing culottes. You have a very hectic schedule of standing on a bin at 3am dancing to Daft Punk shouting 'I AM THE RIFT IN SPACE AND TIME! I HAVE SEEN INTO THE CENTRE OF THE TARDIS!' and trying to buy a cigarette off a man who introduces himself as 'The Breakfast Mindfuck Collective'. Your blackheads can wait until Monday.

8) **'Festival beauty.'** Hey – just because you're at a festival, it doesn't mean you should spend any less on product, er I mean 'skimp on your beauty regime'! Nuh-uh, girlfriend!

While the men might be staggering around barely able to focus, and washing themselves with a slice of bacon, *you* still want to be rocking up like you're about to shoot the cover of *Vogue*. Even though – as discussed before – you're living in a carrier bag in the middle of Valhalla.

'Here's your Emergency Beauty Kit for a festival!' *Grazia* will helpfully say, detailing moisturiser, cleansing wipes, crème blush, mascara, and Guerlain Issima Midnight Secret (£69) 'to cover up the ravages of the night before'.

Now look. I like slap as much as the next man – especially if that man is David Bowie circa *Ziggy Stardust*. But by simply spraying dry shampoo on *everything* – hair, face, armpits, feet – and then applying Barry M eyeshadow in a jolly colour, you're going to come up looking and smelling of hero in less than three minutes.

Don't worry about 'covering up the ravages of the night before' with a £23 serum – a £3 pair of sunglasses will do that. You can also 'cover up the ravages of the night before' by going 'I don't *want* to cover up the ravages of the night before – I am trying to surf into the dark core of mankind. I'm going to sit on this fold-up camp-chair, pour a shot of borderline fatal Polish petrol into my brew, light a ciggie and start singing "212" by Azealia Banks. Because I am a woman at a festival, and I am doing things properly.'

There are, of course, in popular culture, generally two kinds of female characters. The first is, as discussed in the previous essay on Brave, 'a sexy lady'. And the other kind – as discussed now – is 'a dead lady'.

The BBC's drama Ripper Street proved, for me, the last straw, dead lady-wise.

TV REVIEW: NO MORE DEAD LADIES

Ooooooh, Ripper Street. I wouldn't want to live there. Imagine trying to flog a three-bed house on Ripper Street.

'There's double-glazing, off-street parking, good local schools – and ENTRAILS. The rear of the house enjoys aspects over THE SLAUGHTERED DAUGHTERS OF EVE in the alleyways of Whitechapel. Good connections for both City – and THE LOOMING WALL-SHADOWS OF BRITAIN'S MOST NOTORIOUS SERIAL KILLER.'

Or, worse still, a one-bed flat.

'It would be a great first home for the single lady! And, indeed, perhaps the *last* home, too. ENTRAILS. ENTRAILS ENTRAILS ENTRAILS. DEEEEEEEATH.'

Ripper Street sounds, as I'm sure Phil and Kirstie on *Location Location Location* would agree, a bit of a hard sell. Even if you did it up all neutral, and gave it 'kerb-appeal' by painting the front door a 'jolly' colour (but not red: might look a bit like the Ripper grabbed a suppurating innard and wiped it all over the letterbox, in a fit of demented psycho-sexual release), it still might … linger on the market a while.

Fittingly, BBC1's new six-part series of the same name was an equally unappealing proposition. It wasn't inevitable, by any means: the combination of a high-end BBC period drama, the enduring mystery of the Ripper, and rumble-voiced sex item Matthew Mcfadyen leading in a tight weskit and bowler could have been a smash hit.

As a look at the early days of the Peelers in Whitechapel – when policing was both in its infancy, and being tested to its limits by a demented serial killer – it could have been one of those 'Only the BBC could pull this off' jobs. Dark, detailed and compelling. A bit like *Life on Mars,* but with *everyone* having hoops (the extravagant hooped skirts of the Victorian woman) for tea. Imagine.

And to give the writers (four of them) and directors (three of them) their due, they really went for it. There were no holds barred in the 'examining the sordid brutality of Victorian crimes' area. The darkness and 1899-ness were turned all the way up to eleven. The dialogue was up for a bit of 1899-ery like you wouldn't believe. Believe me, good sir, that the intentions of that dialogue were to pay all due honour to the sesquipedalian glory of over-ripe Victorian communiqués, intercourses, promulgations, confabulations and divulgences.

So here we are: six months after the Ripper's unsolved reign of terror, and another girl is found, mutilated, on the backstreets of Whitechapel. Understandably, the locals are *freaking out.* They are *doing their nuts.* They think the Ripper is making his '99 Comeback Special.

'This girl has been caaaaaaaaaaaaaaarved,' sexy Detective Inspector Edmund Reid (Mcfadyen) says, in his customary, rumbly, mahogany bass. 'And this populace is still without a culprit – so it is to *our* uniform they direct their fury.'

Sure enough, in the background, we can hear nine actors shouting 'RHUBARB! RHUBARB!' tetchily at the Peelers, in a 'harbinger of riot' way.

Mcfadyen looks down at the latest victim. With her long auburn hair and ripped-up, floor-length dress, it looks like someone with a massive grudge against Florence from Florence & The Machine has left her dead on the floor, with her intestines wrapped around her like a string of sausages. Perhaps it was someone who heard her honking version of 'You've Got The Love' one too many times. You ain't going to be throwing your hands up in the air any more, love.

Removed from the pre-rioting locals, the dead Florence is carted off to the police station, for a primitive Victorian autopsy. This is conducted by the 'maverick' American surgeon Captain Homer Jackson (Adam Rothenberg), who has that unmistakable vibe of an American character chucked into a British period drama, in order to get co-funding from a US production company.

Have I told you how maverick Jackson is? When we first see him, he's in a brothel with his favourite saucy sex-worker – but he's not mindlessly riding her like a pony for cash, as an oppressive tool of the patriarchy. No. Instead, he's pleasuring her in a most modern way. He's doing some of that … face-sex stuff. You know. That the modern ladies like. He's got his head up her skirt. So rude.

So, yes, he's a user of whores – but in a considerate and hot way. What do you make of *that*, feminists and scholars of common Victorian sexual behaviour? You're pretty shocked, yeah?

Well, not as shocked as you'll be by his dazzlingly futuristic autopsy techniques! For while British surgeons are all, apparently, 'drunks and incompetents' who don't bother to examine murder victims, Jackson is in there with his examining tools – most of which look like the spork that comes with an M&S Five Bean Salad – examining her nethers. All this, *and* he's a great lay! This is prime future husband material, right here!

'What did fall her?' Mcfadyen asks Captain Jackson, ripely, which I trust is exactly how Victorians said, 'Cause of death?'

'Asphyxia,' Jackson says, briskly, staring up her parson's nose. 'But she is no tart. Examine her … apparatus. Even the most costly [whore's] are worn through at that age.'

In news that will surely delight the dead Florence, it turns out her tuppence is in really good nick for her mileage – despite its owner having been 'recently and energetically squired'.

Anyway, the plot proceeded to advance with all the confident ticking of a grandfather clock in a parqueted hallway, being dusted by a period-accurate maid. As Florence's well-maintained vagina had suggested, she was *not* a whore, after all – merely an impoverished violinist from North Finchley, who'd made up the rent money by starring in one of those newfangled pornographic zoetropes. Mcfadyen and his maverick doctor moved through all the scenes that allowed them to come to this conclusion – but, alas, to a growing and unstoppable hysteria from me. For it turns out that it's just quite hard being a Victorian copper and not being inadvertently amusing.

Instance: whenever the coppers burst into a room, to apprehend a suspect, or search for evidence, the first thing they had to do was light candles, in order to see – which made it look like they'd arrived on a very urgent appointment to make a romantic atmosphere. Like some kind of Flying 'Vibe' Squad.

Likewise, the barked instruction 'Make haste, Tucker!' prompted a mid-paced carriage pursuit across authentic cobbles, at approximately the speed of Maggie Smith coming down the stairs in *Downton* – not exactly *The Sweeney* handbrake-turning into a massive wall of cardboard boxes.

Right at the end, however, all my amusement at the overblown language and *Juliet Bravo*-meets-Dickens culture-clash dissolved, as *Ripper Street* suddenly tanked down into real, Mariana Trench darkness. History was repeating: just as Florence had accidentally been strangled while making asphyxia-porn, so, now, was Jackson's favourite sex-worker, who we'd seen at the top of the show.

She was kidnapped, and dressed as a slave – drugged, scratched, with a split lip; being filmed as someone raped her. The leather collar around her neck was attached to a chain – every time her assailant moved, she choked. All props to the acting, but it was genuinely distressing – there wasn't really any difference between watching these two minutes of *Ripper Street* and watching a 'real' snuff porno.

I know *Ripper Street*'s objective was to show just how depraved, unequal and violent Victorian society was, but the preceding sixty minutes had been so clunking – I haven't even told you about Jerome from Robson & Jerome being in it, as a copper and part-time bare-knuckle boxer. Without fail, he punched someone, violently, in the face, in every scene. He left everyone's face a spray of blood and mince – that I just felt a faint, nauseous mutiny at most British dramas, rather than the Victorians.

I'm going to square with you, telly in 2013: I don't think I can see any more sex-workers being beaten, tortured or murdered. I'm done. I'm all in. As a female viewer, it's doing my head in. I reckon, in thirty-seven years, I've seen over 100 tarts screaming in agony, or being slammed against car bonnets before being stabbed, or being kicked across a dingy living room by a husband or pimp, and I've finally reached my limit.

Guys, could we have a moratorium? No more high-end call girls, no Regency strumpets, no crack whores in the waiting room of *Holby City*, no sex-workers eviscerated in American cop shows, no titty good-time girls in wartime serials? I don't know what other kinds of female characters you could replace them with – what other jobs do women have? Do women even have jobs? I find it hard to remember. Maybe we should just have all-male casts, to be on the safe side. Perhaps everything should just be set in either an all-boys boarding school, the army, or the Green Room of *QI*. No one's going to put Stephen Fry in a dress cut down to *here*, put him out on the streets, garrotte him and then leave his body sexily splayed over some bins.

In the meantime, I would really, really like to have episode one of *Ripper Street* mark the last terrified, choking prostitute I ever see.

And this is where these dumb, limiting, repetitive representations of women
leave us: with a large number of men unable to see women as real, living,
clever, amusing, weird, faulty, extraordinary, normal human beings.

One of the most perfect examples of this came in 2012, with a Danish
TV series called Blachman. *Oh, Blachman. You are a confused, damaged,*
damaging man.

THE MOST SEXIST TV SHOW IN THE WORLD

There is an extraordinary television programme broadcasting in
Denmark at the moment. Called *Blachman*, it features the eponymous
host and his friend sitting in a darkly lit room. On their command,
women are ushered in, and take their robes off.

Over the next half-hour, Blachman and his friend then 'review' the
women's bodies – commenting on the skin, the breasts, the hair, the
fat. The veins.

We get close-ups of the men's childlike joy when a cheerful, large-
breasted young blonde disrobes.

We see their more charitable, 'Ah well – you've probably had a
good innings' disappointment when it is an older woman, whose
breasts are not so excitingly buoyant.

Although the world has been pretty much unified in outrage
against the show – the *Mail*, of all people, asked, 'Is this the most
sexist show ever?' – Blachman himself is convinced of humanity's need
for *Blachman*.

'The female body thirsts for words. The words of a man,' he insisted,
going on to warn critical Danes, 'Ungratefulness is the only thing that
can really wear down the few geniuses who reside in our country.'

Amusingly, it seems that Blachman himself is a trifle touchy if
people seek to critique *his* metaphorical tits. He likes to answer back,
angrily.

The women on *Blachman*, by way of contrast, do not answer back. They are not allowed to speak. But I ask, in all confusion: how can you understand a woman's body, if she's not allowed to speak? How would you know what it is you're looking at?

I like to imagine myself on Blachman's show. I would be interested in what he would say about me. I would be interested in what he would *miss*.

I suspect, when I first took my robe off, I would get his 'charitable disappointment' face. I think he'd presume I was probably a bit ashamed of my body.

For starters, my belly is a good four handfuls – lying in the bath, I like to crush it between my palms, to make a soft, pink sandcastle. Once, I was very fat. This belly is all that remains of that vast empire, now – the bit I did not want to run off, because I find it luxurious to gently fist my hands into it, like a mink stole.

Then there's my scars – across my body, like an editor's corrections on a manuscript. Odd symbols – shorthand for different things. The long one across my belly is for a girl who's twelve years old, now: how surgeons had to go in with the knife, with a Caesarean, as she was dying. Fear, and joy, and then opiates, and milky staring.

The scars on my arms, on the other hand, are from my father's razor: I was an almost cheerful teenage self-harmer, in 1993. I criss-crossed my forearms repeatedly – curious to see if it would stop me feeling trapped, and useless. I did it for attention, even though I hid the scars most assiduously, under jumpers. Twenty years later, I know the person whose attention I was actually trying to seek: me.

By now, if I were on *Blachman*, I wouldn't be able to stand still, and silent, any more. I would drag another chair over, and sit between Blachman and his friend – I couldn't bear him missing all the gossip, and the glee, from my nakedness. Yes, Blachman – I know one breast is bigger than the other. I don't need you, Salacious Crumb sidekick, to point it out to the viewers, while I stay mute, and somehow unknowing of my own self. I call my breasts 'Simon & Garfunkel' – their wonkiness stopped upsetting me by the time I was twenty-one.

'They make me laugh – I'm very fond of them. I'm fond of my whole body,' I would tell Blachman – my legs draped over the side of the chair, in a chatty manner; flashing my fur because it was his idea for me to turn up naked. I would have arrived in a nice dress, otherwise.

But Blachman would be very uncomfortable having me next to him. And when I invited all the other naked women on the show to come over, too – to sit down, and talk about their bodies, and laugh, and grab their thighs, and remember awful things – I suspect he would wish to leave.

Because, whatever Blachman says, this show isn't *really* about female bodies. What Blachman talks about when he talks about women's bodies is – Blachman. How naked women make *him* feel – what naked women make him want to do. He believes that it's an important thing to tell a woman whether or not he would like to fuck her – the belief held by a million male internet commentators, typing 'Wouldn't' under pictures of women – women who, I'm sure, if they could be arsed to reply, would type, 'Thank God – I'm really busy today, byeee.'

You could do all this without the naked women, Blachman. *Blachman* could be just that. Blachman.

But, then, who would watch a man sitting in a chair, alone, talking about women's arses? He'd look insane. Blachman is nothing without women's arses – and a man's opinion thirsts for viewers.

Of course, for every Blachman there is a woman like Lucy-Anne Holmes, who founded the 'No More Page 3' campaign: working to end the frankly weird anomaly in which the Sun *— ostensibly a family newspaper — features a young, naked, usually white, topless girl, Monday to Friday. (There are no tits in the Saturday edition. When I inquired about this, I discovered that the logic is that the 'working man', at his workplace, is thought to need 'cheering up' with tits on weekdays, but on Saturday he has football, instead, and so can give knockers a rest until Monday again. Oh, men! Other men represent you so badly! You should be furious at the patronising way you are thought of.)*

Fighting a long and often brutal online campaign, No More Page 3 eventually won in 2015: there are no more topless Page 3 girls in the Sun *any more. It was a beautiful example of how feminism works: there are a million small tasks to be completed, and we all pick one, according to our interests and abilities, and fight it, calmly, correctly, with determination and humour.*

And that is how the future is made.

NO MORE PAGE 3

Look, who knows what will be happening with Page 3 of the *Sun* by the time this column is printed. The bosoms are out, the bosoms are covered up, the bosoms come out again – it's like sitting on a nudist beach on a particularly changeable day, weather-wise.

But whether they stay or whether they go, I still feel it's important to clear up just why something as ostensibly 'innocent' as a lovely girl showing off her smashing duckies in a newspaper has 'incurred' the 'wrath' of 'feminists', although tbh whenever you see that phrase you should imagine not Medusa riding her Man-Hating Chariot out on to the battlefields, waving a staff made of severed penises and screaming 'I AM FURIOUS! I COME TO CHANGE THE WORLD

AS YOU KNOW IT, AND DESTROY ALL CIVILISATION!', but, instead, some tired-looking women sadly sending off some polite emails, while whispering, 'I'm so tired of this shit. Batman never had to get together a petition with 250,000 signatures on it when *he* wanted to change things. He just went and rammed the Batcar into the Penguin's den. Why can't I ram a Batcar into the Penguin's den? I wish I was Batman.'

So. First things first. Why do feminists want to ban Page 3? Is this because they're all UGLY JEALOUS LESBIANS? Well, no – although I must remind everyone that the opinion of an 'ugly', 'jealous' lesbian is absolutely equal to that of a horny straight man who wants to see some breasts. There's absolutely no moral superiority in wanting to look at young girls' tits. You're not Nelson Mandela here, dude. You're as emotional and biased as the 'ugly', 'jealous' feminists.

The reason a lot of women are down on Page 3 is simply down to context. In 2015, there are naked breasts everywhere. We're living in a boom time for boobies. No one is running short on tits. We're up to our tits in tits. You can type 'tits' into pretty much any piece of technology you have and see some.

And as far as I'm concerned, having porn in the porn places is fine. Carry on. It's just having it *in a newspaper* – surrounded by war and economics, and high-profile celebrity rape cases – that looks weird, because it's essentially demented admin. It's incorrect filing. Because if you put tits in the wrong place, they're going to cause trouble. Tits on a railway track = trouble. Tits in a microwave = trouble.

For here's what happens if you have young girls' breasts in a newspaper. You're ten, at school, laying out newspaper on the tables, in preparation for art. And some boys find Page 3, and gather round it, making jokes. And then they turn to the girl who's most 'well-developed', and say, 'Do *yours* look like that? Show us!' or – to the flat-chested girl – 'Haha! You need a boob job!'

And it's probably your first experience of that awful, incoherent rage/shame that you feel when your body is objectified. And you're ten. And you wonder how those boys would feel if Page 3 was pictures of huge, hard cocks on sixteen-year-old boys, instead – and all the girls were gathered around it, going, 'I bet you wish you had one of those, Mark – instead of what looks like the worm in the bowler hat in the *Mr Men* books.'

You suspect their dads might want to sign a petition, too, when *they* came home crying.

Because it's just an unnecessary bit of hassle – having to deal with a world where little children see pictures of naked girls in a family newspaper. Page 3 makes needless problems.

Then there's the suddenly concerned men who are 'upset' that removing Page 3 will take jobs away from working-class glamour models. I don't worry about these guys so much, because I presume that their concern has been long-standing and well informed, and that they have a checkable record of campaigning for the employment rights for young working-class women – that they are members of the Fawcett Society, speak out in favour of gender quotas and are vocal about the 19 per cent disparity in male/female wages.

I presume that, because it would be weird if the only time they'd ever spoken out about their concerns was solely and specifically about the jobs for *topless* working-class girls. You probably wouldn't be asked on to *Newsnight* as an economics analyst with that kind of very narrowcast speciality: pervonomics.

What else? Well, it's so bafflingly narrowcast, isn't it? Online porn has a wide-ranging and ardent love of big chicks, black chicks, Asian chicks and lesbians. Page 3 has the air of being curated by one old man, sitting obdurately at the Page 3 Decisions Desk, commissioning endless shots of slim, straight white chicks and saying, 'I *knows* what I *like*,' over and over again.

A whole, controversial page in a newspaper, tied to this odd, narrowcast vision of sexiness. Alienating 52 per cent of your potential readership. Looking, culturally, in 2015, like a misplaced item in the bagging area.

Both glamour modelling and sex-work fall into the same area for many feminists – they find them problematic. This is an unequal world, the argument goes. Any situation where a women is objectified for her fuckability, and then paid for it, as a commodity, both reinforces the wider inequality of women, and perpetuates female sexuality as something more than just a woman's own desire: it makes it manipulatable; purchasable. Something that can be turned on and off at the whim of men, and denies women the simple, vital ability to own their own bodies, passions and emotions. It puts women's sexual autonomy in a lesser ranking than male sexual autonomy. It makes it clear that male sexual desire is the ruling force in society. It is, simply, oppressive.

And I would say that's all pretty much right.

But. My personal take on this, as a working-class woman who's skimmed a fair chunk of the Wikipedia entry on Marxist labour theory, is that I feel about it roughly the same way I do about Formula One. Do I like it? No. Would I be happy for my daughters to do it? Probably not. I'd certainly worry about their safety, and I personally find a lot of people involved in both industries to not be the kind of people I'd want to hang out with. If it didn't exist, would I invent it? Nah. It's clearly something the world wants, rather than needs. Would I do it? Not unless it was the only way to keep myself, and/or my family, housed and fed and safe, no.

But that's the key part, isn't it? Money. It all comes down to money. 'Bitch got to pay rent' is the simplest, truest thing on Earth, for the majority of people who weren't born into any wealth. Let's face it – there are many, many miserable jobs out there. Rare is the person who enjoys their labour. For most people – without great educations or contacts – your career is something chosen from a fairly limited range of options, most of which you find quite dreary. Not immoral, or evil, or corroding to your soul. Just dreary. Just something in which you would wish to be safe, and respected, while you pay the rent.

This column was written in 2012, as London prepared for the Olympics.

OLYMPIC PROSTITUTES

This week is all about the Olympics prostitutes. This is not, sadly, a new part of Team GB – eventing in Track & Feel, Mollyball, Synchronised Women and Table Penis – but a massive crackdown on prostitution in advance of the London Olympics, instead.

Sex-workers' pressure group x:talk have drawn attention to the fact that, in the last year, eighty brothels have been closed down in the Olympic borough of Newham, and that these 'clean-up' initiatives are putting sex-workers at risk – forced out of brothels and familiar soliciting areas, and into new and more remote locations, away from the Games.

Firstly, I am surprised that sex-workers are being moved *away* from the Olympic site. If there's anything I've learned, over the years, about multibillion-pound events – involving thousands of international sponsors and dignitaries, on a massive month-long corporate freebie to a foreign city, away from their wives and children – it's that a lot of them will *definitely* be up for a prostitute at the end of the evening.

Frankly, I'm surprised they're not bussing *more* prostitutes into Newham – perhaps on those 'priority' Games Lanes that VIPs can use, but buses and ambulances can't. Just to make sure the prostitutes get there fast, while they're still nice and hot. No one wants to take delivery of a cold prostitute. That would be dispiriting.

The whole issue of prostitution in the twenty-first century is a bemusing one. I've sat here for a long time, now, with this cup of tea, and in all honesty I cannot see any logic in prostitution still being, essentially, illegal. In Britain, you recall, it's legal to sell sex – but illegal to *either* solicit on a street corner *or* work in a brothel: essentially making it impossible to earn a living without putting yourself at continual risk, somewhere hidden from police detection/protection.

Why is prostitution treated with such repulsion? Why, in an era of space travel and string theory, do we still have women standing on the side of A roads at 2am: left in the dangerous places, like sacrifices offered to the bad men out there? When a woman's murder is announced on the news, there's often an odd relief that follows the declaration of the phrase '… and a known sex-worker'.

Because those are the girls who kind of … *do* get murdered, don't they? We build a certain amount of inevitable death into their statistics. Not like civil servants, or teachers, or nurses. And not like any male profession on Earth. No legal job that men do has an implicit acceptance of being beaten, raped or murdered. That one is solely and only for the women who get paid for sex.

Of course, I understand why prostitution *used* to be socially unacceptable – how those girls got so ill regarded, and disposable. In the days before contraception and antibiotics, society needed women who would run the risk of syphilis, abortion, and death in childbirth in exchange for cash. For a woman in a pre-medical age, sex was as risky as going to war, and prostitutes were the serving soldiers. We thought of them as expendable, because, essentially, they were. Before condoms were disposable, women were, instead.

Plus, on top of that, we can't forget religion. Oh, religion. So good, for so long, at architecture; so weird, for so long, about sex. Man-made rules, done up to look like ineffable laws of Nature. It's wrong to pay for sex? Why? (vaguely): The Moon will not like it.

So in the twenty-first century, it is odd that we are still confused and panicky about women being paid to have sex. Banishing them to industrial estates at 4am, out of a medieval strain of fear, or spite. We have contraception, and safe sex, and antibiotics, now. We know the Moon does not mind us having sex. For the first time in mankind's history, sex has no overtones of death, or disease, or pregnancy. Sex is just … sex. The health and safety regulations on running a modern brothel are, amusingly, identical to those for running a municipal swimming pool. Being a miner is physically more dangerous; being a personal assistant to Anna Wintour more injurious to your sense of self-worth. We will pay people to love our newborns, and nurse our elderly, even as they die – and yet, of all the daily, normal things humans do, it is sex, and sex alone, we consider to be above legal business. Beyond monetary compensation.

It can't be because we think women must be forced, by law, to only have sex with someone they love, or desire – that women must only ever *enjoy* sex. We've never been either that innocent, or that enlightened. Hundreds of thousands of years have shown us that women cope, effortlessly, with having joyless sex – whether it's in exchange for money or not. The sex isn't, and has never been, the problem.

Tonight, women will be forced out to somewhere distant, and they will be scared, and they will be hurt, because we still haven't realised it's 2012, now: 2012 – the year of the London Olympics.

And the big question you have to ask yourself about the stigma around sex-work in the twenty-first century is: would we invent this system *now*? Forget everything that has gone before. If – in some mad, sci-fi world – sex had only been invented yesterday, in an era where women are legally equal to men; with contraceptives and condoms; where married couples are encouraged to do it at least twice a week, and there's dating, Tinder and *Girls* – would we outlaw the invention of sex-work *now*? If there was a man who wanted to have sex with a woman, and a woman said, for the first time ever, 'Okey-dokey – I'll do that, with a condom, for £100,' would we prosecute him? Would we say she could only do this business transaction with him if she stood on the outskirts of town at 2am, picking up customers blind? For having *sex*?

It is perfectly socially acceptable – indeed, desirable – for a woman to walk into a beauticians and have her anus waxed by someone she's never met before. During *that* exchange, you're supposed to keep up a flow of polite chit-chat about the weather – a *far* weirder idea, to me, than having sex with someone who wants to keep the conversation down to a much more honest and basic 'Yes, yes – more'.

We pay therapists to listen to our most intimate secrets; women to host our surrogate pregnancies; men to donate sperm to make our future children. Is having consensual sex for cash really in a radically different physical and emotional dimension from all these legitimate human exchanges? Only if you believe that all sex should be done purely and solely from deep and loving motivations. A quick conversation with all your married/dating friends should remind you that most people in this country have transgressed that unsaid rule on a fairly regular basis – yet continue not to be socially shunned.

One of the biggest sticking points in the sex-work debate is, understandably, the issue of sex-trafficking. The last estimate suggested 2,600 women had been trafficked to the UK for sex-work in the preceding year.

But sex-trafficking isn't inherent to prostitution. That's an abhorrent and illegal practice of the current sex-work *industry* – not sex-work itself. By the same chalk, parts of the fashion industry are reliant on trafficking, and slave-work. But no one would suggest for one moment that we criminalise the entire fashion industry – we merely lobby for human rights, instead. What's one of the main things that keeps the sex-trafficking industry in such rude health – with each woman earning an estimated £48k per annum for their kidnapper? Trafficked women knowing that they cannot approach the police, because their work is criminalised.

Make sex-work legal – create a world where women can run their own, secure and regulated brothels, pay tax on that respectable middle-class £48k a year, and be seen to be doing a job no more socially unacceptable than the person who is, even now, putting a clean nightshirt on your grandmother – and it would be very difficult to continue keeping these women hidden and imprisoned.

I really don't think we would criminalise sex-work if it had been invented yesterday. And so, today, we must look at it again, as twenty-first century people – and not scared, sex-fearing medieval peasants.

While we're talking about the darker side of sexuality, we must talk about what women fear the most: rape. Rape, which will come to one in four of us – as Sarah Silverman puts it, 'When you're walking down a street late at night and you hear footsteps and you think: "Is this my rape? Is it now?"' – and yet which still, so often, shames us, rather than the rapist. Rape, which is still seen as something almost 100 per cent preventable by women, so long as you do the 'right' things. Rape – which has the bastard's curse of being to do with women, and sex, and therefore lying on terrible fault lines in our logic, and compassion. Rape, which I would like to rename.

This piece was written in the aftermath of the Delhi rape case in 2012, which horrified the world: 23-year-old physiotherapy intern Jyoti Singh Pandey was attacked and gang-raped on a bus, on which she was travelling with a male friend. During the astonishingly, incomprehensibly brutal attack – during which six men, including the bus driver, raped her – Pandey had a metal pole forced into her vagina, and her intestines torn from her body. She later died from her injuries.

LET US FIND ANOTHER WORD FOR RAPE

That broken, post-facto bastard's curse – 'She was asking for it' – reached its spiteful apogee last week, in the wake of the Delhi gang rape.

The lawyer representing three of the men charged with her murder, Manohar Lal Sharma, gave an interview you will want to hide from your children – but whether more urgently from your sons or your daughters, I cannot say. Both become more doomed if they read it and believe it.

'Until today, I have not seen a single incident or example of rape with a respected lady,' Sharma said – insisting that the partner of the dead woman was 'wholly responsible' for her death. The unmarried couple should not have been out so late at night, using public transport.

This woman, now dead, had brought this upon herself. She left the house, intending to be fucked on a bus. She had essentially walked through the streets, looking for six men to help her commit suicide via an iron bar. She was searching for the quiet sound of a fly zip, as ruinous as the sound of a bullet being thumbed into a gun. This is something women do.

The idea of 'asking for it' – whether said by an Indian lawyer in Delhi, a drunkard in a NYC bar, or a careless woman in an office in Slough, tapping through the *Daily Mail* website – is the single, toxic pathogen from which all our problems with rape blossom. Culpability. Blame.

It's so hard to dispel the notion that rape happens wholly unprompted, with the lights on, to a cheerful woman who had done everything 'right'. Surely she had a token of ill luck somewhere on her body? Some evil glamour left in a pocket; a glance that had been better off left at home? Even though a new report shows one in twenty British women have been raped – someone you have been in a room with, today – we think black lightning cannot fall on a sunny day, although we know it can with all the other crimes: on the bonnet of the drunk driver; in the nursery, with a shotgun.

The awful issue of victim-blaming the injured is what makes rape so iniquitous – like telling children in care they should simply have picked better parents in the first place. Why does this happen?

Well, the problem with rape is the sex. As a species, we are still confused, overwhelmed, afraid of, and intoxicated by, sex. It is a cocktail, mixed in with religion, politics, suffrage, power, love, magic, fear, self-loathing and things left widely unspoken. It makes us drunk. It makes us dumb. It confuses us in manifold. Look here, at this pile, in merely its non-fatal complications: *Fifty Shades of Grey*, with its duct-tape. Happy marriages, with their rape fantasies. Count the sex counsellors, and agony aunts. Rape couldn't happen on a bigger moral and philosophical fault line. Rape couldn't strike in a worse place.

That's why I sometimes think we should do away with the word 'rape' altogether. Let's not call this a sexual crime any more – with its baggage of shame, and blame, and ruin. A word so hard for an injured woman – or a man, or a child – to say, now that we've used it in too many places, for too many disparate things, for it to be functionally descriptive of a crime.

Let's call this crime something simpler, and less confusing, instead: internal assault. Intramural attack. Regard it just as we would an assailant violently forcing a hammer handle into a mouth; or puncturing an eardrum with a knife. Does it make any real difference if it's a vagina being brutalised, or an eye? If the weapon is a penis, or a cosh? This is punching, but inside. This is the repeated piercing of someone's body. When you put it like that, suddenly the issue of rape becomes very clear: how many women would ask for that?

The phrase 'sexual assault' confuses a million men, and women, like Manohar Lal Sharma, right across the world – that troubled word, 'sexual', casting a shadow so deep that it hides the 'assault' part altogether. It makes people think of rape merely as some sex that just 'went wrong'.

The police report of the Delhi gang rape alleges that the victim was so badly broken, one assailant 'pulled her intestines from her body with his hands', before throwing her from a moving bus.

And yet, still, everything we debate about this incident is framed around it being a sexual assault. That they attacked her below, before they attacked her above, has defined it. It's become another argument about men and women and desire and politics and culture. Rather than what it is – what all rapes are: one human ripping another human being to pieces.

Not sexual assault. Just – assault. Not a sexual crime. Just – crime. Not rape – with all the confusions we can't afford, can't bear, another generation to painfully sift through, as we have had to.

Just a violence, like any other.

The awfulness of being a female writer is that you know you will not write about rape just once. There will always be terrible new outrages to respond to; another extraordinary story to make you simultaneously fearful and furious for your daughters; for yourself.

This next piece was written after the high-profile case of footballer Ched Evans. Evans' friend, Clayton McDonald, took a drunk, nineteen-year-old woman back to his hotel, had sex with her, then texted Evans, saying, 'I've got a bird.' Evans then arrived in the hotel room and had sex with the victim as his friends filmed them through the window. He then left through the emergency exit.

He was subsequently convicted of rape, after it was deemed the woman was too drunk to consent to sex.

For many reasons – the main one being Evans' utter unwillingness to repent or apologise – this felt like a tipping point for me.

PERHAPS I DON'T BELIEVE IN REDEMPTION ANY MORE

I have always believed in redemption. That however awful life may be to us – and, indeed, we may be to life – at the core of every human being there is an inextinguishable atomic core that wishes to be good – to progress – to change. And that to deny that is, in some way, to try to negate the essence of humanity.

Why would we *not* believe in redemption? Why would we not believe in a troubled human's desire to burn all their old clothes, and diaries, and start again: clean; newborn; determined to be better?

If we need to believe that is possible for ourselves – and I think we do – then we must believe it for everyone else. We must defend it for everyone else. And I do.

Recently, when Jamie Oliver's charitable rehabilitation scheme, Fifteen, took on a former sex offender as an apprentice, there was the predictable outcry.

'It's disgusting that [this lad] can be gifted the kind of opportunity that honest, hard-working youngsters across the country are crying out for,' one of the sex offenders' 'friends' told the *Sun*.

In reply, Andrew Neilson of the Howard League for Penal Reform said, with calm logic: 'If we expect people who commit crimes to never do it again, then we have to accept that once someone has served their sentence, they deserve a chance to be a safe and productive citizen.'

And I was totally behind Neilson. I have always believed in redemption.

But. But. Ched Evans. The Sheffield United footballer convicted of raping a nineteen-year-old. Ched Evans, who is still unrepentant – no apology to his victim – but has now served his jail term, and wants to play football again. To become a safe and productive citizen. Ched Evans, who – by combination of his fame and continued lack of remorse – has now become a lightning rod for female protest.

For when Evans left prison it was rumoured that Sheffield United had offered him £500,000 to rejoin. In protest, Sky Sports presenter and Sheffield United patron Charlie Webster, who herself was abused as a child, resigned her patronage of the club.

The next day, another club patron – Lindsay Graham – also resigned. The day after that, Jessica Ennis-Hill – one of our greatest Olympians – asked for her name to be removed from one of the club's stands, should Evans be rehired.

And at this, I was torn. These women had decided the club's attitude to Evans, and rape, was so intolerable that they could no longer publically support it any more. Powerful women who know both about Sheffield United, and abuse, had left the club they loved – to stand with this woman who they have never met, but wish to protect.

And while I loved the solidarity, I was also troubled – for this means, surely, that these women do not believe in redemption. They would take from Evans his livelihood, and make him an unemployable pariah in this country: ruined by raping one girl, one time.

And here's the thing: perhaps this is how it will be, now. Perhaps it must. Perhaps 'raping one girl, one time' should be the moment the rapist's life is ruined – rather than his victim's. Perhaps this is what women are deciding we have to do, as we get a little bit of leverage, and a little bit of power: we make raping women risky. We make it outright dangerous – because we stop believing in redemption. We become unkind. We clench our fists, and wrap them in steel, in order to protect ourselves: to protect women everywhere.

For those rape statistics remain monolithic. One in five women will be sexually assaulted: 85,000 reported rapes in Britain every year, 85,000 raping men.

And yet, the nearest we have come to dealing with this small army of sexually violent men is to instruct girls on how not to get raped. We give them rape alarms, and Mace, and fear. So far, in the twenty-first century, our best idea has been to try and make the victims more difficult to catch – instead of stopping the source of the problem, instead: the brutal, entitled, fearless greed of the boys who go hunting.

So – maybe this *is* what we do now. Perhaps young, rich, fit, unrepentant men who have raped *do* need to see their lives reduced to ash – without prospect of forgiveness, employment or absolution – until the day they die. I'm starting to see the sense in choosing, say, a hundred rapists and making their lives publically, endlessly awful – unrelentingly humiliating, without prospect of absolution. Of making them famous for being appalling – recognised everywhere they go, regarded as untouchable. So that cold, hungry men become terrified of raping – in exactly the same way women are terrified of being raped. So that rapists spend their lives dealing with the night they raped – in the same way raped women currently do. We reverse it. We turn everything upside down.

Perhaps the only way society *can* be good – to progress – to change – is to stop believing in redemption for a while. Perhaps redemption does women no good at all.

So much of what is onerous, or dangerous, to women, comes down to 'custom'. 'Traditions.' In this piece on FGM, I tried to follow the logic of 'tradition' upstream, to defuse it.

FGM – IT TAKES JUST ONE PERSON TO END A CUSTOM

'Custom' and 'tradition' are odd concepts, aren't they? When you come at them from the side – curious, but emotionless.

What does the dictionary have them as? 'A long-accepted belief that has been passed on from one generation to the next.'

So – these aren't *necessary* things, then. We do not *need* our customs and traditions. We do not talk of the 'custom of breakfast', for instance – or the 'tradition of sex'. These are things that must happen, for us to survive. They are not custom, or tradition. They are needful.

A tradition, or custom, on the other hand – they are simply a thought. An idea thought up by someone, somewhere, and then able to survive through the millennia because it has had fierce weapons, and traps, bolted to it.

'Traditions' and 'customs' are basically old, prehistoric clockwork bombs – the kind of thing you would see in *Raiders of the Lost Ark*. They defend themselves from obsolescence by being rigged out to trigger all manner of fear, anger, revulsion and determination, should you try and reach your hand into the centre and decommission them. If you try and switch them off, traditions are programmed to clamp around your arm, like thousands of teeth, and rip your skin down to the bone. A tradition will do anything it can to keep on surviving. Because a tradition that does *not* survive just joins a billion, old ideas, now forgotten. The primary directive of a tradition is to just keep being passed on. To stay alive. That's all it wants to do. It fears its own death.

Female genital mutilation is a custom – a tradition. Like Christmas, it has a season, and in Britain that is summer. Girls go to 'visit relatives' in their parents' home towns, during the school holidays, and come back with the centres of them cut away and left on the floor, like scraps of meat, in North Africa, Asia and the Middle East. The WHO estimates 140 million Muslim women and girls have undergone the operation, including a very conservative estimate of 66,000 in Britain. There has never been a prosecution for FGM in this country, despite it being illegal.

People often used to call it 'female circumcision', but it bears no resemblance to male circumcision – which is essentially cosmetic, and does little more than change the appearance of the penis. As with most of the female reproductive system, most of the female genitalia is hidden from view – kept safe, unseen, under skin. The difference between male and female 'circumcision', then, is the difference between merely pruning the branches of a tree, and coming at it with a bulldozer, and taking the roots up. Girls who are circumcised are girls who have been hollowed out, as by a machine.

I don't know if you have ever seen a picture of a girl – maybe four, eight or twelve years old – who has just been 'circumcised'. Unanaesthetised, held down on the floor by relatives and cored, with a razor, or a blade, they walk out of the room transformed by not only the pain, but what they just realised they are.

A girl, this tradition has it, is born wrong – the centre of her body has a physical mistake, as ugly and fatal as a cancer – and those who really love her are prepared to cut it away, to save her. Because the lifetime of painful sex, repeated infections, traumatic childbirths and utter physical muteness, where desire should lie, are nothing compared to the shame of not circumcising. If that is your tradition, of course.

For many years now, anyone who criticised the practice of female genital mutilation has been cautioned not to comment on the tradition, and custom, of others.

But remember – when you're arguing against custom, or tradition, you aren't arguing with the millions of people who have followed it, or a whole country. You're not arguing against a force field, a law of nature, or the word of God.

Instead, you are reaching back through time to the first person who ever came up with this idea – some woman, or man, hundreds of years ago, in a world infinitely more terrifying than this one now, who was so scared that their best survival plan seemed to be to core out their girls – and going, 'No. No. Your idea is that this *should* happen. And my idea is that this *shouldn't*. Let us now argue this out, as equals.'

And this deactivates all the weaponry of tradition, and custom, until we all just become humans again – talking about which ideas we want to take on with us, usefully, for the next hundred years.

Last month, Bristol-based activist Nimko Ali succeeded in getting ChildLine to set up FGM phone lines for girls at risk, during this long, dangerous summer.

Ali's parents' idea was that she should be cut. Her idea, in turn, is that the next generation should be able to find help, so that they are not.

So now we will see which idea – not 'custom', not 'tradition': just an 'idea', by a person – will eventually, over the next decades, win.

Let's face it – we could easily have called this section 'Why Having a Vagina Is Often Terrifying'. Here is a piece on one of those other subjects feminist writers find themselves having to revisit, over and over again: women's right to control when they become mothers.

THIS IS A WORLD FORMED BY ABORTION – IT ALWAYS HAS BEEN, AND IT ALWAYS WILL BE

In 2013, in Spain, the ruling Popular Party drafted legislation to radically tighten the country's abortion laws. They proposed to make it illegal for Spanish women to seek an abortion save in cases of rape, incest, or risks to physical or mental health. Following an international outcry, the PP eventually backed down – but this came at the same time as American women began to experience notable restriction to abortion-access in many states, and British clinics started to see regular protests on the pavements outside, with clients – many of them young, and traumatised – being met with a barrage of abuse. There seemed to be a surprising re-framing, in many otherwise advanced countries, around the subject of abortion. It was as if abortion were some relatively recent, morally licentious activity that blew in on the same wind as disco, homosexuality and *Dallas*, and which must now – in more sore, sober and reflective times – be curtailed once more. That the only abortions are these modish, legal abortions – these clinics, and these doctors – and that now, enough was enough, and they must be stopped.

This is an odd logic for modern countries to take – as it ignores the constant, immovable, historical presence of abortion. Its commonness, currency and necessity. We live in a world formed by abortion – and we always have. Examine the social records of any time and they have their abortion remedies: pennyroyal, tansy, hellebore. Silphium was the remedy of the Ancient Greeks – the main export of Cyrene, demand was so huge for Silphium that it was harvested into extinction – but not before its image was imprinted on to the Cyrenian coinage.

Coat-hangers, candles, carved wooden tools – fasting, bloodletting, pouring hot water on to the abdomen. Hippocrates recommended jumping up and down, so that the heels of the feet made contact with the buttocks.

And, of course, in all this there is no pictorial or documentary record of the most common thing of all: desperate, terrified prayers, over the millennia, from girls and women, desperately hoping they will miscarry.

Women trying to control their fertility, in order to have mastery of their lives, is as ancient a practice as humans trying to control their fields in order to eat. The society we live in is shaped by abortion – how can it not be, with a third of women now having an abortion in their lifetime? That is a gigantic force in the way we live – it informs every aspect of our economy, industry and sexuality – but the merciful, positive aspects of it are never seen, or discussed. Squeamish and frightened, we only *ever* discuss abortion when someone seeks to curtail safe, legal access to it.

And legal access is the key thing. Of the 40 million abortions that happen worldwide every year, half happen in countries where it is legal. The other half happen anyway – illegally. Unsafely. Of the 20 million women who abort illegally, 47,000 die. Whether it is legal or not, across the world and throughout time, women abort. And when you look at the reasons given to the World Health Organisation by these women, you can see why. It is a list that invokes mercy, and solidarity with the women, in all but the most determinedly ideological of hearts: 73 per cent 'cannot afford a baby now'; 48 per cent have relationship problems; 13 per cent have an unhealthy foetus; 1 per cent were raped.

The simplicity of why women choose to seek an abortion is devastating: they feel they cannot look after a child. *Cannot.* I assure any anti-abortionist they may disregard their sneaking feelings that 40 million women a year have abortions foolishly, recklessly – that it is done with the same selfish giddiness as binge-drinking, or twerking, and therefore to be discouraged by the high-minded, for the greater good of society.

A woman who is so convinced she would be a bad parent that she is prepared to take a pill and bleed for four days, or else find herself with her legs up in stirrups, has made a very serious decision about what is both good for her and society. And yet because abortion is shameful, women stay silent over their grateful need for legal access to it, and we continue – despite that 40 million – to think of abortion as some fringe activity, done by 'others' – never our daughters. Our mothers, wives and sisters. Our bosses. Our politicians.

When those American states voted to curtail access to legal abortion, I wanted every woman in that building who'd had an abortion to stand up and say, simply, 'I have had an abortion.' Not just the politicians – the PAs and the cleaners, the electricians and the press officers.

And then on – outside the buildings of legislature, and into the streets: every woman – one in three – on strike that day, in a symbolic withdrawal from the running of the country. Spanish women should have done just the same. Both countries would have ground to a halt.

And the symbolism would have been apt – for when women are denied safe access to abortion, *their* lives grind to a halt. Our societies grind to a halt. Forty million a year suggests nothing less. What do anti-abortionists think, exactly, that the world would do with those extra 40 million children a year – born to unwilling mothers? For whose benefit, exactly, would we be assembling this unhappy battalion?

Women have abortions. They always have, and they always will. The only question is: in safe, legal clinics – or back to pennyroyal, hot water and desperate prayers?

The thing about feminism, though – thank God – is that it's not all heartbreaking, horrible stuff about rape and fear and lack of control. This is, still, the best time it has ever been to be a woman: there are extraordinary forces at work out there, bringing change seemingly every day. Our daughters will be, at a rough calculation, 37 per cent less fucked up than we were – they live in an age of miracle, wonder, Beyoncé, Taylor Swift, Aung San Suu Kyi, Melissa McCarthy, Caitlyn Jenner, and Hillary Clinton running for the White House.

OH, HILLARY. SUDDENLY, I LOVE YOU

Look, I like the woman – but I've never been a *super-fan* of Hillary Clinton. You know? I like a couple of her singles – but I've never seen her live, or bought a t-shirt.

Previously, I liked her in the way I suspect most bright, ambitious women who, at some point in their teenage years, *also* had to wear a massive pair of unflattering spectacles, like her: a nod of recognition to a fellow traveller on the same, difficult path. Someone who has also tensed up every time the men start talking about who they want to bang (never you. But still discussed in front of you. Thanks). Being called a 'ball-breaking bitch' for wanting to work hard. Becoming increasingly depressed as you realise just how prepared society is to allow generation after generation of brilliant young women – women who could transform the world – go to waste, because of institutional sexism and fear of their otherness. Going blind every time you drain a boiling pan of pasta, because it steams up your glasses real bad.

I did go through one, brief 'big love for Hillary' phase, back in 1992 – when she got into all that shit for explaining why, despite her husband running for President, she wasn't giving up her job as a lawyer to 'support' him.

'I suppose I *could* have stayed at home, and baked cookies, and given teas,' she mused, 'but what I decided to do was fulfil my profession, which I entered before my husband was in public life.'

At the time, this caused *massive* controversy. It was presumed that Hillary was throwing shade on all stay-at-home, baking wives – despite that sentence not running: 'I suppose I could have stayed at home and baked cookies and given teas – *like a loser.*'

Or even – which would have been more truthful – 'I could have baked cookies – but I cannot cook them faster than Bill eats them. He is The Big Dog, and, frankly, you can just buy cookies for 69 cents a packet in WalMart so, you know, my gigantic IQ made a decision there.'

The logic of the fury against Clinton essentially centred on the fact that she had been able to make a *choice* about her life. It was sobering, as a seventeen-year-old, to witness this: that women just can't say they don't want to make biscuits, and would prefer to be a lawyer, instead.

(Let's flip-reverse this for a minute: imagine if Andy Murray's new wife announced she intended to run for Parliament, and Andy Murray gave an interview explaining that he would still continue to play tennis – and people became utterly *furious* about this, and accused him of shitting on all other, 'normal' men who don't play world-class tennis. That he was *shaming* them. The whole thing was berserk, recidivist nuts.)

So, yeah – I was wildly pro-Hillary, for those bad months. The months of insanity. Then, for the next twenty-three years – whevs. No Hillary thoughts at all.

But last week – when Hillary announced that she would be running for first female President of the United States – I felt a sudden joy. Actually, it was more than that – it quietly and unexpectedly blew a small part of my mind. Fizz. Crack.

Because in that one second – as I imagined the very real possibility of her becoming President – she rewired my entire, subconscious chronology of being a woman.

I hadn't even realised it, but my unexamined presumption was that for women, it's all downhill after the menopause. You make your big bang – you do all your running and fighting and growing and deal-making – in your fertile years, and then, when your ovaries quit, you step back to grow herbs, retire to a cottage-cum-hovel, and do a bit of soothsaying on the side.

Don't get me wrong – I was looking forward to my years of 'going hag': I had intended to finally accept all those invitations to appear on *Never Mind the Buzzcocks* and *8 Out of 10 Cats*, where I planned on terrifying all those young cocky male comedians by appearing with my hair all massive and white, like Mad Madam Mim, and schooling them in how to deliver a Marxist/feminist dialectic monologue that was still twelve times funnier than whatever spiteful, ass-clown lolz they were milking out of the concept of Kim Kardashian being a whore with a big arse. It was gonna be ace.

But! With Hillary's announcement, that all exploded. For suddenly, there is the very real possibility that we will live in a time where a woman becomes the leader of the Free World at the age of sixty-seven.

And in a stroke, this gives women a *whole extra act* in our lives. Another thirty years, minimum, in which we can continue to grow in power, wisdom, accomplishment, ambition and balls. The whole female narrative arc is reinvented like *that* – from slow decline to soaring upward thread. Clinton has made the sexual power of being a young woman – so often our gender's greatest currency – look as nothing compared to what you can get in your seventh decade: the *world*. You have chosen the world over baking cookies.

That's what can happen from now on.

Some of the revolutions are smaller than a female President, of course.

I HAVE GIVEN UP HEELS. LIKE, TOTALLY

I came to a decision last week that, frankly, I'm surprised I didn't make years ago: I've given up on high heels. I've taken them all from the box under the bed, and put them in the kids' dressing-up box. The silver wedges, the green velvets, the black leather peep-toes with the bondage straps around the ankle. Even the canary-yellow ones that looked like they were from the 1930s, and made me feel like a Broadway chorus girl called Lola. All gone, now.

All gone, because I just can't summon up the energy to lie to myself any more. The lie I've been telling myself for thirty years is that, while I cannot wear these shoes in the daytime – to go shopping, or to work, in them would, obviously, be painful – I *can* wear heels in the evening, to 'important' events.

'You look great!' I would say to myself in the mirror, as I adjusted the buckles, and made sure my stocking seams were straight.

'You're totally walking in these shoes in a sexy way!' I would say to myself as I walked very, very carefully down the steps and on to the pavement. And got into a cab, because I couldn't walk to the Tube in heels.

'Spending nearly £50 on cab fares in order to wear heels to a party is totally fine!' I would say to myself as I arrived at the party – regarding any further staircases with gloom, and hand-rail-clutching totteryness.

'Dancing wouldn't have been fun anyway!' I would say as I remained sitting on my chair, when the disco started.

'I'm sure you haven't looked like that *all* night!' I would think, when I looked up and caught my reflection in the mirror, and realised that my aching feet had made my posture terrible, and that I looked like an old, paunchy woman. Well, an older, paunchier woman.

I thought I had no option, you see. If you're going to a black-tie event, that means wearing a dress – and if you're wearing a dress, you have to wear heels. Smart black cocktail dresses look weird without heels. Most evening wear looks weird without heels. You *could* boldly wear trainers, like Lily Allen in 2005 – but that seems too contrary. You're not trying to make a massive style statement. You just want to look *normal*, and nice. Appropriate.

And so you put on the Blisteze pads, and the heels, and the dress, and pay the cab fare, and don't dance, and gradually slump in pain, and then – if you're me – fall down a flight of stairs and break three ribs, and think, 'You know what – fuck this. I'm tired of being scared of stairs, and spending every important event I go to worried I'll fall over and show my knickers. I'm going to do what *men* do.'

For when men go to evening events, they can run upstairs, and dance, and get the Tube there and back, thus saving £50 – because they wear a suit, and some nice shoes, which they might have polished; but that is pretty much the extent of their primping. They are safe and comfortable and happier and better off, simply because they are not wearing a short tight dress and a pair of heels. And they can wear the same suit over and over – they would be utterly confused by the common female panic of fretting that we cannot wear a dress, or a pair of shoes, 'Because I wore it last time.'

Men spend no more than ten minutes thinking about how they will look at a black-tie event. Women start thinking about it *weeks* in advance.

Recently, I have started thinking that the answer to most of my feminist questions is: 'Just do what the men do. All that shit they do really seems to be working for them.'

And so I have. At the last two events I went to – award ceremonies, black tie – I did as men do. I wore a suit. A tuxedo jacket, shorts, a silk blouse, and flat shoes: flat green-and-gold brogues from Marni, that I can walk to the Tube in, and dance in, and stand in with perfect posture, enjoying my evening.

And it felt *amazing* – to be able to walk around with my hands in my pocket, whistling. To feel *ease*. To know I need never feel anxious about what to wear to a posh event again – I've got my outfit, and my shoes, and I don't really need to think about them again for the next five years – unless it's to go wild, and maybe buy a new blouse.

I felt like I'd discovered an astonishing secret. Women kept coming up to me, and going, 'I wish I was wearing what you're wearing. I'm going to have to take these shoes off in a minute.'

And at the end of the evening, they all got into cabs, to go home. I, meanwhile, walked to the pub with the men, and stayed out until 3am – spending my cab money on champagne, and dancing.

So, yes. I have finally given up heels. And it is just jim-dandy.

For a while, I pondered – will we actually know *when we have achieved the revolution? Will we ever be actually told? Fearing that there was no official index for The Great Glorious Day of Equality, I quickly knocked together my own checklist, for ascertaining exactly that thing.*

THE REAL EQUALITY CHECKLIST

I was pondering, last week, how – in a complex and busy world – we would actually *know* when women have become equal to men. Some people argue women have already overtaken men; other people argue women are still at least two generations from parity; statistics often show a confused picture; and, as yet, there is no gigantic golden bell that will be rung out on the day that it's conclusively proved, once and for all, that we're all on a level playing field, with adjacent toilet facilities, sufficient for both sexes, to boot.

In the absence of someone forging The Great Golden Bell of Equality, I've made a quick tick list of things we should be keeping our eyes on, viz. female status in Western society, which I've now pinned up on the fridge, with a Sharpie, to tick off, as and when they occur.

1) Wages to reach parity (white women still earning 85p to every male £1 in the UK, women of colour earning even less – 64p).
2) Equal number of female CEOs in the Forbes 100 (current score: fifteen. Out of 100).
3) Houses of Parliament to represent the blah blah blahdy blah.
4) Women to be able to eat a sausage for breakfast when they fancy it, without feeling bad about it, and wanging on about it for the rest of the day like they're a lay sister who's just killed a unicorn ('I should probably go for a lunchtime swim … and just have Cup-a-Soup for tea … just nibbling on a rice cracker …. oh God

my trousers feel bad I SHOULD NEVER HAVE EATEN THE SAUSAGE.') Ladies, fyi – you should always eat the sausage.

5) A woman to go up and collect her Oscar in a comfortable pair of shoes, like all the men – rather than turning up already in agony, then spending the rest of the evening leaning against walls, tables, chairs, etc., missing out on important business-deal conversations, while her iPhone beeps with Google updates from bitchy tabloids about how her red carpet look was 'a howler', and how she looks like she's 'spilling out of' her dress, when Russell Crowe is 'spilling out of' his trousers and no one gives even half of one shit.

6) For everyone to realise how weird it is for every TV show to pair a man 'of golfing age' with some hot chick who could be his daughter or granddaughter (*This Morning*, *The One Show*, *Strictly Come Dancing*, every *Children in Need* ever, particularly the one with Terry Wogan (498) and Fearne Cotton (12): *brrrrr*). The BBC's Light Entertainment department often looks like one long 'Bring Your Daughter to Work Day'. Why can't we have some bad-ass woman in her sixties bossing some pleasant-on-the-eye boy-faun around? I'd set the Sky+ for Joan Bakewell showing Barney Harwood from *Blue Peter* a thing or two.

7) No more references to a woman who likes alcohol, sexual intercourse, opinionated conversation and partying as being 'laddish'. For anyone who thinks these are the sole preserves and interests of men – the Wife of Bath wants to have a word with you. Put your curly-toed drinking shoes on.

8) For a female former child star to come along who indicates her shift into adulthood not by suddenly rocking up in her pants, and doing a video where she fellates random objects – but by making an album about, say, parallel universes, the Underground Railroad, or that bloke who built Monument in London as a massive telescope, and then lived in it, instead.

9) But, on the other hand, for everyone to also be cool with the fact that a certain proportion of former child stars *will* want to express their new-found adulthood by exploring their sexuality in a series of red-hot videos, and it not being subsequently discussed, for months on end, as if the world is going to hell in a hand cart (see Miley Cyrus).

10) It being perfectly acceptable, in an office environment, to rest your breasts on the desk when they hurt.

11) A female hero who is as complex, odd and sometimes unlikeable as Batman, Sherlock Holmes, Holden Caulfield, John Self, or Jack Bauer.

12) And who doesn't have a single scene where she faffs around on a MacBook in a vest-top, showing side-boob, late at night.

13) For us to *never again* find out, at the mid-point in the story, that the reason a female protagonist is driven is because she was sexually abused as a child. Do women *really* only want to achieve things if they've been horrifically traumatised in their earlier lives? Must the Hero Origin Story *always* be one of shame and ruin? Suggestions for other things that could motivate a female character: she's a sentient adult in the twenty-first century who needs to pay her rent; she has a very annoying mother; *it's her job.* Just imagine, for a minute, how weird it would be if, in the middle of *The Maltese Falcon*, Humphrey Bogart suddenly broke down and admitted that the only reason he wanted to find the Maltese Falcon is because, actually, he had a 'bad uncle', who touched him in the wrong place once on a caravan holiday. Exactly. This is how weird women are made to feel *all the time*. Until the Great Bell rings out.

As a child, I lived in musicals. We had a 3ft-high stack of pirated VHS by the video player: Gigi, The Sound of Music, On the Town, Annie, Easter Parade, Hello, Dolly!, Oliver!, Jesus Christ Superstar, Wizard of Oz, Meet Me in St Louis, American in Paris *(boring; too much jazz-ballet)*, Grease. *I am pretty sure that my eternal ebullience and optimism stem directly from being raised on these, practically from the moment I hatched out of my egg. In all musicals, a generally working-class heroine rises up to joy and success in almost exactly ninety minutes. That was what I thought life would be like, when I was an adult. And you know what? It should be.*

WHY CAN'T LIFE BE MORE LIKE A MUSICAL?

'Why can't life be like a musical?' is a mug-slogan I have a lot of time for. To be honest, more often than not I'm pretending my life is a musical anyway. When I wake in the morning, I'm Tracy Turnblad singing 'Good Morning Baltimore' to the rats in the street. When I'm in a self-pitying mood about work, I like to channel Christ in *Jesus Christ Superstar* – when, in 'Gethsemane', he's on his knees doing a power air-grab with his hands and screaming, *'WHY? Should I DIE???'* at God. And whenever I'm losing an argument, I'm Barbra Streisand in *Hello, Dolly!*, in a massive gold-feather head-dress, shouting, 'Horace – DON'T TRY TO STOP ME!' as the put-upon Walter Matthau just walks away, shrugging.

And I'm scarcely alone in this – for nearly all women love musicals. It's one of the things about us – like having tits and being a bit oppressed. Rare is the tipsy woman who won't give you her 'Edelweiss' at 1am. Rare is the woman who has not, at some point, hung on till tomorrow, come what may.

Last week, I realised just why it is that women – particularly of my age and older – love musicals. And it's very simple: it's because classic musicals were the first feminist movies – *way* before we had *The Hunger Games* and *Thelma & Louise*. If you were raised on whatever movies BBC2 showed on rainy Saturday afternoons, musicals would be the only films you ever saw where you got to watch women actually *doing* stuff – instead of just '*being*'.

Watching female characters just *be* is one of the most depressing things for a young girl to absorb: all those women – usually played by Olivia de Havilland – who make their first entrance at the top of a flight of stairs, pausing to stare bashfully around the room as we clock the reaction of the leading man, which might best be described as, 'Respectful hubba hubba. She make clean, quiet wife.'

She then spends the rest of the movie being inspiring by speaking in an annoyingly 'gentle' voice and having lovely hair. She never argues. She never has her own plans. She's just there as a prize, for boys to win. At some point the silly bitch will probably faint and have to be carried somewhere to recover – which is usually the moment the leading man kisses her. What a rubbish pulling technique – being unconscious. For any unkissed girls out there – I heartily disrecommend it. Stay conscious *all* the time during the romantic process – that's basic but necessary advice. That's a 'Being a Human Being 101'.

Compare all this, then, to the women in musicals. The first time *their* leading men see them, they're in a bar with a gun (*Calamity Jane*), sailing out of the sky with an umbrella (*Mary Poppins*), mind-fucking a load of spoilt, feral kids (*The Sound of Music*), driving a cab and ogling sailors (*On the Town*), dancing with a load of black teens in segregated Baltimore (*Hairspray*) or sassing a drunken customer in a bar (*Easter Parade*). They argue. *Their* plans are usually the *entire plot* of the movie. And they *never* faint – because they're insanely charismatic, super-fit tap-dancing athletes, bouncing off the ceilings, and flying across floors, and dancing through the night, with blood in their shoes, until the sun comes up over Hollywood, and it's time for them to rescue Gene Kelly's ill-fated talkie.

The thing is, in musicals, women *do* stuff. They show off their talent – you know, the way men do in man-movies, when they're fighting each other, or solving crimes. Indeed, their talent usually dwarfs that of their male co-stars. Gene Kelly and Fred Astaire were the two biggest male musical talents ever seen – and while they undoubtedly dance like the definition of joy, everyone's a bit 'Oh dear' when they start singing.

The female musical stars, on the other hand – man, they do *everything*. Judy Garland, Julie Andrews, Liza Minnelli, Doris Day, Ann Miller – those dames could sing *and* dance *and* act, and they *all* have the oddly modern, adroit comic timing of a Jennifer Aniston, or Tina Fey. Indeed, they were so talented they didn't *just* make musicals, like Gene, and Fred – they could do 'straight' drama, too; *and* make best-selling records, *and* do sell-out concert tours. Inspiring as the saying is, women in musicals were never just doing everything Fred Astaire did, but backwards, and in heels. It was 'backwards, in heels, with three other careers, and being fifty years ahead of their time'.

Why do women love musicals? Because a list of 'The 100 Greatest Movies of All Time' will be 90 per cent male leads, while 'The 100 Greatest Musicals of All Time' will be 90 per cent female. Musicals are one of our unique, cultural aberrations – the sole, mad, Technicolor, joyous oasis where women make the weather and call the shots. If life *was* more like a musical, half of feminism's work would be done.

In the twenty-first century, we generally seem to believe that in order for a woman to feel confident she needs a shopping list. Well, balls to that.

WHAT REALLY GIVES ME CONFIDENCE

There are days in everyone's lives where they need a little more confidence than normal. An important meeting here. An event which requires public speaking there. Or maybe your laser-guidance system has just bust, halfway down the ventilation shaft of the Death Star – and now you're down to using 'The Force only' to finally bring peace to the galaxy. What a mare.

Either way, humanity has long acknowledged that, in these circumstances, there are certain things that can give a body confidence. Items, and refrains, that can raise the spirits – carry you through a difficult moment, comforted by their mere presence.

Unfortunately, if you're a modern woman, these things tend to be incredibly expensive/difficult. Were you to believe what you see in movies, and magazines, you would believe that a woman's first line of psychic defence comes in her outfit and accessories. No one can say no to a woman holding an 'It Bag'! Success is guaranteed in this bright, silk 'day-to-evening' dress, £399! On top of this, a woman will become undefeatable if she walks into a difficult situation thinking, 'I am hot. I have a mind for business, and a body for sin. Put the blame on Mame. Let's go!'

And if these things do work for you – then hurrah! I am cheered by your methods! After all, even £600 for a Versace quilted tote is still cheaper than a year of cognitive behavioural therapy – *plus* you can put your packed lunch in it, too. There is no way to store snacks in 'a well-balanced personality'. I know. I've tried.

However, we do need to acknowledge that, for many women, the way to confidence and, indeed, joy, is not through in some way becoming invulnerable through fashion. Here, for instance, are the things that get *me* through anxious days:

1) Lowe Alpine's 'Ceramic' Gore-Tex jacket, in green. Bought: 1996. Shoulder pads may come and shoulder pads may go – but, personally, I can think of no instance of 'power dressing' that could ever be more potent than when I stand in my hallway – cab waiting – and put on my four-seasons, all-terrain Gore-Tex anorak, with two layers of zippers and drawstring hood. There's just a certain, insouciant air a woman projects if she rocks up at a major media meeting in Soho in a coat that she's climbed a mountain in, while eating a ham sandwich. A slightly shabby super-cagoule says, 'Yes, yes – you may look more glamorous and sleek than me, Andrea, in your boy-style tuxedo-coat – but, come the apocalypse, Andrea, *I* will be standing in a fully breathable fabric, dry right down to my vest. And *you*, Andrea – you will be damp. And then, after a very long time, and complications with pneumonia, probably dead. Sign these contracts and good day to you, sir. Andrea.'

2) The knowledge that it all worked out all right for Anne from *Anne of Green Gables*, in the end. Obviously, I don't mean *just* Anne from *Anne of Green Gables* – by gesturing to her, I mean to include a whole pantheon of women and girls: Little Orphan Annie, Maria from *The Sound of Music*, Jane Eyre, Lizzie Bennet, Doris from *Fame*, Judy Garland in *Easter Parade*, Jo from *Little Women* and the be-booted lady Weetabix in the 'We're the Weetabix – okay?' advert, from 1986. All pointedly described as 'not beautiful', all of humble origins and a bit gobby – but all of whom triumphed by being hard-working, cheerful, non-conformist and able to crack a joke. On my wobbliest days, I think, 'If Anne of Green Gables could succeed in a pre-feminist era as a ginger orphan, then by *God* I can.'

3) My iPhone. Or whatever gadget that, in an emergency, on the way to a meeting that terrifies me, lets me iTune the Jesus and Mary Chain's screeching, unlubricated 'Upside Down', and cranks it out so loud that it sets fire to all fear and leaves it as ash. I did buy an expensive handbag, recently – neon orange, from Marc Jacobs – in order to 'help' me through a big day. And it's very nice. But in the cab going over Waterloo Bridge, it wasn't the bag, but the band who had me bunching my fists inside my anorak pockets, shouting 'Come on! COME ON! My head's full of feedback! I've got all of rock'n'roll inside of me! You going to mess with the Jesus and Mary Chain? ARE YOU?' The bag was £350. The download was 99p.

That's the thing about pop, and literature – they're both cheaper than fashion, and more effective. *And* you don't have to dry-clean them.

If I were going to give any young woman advice on how to feel confident in the twenty-first century, I'd point out, 'Two women at the same event, wearing the same outfit, is a disaster. But two women at the same event, singing the same song, is a party. And two women at the same event talking about Doris from *Fame* is a friendship for life. Fill yourself with words, choruses and heroes, like you're supposed to fill your wardrobe with shoes, brooches and belts.'

Ah, the internet – so often women's friend, allowing her to run campaigns such as No More Page 3, the Daughters of Eve anti-FGM campaign that changed legislation and brought about the first prosecution for FGM in Britain, Laura Bates' hugely successful Everyday Sexism project, the tidal wave of pro-trans* blogs and activism, Writers of Colour's directory of media experts of colour, and the uniting of millions of angry, hopeful, active, clever, silly, future-making women, across the world.

But then, on the other hand, the internet – so often a woman's enemy. The rape threats. The death threats. The constant, casual misogyny. Gamergate.

In Britain in 2013, we had a Bad Summer. A long, hot summer of hating women on the internet, triggered by one woman's very simple, seemingly innocuous quest: to make sure there was at least one woman on British banknotes. What happened next was three months of 'Humanity, we're looking quite bad here' bullshit.

WOMEN GETTING KILLED ON THE INTERNET

So. Recap. Caroline Criado-Perez runs a campaign to make sure that the forthcoming redesign of British banknotes includes at least one British woman. However, around the time the Bank of England announce that they will, indeed, include Jane Austen on the new tenner, Criado-Perez became the target of a group of Twitter users, who started sending her messages, threatening to rape her – sometimes numbering up to 200 an hour.

At the time of writing, this has now been going on for six days – despite a 21-year-old man in Manchester being arrested after sending Criado-Perez a threatening Tweet.

I think it would be good to show here the kind of messages Criado-Perez has been getting, as there are those who have discussed these kind of messages as part of 'the rough and tumble' of the internet – suggesting women just need to toughen up a bit, and deal with the unpleasantness of the 'real world'.

'Everybody jump on the rape train – @CCriadoPerez is conductor.' 'I love it when the hate machine swarms.' 'Rape rape rape rape rape rape.' 'Everyone report @CCriadoPerez for rape and murder threats and also being a cunt #malemasterrace.' 'Wouldn't mind tying this bitch to my stove. Hey sweetheart – give me a shout when you're ready to be put in your place.' 'Rape threats? Don't flatter yourself. Call the cops. We'll rape them too. YOU BITCH! YO PUSSY STANK!'

So that's fifty of those an hour. For a week now.

In the last twenty-four hours, these rape threats have expanded to include MP Stella Creasy, who has been vocal in both defending Criado-Perez, and calling for changes in the way Twitter is run, and Creasy – along with the *Independent* TV critic Grace Dent and *Guardian* fashion columnist Hadley Freeman – have received bomb threats. Again, this is all *after* an arrest has been made for abuse on Twitter. *After*.

Many commentators have suggested that, when women – or, indeed, anyone – get abuse like this on the internet, that the only and best solution is for them to simply 'block' the abusers and get on with their lives.

But consider the logistics of this. If a woman is getting fifty of these messages an hour, blocking all the abusers becomes something of a thankless, full-time job.

By the time a woman has finished defending herself from her abusers, and actually gets around to doing what she came on Twitter to do – to talk, to communicate – she's already exhausted. And, also, a little more angry, paranoid, defensive and, frankly, rattled than the non-abused people her Tweets appear next to. There's nothing quite like being repeatedly told you're violatable and worthless to send you to bed anxious and unhappy.

On top of this, there's something that would offend most people's notion of how we want a society to function in the idea that if groups of people – in this case, women – are being regularly attacked, and their voices shut down in public, that – when they ask for help – we shrug, and say, 'Sorry. Every woman must deal with this on her own.'

I don't think most people would want someone they loved to be told to deal with this on their own. And I'm pretty sure most people would agree that this would be a better world if women did not get besieged with threats of rape and death after running a genteel campaign to have a picture of Jane Austen on a banknote, or reviewing a restaurant, or dress.

So: some solutions were suggested. Maybe Twitter could have a 'Report Abuse' button? Maybe Twitter could run algorithms, to spot the traits of multi-account-opening trolls? Perhaps, for twenty-four hours, supporters of Criado-Perez could quit Twitter, to show solidarity – and focus Twitter's minds on coming up with some solutions of their own?

No one really had a definitive answer, but there was a 'Report Abuse Button' petition – currently signed by 104,000 people – and a general debate on how Criado-Perez, and anyone else like her, shouldn't have to deal with this kind of thing on their own.

But within twenty-four hours of this quiet debate starting up, a whole slew of columns and blogs appeared, firmly rejecting the idea of there ever being any curbs on 'freedom of speech' on the internet.

'This isn't a technology issue – this is a societal issue' a *Telegraph* blogger said – adding, in a later blog, that people who wished for better regulation on Twitter were behaving 'like Mary Whitehouse' and that this was a simple matter of censorship. 'This is a curtailment of freedom of speech' was a very popular refrain.

Handily, this neatly abutted with what has, over the years, proven to be a fairly infallible rule: that anyone who says 'Hey, guys – what about freedom of speech!' hasn't the faintest idea what 'freedom of speech' actually means.

There is no such thing as 'freedom of speech' in this country. Since 1998, we've had Article 10 of the European Convention on 'freedom of expression', but that still outlaws – among many things – obscenity, sedition, glorifying terrorism, incitement of racial hatred, sending articles which are indecent or grossly offensive with an intent to cause anxiety or distress, and threatening, abusive or insulting words likely to cause harassment, alarm or distress.

As you can see, if you are suggesting that you are allowed to threaten someone on Twitter with rape or death under 'freedom of speech', then you do not – as predicted – have any idea what 'freedom of speech' means. Because it's prosecutable.

Anyway, let's move on – for if we got upset with bloggers and columnists who chucked around portentous-sounding phrases they'd heard on *Legally Blonde* without really knowing what they meant, we'd be here all day. The *key* thing here is the odd, underlying attitude that has permeated so much of this debate about women being harassed – to the point of paranoia and exhaustion – on social media. There is an air about this that is bizarrely ... exhausted, and cynical.

Currently, an air of jaded world-weariness drives the debate about what we want the internet to be – an affectedly sardonic edge, which the practitioners seem to wear as if it were a black biker jacket, or an edgy nasal piercing.

Wielding what amounts to a massive cynicism boner, these people are adamant when they say, 'NOTHING CAN CHANGE. THE INTERNET JUST IS WHAT IT IS!'

People who, in 2013, who say, with utter certainty, 'nothing can change!' are one of the more discombobulating developments of recent years. I'll be frank – it does my head in to see someone who lives in a democracy, wears artificial fibres, drives a car, has a wife who can vote and children whom it is illegal to send to work up a chimney, saying, on the internet – invented in 1971!!!! – 'NOTHING CAN CHANGE!'

Dude, everyone in the Western world lives an existence wholly defined by *constant* change – change that was brought about by people going, 'I tire of people dying young. That sucks. I will invent antibiotics,' or 'I have thought of a marvellous thing – global communication, via a glorified typewriter!'

It is a particular quirk of egotism/a lack of any sense of history or perspective to say, confidently and crushingly, 'Things cannot change.' What someone who says 'Things cannot change' means, more often than not, is '*I* do not *want* things to change.'

There is a neat squaring of the circle when you notice that, on this issue, those who say 'Things cannot change' are, in the overwhelming majority, men – and that the people they are trying to shut down who are saying, repeatedly, 'Things must change', are women.

And this is all particularly inappropriate when the conversation is about how, of all things, it is *the internet* that cannot change. The internet, which was invented, within our lifetimes, by hippies. Tim Berners-Lee, who gave away the coding for free, with the words, 'This is for everyone' – the sentence that was so astonishing and inspiring when it lit up the stadium at the Olympics Opening Ceremony.

In short, the internet was invented, very recently, for people, by people, and founded in optimism and idealism.

For this odd new groundswell of commentators to start claiming that the internet is inherently dark, cruel and cynical is a gross misappropriation of one of the wonders of the modern age. It misunderstands what it was, is and, most importantly, could be.

Shame on anyone whose argument basically boils down to saying that: 'The thing about the internet is, it's a place where hundreds of anonymous men can threaten to rape women – and that is how it will always be.'

That is in an odd, dark denial of the fundamental decency of human nature and the law. It is illegal to act in this manner on the internet, and the social networking sites on which it happens need to be reminded of that unambiguously. As Andy Trotter said on Monday, of internet platform providers, such as Twitter, 'You can't just set them up, and then walk away.'

I'm pro the mooted twenty-four-hour walkout on 4 August, because not only is it a symbolic act of solidarity – which are my favourite kinds of symbolic acts – but because it will also focus minds at Twitter to come up with their own solution to the abuses of their private company.

You know – the popularity of social networking sites waxes and wanes with ferocious rapidity. Twitter might currently be the hot thing – but it only takes a couple of bad months for it to become the new Friends Reunited, the new MySpace, the new Bebo. Another ghost town, left empty when women, and their good male friends, tire of this horrible clown caravel of rape and death and threat and blocking and antagonism and cynicism and the shrugging insistence that this is how it will always be.

If 52 per cent of Twitter's customers – women – see other women being repeatedly left to deal with abuse on their own, then when a new social networking site appears that *has* addressed this issue, I suspect they will drain away from Twitter in a way that makes a twenty-four-hour walkout look like a mere bagatelle.

The main compass to steer by, as this whole thing rages on, doubtless for some months to come, is this: to maintain the spirit that the internet was conceived and born in – one of absolute optimism that the future will be better than the past. And that the future will be better than the past because the internet is the best shot we've had yet for billions of people to communicate equally, and peacefully, and with the additional ability to post pictures of thatched houses that look 'surprised'.

As you might have guessed from the last piece, the building storm of threats against women on Twitter was something I felt like I wanted to act upon. The day after I wrote that piece, I did: I suggested a thing called #twittersilence, and, in the process, launched my first ever – but I'm sure not my last – half-arsed global internet campaign. On 4 August – International Friendship Day – I suggested a twenty-four-hour withdrawal from Twitter, to both show solidarity with those being threatened, and put pressure on Twitter to make their site safer for everyone to communicate on. #twittersilence trended worldwide, and made Channel 4 News, *but led to, ahem, let us say a 'varied' reception in the media.*

Below is a report on how it went. Tldr: a mixed grill.

HOW TO RUN A HALF-ARSED GLOBAL INTERNET CAMPAIGN

1) **Don't come up with a half-arsed internet campaign while on holiday.** After three big lie-ins, you will be dangerously over-positive – and, also, quite simple, from over-exposure to the sun. 'Let's have an old-skool, 1970s-style strike!' you will say, eating your second lunch of the day. 'Withdrawing our labour – i.e. the posting of pictures of owls looking angry wearing hats, and re-Tweeting amusing cover versions of "Get Lucky"! That will show Twitter what's what! *And* send out a message of peace'n'shizz! *Everyone* will love, and get behind, this idea!' Unless …

2) **When you pick a 'symbolic' date, you fail to check that this isn't also the day the BBC announce the new Doctor in *Doctor Who*.** As soon as you Tweet about your great 'twittersilence' idea, half your potential supporters reply, regretfully, 'Any other day, dude, and I'd be there. Totally. Totalmo. But – IT'S THE NEW

DOCTOR. Gotta Tweet it.' You cannot blame these people. You have made a massive, fundamental error. When, at 7.30pm, the BBC announce it is Peter Capaldi, you regret your own, self-imposed silence. You have a great joke about Malcolm Tucker and the Daleks which, subsequently, other people make on Twitter, leaving you feeling incredibly bitter, and resentful.

3) **It is almost impossible to prevent people from fundamentally misunderstanding the point of your campaign.** Within twenty minutes of suggesting a peaceful vigil, you get people saying, 'I said I didn't want to do it – and now *I'm* getting death threats!' You go on Twitter to say, 'Hey, chill! Don't hassle anyone who doesn't want to do this! I support all methods of protest and support!' Five minutes later: 'My sister's just been threatened with rape. Thanks.' It's at moments like these you can imagine how many times Jesus must have had to say, over lunch, 'Marty, Marty – hey. While no one is more admiring than me of your passion and commitment to my cause, I gotta say, this "Breaking Noses with Bricks for Jesus" campaign is not really where I'm heading to right now. I'm kinda … "parables and martyrdom only".'

4) **When other campaigners make it clear they don't agree with your campaign, try not to take it too personally.** Don't reread what they write, over and over again, going, 'But – why don't they like me?' Don't think about it for four days, solidly, crying and eating Madeira cake out of the packet. Don't start going off into weird fantasies where specific people who've slagged you off happen to see you carrying a stranded dolphin back into the sea, which makes them have the guilty revelation that they have got you all wrong. Don't do that to the point of imagining the best soundtrack to this scene ('Rainbow Connection' from *The Muppet Movie*). You're a campaigner now! Just suck it up!

5) **When the *Daily Mail* runs an online poll called 'Is Caitlin Moran's #twittersilence the action of an attention-seeking egotist?', don't click the 'No' button on the poll.** Don't do that seventeen times. That is a classic trap, dude.

6) **Don't get so upset about the backlash – six *Telegraph* blogs in six days, Toby Young calling you a hypocrite on *Channel 4 News*, thousands of abusive Tweets – that you start bidding on weird things on eBay, at 1am, to comfort yourself.** When, three days later, the £7.99 viscose sky-blue jumper covered in horses arrives, you will be unable to wear it – as it will essentially be the 'Massive Bad Memory-Trigger' jumper. You put it in the bin, thinking, sadly, 'In the bin – *like my idea*.'

7) **Your friends will worry about you.** This will peak when you receive an email from your friend whose partner has a Grade 4 brain tumour, that starts 'Oh GOD are you okay????' You find this difficult to cope with.

8) **But don't regret what you did.** Is the world anywhere near having too many peaceful, well-meaning, *utterly* half-arsed internet campaigns? No. No. And you clearly have a genuine knack for it! You could do it again!

Of course, you don't need the entire internet to bring you low, if you're a woman. Sometimes, your urethra will do that for you.

SLASH & BURN – MY LIFE WITH CYSTITIS

When it comes to teenage girls learning about life through the novels of the late nineteenth and early-to-mid-twentieth century, there is a lot to recommend the notion. Pre-internet, it's how I learned, and it learned me good. I know deep wisdoms, such as, 'If you fancy someone hot who is already married, just wait a while – their wife might catch fire.' (*Jane Eyre*)

However: one aspect that raising yourself on classic novels massively and notably fails in is in the diagnosing of medical conditions, and their subsequent, safe and swift methods of remedy. Because, of course, in the olden days, there *were* no cures. You couldn't do anything about pain, or illness, except divert yourself with time-consuming and disgusting things while your immune system battled away on its own: slathering your chest with hot goose fat, then wrapping it in brown paper and string. Or burning feathers under the noses of the unconscious. Mmm. That's going to cure my fatal heart condition. Smouldering wings. Thanks.

And, so, inexorably, to cystitis. Everyone has their weak spot, and mine is my urinary tract. I suffer from recurrent cystitis. I am versed in the malfunctionings of the bladder. I have an Achilles urethra. Please do not turn away from this page, believing I have been vulgar, or uncouth. None of us chooses our illnesses, and I certainly didn't choose mine the first time I was struck with pain, at the age of fifteen, on a beach in mid-Wales.

As the sun beat down upon my head – mirroring the burning in my atrium – I ran through my internal grimoire of illnesses, culled from the books by my bedside. Was this 'the vapours'? 'The fever'?

'The ague'? 'Dropsy'? 'Furuncle'? 'Grippe'? 'Quinsy'? Was I suffering 'ill-humour'? I certainly felt ill humoured. There weren't many gags to be had in the igneous distress I felt, 12 inches down from my soul. I sat in the sea, and cried.

Three hours later, back in our caravan – after a journey home my memory has kindly scrumpled, and binned – I told my mother I believed I had some manner of quinsy, but in my pants.

'It is the curse of our family,' she said, sadly. 'I have it. And your younger sister. She has suffered for years. It is called cystitis. You will always be slightly unsure of how to spell it.'

'Caz has it, too?' I asked, surprised. I thought back, over the last few years. I just thought she had a generally negative attitude to life. But thinking about it, locking herself in the toilet for hours on end shouting 'Fuck off!' *might* have been cystitis, instead, after all.

My mother then explained, with an even greater sadness, that there was neither cure nor palliative syrup for cystitis, and that the only thing the world had to offer sufferers was a hot-water bottle, clutched between the knees.

Over the twelve years of agony that followed, I learned to loathe the family's hot-water bottle: a pink one with a teddy bear on the front, which came to stand, in my mind, as the coat of arms of pain. I learned that the only real relief came from sitting in a bath – once, for eleven hours, nonstop – topping it up with hot water, and crying.

In 1999, a rumour went around that a foul remedy called 'potassium citrate' would help, and I swigged litres and litres of the poison – a viscid, bitter treacle that promoted impressive retching, and shuddering. The experience was roughly akin to drinking gryphon urine.

I came to share with Caz terrible stories of cystitis's evil. Caz had felt the first, warning twinges twenty minutes into a seven-hour train journey from Euston to Edinburgh, and had no recourse available other than taking a bottle of whisky into a toilet, and drinking herself into numb stupor. I had it at the Glastonbury Festival, and sat in a washing-up bowl of lukewarm water, in a tent, attending the far-off 'whump-whump' of the Manic Street Preachers playing, fittingly, 'Slash and Burn'. Once, I had it at my husband's boss's garden party, in Henley-on-Thames, and had to sit, knickerless, skirt spread wide, on his lawn, releasing tiny teaspoons of terrible hot vinegar, and crying behind my sunglasses while making chit-chat with middle management. That was a low.

We've come to refer to it as 'The *real* Big C', and fear its panging advent like a tiny, pointless childbirth.

Then, when I was twenty-seven, I actually went and saw a doctor about it – bent double and weeping in his chair.

'Your mother was wrong,' he said, briskly. Turned out she, too, had relied on the novels of the nineteenth and early twentieth centuries for her medical information. In the glorious, blessed, holy present, you could actually knock Pants Quinsy on the head in three hours flat with a massive dose of Nurofen, and a course of antibiotics.

In conclusion: classic literature – good for the soul beset by philosophical quandary, bad for the urinary tract beset by E. coli bacteria. I shall be presenting my findings to both the British Medical Association, and the British Library.

Sometimes, it's glorious to be a girl – not least since Lena Dunham's Girls *started airing, in which a host of female characters are allowed to be as venal, dim, misguided, overweight, deluded, amusing and real as men. A huge fan of the show, I went out on to the set for the second series of* Girls, *and I touched Shoshanna's trousers. Bite me.*

ON THE SET OF *GIRLS* WITH LENA DUNHAM: 'SHE IS THE VERY THING'

Brooklyn, July 2012. The Modish Neighbourhood of Williamsburg – 'Billyburg' – the Shoreditch of NYC

It's July-hot – all the rest of New York is bare-legged, and lazy – but this particular residential street bustles, as the caravel of a location shoot has come to town. The street is lined with Winnebagos, generators, and the mandatory sprackling of hot young runners in beanie hats, lolling on doorsteps, languidly thumbing at BlackBerrys.

As you duck under the tape sealing off the street, and walk towards a small, square church – the epicentre of the hustle – you wonder, again, at the sheer logistics of making a television show. All the call sheets and vehicles and phone calls and electricity; the towels and taxis and batteries. All these *people*. A whole village, called into being for months on end. Someone, somewhere, bears a lot of responsibility. Someone, somewhere, made this happen.

Walking into the church – momentarily gloomy – you find that someone, sitting in the control room. This is where the director, and the writer, are glued to a monitor, flanked by a coterie of coffee-bringers, note-takers, technical assistants and producers. This is the pressurised core of the whole show.

Every time I have ever walked into this still, quiet eye of a shoot, the person at the centre is, without exception, a man – a man, in his forties, or fifties. A man, slightly dishevelled, bullishly confident, running things. This is as natural and as immutable as walking into a beehive and finding some bees. That's just who's always at the centre. That guy, thirty years in the business, who looks like all the other guys.

But here, in the centre of this operation – the hub the whole street is revolving around, for HBO's most prominent show – is a 26-year-old woman, in slip-on brogues and a leopard-print shift dress. She has a round, almost child-like face, and is texting on an iPhone with chipped, burgundy nails. She chews sugar-free gum. She looks like an English student, or the keyboard player in an alt-rock band. She calls for quiet on the set, and begins the next take with:

'Everybody – let's remember – this is a show for *smart* people. I read that, once, in a review.'

This is Lena Dunham. Not only is she the director on this show – *Girls* – but she is also the show's creator, and writer. And, in a minute, she will slip off this chair – with 'GIRLS' written on the back – go into the adjacent room, and take the lead role, as Hannah Horvath, too.

Two days before this shoot, she was nominated for three Emmys, for each position she fills on the show: Lead Actress in a Comedy, Director of a Comedy Series and Best Comedy Series. Her show, *Girls*, became the most talked-about, and controversial, show in the US when it premiered in April.

Next week, it starts screening in the UK to an already-formed cult following, who've been illegally streaming it from the US over the summer, and blogging and Tweeting about Dunham with the fervour one usually associates with a pop star.

There has never been anything quite like *Girls* before. There has never been anyone like Lena Dunham – running a massive, pop-culture phenomenon, on her own, at the age of twenty six. To a generation of girls, she is the thing. The very thing. The absolute thing.

'Welcome to the "Women of Excellence Lounge"!' she says, gesturing to an empty chair. 'Come and watch. We're shooting a very exciting scene, about some delicious cookies. And, later, someone dies.'

So what has Dunham done? Two things, really. Firstly, she's brought a wholly new depiction of women to the screen – one which women will find as thrilling, liberating and homage-provoking as men found, say, Woody Allen's characters, three decades before.

There are scenes in *Girls* that will make you gasp. In the second episode, Dunham's character, Hannah, has pretty much the worst consensual sex you will ever have seen with her on/off boyfriend – which includes him vocalising a fantasy that she's an eleven-year-old, and her gallantly trying to go along with it, but failing, before he ejaculates on her chest. You are allowed to find this scene both fist-bitingly unacceptable – but also very funny.

In the third episode, Hannah's more worldly, rock'n'roll yet brittle cousin, Jessa, gets pregnant, skips the abortion appointment her friends have arranged for her ('I can't believe she's late for her own *abortion*'), gets drunk on White Russians in a bar, pulls some guy and, while having sex with him, in the toilets, realises her period has started, as she stares at his bloodied fingers. You are allowed to both find this disgusting – but also thrill at an incident previously wholly unrecorded on television.

In the fourth episode, Hannah contracts a sexually transmitted disease – 'Not one of the famous ones' – and has to contact all her ex-lovers, to tell them the news. She spends the whole episode trying to work out how she feels about having a sexually transmitted disease, before ending the episode changing her Facebook status to the message 'All adventurous women do' – Jessa's laconic comment on how common STDs are with a certain kind of woman.

As the credits roll, Hannah is jumping around her bedroom, in her slightly-too-tight, slightly-too-short plaid dress, to Robyn's euphorically sad Europop anthem 'Dancing On My Own'. You are allowed to feel both sorry for Hannah – and oddly proud of her. The ambiguity in *Girls* is the thrill. It constantly makes you feel two things at once. This comes to its visual exegesis in Dunham's face. As Hannah, the majority of her big reaction shots show her looking – ambiguous. Hannah's only twenty-five. She doesn't know. We don't know. This is not a show shouting out answers but throwing out question marks, instead.

Because of this rawness, there is a pirate swagger to all this stuff – an outlaw edge, made all the more interesting by the fact it's 'just' a sitcom about middle-class girls, where nothing much happens ('It's not like, this week, the gang go to a spa! Next week, the gang go to the Moon!').

In a world full of 'television that looks like television', the absolute sticky, honest ordinariness of it makes it revolutionary. I don't know a woman who has seen it and not immediately texted all her friends, going, 'There is a show about all the things we do, but don't say! This is a show about all the secret things of being a woman! It shows the confusion! This show will make you feel like you are *normal*.'

We are in Dunham's trailer, in her lunch break. She, obviously, looks a lot like Hannah from *Girls* – but more upright than Hannah; less slouchy, brighter, and not in the least petulant. She looks, in fact, like the show-runner of a flagship HBO show – albeit one wrapped in a rather filthy looking fleece, covered in CND symbols.

'It's my snuggie,' she says. 'I once didn't wash it for nine months. I wore it while I was sick, I wore it while I was working. In the end, they had to tell me straight out it smelt terrible. It had the smell of my anxiety on it.'

Dunham's lack of confidence belies her background – she is the daughter of wealthy, middle-class, boho artists (her mother, Laurie Simmons, is a photographer and designer; her father, Carroll Simmons, a painter), whose self-financed 2010 film, *Tiny Furniture*, shot for just $43,000, won the Best Narrative Feature at the South by Southwest Film Festival.

Tiny Furniture is about a self-obsessed artist, Aura (Dunham), who still lives with her parents, has experimental, uncommitted sex, and runs with a close group of friends who are as equally confused about life as she is. In the film, Aura's mother was played by Dunham's real-life mother, and Aura's sister by Dunham's real-life sister. At the time, Dunham was still living with her parents.

Girls, commissioned the same year, under the aegis of executive producer and *Tiny Furniture* fan Judd Apatow, is, essentially, *Tiny Furniture: The Dramedy*. In Hannah Horvath, Dunham plays, again, a confused middle-class, solipsistic NYC girl, running with half the cast of *Tiny Furniture* in barely rebooted roles, still having experimental sex, and still overly dependent on her parents.

Given that Dunham has been dealing with roughly the same material, and characters, for three years, over two projects, it's interesting how controversial *Girls* has still been. For a show in which there are no fight scenes, robots, time travel, espionage, explosions, spaceships, dragons, guns or vampires, *Girls* has had two incongruous charges repeatedly levelled at it. Firstly, that it sets out to be deliberately controversial. And secondly, that it is not realistic. That this – disgusting, ambiguous, venal, oddly innocent, walking around in their pants, with small pot bellies, dancing – is not how women are. That Dunham is doing all this solely to *provoke*.

'I find it all odd,' Dunham says, sitting on the sofa. 'Take the abortion episode. In my life, my mum's had three abortions, my friends have all gone through it without asking a lot of questions. I live in a pro-choice world. So I didn't even understand that it would be a debate – because it was so obvious to me that what we were doing wasn't scandalous. You know? And yet it's "the abortion episode" – in which, ironically, no one even *gets* a fucking abortion in the end, so …'

She raises her hands.

What about that sex scene with Hannah and her on/off boyfriend, Adam – where he wants her to pretend she's a child, and then ejaculates on her breasts?

'Well, this is a show about the kinds of situations women will put themselves in. In that scene, that is one girl with a complicated relationship to sex. It's not *every* woman. Lots of people were like, "Really? Girls your age let boys come on their chests?" And I'm like, well, I don't know, because I haven't had them all check a "yes" or

256

'no" box – but I guarantee it's at least 60 per cent more than are admitting to it.'

It's noticeable that those levelling these charges at *Girls* are always men, or older women. Dunham's own generation, by way of contrast, fell on it voraciously, with cries of self-recognition. It seemed odd that other generations and sexes wanted to just … deny what younger women are up to.

'That was always so shocking to me – because I prepared myself for almost every argument somebody could have except for the one where someone goes, "This isn't real – this isn't your world." The one thing I guarantee I do know is about being middle-class, a half-Jew, half-WASP in New York in 2012.'

The sex scenes in *Girls* – all different, all unusual, in some way or another – are an important part of the show. They're not ever there in the 'happy ever after', 'they have sex THE END' way you see in most shows – something that happens at the end of an episode, as a resolution. In *Girls*, each sex scene is like a number in a musical – moving things on, revealing things about characters. You are never in the same place you started after a sex scene in *Girls*.

'That musical analogy is very gratifying to me,' Dunham says. 'I don't want to see anyone sensually engaging for the sake of it. That's how we move the ball forward, emotionally. That's where we see the characters more deeply.'

Certainly, Dunham seems to view sex in an oddly complicated way – as both a thing to be theoretically prized, or enjoyed, certainly – but also like a puzzle to be solved – something inherently mysterious, and perhaps slightly worrying, in a way that, again, reminds me of Woody Allen. Dunham's characters are constantly trying to work out *why* people want to have sex with them, and how they feel about that – both before, and after. Sex is a question, not an answer, in *Girls*. Do I like bondage? Is this a bad idea? Should we split up? Who wants who more? What does this sex, with this person, mean? What does it say about *me*? Can we have sex in a bunk bed? What about if we have sex in a huge, disused pipe, in an alleyway? It's almost like having sex is like filling in one of those 'Your Personality Type Revealed!' questionnaires in *Cosmopolitan*.

'I feel like I started thinking about it really early,' Dunham says, snuggling deeper under her fleece. 'Not in a "I'm a horny child, I'll hump the armchair" way, but more, "Isn't this so crazy – that this is where we all come from, and this is what we're going to do?" I feel like my whole life from when I found out about sex, to when I finally *had* sex, was like a terrified countdown, to when this would … *befall* me.'

She laughs.

'I remember sitting in my house as a kid and being like, "In ten years, *I might have to have sex.*" I saw an episode of *My So-Called Life* where her best friend goes, "It's terrible once you have sex – because you can't just try it once. You've got to keep on doing it." I was worried about sex before any of my physical instincts or desires had kicked in. It just seemed like … a problem.'

The way Dunham found out about sex may well have contributed to this:

'My friend Amanda told me, and it was terrible! Because she didn't just tell me, she kind of … acted it out on me, like she was the guy. We were in a little house in kindergarten, and she held an invisible penis and said, "It's in your vagina." So I was sitting there, horrified. I went home going, "Amanda put her invisible penis in my vagina!"'

Dunham's boyfriend appears to be a kindred spirit when it comes to this bemusedly uncomfortable view on sex and procreation.

'On our first date, he said he was really upset by the fact that babies come from, in his words, "Sexy fucking", and that he'd like to get his baby at a business meeting, and do sex separately. To not have sex have anything to do with his child at any point. He said he's come to terms with the fact he's going to have to do it, because he wants a child – but he's upset those two things are connected.'

It's tempting to use this as an opportunity to talk about the nudity in *Girls*, by saying, 'Aside from sex, the other issue of note in *Girls* is Dunham's nudity' – but the truth is, *every* aspect of *Girls* is an issue of note. She's called it for a whole generation – for there are boys in *Girls*, too. A lot of them – impressively early. If it took thirty years from the coining of the term 'Generation X' to Douglas Coupland writing a book about it, then Dunham has defined *her* generation, brought it to screen, and been nominated for three Emmys for it – all before anyone has even come up with a name for it.

Her generation, then, is roughly seventeen to thirty: their childhood TV riding the currents between the over-analytical comedy/drama tropes of *Sex and the City*, *Dawson's Creek* and *My So-Called Life* box sets; and the no-holds barred, bare-everything, your-life-is-currency atmosphere engendered by Facebook, *Big Brother*, Twitter, and the Kardashians. It's an age where everyone is an expert on themselves ('The thing about me is …'), and vaguely feels like their life is a movie, or a reality TV show, or a blog. It is a generation constantly set to 'broadcast'.

But, of course, since the economic downturn, and the recession, the only news they have to broadcast is bad. They can't get jobs; they're broke. As they came into adulthood, all the usual markers of growing up – employment, social progress, the chance of owning your own property, and doing better than your parents – have caved in under their feet. There's the sense they don't know what to do with themselves – they are big personalities, raised in a time of expansion, boom and comfort, now dealing with a shrinking, bony world.

As Dunham is the first to chronicle their lives, everything that happens to the men and women in *Girls* is of note: their casual preference for prescription drugs over alcohol. A reliance on their parents previous generations would find shaming, and bewildering. An idea of sex as something both theatrical, and theoretical. The normality of anal sex. Everyone being massively in debt. The proliferation of unpaid internships. All the women greeting each other, habitually, with 'You look *beautiful*!' – an automatic, oddly loaded salutation: 'looks' are being monitored. The pecking order of online social networks – when the cool cousin, Jessa, explains that she's not on Facebook, the others are blown away: guileless Shoshanna gasps, 'Oh my God, you're so *classy*.'

Perhaps the most obvious novelty in *Girls*, however, is Dunham herself, and how she looks.

In a world of pointy-faced, orange ladies with thin, hard legs, she is round-faced, pale, and soft.

The first publicity stills for *Girls* showed her on a park bench with her gang – thick tights, skirt riding up over her thighs, belly gently rounding up to a cheap belt. Fetishably real. The confidence she had for this to be the publicity shot going out to thousands of journalists extends to the show – in *Girls*, Dunham is regularly semi-dressed, or naked: talking to people while pulling a skirt up over Spanx, sitting in a bath eating cupcakes, having terrible sex with a man who grabs her belly and wobbles it in his hands, telling her he knows how she could lose seven pounds. In a 'Circle of Shame' world, where the greatest crime a female celebrity can commit is to put on weight, or wear an unflattering outfit, unembarrassed, casual nudity is Dunham's 'thing'. Along with her frequently looking dishevelled, or sprinkled with acne. Her lack of fear, and vanity, is bracing. What does it mean to her?

'Hahaha!' she laughs, slightly awkwardly. 'It's funny, because it didn't come out exactly the way I saw it in my head. When I imagine myself walking down the street, and then see footage of myself walking down the street, it doesn't look the same. In my brain, I've always been maybe ten notches more classically beautiful than I am. In my brain, I've always been really gorgeous – and they just don't get it yet. There was a certain amount of … deluding myself.'

The first time Dunham appeared naked on camera, it was with a film she made at university, in which she climbed into the campus fountain in a bikini and pretended to shower and clean her teeth, before being moved on by a security guard. When she put it on YouTube, it went viral, and got 50,000 hits. However, it also sparked a debate, in the comments underneath, about the size of Dunham's thighs, and whether she was fat or not. What she had just seen as a jokey film had turned into a debate about her fuckability, and she eventually deleted it.

This level of debate continued when *Girls* broadcast.

'There is hostility – people saying, "Why do you think I want to see you naked?"' she sighs. 'It's like, you put on the television and watched it! It's like when you're on Twitter and someone goes, "I'm really shocked you said that, you should be apologising." You chose to listen to me! YOU ARE FOLLOWING ME!'

One review of *Tiny Furniture*, from critic Amy Taubin, still makes Dunham reel: 'Dunham walks around her apartment in nothing but a t-shirt, forcing us to look at her ass and thighs.'

For women, the public reaction to another woman's body is always interesting.

'I think my motives are varied. There's a part of me that goes, "You think I'm chubby? Well LOOK AT ME NAKED." Then there's also sometimes some feeling of rage. Where it would be fine for you to do it if you had a more traditional body – but you don't, so you shouldn't. Like fat girls should know to keep their clothes on? And [as a woman], you're not allowed to be fine with yourself. There's one day, in seventh grade – when you're like twelve – when it stops being okay to say nice things about yourself. When you're little you can be, "I love my dress! I'm beautiful!" Then a day comes where all your friends are like, "Don't you know that's *not* okay?" When you get a compliment now, you must be like, "No! I'm so fat and hideous!"'

But the fabulous thing about Dunham is her air of not caring. Yes, she has days of freaking out ('I lose my voice. I think it's a physicalisation that I just need to … stop answering people's questions'), and times where, exhausted, she must rewrite scripts overnight ('I collapsed in a little pile. It was hot, impotent, sad crying. But I did it. And the crying helped me get there').

But when talk turns to the then still-forthcoming Emmys, you see, again, how guilelessly swashbuckling she is about the whole thing. Big award ceremonies are, for women, their princess moment: however much of a sclump you play on screen, at the Emmys, or the Golden Globes, or the Oscars, you lose the weight, get the stylist, put on the shoes and have your duckling-to-swan makeover.

Dunham, however, plans no such thing.

'I never imagine my wedding – but I've always loved to imagine holding hands with a faceless guy on the red carpet. And I want to wear a cape. When I told my publicist that, she said, "I'd rather you didn't." But it would be cool! You'd just feel like a … super-person. And my red carpet pose will be either a peace sign, or star jumps. I might star-jump down the red carpet.'

In the event, when Dunham attends the Emmys, six weeks later, she does not wear a cape, or do star jumps, on the red carpet. She wears a pretty blue lace dress, and stands quite still, being normal. She also loses in all her categories – Best Actress goes to Julia Dreyfuss in *Veep*, Best Director goes to *Modern Family* and best writer to the modish Louis C.K. Has some fear overcome Dunham in the month and a half between? Did the pressure of shooting the second series of *Girls* get to her? Even this early on, is she going to bottle it?

The answer comes in the pre-recorded sequence which opens the ceremony. The camera roams around backstage – and finally finds Dunham, in a restroom stall, sitting on the toilet, naked, cheerfully eating cake. Breasts exposed, belly gently rolling, hair cropped short, like a pirate girl. University tattoos still diary-ed, on her arms, and back. She does not look like anyone you've ever seen nominated for three Emmys before. This film projects on a screen, 20ft high, in front of all of Dunham's peers, and to an audience of 13.2 million people.

All the headlines the next day are about her.

All this pressure, in the tiny eye of the storm – but still she holds steadfast, naked, eating cake. She has absolute mastery of the laughter.

Lena Dunham at an awards ceremony is always a joy. I have, of course, spent years preparing for how I would attend a major awards ceremony. After much deliberation, I've decided I shall dress in a Ghostbusters jumpsuit. One with the 'Venkman' badge on, obviously. Everyone wants to be Venkman. All my family have Venkman badges. Except my brother, who is niche, and has one that reads 'Janine'.

WHEN THE OSCARS WON'T BE EVIL

So it's the Oscars tomorrow – the biggest prize-giving ceremony on the planet. Everyone has had an idle thought about winning an Oscar – whatever their actual job may be. The dress; the hair. The epic, barnstorming, score-settling speech – 'And, now, so we turn to Nemesis Number Fourteen, Rachel Whitmore – who, in Year 5, said I looked like a Moomin. WHO'S LAUGHING NOW, RACHEL?' – until the orchestra has to pointedly play you off.

For years, I couldn't work out why an awards ceremony for the film industry was *the* totemic prize-giving event. Surely awards for international diplomacy, medical advances or technology should be bigger?

But then it struck me: of *course* the awards ceremony for the film industry would be the biggest award ceremony – *because it's the film industry, duh*. The one thing they know is how to put on a show – lighting, costumes, music, stories, stars. These are experts in narrative, and sell. And on Oscar night they sell themselves to the world.

So, given that it is the biggest awards show on Earth, it feels like it's time to look at the Oscars and ask: when are they going to stop being such balls? By which I mean – utterly toxic for women. There are places it's worse to be a woman – Afghanistan, for one; and the men's urinals of Foxy's nightclub in Nottingham for two – but Hollywood runs it pretty close.

Last year, 97 per cent of movies were directed/produced by men. Although men and women are vaguely similar – generally the same number of legs, etc. – the stories men and women wish to tell, and listen to, are very different. One only has to compare and contrast the respective conversations on hen-nights and stag dos to see that.

If 97 per cent of the stories are chosen by men, Hollywood is still 97 per cent unequal. In essence, if news of feminism were a car, driving *from* Mary Wollstonecraft *towards* Hollywood, I would estimate it's still broken down somewhere in the middle of the Atlantic right now.

And this is hugely obvious at the Oscars. Evidence one: all the women there are in pain. For the few women actually succeeding in Hollywood, this is their big night of power and triumph – yet all will have been on a diet since six weeks before the Golden Globes, yanked into a dress they cannot breathe in, and will be wearing shoes they cannot walk in.

Their male peers, meanwhile, are walking around, safe in the knowledge that there won't be whole, live TV shows devoted to how they look fat in their dress, or – thanks to E! Entertainment's peerlessly evil 'Pedi-Cam' – have lacklustre toes.

In recent years – as women's power in Hollywood has risen fractionally – there has started to be an acknowledgement of how women will be deemed to have 'lost' an awards ceremony if they don't take on this extra, female-only job, of physically training for it like self-loathing athletes – lest they be derided and denigrated in the media. Julianne Moore accepting her BAFTA with a whimpered, 'I'm so hungry.' Emma Thompson taking off her heels and throwing them into the crowd. Tina Fey referring to *The Hunger Games* with: 'And that's how I refer to the last six weeks.'

So there's a simple checklist here: we will know equality has reached Hollywood when the ladies start rocking up in comfortable shoes and a square meal inside them. For European award ceremonies held in the slashing rain, this will extend to 'Women being able to wear a coat on the red carpet'. It is amazing that, in 2015, a necessary part of being a successful young actress is 'Being able to repel hypothermia, simply through willpower alone'.

The second sign will come in the introductions. Are you a *man* coming on stage to present an award? Get ready to be described as 'insanely talented', 'dynamic', 'inspiring' or 'hilarious'. You'll like that.

Now, are you a *woman* coming on stage to present an award? Get ready for your introduction to sound like it was scripted by a fifteenth-century diplomat trying to sell a potential bride to Henry VIII!

'The scrumptious Cameron Diaz.' 'The enchanting Anne Hathaway.' 'The ravishing Jennifer Aniston.'

It's always with the physical descriptions. This might seem like carping at chivalry – why is it so bad to say a woman is beautiful? – but think about this: some women aren't beautiful. That's just a fact. Imagine a world where we started introducing all men *solely* with physical descriptions: 'The dewy Martin Scorsese.' 'The lissom Clint Eastwood.' 'The hunka burning love that is Judd Apatow.' See how weird it is?

And hey – while we're spring-cleaning the Oscars of bullshit, let's have a quick chat about people of colour. Last year's running gag was on the unpronouncability of ten-year-old Quvenzhané Wallis's name. Just some perspective here: it's not like black Hollywood has a monopoly on weird names. The white people are representing hard with Benedict Cumberbatch, Arnold Schwarzenegger, Michelle Pfeiffer, Sigourney Weaver and Shia LaBeouf.

If the Oscars *is* the biggest award show on Earth, how about it finally stops acting all *weird* around people with darker skin and/or tits, and starts treating them not as freaky guests, but just as much a part of Hollywood as all those normal white guys?

It's been an amazing couple of years, really. I got 35 per cent famous, cut my hair short, got pissed with Benedict Cumberbatch, had two Number One books, gave up heels and finally worked out what that weird smell in the hall was (the lightshade was incorrectly fixed, meaning the seam – fastened with glue – was near enough to the hot bulb to warm the glue, releasing its disturbingly fishy odour. It wasn't that there was a Hellmouth opening up AFTER ALL! It was such a relief).

But perhaps the most exciting thing was making the sitcom Raised by Wolves *with my sister, Caz. Based on our childhood, of being a huge, home-schooled family in the West Midlands, as we were writing it we realised something: this show wasn't, as we'd originally thought, all about the weird teenage girls in it. It was all about the mum, Della. I tried to explain why here.*

MUMS ARE SUPER-HEROES

'Mum' is a pejorative, really, isn't it? I'm sorry to drop such a Downer Bomb the day before Mothering Sunday, but it is. 'Mumsy' clothes, 'Mum-dancing', 'Your mum' – bad, all bad. 'Mum' as an insult rests on the underlying notion that all mums are dull, knackered, sexless husks who – having reproduced – need to just lie down and rot, so that their bodies may become useful to the world again by e.g. helping a tree grow, or providing carrion for a passing fox.

This is odd, given that a notional 'Mum Island' – back off, Channel 5! I've already copyrighted the idea! – would currently be populated by J.K. Rowling, Beyoncé, Björk, Tina Fey, Scarlett Johansson, the Prime Ministers/Presidents of Chile, Malawi, Argentina, Brazil, Bangladesh and Liberia, Shonda Rhimes, Sheryl Sandberg, and more Nobel Prize winners than I have time to count, as I'm doing the school run in twenty minutes.

Mums can, demonstrably, get things done, wear the correct-sized clothing, be wildly creative and dance in a sexy way. So why do we still think of them as Benny from *Crossroads*, but with tits?

I would suggest that film and TV are the problems here. Mums on screen divide into roughly two categories, thus:

1) Sensible dullards like Mummy Pig in *Peppa Pig*, whose job it is to appear in front of Peppa, Daddy and George, and say, 'Are you having *fun* in here? Well, I've come to end that! Come on – everyone wash their hands, and put all the good times away!'
Or:

2) Mums *just* as buzz-kill as Mummy Pig, but lent 'humanity' and 'character' by constantly complaining about what drudges they are, while allowing the children they raised to treat them like dirt. Watching this, I'm like, 'Hey, screen mom – you're a *formative influence* on that kid's life. You were essentially a *god* to them until they were ten. When did you skip the bit where you teach them some freaking manners? How am I supposed to like you when you raised such hateful, misogynist trolls?'

Basically, popular culture has not served motherhood well. It is fascinating that the onset of male puberty has created the sublimated super-hero imagery of Spider-Man (web shooting), Luke Skywalker (light sabre) and the X-Men, but the incomparably more dramatic shift into motherhood gets the alien bursting out of John Hurt – YEAH THAT'S RIGHT, A MAN – in *Alien*, and that's about your lot.

As an exercise, I'm just going to run through, once again, what becoming a mother consists of. First of all, you casually make *an extra internal organ* – the placenta. Like you're some goddamn intergalactic robot UPGRADING ITSELF.

Then you spend the next nine months being a LIVING, WALKING FLESH-NEST: casually absorbing your foetus's endless excreta while you're busy running an international business – something which, in later years, you will find the perfect metaphor for raising a teenager.

Then, at the point where you've grown a skull and a brain big enough to make humans the dominant species on Earth – but still *just* small enough to emerge from your pelvis without blowing both your legs off – a homunculus will effortfully punch its way out of your 'special flower'.

Here – at the point where, in a comparable exercise, a man who'd just passed a microscopic kidney stone would be wheeled on to a ward, dosed with morphine, treated like a brave hero, then left the hell alone – you magically turn your tits into a milky heaven-buffet, and start cranking out fifteen meals a day into a tiny, screaming, ungrateful creature who resembles an enraged otter in a jumpsuit.

Just to, again, get this into perspective – when the most magic man who ever lived, Jesus, turned water into wine *once*, for *one* party, people went on about it for 2,000 years, and formed a major man-religion around it.

Meanwhile, for millions of breastfeeding mothers every day, turning *their bodies* into lunch, the reaction is, 'Bitch, please – don't do that in Claridge's.'

And then, of course, after the first year, the *really* difficult bit starts. The fevers and the ghosts and the sleeps that won't come – the terrible falls, and the bullies, and the boy who breaks their heart, and the hair that makes them sad. And you have to teach them what jokes are, and what death is, and how to charm – all while putting three meals a day on the table, and money in the electricity meter, and joy between every wall in the house, and never, never, *ever* forgetting to try and love every minute, because suddenly, ten minutes after they were born, they slam the front door for the last time, and you are sitting there, going, 'Where did the baby go? Where is my baby?'

The sitcom I wrote with my sister, *Raised by Wolves*, starts on Channel 4 this week, and it centres around a single mother of six, living on a council estate, in Wolverhampton. We knew we'd found the right actress for the part when Rebekah Staton walked in and said, 'I'm going to play her like Clint Eastwood. Is that okay? Like a fucking glorious super-hero.'

And we were like, 'Yeah. How could you play a mother any other way?'

As I am a mother, I am now incapable of not constantly giving out advice. It appears to be hard-wired into you – as soon as people start coming out of your nunny, you begin doling out tips thither and yon, and you cannot stop. You became an advice machine. You are all like, 'Hints and tips are on me!'

ALL THE LISTS OF MY LIFE

Ten Things About Fashion Every Woman Should Know

1) Never buy a 'jumper-dress'. Too bulky to go under a coat outdoors, too hot and sweaty indoors – it's a perfect storm of uselessness. PLUS: will go super-bobbly within three washes, so you'll look like mad sweaty mohair bubble wrap. Avoid.

2) White trousers will *always* make you nervous – however knowledgeable you are about your current place within your Cycle of Red Doom. It's not worth the aggro.

3) Duffel coats are surprisingly waterproof, give off a pleasingly benign air of 'I am a poor student/Paddington Bear, please don't mug me', and go with everything. You *could* spend your life oscillating between wrapper coats/trenches/pea coats/swing coats/capes and faux fur, spending over a grand and cluttering up your coat cupboard. Or, alternatively, bung £78 on a duffel from Toppers and not think about your outer layer again until 2024.

4) Never get an embroidered bra. Under anything more sheer than a massive thermal fleece, it will look like you have a horrific garland-shaped rash all over your wabs – such as harbinged the Black Death, in days of bad yore.

5) In matters of style, the word 'comfortable' is – contrary to everything you've ever been told – your friend. Likewise, 'jolly'. Look, you're a long time dead, and life is hard – do you want to spend your entire life with aching feet and your knickers wedged up your crack, worrying your tits are about to fall out of your top, and pulling down the hem of your 'fierce' dress over your cold, unhappy thighs? I have drilled my daughters from an early age to appraise their own, and others', outfits on whether they are 'jolly' and 'comfortable'. 'That's a jolly comfortable cardigan!' 'Those dungarees look smashingly warm and bright!' 'Mum – Megan Fox does *not* look jolly or comfy on the red carpet. We feel sorry for her.' Feminism will only have done its job when every high-powered woman at the Oscars is as jolly and comfortable as the men.

6) The area between your big toe and next toe is one of the most exquisitely tender and sensitive areas of the body. You will only realise this one hour after buying your first pair of Birkenstock flip-flops, miles from any shoe shop where you might replace them with something less agonising, e.g. a bag full of wasps.

7) Similarly, although Doc Marten boots are among the finest fashion inventions on Earth, do not even attempt to wear them before you have thoroughly smashed every inch of a new pair with a massive claw hammer, to 'soften' the leather. I'm not joking. Huge hammer. Smash smash smash. I still bear scars on my feet from the first, non-hammered pair of Docs I bought – and that was in 1991. Anyone finding my dismembered corpse would look at my feet and conclude, 'This is a Caucasian woman, late thirties, who came of age during grunge.'

Places Where Lost Things Are

1) That drawer full of random detritus in the kitchen.

2) That drawer full of random detritus in the hallway.

3) The pocket of your other coat.

4) In the car.

5) In the taxi you got, drunk, last night. You won't see that iPhone again. Bye bye.

6) In a bag hanging on the back of a doorknob (NB more than 8 per cent of lost things are in this location. Make it your first port of call).

7) In the bedroom of any girl-child in the house over the age of twelve if said item is a) electrical b) a choice piece of your clothing c) your spendy Eve Lom face cream d) high-calorie snacks you had purposely hidden on a top shelf, in order that only you and other bill-paying adults access them.

8) Outside, in your recycling box, in the rain. Right at the bottom. Hurry! Hurry! Here comes the bin lorry! Go out there in your too-short nightdress, and scrabble through it in an ungainly crouch, against the clock! Oh, look – a fox has done its business on top of your recycling! Now you smell like the drains of Mordor! Enjoy your day!

9) In a box folder marked 'IMPORTANT THINGS' that you have completely forgotten about, and won't remember until you move out of your house, seventeen years later.

Reasons Why There Has Never Been a Better Time to Be a Woman

1) Benedict Cumberbatch's face.

2) High-Lycra-content jeans.

3) Like all voting and stuff like that.

4) The two hottest men in the world (Brad Pitt and George Clooney) married human rights campaigners and strident feminists. Twenty-first century beefcake *loves* kick-ass women.

5) Beyoncé.

6) (But not when she does slow-jams about fancying Jay-Z. DO SONGS ABOUT FEMINISM AND DANCING, BEYONCÉ.)

7) Tina Fey and Amy Poehler's brilliant, ongoing female version of a bro-mance. 'Ho-mance'?

8) The fact that, Louis C.K. and Chris Rock aside, the funniest people in the world right now are all women: Melissa McCarthy, Fey and Poehler, Lena Dunham, Amy Schumer, Sarah Silverman, Kristen Wiig.

9) ASOS.com have a search-category 'dresses with sleeves'.

10) The biggest pop star in the world, Taylor Swift, persistently wears comfortable, yet silver, brogues. By my reckoning, this is the first global diva capable of convincingly running after an ice-cream van since Alanis Morissette, in 1991.

11) Only another twenty-five years until the Equal Pay Act of 1975 is estimated to be legally enforced across the board! Hurrah!

12) There is a sitcom about suffragettes (*Up the Women*, BBC2), an Icelandic socialist lesbian Prime Minister who demanded financial reparation from incompetent banks after the 2008 crash, and while Donna Tartt's started a new book, Hilary Mantel's already halfway through hers. Malala has a Nobel Prize, Laverne Cox is on the cover of *Time* magazine, Clare Balding is the person who most represents the values of the BBC, and J.K. Rowling dropped *off* the Forbes 100 List – because she'd given so much of her money away to charity. The three most exciting pop artists in the world at the moment are FKA twigs, Lorde and Kate Tempest, and we have a black first lady who raps on YouTube about turnips. When I was growing up, my choice of female role models was between Margaret Thatcher or Bananarama. Obviously that was pretty great, but – choice! Increasing the lexicon! The present day! You're amazing!

Things Every Teenage Girl Should Know

1) Self-loathing is the default mode of the teenage girl. You are not alone in this. Contrary to what you think, it's nothing to do with how fat your legs are, or the unmanageability of your hair. You are self-loathing because you are turning into a woman – and this seems, to a thirteen-year-old girl, like something exhausting, joyless and high-maintenance, for which you will be constantly judged. And you are right. By and large, that's exactly what being a woman is right now.

2) But you don't need to be like those women. You can *choose* what kind of woman you want to be. And if those kind of women don't exist, you reply, 'Those kind of women don't exist … *yet*.' 'Yet' is going to be a useful word for you. 'The world isn't like that … *yet*.' 'People don't do things like that … *yet*.' As a teenage girl – as the future – YOU are the 'yet'. You are the one who gets to invent

the future. You are the one who gets to invent new women. The kind of women you'd be excited to be. Refer to this process as 'the revolution', for short, as it sounds more exciting. You want the future to be exciting.

3) Start the revolution with you. If you're self-loathing – invent a you you *don't* loathe, instead. Imagine the thing you would want to be – then be it. Make yourself your own project/pet/pretend best friend. Pretend to be confident, happy, relaxed – and you'll soon realise there's no difference between pretending these things and actually being them. Wear a silver cape. Be obsessed with geology. Don't speak until 11am. Intend to be the world's first Girl Beatles. Learn what every drag queen before you knew: fake it till you make it.

4) Your key hobbies need to be long country walks (get some fresh air in your lungs!), masturbation and the revolution. Between those three, you should, in the long term, stay relatively sane.

5) Don't cut your own fringe. It is far, far more difficult than you could ever imagine.

6) For that matter, don't cut anyone else's, either. Good friendships have ended that way.

7) Every time your heart gets broken, breathe deep – it grows bigger as it mends. Imagine each line of red scar tissue on it with pride – the same pride you'll one day have for stretch marks on your belly, after having a baby. Skin and hearts tear to make great things. Don't be afraid.

8) And if your mind tears, do not fear that, either. Depression takes a layer of skin off – so accept that you feel more of the world than most people. Did you hear what I said? YOU FEEL MORE OF THE WORLD THAN MOST PEOPLE. That's amazing. And anxiety works like electricity in your bones – it keeps you wakeful and driven, so use those extra hours – those extra, sleepless days – that your poisoned adrenalin body is giving you. You are living longer. You live in double time. Insist that that's a blessing. Fake that until you make that, too.

9) When in doubt, listen to David Bowie. In 1968, Bowie was a gay, ginger, bonk-eyed, snaggle-toothed freak walking around south London in a dress, being shouted at by thugs. Four years later, he was still exactly that – *but everyone else wanted to be like him, too.* If David Bowie can make being David Bowie cool, you can make being *you* cool. PLUS, unlike David Bowie, you get to listen to David Bowie for inspiration. So you're one up on him, really. YOU'RE ALREADY ONE AHEAD OF DAVID BOWIE.

10) Go out there and change the world, so it works for you, and every girl like you. I know you will.

Ten Things Teenage Boys Need to Know

1) Everything in the previous list. It's all *exactly* the same for you.

Things Cookery Books Never Tell You

1) Whenever it says 'an onion', you should use ten onions.
2) Whenever it says 'a clove of garlic', you should use twenty cloves of garlic.
3) Similarly upscale vanilla, lemon juice, olive oil, salt, chilli and glacé cherries (the last because they're so astonishingly delicious that you will eat half of the tub before you even open the recipe book). Recipe books routinely underestimate how much of THE DELICIOUS THINGS you can handle. You can handle a lot of THE DELICIOUS THINGS.
4) Whenever it says 'leave onions to brown (for five minutes)', that should actually read 'leave onions to brown (FOR HALF A SODDING HOUR WHILE ALL YOUR TIMINGS GO OUT OF THE WINDOW AND YOUR GUESTS BEGIN TO STARVE AND YOU DESPAIR OF THE SISYPHEAN TASK YOU HAVE GIVEN YOURSELF)'. Be wise to this. Start cooking yesterday.
5) Brussels sprouts with goats cheese on them is an ASTONISHINGLY lovely dish – and yet no one will ever believe you. Ever. For it

sounds like the most disgusting thing invented. Bitter ack ack ack sprouts and BOAK cheese that smells of goat. Even typing about it now, I'm dry-heaving into my mouth. I'm REPULSED. And yet, I know that, next time I make them, I'll be hovering over a dish of them in the kitchen, with a fork, going, 'Oh my GOD, these are so unexpectedly moreish!'

6) You will never use that jar of za'atar in your cupboard. You might as well redeploy it as pot-pourri now.

7) Bovril in Bolognese – amazing.

8) Bovril *and* ketchup in Bolognese – you'll lose your *mind*.

9) Cooking might be all well and good – but the best meal in the world is a cheese sandwich, and you know it.

10) Most people, when sharpening knives, cannot help but doing a 'Yeah – I'm sharpening a *knife*. Check me *out*. This is a *primal skill* face.' Do not be one of those people. All the way through sharpening a knife, say, repeatedly, 'Gosh, I'm so sorry I'm just sharpening a knife. I don't even know what I'm doing. I'm an idiot! An idiot with a tool! I'm just using a thing I bought from Lakeland, for £7.99. I am in no way primal. If a bear attacked me, I'd definitely die.'

11) You know Nigella's Sauternes Custard, Heston's Pine Needle Dust Christmas Pudding and Jamie's Ultimate Trifle? They are all, unquestionably, delicious. No doubt about *that*. But if you squared off the ratio of time, effort and cost in making them against a bag of Milky Way Magic Stars, are they *really* better than giving the man in the newsagent's 42p, then choffing the lot as you take the 43 bus down Holloway Road? Nuh.

Things Not to Say on Social Media, as They've Been Colonised by Annoying People

1) 'Mmmmkay?'

2) 'There are no words.'

3) 'No – just no.'

4) In an argument about 'issues': 'You've thrown [subject matter] under the bus!' Dude, you've only got 140 characters. There's no buses on Twitter. Just say 'Betrayed' – then use the seventeen characters you've saved to CALM THE FUCK DOWN. Tweet yourself an emoji of a panda or something.

5) '[name of town or place] I am in you!'

6) '#blessed' (unless you're doing it as a deliberate parody. And even that will probably be passé by next week).

7) 'Nom nom nom.'

8) 'You won't *believe* this!' Note: Humans are a species that still have to consciously work out if unicorns are real or not. Of *course* we'll believe 'this'. We'll believe *anything*.

9) 'Need. Coffee.'

10) 'David Camer-WRONG', 'Tony B-LIAR'. Yeah, we get it, Rik from *The Young Ones*. Now go and iron your yellow dungarees.

Times I've Had My Heart Broken

1) When Andy Taylor (not the one from Duran Duran) told me that David Vaughan was 'only joking' when he asked me out (1985).

2) When the dog died (1987).

3) All of us on the stairs, scared, crying (1988).

4) Artax the horse dying in the Swamp of Sadness in *The NeverEnding Story* (the book, not the film) (1989).

5) Matty Vale asking me if my nickname is 'Fatty' (1990).

6) [redacted] kisses [redacted] in front of me at the Sony Christmas party, and tells me they're getting married (1991).

7) [further redacted] hits me, and I realise that he actually hates me – despite his shoes being under my bed (1994).

8) The midwife says, 'I'm sorry – we can't detect a heartbeat any more' (1999).

9) Coming home that night – me limping, sore – and playing 'First Time Ever I Saw Your Face'. And it hits me that I will never see that child's face. There will be no first time. Two heartbreaks in twenty-four hours. We cannot stop crying (1999).

10) When my firstborn daughter is two, and is so scared of a cow, she farts in fear when it moves near her. I don't know why this breaks my heart. But it does. I cannot bear it. I pick her up and run away (2001).

11) Empty chair around a table on Christmas Day (2008).

12) Three empty chairs (2009).

13) Deleting a number from my phone (2011).

14) Finding the photograph where, now, it seems so, so obvious what would happen next (2013).

15) Storing the chairs in the basement (2014).

Reasons Why the Future Will Be Better Than the Past

1) It always is.

2) David Bowie might play live again.

3) Telescopes keep finding new, bursting nebulae that look like horses, eyes, lava lamps, sundaes, ribbons and spawn. In tens of thousands of colours, across billions of miles, from a trillion years ago. And yet, the amount of matter in the universe has been constant since the Big Bang. Every atom of you, and me, once swirled around inside them. We are all stardust. We are golden. We are unique kaleidoscope rearrangements of everything that has gone before, and everything that will ever come again. The telescopes show us all there will ever be – and, also, right down inside ourselves.

4) You can put a tincture of marijuana in a vape.

5) Tofu technology is *really* moving on.

6) Western culture's voracious hunger for novelty, and the new, means that, eventually, it will be a thirst for new *stories*, and stars, that open up the media, TV and Hollywood to women, people of colour, and LGBT. It'll be the start of the most joyous transfer of power, money and influence ever. We'll laugh, cry and eat a *lot* of popcorn watching this revolution.

7) Every graph plotting the world's wealth, life expectancy, peace and health has been moving inexorably upwards for the last 120 years. We make light out of waves and lungs from machines, and can grow lunch in the desert, or in space. We're a long way off living in mud, wearing mud, eating mud, and screaming every time the sun comes out.

8) We haven't had our black Beatles yet.

9) Or our female Bowie.

10) Or our lesbian Elvis.

11) Or a city run by women, or an empire founded without genocide, or a company run to save the world, or an endangered species, or habitat, adopted by a billionaire – just for lolz – and funded, and protected, until it thrives again. All these things could happen. All these thing could happen *next year*. The world could be unimaginably different, and amazing. Because:

12) It always is.

MORANIFESTO
part three

And so we turn to arguably the most important decision you have to make in your life after, 'shall I fall in love with this charismatic yet bad man?' and, 'will the name "Khaleesi" date well for my baby?': which party to vote for in the next election.

Which party is for you? Who do you trust? Depending on how long you've been on the internet, and which conversations you've been part of, you might just be starting to think that …

The answer to all this might be to just … make something new. Neither left nor right.

Personally, I like capitalism. I think it's got lots of great ideas. I live in it, and it means I have a *lot* of choices for dinner tonight. I believe in people being able to make their own decisions – being able to help themselves, come up with solutions to their own problems, invent things that would be useful to others and make a living from it. Clearly, 'the government' can't do everything. If you're waiting for the state to make a perfect world, you'll be a long time waiting.

But I also like socialism. I think it has a lot of great ideas, too. I've read what happened to the children of unemployed working-class people in a pre-welfare era – Helen Forrester's *Twopence to Cross the Mersey* is both heartbreaking and pitiless – and I can categorically state that the policies of Clement Attlee's post-war Labour government are the only difference between her adolescence (malnourished, uneducated, in rags, constantly ill, despairing) and mine (off down the library/adult education centre, getting antibiotics from the doctor, wearing clean clothes, working as a writer by the age of sixteen). The state needs to be there to help people who cannot help themselves. That's just obvious.

Both capitalism and socialism have brilliant aspects. Both can often work for the betterment of humanity – which is, at the end of the day, surely the point of everything.

But the thing is, as I've become more politically engaged and informed, I've found it harder and harder to know who to vote for. Like most people, I inherited my vote, Labour, from my father. But I've voted in every election, save the last, without ever actually *reading* the Labour party manifesto. I just … believed in them. I was born into it – as you are born, by default, into your parents' religion – without ever making a decision for myself.

How many people have actually read a manifesto? How do we decide to vote? Often, because we're busy, and politics is boring, it's on the back of one TV debate, or because our peer group favours one party over another, or because we just kind of 'like' the leader – he seems like a nice guy, with his kids, and his kitchen.

Really, we often put less thought and research into our party allegiances than we do planning a holiday.

And – if you *are* one of those weird, rare, perverted manifesto readers – how much did you actually *agree* with, and then vote for? People tend to vote for two or three issues – tax, education, healthcare, immigration, the environment – and ignore, or are ignorant, of the rest. We *have* to remain ignorant – or ignore – huge chunks of party policy when we vote. Very few people are purely left-wing, or right-wing. More pertinently, increasingly few people actually know what 'right-wing' or 'left-wing' mean. Ask someone under the age of twenty, and they'll stare at you with the rainbow pinwheel eyes a Mac displays, just before it crashes.

As Armando Iannucci put it in a column in the *Observer*, 'A generation that puts whatever it likes on its playlist, or in its wardrobe, must be asking: "Why do I have to pick between two parties?"'

And – to take his point further – pick between two parties, both founded more than a century ago, when we worked, loved, spent, lived and believed in ways utterly different, and removed, from the lives we have today?

Shouldn't we just ... make new parties? Dozens of new parties? Founded on what life is like now? Built from the ground up, with crucial concerns – the society-altering explosion in part-time work, the need for quality childcare and the awareness of the demographic time bomb of an ageing population – hardwired in, as first-strike priorities, rather than tacked on, as afterthoughts, after the economy?

You know, when it comes to the idea of forming new parties, I find UKIP incredibly inspiring.

I mean, look at them. It is no exaggeration to say that, in the cantina scene in *Star Wars*, a booth containing UKIP's leading members would by *far* be the oddest in the room. Even more than one containing that alien who plays his own proboscis like a flute.

Their raggle-taggle bunch of candidates are openly denigrating of, variously, women ('Do you clean behind the fridge?'), immigrants ('Send the lot back'), and homosexuals (the councillor who, winningly, blamed the recent floods on the introduction of gay marriage) – thus alienating a good 60 per cent of a possible electorate before they even start. It has all the logic of launching yourself as the 'We Hate *Coronation Street*, Biscuits & Sex' party.

In an image-conscious age, meanwhile, UKIP's logo looks like the kind of shonky thing that would be invented by a drunk butcher using an Amstrad in 1998 – a purple pound sign on a yellow circle, that looks like it should be thrust into a window display of meat, next to a sign saying 'MONDAY MINCE SPECIAL'.

Their manifesto declaration claims that 'Political correctness is stifling free speech' – suggesting that the rights of a builder to shout 'Oi! Tits McGee!' at passing schoolgirls without remonstration is the biggest problem we currently face.

Even their name is a bit 'Wha?' 'UKIP' sounds like the kind of acronym you'd find on a dogging website, that refers to a practice so awful, you can't even bring yourself to Google it. 'Couple – he 47, she 42 – seek bisexual younger f for UKIP on Cannock Chase.'

But – *think* about it. If a party as awful and weird as UKIP can build themselves up out of nowhere, fronted by a series of bluff wankers, operating without any credible kind of economic plan, and derided by the rest of the world – yet now command 30 per cent of the vote despite being in total disarray – what could a new party with *noble* intentions, and a *proper* plan, do?

In short – what if there were a good, clever UKIP? A group of ideologues who came to lead political debate with – rather than diatribes against immigrants, smoking bans and Europe – ideas on housing, economic disentanglement from Russia, a living wage and the simple, honourable pursuit of human progress, and joy?

Yes – if I was a young, liberal firebrand, sitting at home, planning to start a new party – planning the revolution – I think the 'inspiration poster' I'd have on my wall, right now, would be of Nigel Farage. Because if he can do it, *anyone* can.

How would we do it?

I believe everyone should write a manifesto. *Everyone*. Even if it's only fifteen words long, and simply consists of the words, 'My manifesto: I would have more shops that sell tea, and fewer that sell coffee.'

This information is important.

Maybe you would be the only person who put this in their manifesto. Or maybe we would find, to our surprise, that *millions* of people *also* put this in their manifesto. We suddenly find – wholly unexpectedly – that this is one of the burning issues of the age. *Millions* of people want more tea shops, and fewer coffee shops.

The next exciting bit is finding out why. Why do people want more tea, and less coffee?

Perhaps it is because they are furious with multinational coffee chains avoiding tax in foreign territories. Perhaps they are enraged by coffee chains' tactics of deliberately opening up next to independent cafés, in order to close them down. Perhaps they believe that the higher caffeine content in coffee, coupled with its rising popularity, has noticeably changed the personalities of people in previously tea-drinking countries: making them more short-tempered, anxious and prone to headaches. Perhaps they wish to reclaim an important aspect of British identity – a brew – that they feel is being eroded. Or perhaps they just prefer tea to coffee.

The *important* thing would be suddenly having the information that *millions* of people are both concerned by this issue and are offering a solution – 'They should serve tea in libraries, with profits funding new books!' 'Companies should be compelled to have signs on their doors stating their tax status and last payments!' 'Independent businesses should receive preferential business rates, in order to encourage British companies!' 'They should bring back hanging!' – all discovered because everyone now writes a manifesto.

I would then have all these manifestos uploaded into a database.

I know I am slightly unusual sexually – I still have a thing for Gonzo from *The Muppet Show* – but I find that quite arousing. The ability to see into the hearts and minds of all my fellow citizens – see their worries, and fears, and hopes – and then scroll through thousands of mad, brilliant, useful, stupid, genius solutions.

Currently, the only way we have to see what people want, and are worried by, are a) polls b) the markets. The reason that capitalism has been, so far, the most successful way to run a society is because the markets show us what people want. Someone invents something, someone else buys it – now we know it was needful.

Compared to communist systems, where it was centrally decided what bread should be made, and where it should be sold – resulting in empty shops and millions of unhappy communists being left without toast, or freedom of speech – the market system palpably works better.

But it's not perfect. For one, it's incredibly wasteful: the millions of tons of unsold clothing, food and goods going into landfill, or being incinerated, tell us that. In the current system, however much research a company does it still can't pre-empt everyone deciding not to buy 2007's ill-advised venture into fluoro vests, and them all ending up on a recycling boat to China. The market provides and the consumers reject. It's a fairly simplistic system – a brutal and dumb tool.

And secondly, it is highly calibrated to *want*, but doesn't really register *need*.

In screenwriting, 'Want vs need' is a key concept for your characters and plot. In *Gone with the Wind*, Scarlett *wants* Ashley Wilkes, the anaemic fop – but what she actually *needs* is to learn to become independent by her own means, and take over Tara. In *Star Wars*, Han *wants* to earn money running a cash-in-hand mission for the Rebel Alliance – but what he actually *needs* is to become part of something bigger, and overthrow the Imperial Forces.

And so it is with, broadly, capitalism vs socialism. We *want* a £3 latte, we *want* an iPhone, we *want* a cheap top from Primark. These are the things that drive us. We don't mind paying for them. Indeed, culturally, to spend money on these things is a signifier of self, and status.

But what we *need* is a well-run society, with infrastructure, healthcare, education and justice. The thing is – as Scarlett and Han could tell you – your *wants* are what tend to get you out of bed in the morning, and motivate you in the short term. You tend to find your *needs* – possibly accidentally – later on. They are part of a grander narrative. And, in the beginning, they tend to be harder to sell. Han would never have put his life, *Falcon* and Wookiee in danger to fight for freedom at the beginning of the movie.

We're far happier to pay for *wants* instead of *needs*. No one ever got angry with society for Kit-Kat Chunkies going up to 52p. But suggest an income tax rise to pay for sustainable fuel, and the outrage leads to it being scrapped – despite the fact that a) we will palpably run out of oil in a way we will never run out of Kit-Kat Chunkies and b) Kit-Kat Chunkies are arguably less useful to us, in the long run, than the polar ice caps.

Also – annoyingly – we tend to find out what we *need*, and learn it's not available, at times in our lives when we are too busy to protest much about it.

By the time a big *need* kicks in – say, emergency psychiatric care for a loved one undergoing a massive psychotic breakdown – you're too busy talking them down off a multi-storey car-park roof to organise a protest against mental healthcare provision in this country.

That's the big difference between a 'want' and a 'need', when it comes to using the market as your main metric. It doesn't make any difference to the market how much you *need* something. The markets are blind to *need*. The markets are, bluntly, wholly unaffected if you die. Capitalism doesn't register, anywhere, loneliness, anxiety, depression, homelessness or death – unless they affect your ability to contribute to the economy.

Here are other things capitalism doesn't register – which it is wholly blind to: birdsong, informal support networks run on love, non-abusive childhoods, jobs with prospects, optimism, peace of mind, stories that change people's lives, pop stars who inspire, pride, beautiful buildings, public spaces, neighbourliness, and having somewhere nearby you can walk to, and sit, and feel content.

And that's why we know capitalism isn't perfect – because humans do register an absence of these things, painfully and viscerally. Humans invented capitalism – but we haven't yet found a way to make capitalism, in essence, *see* us. All of us. So far, only the socialist invention of the Welfare State has done that – has specifically set out to address the non-profitable *needs* of people, when they cannot fix their problems on their own.

And so here we are in 2016 – seesawing, roughly a decade at a time, between left-wing and right-wing governments; capitalism and socialism; wants and needs. Each one coming and largely undoing the efforts of the previous government, in a blunt, unwieldy attempt by electorates to find some kind of balance between the two systems.

The thing about having all this information – all this connectedness, all this processing power – is that it should allow us to, finally, start being able to see what *actually works*.

One of the most alarming things about the 2008 crash was a procession of worried-looking economists appearing on late-night news programmes and debating what to do next. Half argued for Keynesian policies – half argued for austerity measures. But nobody seemed to *know*.

To someone sitting on a sofa drinking a cup of hot Bovril, this seemed nuts. We've had nearly a century of both approaches now – FDR used state intervention during the Great Depression in 1932, the New Deal was one of the defining political ideas of our age, and we've seen a lot of free-market economics since – surely economists can learn from past experience and have *some* idea of which method edges it, when the world teeters on the brink of financial collapse?

I'm well aware there are a billion complicating factors that can skew the results either way – no one can be 100 per cent sure exactly *why* some methods worked, at the time, while others didn't – but we live in a world of fabulous processing power now.

If you were to build a jet engine in the 1950s, as Paul Mason pointed out in *PostCapitalism*, you would design them on paper, stress-test them using slide rules and construct full-sized templates on silk.

'When we designed the tail fin of the Tornado fighter we did twelve stress-tests on it,' a veteran US Army engineer explained.

Since the advent of virtual 3D mock-ups on super-computers, however, the process has changed entirely: 'With [the Tornado's] replacement, the Typhoon, we ran 186 million [tests].'

And all without a single thing crashing, or causing injury. Even if we don't have the processing power *right now* to model the infinitely more complex structure of a global economy, we are surely not far off. And we would surely have it sooner if someone decided to pursue the idea.

And you wouldn't use such a thing just for modelling economic policy. You'd use it to model education, healthcare, social provision, housing, travel infrastructure. And the advantage you would have, in the modern age, is *people*. People, who could interact, and input their decisions into this programme.

If it ran alongside Twitter, or Facebook, or Google, whenever someone went online they could be asked the questions the programme is running that day. Let's face it – people *love* doing this shit.

It could also alert you to key pieces of information – such as 'Britain is experiencing a huge shortfall of electricians' – thus allowing you to tell your child, who is planning their GSCEs, that they might want to change their choice.

And once we had all this information about what things actually *work* – rather than political theories and tribal beliefs – then *that* is what we would form our new parties from. The first ever political party that would have run prototypes, and had peer-reviewed papers. We do this in medicine, and engineering, and in our leisure time – all plays get months of rehearsals and previews. So why not politics?

We would have invented a Wikipedia of politics – an open-source resource to which everyone could contribute. An aggregation of everything we have learned, across the world – all being updated in real time, on a scale unimaginable for any government or business. Really, it seems extraordinary we haven't invented it yet – it does highlight the data shallowness of something like Google, or Facebook. Every day we create as much information as we did in the years between the dawn of civilisation and 2013. Five exabytes of data every two days. The average online citizen creates a data trail that, if rendered in zeroes and ones, would stretch to Mars and back.

And yet, currently, we use this information to do little more than sell advertising. This is the ultimate weak spot of capitalism: capitalism. We are constantly told it sees the bigger picture – but what it does, instead, is simply make the picture of *itself* bigger.

Being of a minxish mind, I would call this huge resource – in size, a rival to Wikipedia, or Google – 'God'. God's purpose would be to constantly try and find the best of all available options, from around the world: suggested and explained by the people who'd invented it; the employees who'd made it work; the patients, pupils and citizens who'd lived through its implementation.

Just as now, on Amazon, one can peruse hundreds of different hosepipes on offer, and then see what the customer rating is, and their comments on the products' flaws and triumphs, so we would be able to peruse educational models, legislation to curb sex traffic, planning regulations, systems of care for children and the elderly.

This system would also defuse one of the most poisonous aspects of our current system: ministers being afraid to make decisions; or being pressured into making them after being lobbied by corporate interests, or their drinking buddies. As a socialist, I enjoy the irony of this, but this system would allow market forces – in the role of citizens' decisions – to finally come to bear on policy.

'But, Cat, people would still lobby!' I can hear naysayers saying. 'It would still be a system open to corruption – interested parties could swamp the site with positive reviews of things *they* have a stake in!'

To which I would reply: yeah, but that happens anyway. At least with this system, you've got a *far* better chance of detecting it happening than with the current system, where it all happens in small rooms, closed from public view. Anyone reasonably proficient in IT would be able to notice what was going on, and track it down – and from their bedroom, rather than going through files in a basement.

(As a sidebar, I would suggest that this model should be the one unions should adopt, if they wish to survive in the twenty-first century, and reinvent themselves for a modern working world dominated not by men, in factories, but women, and part-time work, and zero-hours contracts. Unions should become something not just to block management, but as a repository for ideas and innovation: helping their employers from the ground up, just as the working classes have done throughout the ages.

The union movement needs to refind its intellectual roots – publishing papers, encouraging new kinds of membership and leaders. A union should come to mean the power of crowdsourcing – an organisation with an unparalleled specialised overview of its industry, and a hive-mind of millions. Something *worth* millions, to business – rather than something simply to be battled with, for the sake of the balance sheet.)

(As another sidebar, I'd also invent a 'Local God' – something dedicated to your area, which shows you what's going on, and how you can get involved – like a massive societal 'To Do' list. You've got a Saturday morning free, you feel like you want to do something noble, you log on, and it lists all the things going on in your area: some people are planting up the borders in your local park. There are five kids in the local care home who don't have any visits planned. Your elderly neighbour, five doors down, has posted a request for someone to come and mend her door. A mum has suggested that you come and babysit her kids while she goes for a swim, in exchange for having yours this afternoon.

No community-minded urge – no desire to do good would ever be wasted. Local God would show you every place you could be useful, and make a change. Local God loves the fact that every human being wants to be good. Local God knows you don't want to waste a minute of your life. Local God also probably works some kind of scheme where the more good you do – shown in your profile, in some kind of ranking system – the bigger discount you get at your local, involved shops; thus making any idea of a 'Big Society' both actually practical, and of deeper use and value to the people engaged in it. It would put a financial value on doing the traditionally unpaid care work that disproportionate amounts of women and the working classes engage in, and make the whole system fairer. I've got to admit – I fancy Local God quite a lot.)

So this would be the basis of a new political party – to take the working methods of science, medicine, technology, gaming and art, and apply it to the formulation of policy.

Obviously this – like many of the things here – will probably look hopelessly pie-in-the-sky and impractical, or weird, or demented, or just plain wrong. But I'm going by the principle that, when I read *A Hitchhiker's Guide to the Galaxy*, I thought, 'Oh my God! The *Guide* is such an incredible idea! A small electronic tablet you hold in your hand, which tells you everything you need to know at the press of a few buttons! Douglas Adams is a brilliant man – but clearly one who has smoked a *lot* of marijuana, and is definitely best off making up weird things in sci-fi novels. They could *never* invent such a thing.'

But now, in 2016, I carry my iPhone everywhere, and it tells me what restaurant to go to; how to say 'is this consommé or a finger bowl' in French; and make the Ron Burgundy-themed 'Glass Case of Emotion' cocktail (muddled rosemary and peach, whisky, lemon juice). Sometimes you just need to throw your new, mad, invented balls on the table and see who runs with them.

So, yes: this is a brief summation of all the things I've sat on the patio at 3am, fired up on gin, and ranted about, as friends with slightly more political/economic/social grounding go, 'But, Cat! This is drunken loon-guff! I would stop you right now with a few facts, but I'm worried that you will then return to your activities of an hour ago, where you were crying and saying, "Man, I miss Freddie Mercury," while singing "Under Pressure" in the manner of a wolf being clubbed to death by a duck.'

But then – and I'm going to be blunt about this – I think it is the solemn duty of *every* citizen to dream of mad futures – just as, 100 years ago, they might have dreamed about votes for women, a black US president, being able to marry the person you love irrespective of their gender, heart transplants and *RuPaul's Drag Race*.

The future wants you. Because that's your eventual home. Like Philip Larkin's 'Days', we have nowhere else to live.

THE FUTURE

When you're younger, you don't care much about the future. That's where all the old people will live. But it turns out that the world keeps on travelling forward, unstoppably, at twenty-four hours pver day. And suddenly, BANG! You are the old people now – and it's on you to make sense of the world; uncover truths; fight for better things. Steer the ship. You are the generation in charge of the world, now. This is all on your watch.

This part of the book, then, is about that process: trying to understand what's going on. Who made this future, that we live in now? On what basis did they make these decisions? Do we trust their decision-making process? And, most importantly – do they care about the future yet to come? Do they know how quickly the next thirty years can arrive? Are they planning great, right things? Are they already looking 2050 in the eye, and saying, 'Let's make sure you are better than where I stand now'?

For me, one subject dominates this decade: migration. The summer of 2015 saw the greatest refugee numbers in history – 60 million on the move; boats full of people, escaping cities on fire. Perhaps things will have changed by the time you read this, but at the time of writing, the world does not have a proper plan to deal with this wholesale emptying of countries. Columns of refugees, miles long, walking down roads, carrying children – a whole generation going to waste; whole nationalities becoming like albatrosses – seen as unlucky, never allowed to land.

But the summer of 2015 will be as a mere bagatelle if even the mildest predictions about climate change are correct. By 2100, 150 million will live on land that will either be so regularly flooded as to become unusable, or will be permanently submerged. One hundred and fifty million on the move. What will we do? Build new cities – or build walls around the old ones? Will we welcome them in – or leave them in medieval camps on the edge of twenty-first century cities? Remember, the places that will be flooded will include Miami, London, Barcelona, Istanbul, St Petersburg, New York ... how we deal with Syrian refugees now is how others will be dealing with our grandchildren. Oh, the future! You are already asking us questions. Terrifying questions we must be adult enough to answer.

But! There is hope! Because, as I explain, if we can invent New York, we can invent our way out of anything.

However, we start with the little things, first. Me and Pete, in bed.

I LOVE PETE'S CAR

It's 11.01pm. *Question Time* has finished, and we have decided – as always – that we cannot face the indefinably weird *This Week*, starring Andrew Neil.

I turn the TV off and curl around Pete's back.

'It's our twentieth anniversary in February,' I say, sleepily. 'Two decades since I first saw you! You were the first boy I ever met who made me feel *normal*. But at the same time, you were also the first boy I ever met who made me feel *special*. Isn't it funny how that inherent contradiction lies at the heart of true love?'

I snuggle up close to him. I am glad to have given him the gift of my spontaneous profundity – and at a time when most other couples would just be saying, 'But why has Andrew Neil dressed up as an elf to talk about Europe? I don't understand' instead.

Pete is silent.

I smile, knowingly, to myself. Yes. Yes – there *isn't* much you can say when your wife's just been dead freaking wise.

Eventually, however, Pete speaks.

'And as well as all that "normal" and "special" stuff,' he says – almost as if he can't help himself – 'I was also the first boy you knew … *who had a car.*'

It hangs there for a minute.

'Are you saying that's why I was really attracted to you? *Because of the car?*' I ask.

Pete goes tense, in the way that he does when he's scared. This is how he reacts whenever I say, 'I've had an idea!', or … well, mainly 'I've had an idea!'

'I want to make it *very* clear that was *just* a joke, and that I'm going to sleep now. *Goodnight*,' he says, closing his eyes.

I let a whole minute pass.

'Oh, my God, Pete – you've just negated love!' I say. 'You've just ended a day with Love Negation! That is *poor* relationshipping.'

Pete exhales. I realise he has actually been holding his breath for the last minute. As if, perhaps, trying to die rather than have this conversation.

'This is unbelievable. I'm not into *cars*,' I continue. 'I'm *famously* not into cars. Remember when John bought that new Jaguar – and I wouldn't even leave the house to look at it because *Hello, Dolly!* was on? And that was a fifty grand, duck-egg-blue Jag. Back in 1995, you were just pimpin' around in your mum's red Peugeot. I don't *care* about cars. I'm not a … *Clarksonsexual*.'

'I—'

'I am, however, HURT,' I say. 'As someone who is very deep, I am *hurt*.'

There is another pause.

'It's not so much that you were into *cars*, back then,' Pete says – clearly keen to clarify. 'It's more that you weren't into …. walking around in the rain that much. I remember the first time I picked you up from your house. You got into the Peugeot with an expression on your face which said, 'Wow – I can have love, *and* not be on a bus.' I was part of a package. It was me *and* the car. I'm being self-deprecating here.'

I fall silent as I think back, to the start of our love, in 1995. I couldn't drive, I had no car, and I lived very far from a supermarket. When I met Pete, everything changed.

I can remember the drunken conversation I had with my friend Sian. Opening a bottle of Baileys, exclaiming, 'Oh, my God – he took me up the Big Sainsbury's!' Then explaining that wasn't a euphemism, and pointing at all the heavy, jumbo-sized tins I'd been able to buy – because I didn't have to drag them back on the bus.

I thought about the twenty years since – in which I've steadfastly continued not to learn to drive. The million times I've spent too long backcombing my hair, and Pete's looked up from his laptop and said, 'It's too late for you to catch the bus – let me give you a lift to the Tube station, instead,' and shuffled towards the front door in his Crocs, jangling his keys.

Him doing the school run twice a day, for the last nine years, as I have a lie-in 'just this once' (every day for the last nine years).

How, when we go out, he'll end up giving a lift home to five of my drunken friends – all rammed in the back of his Ford Galaxy.

How he's the one who picks up the parcels from the post office; or gets bread at 9pm, when we run out. Those endless, day-long drives back from holidays in Cornwall, where he's exhausted, while I'm in the passenger seat, going, 'Look! A hawk!'

How, when I'm in the car with him and he accelerates, or reverses into a very tight parking space, I can't help making small, primal squeaking noises of excitement.

And, still, staying nice and dry while I'm taken up the Big Sainsbury's.

'Pete,' I say, eventually. 'I think you might be right. I might actually love you because of the car.'

But I say it quietly, because I don't want to wake him. He's got to get up early for the school run tomorrow.

So much of what is wrong in the world is explicable when you realise one, simple thing: everyone thinks they are the normal one. Everyone thinks they are medium.

EVERYONE THINKS THEY'RE MEDIUM

I've recently swapped running for swimming – my knees are going, and, unused, my arms were starting to get string-like and disproportionate, like a T. Rex.

In all, it's been a pleasant return to the pool. As a keen childhood swimmer, I easily slipped back into the customs of the place – thoughtfully removing the Tribble-like lump of collected hair from the shower drains, in order to make showering more agreeable for the next user, and eating a whole packet of crisps on the bus on the way home, because I'm *starving*.

Indeed, there has been only one floating verruca plaster in the otherwise serene waters of my joy: 'Medium'.

My local pool has three lanes. These are clearly labelled thus: 'Slow', 'Medium' and 'Fast'.

In the 'Slow' lane, adult learner swimmers bob around on noodles, laughing their heads off.

In the 'Fast' lane, meanwhile, three men in tiny trunks speed up and down – giving the impression that they are swimming to a very important business meeting, and must not be disturbed in any way.

And in the 'Medium' lane – everyone else in Haringey, a million people, all packed together, in Medium Soup.

The problem is this: only ten of those people should actually be in the 'Medium' lane, tops. Believe me, I've swum behind all of them, and people – your breaststroke is no 'Medium'. There are people on the International Space Station decanting cold treacle out of tins showing more hustle. You are a SLOW. Your spirit animal is the SLOWTH.

This is not a personal evaluation from me. I would merely draw your attention to the 'MEDIUM' sign at each end of the lane.

'MEDIUM: lengths in twenty-eight seconds or less.'

It's there on the board – the *official* definition of 'Medium'. And yet, everyone swimming slowly in the Medium lane absolutely ignores it – because they 'feel' medium, inside, instead, and that's what *really* counts, to them. They just *want* to be medium, despite all the facts.

Exactly the same thing happens on the motorway. Slow lane: empty, save the odd Polish artic. Fast lane: three men angrily swarming towards a meeting in Donnington at 101mph. Middle lane: 50 million people in a terrifying, tailgating Medium Soup, all the way from London to Birmingham, because they 'feel' middle-lane-ish, despite all the facts.

Because, in this country, everyone wants to be a medium. We *all* feel medium. If I were to choose just one thing that defined 'Englishness', it would be that. We want to say that we are in the middle.

Indeed, the English love 'medium' so much that we put a moral value on it. Being in the middle – neither excessive nor spare; neither too loud nor too quiet; too clever or too stupid; too flash or too dowdy – is the 'right' thing to be. Think of all the things we trust the most: John Lewis, gently rolling countryside, the middle classes, Radio 2. We love a happy medium. We feel most comfortable when we're bang in the centre. Even if, really, we're not. Even if we're eccentric or brilliant or broken or different or angry or pioneering or evil or half asleep – we all like to think we're *just like everyone else*. Wherever we are, that must be the centre. Whatever we are is normal and reasonable and right.

And so, inevitably, to the bit where, in my swimming costume, reeking of chlorine, already thinking about the crisps, I realise I'm actually doing lengths in the middle of a massive societal metaphor.

I'm looking at the pool – at all the stubborn people in the 'Medium' lane, *agonisingly* slower than 'twenty-eight seconds per length'. Women who've come down with a couple of friends, and are all swimming a slow breaststroke together – convinced that they are 'Medium', even as faster swimmers pile up behind them – or stop entirely, in frustration.

And I thought, 'Oh, my God – this is British politics! The 'Medium' lane is the 'middle ground'! The Libs and the Labs and the Cons all claiming *they* are right in the middle, they are the normal ones, they are average. Even with a referendum on the EU, and privatising the NHS, and cutting welfare, and university fees – they *all* still claim the middle ground. None of the three big parties would *ever* say they were being radical, or innovative, or different. None of them will ever move out of the Medium lane, whatever speed or stroke they're doing.'

And I watched the people who *are* naturally 'Medium' – who really *do* do a length in twenty-eight seconds or less – getting frustrated with this bastardised 'Medium' lane, and ducking under the lane separators. Some going left, and harassing the 'Slow' swimmers. Some going right, and getting in the way of the 'Fast' swimmers. And some getting out of the pool completely.

And I thought about Nigel Farage, and last summer's riots, and declining voter turnouts, and how dry this pool is making my hair.

And I thought: 'Medium' does mean something. You can't just claim it if you want it. It means 'twenty-eight seconds per length'.

As a home-educated, part-feral child, nearly everything I am was collated from books. I read myself a new brain, and then a new life – I venerated books like others venerate jewels, or land. And then … I kind of forgot. I spent ten years forgetting what a book can be – and what you are, when you read a book – until I was asked to judge the Baileys Women's Prize for Fiction, in 2014. We gave the award, in the end, to Eimear McBride's extraordinary A Girl Is a Half-formed Thing, *which I recommend until I burst. I am sure there are girls out there reading it, now, who are having their lives changed as surely as mine was by the volumes by my bed, twenty years before.*

READING IS *FIERCE*

Since I had kids I've had the perfect excuse not to read: I have kids.

'Where would I find the time?' I tetched at inquisitors – a sorrowful committee of literary characters in my head, who were sad that I didn't hang out with them any more.

'It's all right for you, Gandalf, Jane Eyre, Oswald Bastable, Boo Radley and the sexy blokes out of *Riders*,' I continued, as they looked accusatory. 'You're all childless. You don't have to walk in the pissing rain to the nursery, then get back in time to put on a wash. Get bent.'

'When you were young, you used to read a book a day,' Prince Andrei Nikolayevich reminded me, sadly. 'Although, to be fair, you did only manage *War and Peace* in a day by skipping through all the passages on farming while shouting, "WHERE ARE THE SEXY BITS?" But now look at you – reading just ten books a year.'

'Yeah,' a random alcoholic man from a Raymond Carver short story agreed. 'You're out of the game, lady.'

The random Raymond Carver alcoholic then started trying to unadvisedly bum a lift from someone in J.G. Ballard's *Crash*, and I had to simply walk away from them, before it got messy, in order to put the tea on.

It was against this perfect excuse, then, that when I was asked to be a judge on the Baileys Prize, I surprised myself by saying 'yes'.

'It means reading fifty-nine books in five months,' they warned.

'I can handle fifty-nine books in five months!' I said, cheerfully. 'I'm going to become a reader again!'

Three weeks later, and I was physically sick with literature. It was a rainy day, and I'd spent ten hours straight reading Eleanor Catton's *The Luminaries*, finished it, put it down, and then did five hours on Margaret Atwood's *MaddAddam*, until 2am. I'd gone from a book set in a New Zealand gold-rush town in 1866 – all muddy skirts, opium, shipwrecked boats and murder – to a dystopian future where human clones and super-intelligent pigs scrabbled in the post-Apocalyptic rubble. My brain reeled like a drunken gyroscope – I was both discombobulated and elated. I was alight. I was exhausted. I was flying.

Because what judging a literary prize did was remind me of what I knew when I was eleven, and was wiser, and forgot as I got older, and stupider: that reading is not a passive act. That it's amusing that 'bookworms' are thought of as weak, bespectacled and pale – withdrawn from the world, easy to beat in a fight.

For a reader is not a simple consumer – as you are listening to a record, or watching a movie. A reader is something far more noble, dangerous and exhilarating – they are a co-artist.

Your mind is the projection screen every writer steals; it is the firing of your neurons that makes every book come alive. You are the electricity that turns it on. A book cannot live until the touch of your hand on the first page brings it alive. A writer is essentially typing blank pages – shouting out spells in the dark – until the words are read by you, and the magic explodes into your head, and no one else's.

Consider me, now. If I type 'dragon' – casually, just six letters, no effort for me – suddenly, a dragon appears in *your* mind. *You* have to make it. Your brain fires up – perhaps your heartbeat will speed a little, depending on if you have had previous, unhappy experiences with dragons. Perhaps you will have given her golden claws – or maybe you have a fondness for tight, black shiny scales, instead. But however closely I have described her, she will still be *your* dragon – in your head, a result of your million tiny acts of birth. And no one else will ever see her.

And so to read is, in truth, to be in the constant act of creation. That old lady on the bus with her Orwell; the businessman on the Tube with Patricia Cornwell; the teenager roaring through Capote – they are not engaged in idle pleasure. Their heads are on fire. Their hearts are flooding. With a book, you are the landscape, the sets, the snow, the hero, the kiss – you are the mathematical calculation that plots the trajectory of the blazing, crashing Zeppelin. You – pale, punchable reader – are terraforming whole worlds in your head, which will remain with you until the day you die. These books are as much a part of you as your guts, and your bone. And when your guts fail and your bones break, Narnia, or Jamaica Inn, or Gormenghast will still be there: as pin-sharp and bright as the day you first imagined them – hiding under the bedclothes, sitting on the bus. Exhausted, on a rainy day, weeping over the death of someone you never met, and who was nothing more than words until you transfused them with your time, and your love, and the imagination you constantly dismiss as 'just being a bit of a bookworm'.

So this is what I remembered, as I judged a literary prize, this summer. Being a reader. The unseen, life-changing duet you sing with anyone who's ever written a book.

I've written about libraries before, in Moranthology *– how my local library was a cross between a life raft, an emergency exit and a festival – theme park of the soul, cathedral of the imagination.*

I went back to my library, in the winter of 2015. And what I saw broke my heart.

AUSTERITY – THEY KILLED MY LIBRARY

I went up and saw some of the austerity last month.

I hadn't intended to – I was just visiting my old home town – but I ended up in my local library: the one I lived in between the ages of five and fifteen. And there, in the library, was some austerity. A visible thing. Something you could mark on a map, with a pin.

I've written about that library before. About how this place was the delight of my life – a thing I would have married, in my pre-pubertal anthropomorphic phase. I would have been as happy as a clam – and, if the gods had so blessed us, in later years, I would have got pregnant by that library, and we would have raised a couple of little mobile libraries together.

It was a 1960s red-brick cube, with the shelving inside packed tight. And the shelving had to be packed tight, for there were so many books inside – that place was rammed full of every and any kind of book you could think of. Carousels of 'trashy' paperbacks. Big shelves for atlases, and illustrated histories of the wars. Smaller shelves for hardback fiction. Audiobooks, which I was very snobbish about. 'I have read 337 books,' I wrote in my diary. 'I mean *properly* read – with my eyes. *Not* audiobooks.'

I learned *everything* there. Sex, witchcraft, baking, butchery, geography, navigation. I read Larkin sitting on the lawn outside, and I cried to be the real girl, in a real place, from his 'Lines on a Young Lady's Photograph Album'.

That library was a Pandorica of fabulous, interwoven randomness, as rich as plum cake. Push a seed of curiosity in between any two books, and it would grow, overnight, into a rainforest hot with monkeys and jaguars and blowpipes and clouds. The room was full, and my head was full. What a magical system to place around a penniless girl.

But then twenty first century austerity. I knew what the cuts had done to libraries – I'd seen the piles of books for sale outside libraries in Swindon, and in Barnet. But they weren't *my* libraries – so I couldn't calibrate what was being thrown out, and what was being kept. I could when I went back to Wolverhampton, though – because that library is the inside of my head. I know everything about it.

And *everything* had gone – or near enough to make no difference. Most of the stern, tight shelving gone – and all that was left was racks of Andy McNab, and *Fifty Shades*, and rip-offs of *Fifty Shades*. So few books. Weepingly few books.

To the side, a single, lonely carousel labelled 'Classics' – in the midst of all the pink and gold-embossed lettering, the Brontë and Dickens looking like martinets in the middle of a hen-night. And, by the door, old books piled high, for sale: the history books, the maps, the novels and poetry.

Now, you may say we have no need for reference books any more, now that we have the internet. Why go to a library (because you need to get out of the house! Because you will *die* if you stay in the house!) when you could just Google something (because you have no computer! Because you are old, or poor, or in a valley where broadband does not venture!), instead?

Well, because a search engine will just show you what is most *popular* – rather than what is *best*. You, like a billion other Googlers, will be herded to the footage of a shark biting a man, or the same shallow Wikipedia entry: we are all reading the same 10,000 words; walking the same paths; thinking the same thoughts; filtered through the single lens of Google. We are approaching a mono-knowledge – diametrics herding us; migrations of thought, as unquestioning as a million dumb buffalo.

But do we need libraries to be clever? What is wrong with a room containing only light modern fiction about mercenaries, and submissive sex? Can the working classes not have rooms of cheap pleasure?

What's wrong is this: it will not survive. If you take the intelligence, and knowledge, out of a library – if you take away the purposefulness, the *usefulness*, so that it is filled only with sugary treats – then when the next round of austerity cuts come in, that library will die. No one will fight for it – no one *can* fight for a room like that. How could you argue to put money into that neutered, monosyllabic, intellectually sterile room when [hand gesture] hospitals and [hand gesture] schools need it more?

This is a tactic we must all grow furious about. That when something cannot be axed straight away – because it is important, because it is loved, because people protest – that thing is then starved, or bled, until it is a weak, mutant ghost. Until no one wishes to defend it. Until no one *can* defend it – because all the words they could have learned, and used, are now heaped up by the door, for sale.

Until, walking into that room again, twenty years later, you cry, 'My God, my love – what have they done to you? What have they done to your brilliant, brilliant mind?'

As discussed in Part One, one of the key things we need to get our heads around is that change doesn't come all at once – it comes in tiny steps. And even though you wish for great steps – giant steps – even though your wellbeing depends upon it – you cannot, in your desire for giant steps, crush those making tiny steps. And, so, 12 Years a Slave.

12 YEARS A SLAVE

During the build-up to the Oscars, there was an interesting debate about race in film, centring around *12 Years a Slave*. While most agreed it was a beautifully made film, there were commentators who were disappointed that this was yet another story where black characters were shown powerless in a white-dominated world – stripped of any joy or self-dominion, and rendered down into little more than a pornographisation of helpless, miserable survival.

At the New York Film Critics Circle awards, in January, Steve McQueen was heckled by black critic Armond White as 'an embarrassing doorman and garbage man' for making a film that was little more than 'a slavery horror-show … torture-porn'.

In the *Guardian*, meanwhile, black commentator Orville Lloyd Douglas explained why he would be seeing neither *The Butler* nor *12 Years a Slave*: 'I'm convinced these black race films are created for a white, liberal audience to engender white guilt.'

In short, these were not films that a wealthy, ascendant black film industry would make for a black audience – but the unhappy product of black creativity having to look for funding from a white-dominated industry, and play out to white audiences, who were mainly propelled to the cinema, popcorn in hand, out of liberal shame.

Or, as Golden Globes host Amy Poehler summed it up: '*12 Years a Slave*, what a film. It *totally* changed the way I look at slavery.'

While it would obviously be to all of humanity's joyous betterment if the roles available to actors of colour could be expanded out from 'gangster' and 'horrifically abused slave', ultimately, I feel about *12 Years a Slave* triumphing at the Oscars the same way I did about *Fifty Shades of Grey*.

For years, we fretted that society wasn't allowing female sexuality free expression – that the conversation was dominated by male-created pornography, and however many highbrow conversations about it we tried to jump-start, it just wasn't crossing over into a mainstream conversation.

Then *Fifty Shades of Grey* became a phenomenon –100 million copies sold – and many went, 'But this wasn't the conversation about female sexuality we *wanted*. This isn't about a powerful woman unashamedly indulging in rococo sexual liberation. It's all about a shy teenage girl being beaten on the clitoris in exchange for an iPad, instead. This is the *wrong* revolution. I don't like it.'

But the thing is, when you're starting a revolution – by which I mean, altering the landscape, so that new voices become dominant – you have to take the longer view. The simple fact is, *Fifty Shades* kicked the doors in and, more importantly, *made a lot of money*. Publishing is a business, like any other. It will go where the money is. Now there is, thanks to *Fifty Shades*, a huge, new market for 'women writing about their sexuality', there will be a lot *more* women writing about their sexuality – and they will write different books; better books; bolder books. But they will all be fuelled by that first, imperfect kick-start of *Fifty Shades*.

Because the history of change is that *someone has to start the conversation*. Someone has to be fearless enough to go to that new place. But if we attack those who start valuable new conversations – the writers, directors and actors – for not delivering the perfect revolution, whole, straight off the bat – we scare off the next generation of writers, directors and actors. We end up having no new conversations at all.

The single biggest mistake made by cultural commentators – critics, academics, bloggers, political activists – is to attack the artists for the failings of the industry they're working in. It's like those moments when the activist Michael Moore bursts into the offices of a multinational corporation, film crew in tow, to tackle that company's appalling record in human rights – and then just hassles the receptionist, instead.

If you don't like the black films that are being made, attack the power – the white studios, backers and distributors – not the few black artists out there breaking their balls to get something bold and beautiful made.

Here's a story I found, a couple of months ago, that encapsulates the whole *12 Years a Slave* affair. Danny Glover – star of the *Lethal Weapon* films – has spent thirty years trying to make a film about the Haitian revolution. The Haitian revolution – the only slave colony in the world that overthrew its slave masters, to form its own government. This is basically as if, in the Second World War, there had been a concentration camp where the prisoners overthrew the guards – and then went on to rule Germany. It's one of the all-time great pitches.

And yet, this film still hasn't been made – despite, at one point, Glover assembling a cast that included Wesley Snipes, Chiwetel Ejiofor, Angela Bassett and Mos Def. Studios could not imagine someone making a film about the first ever black revolution – no matter how righteous a subject it might be. But what's the one thing that might, now, finally get this film made? That the imperfect conversation starting *12 Years a Slave* made $158 million, and won Best Film, at the Oscars. Steve McQueen has started a new conversation. He's opened a new market. That is more – more – *more* – than enough for one film to do.

Sometimes, I get homesick for the future. A time where writing a column like the next one will seem bizarre, as we will have sorted out all this inequality bullshit once and for all.

ALL THE PEOPLE WE'RE MISSING

In my more melancholy hours I tot up what we're missing. What we didn't get, because some people died too young.

I miss Amy Winehouse, man. I would like another *Back To Black* right now. I wanted to see her on Christmas Day *Top of the Pops*, still dressed like a rogue lady pirate going undercover in the Ronettes. I wanted more Winehouse.

Douglas Adams. I miss Douglas Adams. He was the original hot geek – obsessed with science, reasonableness, boggling at the world. What would he have made of 2015 – of Twitter, Gamergate, iPhones, the new *Doctor Who*? I can vaguely imagine his take on it – enough to long for it but not well enough to stop me from mourning that I'll never hear the exact, unexpected, brilliant thing it would have been.

Richard Pryor and Bill Hicks – imagine them on *Colbert*, talking about 'I Can't Breathe' with Martin Luther King – who would *also* not have died young. Jimi Hendrix – wonder-drunk on the million new sounds 2015 would afford him. Sylvia Plath, older, scarred, survived – reviewing *Girls* over 4,000 words for the *New Yorker*.

Those are the known unknowns – the careers of those who died too early. We know what we will *not* know. Or we can, at least, guess. We know the ones we've lost.

But recently, I've started thinking of all the *unknown* unknowns. All the films, TV shows, songs and ideas we *don't* know we're not getting. The people who should be famous, talked about, allowed to create – but aren't.

For *that* is what inequality means – inequality in the media, in acting, in music, in business, and in politics. In 2015, it is beyond obvious that Britain – through a combination of complacency, distrust and blindness, tinged with a *little* Tabasco shot of fear, and malice – is racist, sexist, homophobic, and stacked against the working classes.

We've seen all the statistics by now we see them every week but we do not need to see them to know that twenty-first-century British culture is *not* British culture. It is, rather, a tiny monoculture of straight, white, public-school men, masquerading as the culture of a multicultural, multiclass, multisexual, half-female country.

Now, most of those people would – I hope – describe themselves as 'non-bigoted'. They would say they are for equality; that they are liberal. But egalitarianism is, like love, only really useful when it's an adverb – not a noun. Both love, and a belief in equality, are almost useless if they remain just a feeling in your heart. It's what your love, and your egalitarianism, prompts you to *do* that's the key thing.

I write books, TV shows, films, newspaper columns – and every industry award ceremony I go to, and every building I enter, the whiteness, the maleness, the standard London media accent, is the default. The only Asians are waiters; the only Liverpudlian accent on the Tannoy, on the Tube there.

These are the straight, white, male rooms filled with the blithe, Boris Johnsonian assumption that if there were non-white, non-male, non-public school talent out there, it would have found its way into this building – to this awards ceremony – *somehow*: never realising that *they* are the somehow. *They* are the ones who would have to fund projects, internships, jobs – they are the ones who would have to insist on commissioning being a distribution of power – rather than soporifically reshuffling the money between the same, small group of faces.

Meanwhile, it's embarrassing we have no one – neither playwrights, nor pop stars – who we can call 'the new voice of the working classes', unless it's unwitting reality TV stars like White Dee from *Benefits Street*, who are not telling stories – merely being used in someone *else's* narrative. It's mortifying our best British actors – David Oyelowo,

Idris Elba, Thandie Newton – are having to go to America to make films, because there are no roles for actors of colour here. It's weakening our democracy that politics has remained so white, male, straight and middle class that – a hundred years into universal suffrage – the vast majority of new political ideas will simply die, unexpressed, in people who think Westminster is not for them, and do not enter politics. It has created a void.

We are, currently, a society with an empty, silent hole in the centre of us, where dozens of public figures *should* be, but aren't – because we have simply failed at the infrastructure that would get the best people there. We moan about how bored we are, how everything 'seems the same', 'they don't write songs like they used to' – without taking the simple steps that would allow this country to *explode* again into creativity, thought, joy, progress and change.

That feeling we had during the Olympics Opening Ceremony – where we saw our multicultural, multisexual, multiclass Britain, and fell in love with ourselves? Where Britain felt – for months of afterglow – special, and astonishing, and we pitied everyone who wasn't us? That high is available for us any time. That's what we can be. If we *do* equality – rather than just silently feel it, and then continue, with business as usual.

I am not a naysayer. I say 'Nay!' to naysayers. I believe in giddy, deluded,
intoxicated optimism, because that is the fuel that will keep you going long
after anger, and righteousness, or fear, have burned out. I look everywhere
for things to make me optimistic – and Manhattan is probably the biggest
of them all.

NEW YORK WILL SAVE US

I didn't want to go to New York. I'm tired, and still undergoing a small
melancholy about not seeing any birds in my garden this summer – at
least, not enough for a party, or a bustle in the hedgerows.

I wanted to go to Wales, and marinade in soft drizzle, and do 'some
nature': look at red kites through binoculars, wear a Gore-Tex anorak,
and sit on some limestone, drinking tea from a Thermos. If I could
order that day from Argos, that's the one I would order. Wales. Where
nature is not slowly dying. Where my anxiety about a forthcoming
environmental apocalypse can be ignored, for a while.

But, instead: New York. Manhattan. Steel. Glass. Planes. Gotham.
No nature at all – unless one counts one of those miserable, cancer-
footed pigeons eating vomit next to a man dressed as a Minion in
Times Square. This is where we are. New York.

And, of course, despite my melancholy, I'm not going to *waste* this
city. That would be titanic ingratitude. Never look a gift New York
in the mouth. Bad pigeons or not, New York is like yellow shoes, or
sunshine, or Bowie – it goes with everything. It's never *wrong*. When
life gives you New York, make New York-ade.

On the first day, walking through Greenwich Village as the
children take pictures of everything – the fire hydrants, the homeless
man with no nose ('Girls – don't take pictures of the homeless man
with no nose'), I remember that, when I first came here – seventeen,
with a band, drunk, astonished – I became convinced that New York

was a feeling, more than anything else. You know 'The Moment'? When the fire catches, or the chorus lifts, or the first cocktail hits your nervous system? The short, hot crescendo of the day? Somehow, Manhattan's electrical circuit-board streets have conspired to break all the rules of time, and make the island live in a state of *permanent* crescendo. It's *always* having 'The Moment'. It's always climaxing.

Really, as a city on an island which is perpetually zenithing, Manhattan should be something discovered, on other side of the universe, on a particularly good episode of *Doctor Who*. It can't be real. Nothing can be constantly having The Moment. It's an emotional impossibility. And yet – Manhattan. An impossible heart.

On this visit, however, I don't feel any of that. This time around – still melancholy for the Black Mountains of Wales – it's New York's *physical* implausibility that hits me. I want mountains – and I am surrounded by them: *built* ones. Granite, steel, glass ones – raised up by man, in a century of tearing muscles and sheer, bull-like effort. As Guy Garvey sings in Elbow's 'New York Morning' – a song I listen to a thousand times while walking down the streets, slightly tearful – *'Me, I see a city and I hear a million voices/Planning, drilling, welding, carrying their fingers to the nub/Reaching down into the ground, stretching up into the sky/Why? Because they can, they did and do so you and I could live together.'*

It takes a working-class, northern band to look at a city and calculate, automatically, how long it would have taken their fathers, and their grandfathers, to build it: each hod of bricks; each slam of the sledgehammer; *'Every bone of rivet steel, each corner-stone an anchor.'* To coolly assess each blueprint, welding spark and crushed limb, and *still* love New York. In fact, to love it even more – because you don't see it as a glittery miracle any more. You see it, instead, as the sweating, determined euphoria of people working so hard that it *looks* like a miracle, in the end. The effort behind a neverending, rolling moment.

When you see how much backbreaking work real magic is, you fall in love with magic even more.

And that was when I stopped feeling so melancholic about there being no birds in my garden – when I felt my long-rumbling anxiety about the slow, dull death of the natural world dim down – even as I stood upon an electricity-gorging glass-and-steel blade; the neon impossibility of dirty, hot, fucked-up New York.

Because: humankind is incredible. We built Manhattan, simply because we wanted it. We wanted it like we want hot fatty carbohydrates, and sex, and disco music, and silver heels, and driving fast. So we made it.

So if we can build Manhattan from simple, joyous *want* – a present to ourselves; a treat – in just 200 short years – raising the Chrysler Building, the Brooklyn Bridge and Broadway when our women were still in corsets, and African-Americans still using separate doors – imagine what we'll be able to build when we really *need* something. When the floods start, and the graphs spike red, and we panic. When the last tiger dies, followed by the last polar bear, and the last song thrush, and we are alone – feeling the terrible melancholy, and dishonour, of being the only species left on the planet.

Then – when the apocalypse arrives, finally, on our doorstep – we will galvanise, and raise forests, and refreeze the poles, and hatch and release a billion songbirds into the air, because, because – because if we can make New York, we can make *anything*.

In the summer of 2015, the migrant crisis in Europe became the big, rolling, ever-escalating story – boats full of terrified people, children washed up on beaches, humanity trying to save humanity on the shores of Greece.

The burning out of Syria, and the rise of ISIS in its blackened, abandoned socket, drove so much of this misery. The first piece I wrote about it was before the migration crisis began – back in early 2013, when the UN was still debating whether or not to bomb the country, to bring about peace.

SYRIA: A MAN ON A ROOF

There are a great many people who have stared into the abyss of Syria and seen – miraculously – an answer. Well, one of four answers – the only four formulated, in years of debate. They are:

Bombing, in the expectation it either 1) will or 2) won't actually improve things – but it is symbolically vital to intervene. Or:

Not bombing, in the expectation it either 3) will or 4) won't improve things – but it's symbolically vital *not* to intervene.

And that's it: four answers, all centred around the subject of military intervention, and inevitable civilian death. The only four answers on the table.

By way of contrast, I don't believe in any of the four answers. All I have is questions, instead.

1) Why has so much of the coverage been not about Syria but about us, instead? Like a bad boyfriend's excuse – but with war? The last weeks have been dominated by who betrayed who in the Commons; whose career is now fucked by the lost vote; and who is now closest to the US – Britain or France?

The Syrian crisis has been depicted as a crisis in Western politics and media – where if *we* finally worked out what our tactic was, and the right people triumphed, then the problem in Syria would be over in a matter of months.

But all the way through this, I have felt increasingly discombobulated by the lack of Syrian opinion. Syria has a 94 per cent literacy rate and over two million refugees in neighbouring countries. Where are the Syrian politicians, and opinion writers, and academics? Why was the debate not being largely shaped by what these people there thought, feared and believed? How come I knew what Piers Morgan thinks about Syria – but not Syria itself? It's 2013 – these people are not 'other'. It's a four-hour flight away. It's far closer than New York – and we would know what New York thought about being bombed by the US Army.

2) Are we sure we *really* know how this crisis started? When countries collapse, their implosion often resembles a human suffering a psychotic breakdown. At the point where the neighbours, and emergency services, get involved, they just see someone who had an argument with someone in a shop, and is now threatening to jump off the roof. All the attention is on what the person in the shop said, and how to get the person off the roof.

But of course, psychotic breakdowns begin years before someone gets on the roof. Assad – he's just the argument in the shop. His murderous crushing of protest is what has summoned the emergency services. But according to a brilliant, long-view piece by foreign policy consultant William R. Polk, Syria's nervous breakdown started with a catastrophic, climate-change-driven drought from 2006 to 2011, with up to 75 per cent crop failure and 85 per cent livestock death. Hundreds of thousands of farmers and their families fled to the cities – where they then had to fight for dwindling resources with a pre-existing 250,000 Palestinian refugees, and 100,000 from Iraq.

In 2008, the UN termed Syria 'the perfect storm for societal destruction', described a country for which the fallout from drought was 'beyond [their] capacity as a country to deal with', and requested aid. The request was rejected – and here, four years later, we are.

Syria is a crisis sprung from mass migration and climate change and the effects of neighbouring countries' wars – not just Assad's viciousness. Assad's a nasty, desperate man dealing with something that would overwhelm almost any government. Put into that context, the conversation about whether to bomb Damascus or not seems surreally disjointed. Syria's root problem is in the deserted hillside farms full of cattle bones and neighbours' wars – not in whatever chair Assad is currently sitting in.

3) What if aid agencies were among the most powerful forces on Earth? What if that recent, sobering poll – which revealed the British public believes the government spends over 20 per cent of its budget on foreign aid – rather than the real figure: 1.1 per cent – were true? And aid agencies suddenly had the equal political and financial leverage as arms dealers, and chemical weapons manufacturers?

I know this seems like costly whimsy – but then, in the most awful sense, a single US soldier fighting a disorganised war in Afghanistan, and costing $1.2 million a year in upkeep, is, ultimately, quite a costly whimsy, too. I know these questions seem more and more absurd, but when you look at Syria – a country now so broken, and so far from stability, and peace – is there anything *other* than aid that can stop the next generation being utterly screwed? What if aid agencies were powerful enough to accelerate what the refugee process already, inexorably does, and could essentially .... evacuate the country?

What if, one day, there was a war, and instead of being trapped, and gassed, and bombed, everyone could – run away?

What would it be like to wield a brutal, oppressive regime, and to wake up one day, and find your country ... empty?

And of course, what I wrote did become, awfully, true – Syria did empty out. Not in an orderly way – helped by the UN, and aid forces – but ad hoc, ramshackle and desperate, as whole families, villages and towns started the long walk out of a country that was falling to pieces around their ears. This column came six months after the last, as the first waves of this unhappy tide started to break.

THE REFUGEES ARE SAVING US ALL

It's funny how tiny we think the problem of migration is, really. There are currently 50 million people displaced by war. Fifty million – the most people in transit since the Second World War. Fifty million means an entire country – more than the population of South Africa, Australia, Venezuela, or Spain – has no actual country. Fifty million people have left behind their streets, their schools, the graves of their dead. Syrians, Somalians, Afghanis and Iraqis fleeing extremist Islamic groups; Rohingya Muslims fleeing Burma, and the perpetual, bloody churn on the borders between Mexico and the USA. Fifty million.

And yet – the unhappiness of British holidaymakers in Kos.

Six thousand refugees have arrived in Greece so far this year – and this has, unfortunately, clashed with the British holiday season. For the last two weeks, the press has been full of pictures of British holidaymakers on Kos, looking disgruntled that the definition of 'a holiday' does not include 'complete inoculation and isolation from immense geo-political events'. One imagines similar annoyance on the faces of previous British holidaymakers on encountering earthquakes and tsunamis.

'The holidaymakers feel uncomfortable,' the *Mail* explained, showing well-fed, safe people on holiday claiming the word 'uncomfortable' over people who were lying, with their children, in a doorway, as their home towns burned.

'Fully clothed migrants walk past sunbathing tourists in bikinis,' it tutted – which at least had the novelty of someone being 'fully dressed in a t-shirt and shorts' recast as a threat.

As one might expect, the 'Comments' section below was not creamy with the milk of human kindness. 'Only one solution: send a gunship and sink sink sink.' 'Most of them are cockroaches.' '#shootthemonarrival.'

From the *Daily Mail*'s point of view, it was a perfect storm – they were able to be furious with both 'incompetent Greeks' for not 'dealing' with the problem, and also the immigrants: both groups of which – with their catastrophic economic crises, and war-torn homelands – were conspiring to spoil the vacations of people from the seventh most powerful country on Earth.

As an optimist, I was compelled to try and find the positive in this unhappy situation – and, after six solid hours of pondering, I actually found one. And it is that this story contains the greatest number of ironies ever witnessed within a simple situation. A new record has been set! Alert *The Guinness Book of Records*!

We'll start with the biggest, which is this: what is a refugee doing, when they leave a country that is, in the case of Afghanistan and Syria, being overrun by ISIS – the people we currently regard as being the biggest threat to global democracy and progress? To us?

Well, obviously, in the first instance, they are saving their own lives, and that of their families: they are acting with the understandable and universal desire to not die horribly, or live miserably.

But that isn't all. For they are also preventing themselves from being weaponised in the future. How many of those who *cannot* leave Syria, or Afghanistan, will be coerced into joining ISIS – merely to survive? And how many of their children will embrace extremist Islamic doctrine? How many millions of trapped people will end up making ISIS more powerful – fuelling its armies, serving its businesses?

The world would be a much more merciful and sane place if we saw refugees for who they are – people who refuse to stay around, and be bitten by zombies, or vampires, and be turned into zombies and vampires themselves.

Humanity should have a special place in its heart for people who run away from wars. Who remove themselves, and their children, from any situation where they must pick up a gun, or strap explosives to themselves, and maybe come to wage war against the very disgruntled holidaymakers who wish them to stay under Western-hating regimes. These refugees are inadvertently saving your arses, *and* your ability to go on holidays, *and* your ability to whine in the *Daily Mail*. The dignified response would be to at least nod your head, in thankfulness, on your way to eat meze.

Then there is the presumed economic superiority of British holidaymakers in Kos – who clearly classify the refugees in the same bracket as the homeless and beggars.

However, as the current rate for being trafficked into Kos is between £500 and £2,000 per person, this ironically trumps Ryanair's £79.99 return from Liverpool with an almost blingy manner. Perhaps the refugees could help out the British holidaymakers with a penny, here and there.

The last is the irony of this all happening in Greece. I'm married to a Greek man, and I know how many Greeks refer to British holidaymakers – drunken, arse-flashing, shouting 'Oi! Stavros! EGG AND CHIPS POR FAVOR!' It looks a bit like the comments section of the *Daily Mail*.

A refugee from a war, or a refugee from bad British weather … everyone can look down on someone, somewhere. Meanwhile, a whole country still roams the Earth, earthless.

Three weeks later, and the situation had become more appalling. It became increasingly clear that the 'plan' was to do nothing – that, in fact, the absence of a plan might even be *the plan – for, if enough people died crossing the Mediterranean maybe it would discourage others. And I wondered – what will that do to* us; *those of us just watching this? Were we not condemning our own souls, along with theirs?*

WE ARE ALL MIGRANTS

When I consider the last few weeks, I realise I'm not concerned about the child migrants who are dead at the bottom of the Mediterranean. There is no point in being concerned about them – for they are dead. They think and feel nothing any more – not after that last, terrible panic. After the waves came through the hatch, which was locked, and their mothers and fathers died next to them, trying to punch through the side of the boat, to escape.

There have been thousands of them before, and there will be thousands – thousands upon thousands – more. They died, or will die. My thoughts are not with them.

Do you know who I'm concerned about? Us. Those children – floating underwater, off the coast of Rhodes – they do not play out well for *us*.

Put aside how it makes us look to the rest of the world – our columnists calling them 'cockroaches'; our government withdrawing funding for the rescue ships: a cold, unspinnable decision that could only have ever had one result: people dying.

Put aside, also, our reputation as a nation: for we still have enough friends – friends who agree with our policy: well, Australia, at least – to brush that off.

No – I worry about us. Every individual in this country. I'm worried about us being part of a nation that goes along with this being the plan. I'm worried about our mental health. I do not underestimate anxiety, and guilt, any more – how they can torque up inside us, as we get older. How things we thought we could ignore – things that would pass – can get lodged in your heart, burning you for twenty bad years, before the world turns sour, and you collapse.

How much energy are we using, to not think about those children? Would funding those rescue boats cost us more, as a country, than it will cost our souls and minds to think of those children in the sea? The Mediterranean – previously for holidays, and Cannes – is now to be fashioned into a siege trench, in which thousands and thousands of people will die. Is this what we do now? We protect the economy of Europe by letting the beaches of Greece and Italy fill with the corpses of families? How do we feel about that?

I know how we're *supposed* to feel: like it must happen. That we are a small country, in a world full of misery, and we must protect ourselves. We are supposed to feel grateful we are being protected from these waves of migrants, coming at us from the north, east and south. There is a place for everyone, on this Earth, and everyone must stay where they are. Or, at least, not come here. Politicians have made hard decisions to keep our country safe for us. The birds may migrate, but we must not.

Except we do. Humans *are* migrant. The world is only full of towers and minarets and gardens and pathways because we spread across the world, in flocks: murmurations of humanity that came in waves. Almost all our history is simply about movement: trade routes, new lands, exchanging silk for flints; founding empires, America, mountain conquering, travelling to Disneyland, or the Moon.

Perhaps it's because I am the grandchild of migrants, married to the child of migrants, but I am hyper-aware of the plasticity of a 'homeland'. I am aware of how much people move, and why. I note how the ones who migrate – away from trouble, away from war, or repression – are the ones obsessed with peace, stability, educating their children, fitting in, and getting on: the kind of super-citizens who recharge cities. I obsessively catalogue all the reasons why migration is argued to 'not work', when clearly it *is* working, because it has, all through history. It *is* history. I note how migration to Britain in particular is deemed inappropriate, because we are small, and crowded – despite only 2.27 per cent of Britain being built upon, and our economic system being dependent on constantly expanding consumer demand.

But none of that really matters – not now. The thing that *matters* is this: people will not stop migrating out of fucked-up countries. There are currently more humans in transit – fleeing wars and repression in Syria, Eritrea, Libya and Iraq – than at any point since the Second World War. Fifty million, according to the International Organisation for Migration.

And if even a quarter of the predictions about climate change are true, they will be joined, within a generation, by millions more fleeing drought, flood, or countries that have been inundated by the sea. Most of this migration will be from the south to the north. The boats will not stop coming, because there is nowhere else for these people, with their children, to go.

And so my question is this: won't we, as a country, go mad if our sole and only plan, for the next fifty – the next 100 – years is to sit here and keep watching children drown? Isn't that – just a little – like turning the unstoppability of migration into murder?

And then, finally, the crisis seemed to peak in one awful moment – David Cameron, the Prime Minister of Britain, referring to the migrants as 'a swarm'. And this made me wonder, what is it, in the language we use to describe others, that gives away so much about ourselves?

SWARMS

In *The Hitchhiker's Guide to the Galaxy*, Douglas Adams sketches, with loving detail, one of the minor characters, Mr Prosser, a council worker charged with knocking down Arthur Dent's house.

Although Mr Prosser is a classic jobsworth – 'fat, forty and shabby' – with a clipboard, the unusual thing about him is his ancestry. He is a direct male-line descendant of Genghis Khan, King of the Mongols.

As a consequence, whenever stressed, Mr Prosser – an otherwise unremarkable man – is apt to have visions of people's houses being consumed by fire, and his enemies 'running screaming from the blazing ruins, with at least three hefty spears in [their] back'. Mr Prosser, Adams tells us, 'was often bothered by visions like these, and they made him feel very nervous'.

I've been thinking about Mr Prosser a lot, recently, as the migrant crisis rolls on, and we see the language that's being used around it. Over the years, one of the most useful rules of thumb I've found is that, when people talk about *other* people, they reveal an enormous amount about themselves.

This is particularly pertinent when talking about people we dislike, or fear – when we discuss their presumed motives. When the language gets heated, we talk a little quicker, and the words tend to come not from our minds – measured things, latterly learned; the correct things; the formal things – but from our bones, instead. From centuries down.

And, so, to migrants. The language used around the crises at Calais, and in the Mediterranean, has been telling: 'Swarms.' 'Floods.' 'Invasions.' 'Economic migrants.' 'Endangering our national identity.'

The people using these terms are, fairly consistently, white British – that is to say, of Anglo-Saxon, or Norman descent. Perhaps it's because I am of Celtic descent, but the language they use to describe migrants aren't terms I would ever use. Partly because my grandparents were migrants here – from County Mayo to Liverpool, at the turn of the century – so, you know, I'm migrant-friendly, along with – as a general rule of thumb – all my other migrant-descending friends, i.e. Jews, Greeks, Sikhs and, in one case, a proud, possibly-too-embedded-in-Ancestry.com Huguenot.

But it's also partly because, as a Celt – and I don't want to make all you Anglo-Saxons and Normans feel bad here – *we were here first*. The Celts were the ones who lived in England before the swarms of Anglo-Saxons and Normans came over – some *invading*, some *as economic migrants* – and *disrupted our way of life, flooding our towns* and *endangering our national identity*, to the point where we only lived on in areas so wet and remote (Ireland, Scotland, Wales, Cornwall) the Anglo-Saxons and Normans couldn't be bothered to deal with the travel, and the mildew, and left us alone to be pale, and ginger.

Yes, this all happened centuries ago. But I do wonder if, like Mr Prosser, these things are embedded somewhere, deep in the psyches of Anglo-Saxon and Norman Britons.

When I drive through tiny, classic British villages in Suffolk and Surrey – householders tending their rose bushes, before strolling off to the pub, for a pint – I wonder if, underneath all of this, there is a deeply buried tribal memory of their ancestors coming to claim Surrey and Suffolk. The battles, and invasions – the conquering, and the taking of a whole country.

It would be weird if there weren't. We are, after all, taught our history. We all have a sense, somewhere inside us, of how we got to where we are today. And here it comes out in our language, when we see others, across the sea, staring at our country – although these people, ironically, do *not* wish to invade, or subsume, us. They want to be *part* of our culture. They want to open a corner shop, or be heart surgeons. They are coming here not to kill us but so they themselves don't die.

And yet, in our language, we ascribe to them the behaviours of our forefathers. Well, *yours*. Mine were busy heading west, in order to get rained on, then be oppressed.

'Swarms.' That was the biggest one, for me. Our Prime Minister, David Cameron, referring to the migrants as 'swarms'. Of course, it's just one word, and he might later have regretted it. But to see someone from a background of immense privilege, talking about these terrified, traumatised families as 'swarming' seemed like both a brutal, and inadvertently revealing, word.

For I could talk about white public schoolboys 'swarming' – cherry-picking jobs in the media, the City, Parliament and business, at the expenses of women and the working classes. The figures are there, every week: 48 per cent of Tory MPs privately educated, against 7 per cent of the population; Britain coming fifty-sixth in the world rankings for its proportion of female MPs – just below Kyrgyzstan. Etc. Etc. You know the figures by now.

But I would not use the word 'swarm' – because then I would be revealing something – that I am a chippy, Celtic, working-class woman – about myself.

That's the thing about talking about other people. You end up talking, really, about your darkest self. You are the migrant. You are the swarm.

When you are watching something like the migration crisis unfolding on the news – when turning on the TV at 6pm, or 7pm, or 10pm, becomes a nightly event, that leaves you crushed, dispirited, blank and despairing – you are apt to think, after a while: maybe the news – the actual *programme – needs to change. Maybe we need a new news. Maybe that is part of the problem.*

WE NEED A NEW NEWS

I love Yoko Ono. I remember reading an interview with her – possibly in *Smash Hits* – where she did that thing of pointing out something, with a very tiny question, that demands a big answer.

Why, she mused, is the news like it is? Twenty-five minutes of news – awful, visceral, news of war, and fear – rounded off with five minutes of sport.

Why *sport*? Why does our most 'important' television programme of the day include updates on, quite randomly, sport? What makes sport worthy of being included in *the daily news about our world* – when, say, art, or fashion, isn't?

Yes, sport is a massive business – £20 billion in the UK – with millions of passionate fans. But that is exactly the same description you could use for art (an industry worth, *without* being on the news every day: £71 billion) and fashion (likewise, £26 billion).

Could it be, Ono suggested, that it's because fashion and pop are seen as for *girls* – and sport is for men?

In the twenty years since I've read it, I haven't decided if it *is* sexism – but it's a thought I keep coming back to. How do we decide what 'The News' is – and, subsequently, how does that decision affect us? In that half-hour, what are we telling ourselves about ourselves?

Would we be a different culture if, instead of rounding off our bulletins of death and war with sport, we had arts news, instead? After all, it is an odd echo to the preceding news, sport: another male-dominated world of physical power, centred only on winners and losers.

Imagine if we ended news bulletins by entering the intellectual, and emotional, world, instead: a dazzling paragraph on love from Donna Tartt's latest book; a new poem on grief; the huge new pop single that makes people dance when they hear it. No winners, no losers. Just a joyous celebration of revelation, insights, skill, genius. Would that change us? If we changed the news to a new news? Why *did* we ever choose sport, anyway?

It needn't be art, of course: tech news would be just as different – what's been invented; what's spectacularly failing; what's coming over the horizon. Or we could have ecology news: the latest panda born; the bleaching corals; the comeback of the bees. Really, those five minutes could be anything we wanted. With no winners or losers at all.

And, of course, once you question the last five minutes of the news, you start to question the first twenty-five minutes, too.

I had always thought, until recently, that those twenty-five minutes show you everything that's going on in the world.

And they don't, of course. They're just showing you everything that's going on in the world *that has reached a crisis point*.

And that's a different thing – being shown what has basically gone beyond the ability of any agency to resolve it. Wars, famines, terrorism. Continents of melting ice; archipelagos of plastic. The collapse of markets; of economies; of industries. The collapse of – in so many awful valleys, or on mountain tops, or in burning cities – humanity itself.

Of course, the news can't help being the news – it can't help showing you every black, smoking hole that has become some unstoppable Hell on Earth. It can't stop showing you the end of hope. But, in turn, it is becoming, I think, the end of hope itself. Because the news is, essentially, screwing us up. Crushing us.

The remorseless delivery of each new crisis by twenty-four-hour news channels, and social media, leaves us exhausted, and bleak – battered and out of love with our own species. We have no perspective on how lucky we are – how things are improving, how things might be prevented.

Twenty-first-century technology allows us to sit in this panopticon and the pounding bleakness of what we see has made us fall back into an almost medieval analysis of what is going on. We are as resigned to our inevitable climate crisis as we were to God's inevitable apocalypse; our world leaders use the word 'evil' to describe their enemies – as if evil were something that roamed the world in a miasma, rather than grew out of a dully predictable and age-old recipe: famines; corrupt leaders; prejudice; poverty; instability; disputed borders; fear.

That's why I want a sister programme to the news – that might be thought of, if not called, 'The Perspective'. Every study states we are living in the period of greatest stability, illumination, tolerance, longevity and progress mankind has ever seen. So let some kind of news *show* that.

We need a new kind of news programme, to show us the news five years *before* it becomes 'the news': when it's still a manageable, budding problem that can be solved with technology, aid, diplomacy. Where someone watching the news could, feasibly, be the very person to solve it. When there is still some kind of hope that love, insight, skill or genius could provide – rather than just another, dispiriting, numbing reporting of the winners and losers.

First on the battlefields, and then, mysteriously, in all that sport.

Because, of course, how we report on ourselves – what we deem 'news'; the stories we tell ourselves; what we, in essence, publicise about our species – has knock-on effects.

This was never more apparent than in the spring of 2015, when gunmen burst into the satirical Parisian magazine Charlie Hebdo *and killed twelve cartoonists, journalists and employees.*

JE SUIS CHARLIE

And so terrorism reaches the media, with the murder of twelve journalists, cartoonists and satirists in Paris. A precise and deliberate move – to silence those commentators' voices, and opinions, forever.

Speaking coldly and unemotionally as a journalist, it's a fantastic, dark PR job. Headlines around the world, instant heat, endless traction. For one hour's work. For one big stunt.

It seems, looking back now, inevitable that there would be a terrorist attack on a media organisation – because terror has always, in the end, been about PR. Look – you can't kill everyone who disagrees with you. Islamic fundamentalists know this – for all their Twitter-savvy and caches of weapons, they're still a tiny minority, opportunistically picking off the easiest of targets: journalists at their desks, aid workers. A school. They know they can't personally slaughter everyone in the Western world who disagrees with them. Extremists don't have the numbers. They can't end Western democracy – it's already won. It's huge. It might be ragged, and often wrong, and still in the very early days of working out how to be halfway fairer and more inclusive – but it's just going to carry on: a multiplicity of voices and ideas, all vying for space: different. Together. All just … talking, and creating.

For the Western ideals the extremists fight against aren't just embodied in a couple of politicians, or a couple of pieces of legislation, or twelve cartoonists in Paris – they're in millions of books, movies, stories, songs; the clothes you have in your wardrobe, the food you eat, the parks you walk through, the libraries you use, gay marriage, women's careers, the free-ranging, illuminating conversations people all over the world have on Facebook, and Twitter. However awful, and terrifying, the shootings in Paris are, there are no guns that can stop all of this, now. A billion lives will roll on. Like the catastrophic, foolhardy, damaging 'War on Terror' it inspired, extremist Islamic terrorism is *also* a war that can't be won. Two unwinnable wars, at war with each other, while the *real* war goes on, regardless.

Because the *real* war is PR. That's why it's awful and inevitable the terrorists finally struck against the media – against an organisation, *Charlie Hebdo*, that deals in perception. For the awful truth is this: there will always be a certain number of young men – and it is almost always, sadly, young men – who are miserable, and damaged, who want to kill people. And those young men will look for a reason for their unhappiness, a target for their anger, and an action they believe will bring 'justice'.

Young white boys in America take guns into school and kill their peers – one shooting every five weeks, on average; 486 killed since 2000. The story they tell – in interviews and suicide notes – is that they feel rejected by society; sneered at; belittled, and that violence is their only recourse. But we do not weave them into a story of young, white American men at war with their generations, or schools, or their society.

Young Islamic men – no less miserable and damaged – have a different narrative they latch on to – that they are avenging their Prophet – but their ultimate recourse is just the same. But because of Islamic extremism's dark, effective PR job, they are 'inspired by', and we place their acts within, a narrative of a grand, global problem – that things, and people, are getting worse, that we never had these problems before; that this is an oncoming storm.

And this is feeding into our very worst instincts, as a planet. The rise in right-wing xenophobia, fear and racism across Europe is rooted in a belief that things were somehow better, and calmer, and more peaceful, at one point – when cultures didn't mix. That everything was fine until we started travelling, mixing, blending. That before multiculturalism Europe was peaceful.

But it never was, of course. Even a hundred years ago, Europe was far more repressive, bloody, bigoted and fearful than it is now. Homosexuality illegal, women denied power, paupers in workhouses, Catholic repression, Fascism rising. For this will never end, you know. This battle for freedom. The mistake of the right is to believe in a prelapsarian Europe – but there is no point where civilisation is complete. Ever. The past was never perfect, and we never reach the future. It is always ahead of us, being built. The story of mankind is that every achievement we have ever made was built while running. We never rest. We do not pause. We are always in motion. We are countering as much 'terror' now as we ever have. There are always unhappy people who want to destroy, and kill. There always will be.

And this is why we must not let an inhuman PR act dictate our course of action. We don't dignify it and magnify it by calling it a 'war'. We don't give in to fear, or hatred, or become more insular – because that is the ultimate aim of the terrorists' PR job. Division. We must never let it become as solid and powerful as that. We just counter it with bigger, better, more glorious ideas. That's how you win a PR war. You make a better alternative.

News used to travel more slowly – physically, visibly. This was something I realise while thunderously, inappropriately, dressed on the side of a mountain in Cumbria.

PATHS

Busk Pike, Lingmoor Fell, November, 2.30pm

We've been lost for a while, now. However often I turn the map, it does not look like the bit of Cumbria that is in front of me.

I *want* to look down on a lush valley that contains a footpath that leads to a waterfall, and then a pub. That's what the map has promised me. That's why I left the nice hotel.

Instead, all I can see is a very blasted hillside, a series of disused quarries, and a wall of rain moving towards us, like a sheet of blindness. The rain looks very non-negotiable.

Of course, I know there's no such thing as 'bad weather' – only 'inappropriate clothing'. Although not an exhaustive list, I feel I'm probably wearing a good percentage of the world's most 'inappropriate clothing' for this fell-walking expedition: a Topshop duffel coat, Doc Marten boots inexplicably spreckled with pink paint since last year's Gay Pride, and a *Ghostbusters* t-shirt. Because this is a weekend away with my husband, underneath my jeans, I'm also wearing sexy lingerie, 'for later'.

I can hear Michael Buerk's sorrowful voiceover, on *Emergency 999*: '… and when they found her body, it was clear the hypothermia set in in the *unhappily unprotected area* above the stocking-tops'.

I pity the poor actress having to re-enact my stupid day. She'll never move on to *Holby* with material as poor as this to work on. 'Gigantic cold dead idiot dressed as sci-fi nerd/exotic dancer.'

An hour earlier, before we got lost, it had all been so different. Walking the Cumbrian Path between the burning red maples and white, pre-Christmas frosts, I'd turned into 'Brilliant' from *The Fast Show*.

'Aren't paths *AMAZING!*' I'd been shouting. 'One of the first big ideas humans ever had! Psychological and engineering evolution!'

On these paths, you walk inside the ghosts of every other person ever here: barefoot, hob-nailed booted, cloaks swishing. In the days before printing press, telegraph and phone, this was how ideas and news travelled: knowledge of a forthcoming invasion a plague – a new poem – moving at the speed of shoes.

If you could see it, speeded up, from space, you'd witness the whole of Britain slowly lighting up over the centuries, as communities connected like neural pathways, along these tracks. We're at war! We're at peace! Cholera is not a vapour, but hides in the water! Dr Frankenstein's monster lives!

Each idea held like a torch in someone's head as they walked towards villages of new people, who would then also be lit up by them. Each of these old ways are the delivery system of the future, illuminating us from Neolithic, to medieval, to Georgian.

I felt the same rush of history twenty years ago, on the Byzantine Road, in Paros. Built by Christian Romans, the stones first smoothed by soldier sandals, crushing the same Greek myrtle my cheap gladiator-style sandals were crushing now.

In a hot, oily, herbal fug, we passed the broken, hillside marble quarry that Alexandros of Antioch bought a block of marble from, and made his Venus de Milo. The nearby churchyard was full of white gravestones made of the same marble.

'If we took one of those gravestones, and got creative, we could give her her arms back,' I pointed out to my husband.

Back in Cumbria, in the otherwise empty moorland between Wilson Place and Colwith Force waterfall, we passed a joke. A huge, dead tree hangs, perpendicular, over the route, and into its sponge bark, someone, a long time ago, pushed an old twopence coin, now verdigris-green. The next traveller had obviously smiled at the idea – a rotting tree, leafing coins! – and pushed his coin in, next to it.

Now, hundreds of coins stud the tree – a little, decades-long gag, for every walker who passes here, and joins in. Another simple transmission of human ideas, even when the valley is silent save the hawthorn, and the robin.

And sometimes, the idea that pathways transmit is the idea of pathways themselves. The Lakes now live as a network of tracks, laid down over fell-tops like lace, that people fly the world to walk. But whose idea were these paths? They lay, useless, on private estates, until 1932, and the mass trespass of Kinder Scout – when factory workers from Manchester and Bolton and Sheffield and Liverpool broke the law, and walked the hills, and showed Britain how much more beautiful a hillside looks studded with a line of knitted bobble hats, sitting on a drystone wall, drinking from a Thermos – hearts full of love for the slate and the rowan and the poetry and the cloud. These pathways pumped blood up into these hills again, like veins, and brought them alive.

It was one of those knitted bobble hats who found us on Busk Pike, at dusk, and took us back down to Little Langdale. Eighty-two years old, from Manchester, he was walking through the rain on the path like it was just popping round the corner, for milk.

'Nice day for it!' he said, cheerily, as we waved him goodbye. And even though it was raining and we were exhausted, he was right.

We don't really tend to think of much as happening in the countryside – the cities are the places for people; the places where we think, and where things change.

But just as those footpaths on blasted hillsides were the first neural routes for news, so the blasted hillsides now are full of the things that might just set us free: wind turbines.

HOW WIND TURBINES KEEP US FREE

Holidays – Cornwall, then Wales, and all the great stretches of motorway in between. The kids are on their iPhones, showing each other pictures of themselves on Instagram that they took thirty seconds ago – twenty seconds ago – *now*, right *now*.

I cannot believe the kids are looking at their phones, rather than what is out of the window. Out of the window is astonishing.

'Look! Look at those *windmills*!' I keep shouting – pointing at what would have blown my mind when I was their ages.

There are vast, handsome wind turbines lining the cold corridors of the M4, the M5, the A30, the A470. Alone, in clusters – massed, and marching across the top of ridgeways, and mountains. Each one 200ft of sheer metal muscle, scything at the sky – like the Seattle Space Needle, angling for a fight.

Turbines are the recurrent markers in exposed places, now – our odd companions whenever the landscape veers towards the bleak. Huge, white priests, praying above the tiny tin cars on the tarmac below.

If I'd seen just one of these in 1986, I would have *freaked out*: back then, the tallest thing you'd see from a car window was a tree; or maybe a large dog. Now, we line our travel routes with skyscrapers, and Angels of the North, and these buff swords, tearing at clouds. Do the children know how amazing they are?

'Yeah, yeah – it's a windmill,' Nancy confirms, when I make her look at the eight, 100m high giants that stand guard over Bristol – facing out into the Bristol Channel, stealing the breath out of Wales. 'Big. Whevs.'

The thing is, I can understand why the children are offhand about them – they are, after all, teenagers. Their job, for the next seven years, is to be studiedly unimpressed by everything, lest anyone discover their most passionately concealed secret: they are so terribly, terribly young.

But what I can't understand is any *adult* who dislikes turbines. Even more – becomes convulsed with hatred for them: fulminating against wind power as others might fulminate against cancer, or locusts. Every possible antagonism towards them seems bizarre. To argue that they're ugly recalls people arguing that the young Barbra Streisand was ugly. It may not be to *your* taste, dude – but many of us have pictures on the wall, and would travel for a glimpse, and swoon, just a little, when we see them at sunset. Children still buy bright paper windmills to top their sandcastles; adults dream of living in Caractacus Pott's windmill home. A windmill is often a loved thing.

Then there's 'Ban turbines – turbines kill wildlife', championed by those who have previously kept their mad passion for nature on the down-low, and have notably never followed up their concerns by suggesting Britain outlaw pet cats, which kill an estimated 275 million wild animals a year – and all without powering a single dishwasher, to boot.

The third complaint is equally odd: to argue turbines are so ugly that they ruin the countryside is, I think, to betray a quiet, unrecognised self-loathing of your own species. The British countryside is all a confection of man – the sheep-stripped hills of Wales and Scotland; the fishing harbours of Devon and Cornwall; the patchwork, hedge-hemmed quilt of Gloucester, Shropshire and the Cotswolds: all made by us. All fashioned, by us, out of what was before: forests filled with wolves, and the sea bashing at rocks, and neither place good for a person to live. We have always done with the land what we want, and need, to survive – and is there anything right now we want, or need, more than these thin, white, humming windmills, across our hills, and alongside our roads, giving us not just our power, but our freedom?

Because that is what you are looking at, when you look at a wind turbine – freedom. A certain measure of freedom from the bloody, terrifying events exploding in Russia, Ukraine and the Middle East. While this country's energy supply rests on careful diplomatic negotiations – pipelines across Afghanistan and Europe, nuclear power stations built by China, careful meetings with cruel potentates, turning a blind eye to the abuse of human rights – the potential for Britain to do good in the world is horribly compromised. We cannot speak freely – we cannot be wholly *moral* – when we know that unwelcome honesty with another country might result in our streetlights going off; our cities going dark, in winter. And that's before we talk about the morality of dirty fuel and global warming: all those floodlights in Glasgow, during the Commonwealth Games, flooding the very Pacific island nations that had come to compete against us. A tiny, terrible circle of causers and effectees.

So that's why I love wind turbines. Why I basically fancy them, *and* their cousins – those fields full of solar panels, basking, like lizards, in the sun. It's not just that they're sexy, nerdy inventions: rivets and wires, rigged up to catch the explosive energy that has been swirling around us since the Big Bang. It's that they will allow us to be better people, too.

An interview with the man who's done more to change the way that I write than anyone else – Russell T. Davies, the man who made sci-fi not only sexy – cor, David Tennant! Doctor PHWOARGH, more like – but also inclusive, limitless and all about the human spirit.

I met him once, at a party, when I was but a young writer, and he greeted me, hooting, and crying, 'Do you know what you are, darling? You're an ENTHUSIAST!' And it was like getting Glinda's kiss, while lost in Oz. I'd been identified and named as a thing. 'An enthusiast.' No more snark, or dolorousness. I was for joy, excellence, playfulness – the future.

Russell's passion for social change through the medium of a bloody good time on television is genuinely inspiring. He knows you can have your life changed by a line, a look – a kiss – all beamed to you from the corner of your living room, and shared with 7 million other people. His last project, Cucumber, *had both an extraordinary purpose, and an extraordinary story.*

RUSSELL T. DAVIES: THE MAN WHO CHANGED THE WORLD, JUST A LITTLE BIT

'Ooooh, I tell you what,' Julie Hesmondhalgh – best known to the world as the late Hayley Cropper from *Coronation Street* – says, sitting in the dazzling late September sunshine, smoothing her skirt over her knees. 'They've spent some money on this.'

We're sitting outside a cricket club in the posh outskirts of Manchester – 'This is where all the footballers and the WAGS live. It's all beauty salons, and fine dining,' Julie explains.

The lawns are immaculate – the old oaks starting to bronze. The roses are full, and well attended.

There are around fifty extras, all dressed for the occasion, smoking in between takes. There's a large buffet which, to everyone's sorrow, can't be touched – 'Continuity!'

The demographic spread of the extras is extraordinary, and unusual – more than half are black, and the other half is made up of gay men in their mid-forties, teenagers of every subcultural and sexual persuasion, and ballsy, capable middle-aged women. I have never seen this kind of diversity on any drama I have ever written about.

But this explosion of amazing, and previously unseen, characters is no surprise when you know where we are: for this is a location shoot for Channel 4's new flagship drama, *Cucumber* – the eagerly awaited return to adult drama for Russell T. Davies, arguably Britain's most influential, and inarguably Britain's most exciting, entertaining and inventive screenwriter, after a five-year absence.

I can't tell you any more details about what's happening here, as it would spoil a massive plot twist – but suffice to say, the man who made gay drama mainstream (*Queer as Folk*), resurrected Jesus in modern-day Manchester (*The Second Coming*), reinvented Casanova as a scrawny, gobby, charming David Tennant (*Casanova*) and rebooted the long-dead and derided *Doctor Who* as one of the world's biggest and most thrilling shows, is not coming back quietly.

Hesmondhalgh talks about how, when she first read the script, there was a flashback to a wedding:

'The full thing – in a church, dozens of extras, big wedding dress, everything. For this five-second flashback. And I thought, as an old pro, "Well, that'll be the first scene they lose. A half-day shoot in a church for a five-second flashback – they'll never cough up for that." And it was one of the first scenes we shot. They've gone full out for this.'

'When Russell comes to you with an idea, you just go for it,' executive producer Nicola Schindler says, joining us on the terrace. 'Anything and everything he writes, I want to shoot – because there's no one else like him. Russell tells stories no one else would dream of. And it's a word people shy away from using, but what he does is important. He tells us who we are. And who we could be.'

At this point, Davies himself comes over – approximately 900ft tall, in a suit, hooting, as is his wont, in mock fury.

'They wouldn't let me take a Cadbury's Mini-Roll from the buffet. I said, "That buffet would not be *here* without me! I *wrote* that Mini-Roll!"' he roars. 'Oooh, it's just like when I worked with [redacted] and they swanned off and won [redacted] – no gratitude! No gratitude at all!'

He dissolves into laughter – a big fizzing, hooting laugh.

So what *is Cucumber* all about, then, I ask – gesturing to the hive of industry around us. Why are we all here today?

'Sex,' Russell says, immediately. 'This whole thing is about sex. Gay sex. That is its subject, in great detail. In every episode. Its stare is unwavering. It is *all* about fucking. So, it will provoke a bit of a … *response.*'

And then he starts laughing again.

When Russell T. Davies left *Doctor Who* in 2009, it was to start a whole new life. The last five years had been spent coping with the kind of workload that would cripple most writers – not only show-running *Doctor Who*, but also creating, writing and overseeing both the darker, for-adults *Torchwood*, and *The Sarah Jane Adventures* for CBBC.

At the time, he explained why he had taken on what were essentially three full-time jobs, concurrently: 'In this industry, more than half of your energy goes into getting things made. Most writers would *kill* to have their projects made. So when you're hot, you just go for it. Because if you wait until a point where you have more time to write these things, you won't be hot any more, and those things won't get made. Ever. And that's all you ever want. For people to see your stories.'

At this point, Davies had been voted the fourteenth most influential man in British media – he'd been given an OBE, and become one of the biggest revenue streams, via an unstoppable flow of *Doctor Who* merchandise and spin-offs, for an otherwise beleaguered BBC. Exhausted but triumphant, he left Britain to start a new, golden life – he gave up his great love, smoking; moved to Los Angeles with his partner, Andy; and started work on a new project, *Cucumber*, for an American network.

These were to be the glory years – finally enjoying life, in the sunshine, with a partner he just 'Hadn't seen that much. Because *Doctor Who* takes up everything. There was always an edit to attend. A Judoon whose head had fallen off, hahaha.'

America loved the scripts for *Cucumber*. Huge names were being discussed for casting. This was to be the next stage of Davies's career.

But then, Andy started saying odd things.

'The problem is, my boyfriend has always been mad,' Davies says. We have left the shoot, now – we're in the back of a black cab. Davies's legs are cramped up, despite the car being so roomy. He is approximately three miles tall.

'He's fucking nuts,' Davies goes on. 'He's always had synaesthesia – saying random things like, "You know the name Richard? That's a bunch of twigs in a pot in a white kitchen." Completely bizarre and annoying. I would always tell him to shut up. It's an annoying trait. You say "Susan", and he'll say "Fudge". Gah! So when he started saying, "I keep seeing an Edwardian lady smiling sarcastically at me," it seemed quite normal. I ignored him.'

Davies continued with his first draft of *Cucumber*. The spark for it had been unexpected: Graham Norton.

'Graham Norton shamed me into doing it!' Davies hoots. 'Shamed me on Radio 2, live on air, while I was doing promo for *Doctor Who*. "Why don't you write something proper, about real gay men, again?" he said. "Like *Queer as Folk*?" I walked across Manchester's Media City feeling *chastised*. But he was right. Graham Norton was right, thank God.'

Ten years before, *Queer as Folk* had been Davies's calling card to the wider world. Despite having spent the previous ten years writing *Children's Ward*, *Why Don't You?*, *The Grand* and *Dark Season* – which starred a very young Kate Winslet – *Queer as Folk* was clearly a whole different league: something so unmistakably from the heart; so wildly inventive; so joyous, angry, filthy and funny, that it changed people's ideas of 'gay drama' overnight. It was genuinely revolutionary.

'Before it went out, everyone thought it was going to be Channel 4's worthy gay drama,' Davies recalls. 'All vegan protestors and AIDS, hahaha! The only gay characters we'd had [on British TV] before were ones dying on *EastEnders*, God bless them. People weren't expecting this.'

For 'this' was a gigantic, classic love story between sexy, handsome Stuart (Aiden Gillen) and reliable, lovelorn Vince (Craig Kelly), set in Manchester's Gay Village – a place which came across as a hi-NRG Narnia, or Oz. A place where young gay men and lesbians could reinvent themselves as the heroes of their own stories, and feel, for the first time, normal. More than normal – amazing. Watching it, as a straight teenage girl, it made me want to be a gay man. To feel I was a part of a world as connected, joyous and fearless as Davies's.

One scene still makes me catch my breath, with glee, fifteen years later. The swaggering Stuart comes out of his house to find someone has sprayed 'QUEERS' all over his Jeep. Rather than being shamed, or cowed, to the horror of his teenage one-night stand, Nathan (Charlie Hunnam), Stuart leaps into the car, and drives Nathan up to his school gates – horn blaring as his schoolmates scatter. When they jeer – shouting, 'Give us a kiss!', and mincing around – Stuart shouts back, 'I'll give you a good fuck, you virgins!' before driving off again, gravel spraying – leaving Nathan staring after him, lovelorn.

Queer as Folk showed gay men, for the first time, as heroic, venal, clever, stupid, horny, heart-broken, foolish, noble – in short, as proper human beings, rather than just 'hilarious camp best friends', or 'an issue'. It changed things overnight.

'People having televisions in their bedrooms was quite a recent thing, at that point,' Davies recalls. 'So there was a generation of teenage gay boys who were actually deciding on their viewing habits, and watching this, in secret. And to this day those boys – now grown men – will come up to me and tell me how it changed their lives. Well, how much they wanked to it. Which is the same thing, let's face it! Hahaha! I'm never sure how to respond to it. It depends on if they're handsome or not, to be honest.'

Davies knew how important the show was: 'To live as a gay man in the twenty-first century is a political act,' he says, simply. 'There is a resonance to your existence that straight men just don't have. It is a conversation. It is a topic. It needs TV shows.'

Davies didn't exactly give up on writing about gay men after *Queer as Folk* – *Doctor Who* featured the ground-breaking Captain Jack Harkness, played by John Barrowman, as a swashbuckling pansexual super-hero who kissed the Doctor, on prime-time BBC, and thereby, as I said earlier, did the unthinkable – made ten-year-old boys in school playgrounds fight over who was to play him in their games. This is something I would argue is one of the single greatest acts of cultural influence in the last fifty years.

Davies had, simply and beautifully, shown us love as being something universal, fundamental and worth fighting for. In among all those aliens, love was an inalienable right – however you loved.

But Davies always knew he'd come back to a wholly gay drama one day.

'*Cucumber* is basically *Queer as Folk*, fifteen years on,' Davies says. 'What are they doing now? How are they coping with middle age, careers, relationships, family, love? And, most of all, sex. What sex are they having?'

And it is sex – gay sex – that is *Cucumber*'s territory, fuel, and language.

'The first response about [gay issues] is always, "Why does it always have to be about sex?" And I understand that. As a viewer, my heart sinks when bad stuff is just about sex,' Davies confesses. 'But the only reason I wanted to write this is because Henry [the hero of *Cucumber*] *doesn't* have sex – even though he's been in a relationship for nine years. He doesn't fuck. And to me, that's new territory. I think it's true of a lot of gay men. It was a story I was hearing over and over from friends. But it's a huge secret – maybe our biggest. The only person I've ever seen publically stand up and say that he doesn't have sex is Stephen Fry, and when he did [on a documentary last year], I was shouting, "SHUT UP! SHUT UP!

THIS IS MY MATERIAL!" I'd started writing this three years ago, and I was ahead of the curve then! I'd *invented* gay men not having sex, hahaha!'

Time and again, the biggest hinge on which homophobia's gate hangs is sex – the fascination with, and horror of, penetrative sex. And it's an unease with the subject that goes both ways.

'We had an early screening for *Cucumber*, and one man from *Attitude* got very upset, because he has the same sexual problem Henry has. And he apparently left the screening saying, "I don't think that should be shown." *Attitude* magazine! The gays want to ban me! Hahaha!'

But while *Cucumber* is about sex, it is not *just* about sex. Rather, sex is seen as the animating force that connects everything – like the Dust in Philip Pullman's novels. And so *Cucumber* is also about families, mid-life crises, stalling careers, reinvention, racism, the internet, pornography, being transgender, mortality – hope, and love, and loss, and joy. It's also – and this is a given with a Russell T. Davies show – incredibly funny. The end of the first episode, which I don't want to spoil, ends with a titanic nervous breakdown sound-tracked by Boney M – something you just don't get with Stephen Poliakoff.

Cucumber is about what a continual, never-ending, confusing, glorious, heartbreaking surprise life is. A series of waves we paddle on the surf board of our desires – trying, once in a while, to stand, and surf to the shore. Sometimes we make it on to the sand. More often than not, we fall, and go under, and start again.

Davies got the call when he was at Heathrow. It was 2011, and he and Andy had come home to the UK for two weeks, as Davies was midway through writing the first episode of *Cucumber*. Andy had taken the opportunity to go to his doctor, and check out the headaches he'd been having.

Davies was returning to LA early and called him – just before he checked his luggage on to the plane.

'Standing outside, leaning against the wall,' Davies recalls, with the vividness of those recalling something truly awful.

It turned out that Andy's 'sarcastically smiling Edwardian lady' wasn't a charming form of synaesthesia at all: he had a glioblastoma multiforme – a Grade 4 tumour, pressing into his brain.

'And there is no Grade 5,' Davies says. 'After Grade 4, you just … die.'

And so all the plans were cancelled. They couldn't return to LA – Grade 4 brain tumours are not allowed on planes. Everything in LA was shipped back to Britain – to the house Davies had kept in Manchester. *Cucumber* was cancelled. Everything was cancelled.

'And thank God for money – all that money I had earned from Judoons, and farting Slitheens, and never spent,' Davies says. 'Money I'd always saved for a rainy day. Because this … this was the monsoon.'

The prognosis was as simple as for there to be no prognosis – they would open up the side of Andy's head, operate on him and, after that – if he survived the operation – he would still only have a 3 per cent chance of living.

'He was mad – quite mad,' Russell says, staring out of the window of the taxi. 'He had a stroke, he was ranting and raving – one night, there was brain fluid pouring out of his ear, like a tap. And however marvellous everyone is – and you really do discover the goodness of your friends – true goodness – you are alone. Fuck me, you are alone. In that hospital. At 3am, thinking, "He's going to die." Planning what you'll do next.'

Davies's friends knew what he would do next: 'They thought I was going to leave him!' he hoots. 'They did! They all slowly admitted it! What the fuck did I look like? As if I'd go!'

The cab pulls to a halt, in a pleasant street, outside a well-kept, normal-looking 1930s house, with bright glass in the door.

'Come in, come in,' Davies says, opening the door.

We walk into the hall. Through the window, straight ahead, is a small back garden. It has a full-sized Dalek, under a tree, in the rain. The plunger points straight at the house.

'I'm home, love,' Davies calls out.

And there, in the front room, is Andy – sitting on the sofa, with a seven-inch scar on the side of his head, beaming. He survived. He was one of the 3 per cent. He was the unlikely happy ending most screenwriters would demur from writing.

'Good day?' he asks Davies, as Davies kisses him.

'Yes!' Russell says, adjusting the blanket over Andy's knee. 'What are you watching? *Eggheads*? How *marvellous*. Tea, anyone?'

So this was how *Cucumber* was written and made, in the end. A show not for LA, and America, and a new life, after all – but back to Manchester: the world Davies has chronicled for so long, so brilliantly. Written between hospital appointments, and fear, and changing the bedclothes at 2am – for Channel 4, now; now that Davies knew he would be staying in Britain. Written when Davies finished his day as Andy's carer, and could start writing – at 11pm, 12pm, 1am.

This forced return, and these intense, late-night writing sessions explain, perhaps, *Cucumber*'s particular vividness, and astonishing innovation. For *Cucumber* now is not just a single show, but a whole, ambitious world – it has a secondary drama, *Banana*, that runs alongside it, accompanied by a talk show, *Tofu*, to discuss the issues that are raised in every episode. There has never been a drama quite like it.

Glancing incidental characters have whole, stand-alone stories – a line in *Cucumber* triggers a whole, life-changing episode in *Banana*. The detailed, interconnectedness of everyone's lives. Drama attempting to mirror the true warp and weft of our astonishing, complex lives – painfully aware of how, even if you are the extra in someone else's story, you are always the hero of your own.

Davies has brought, to the lives of ordinary middle-aged gay men in Manchester, the same sense of intricate universe he once brought to all of space and time in *Doctor Who*.

'Well, I realised something,' Davies says, bringing the teapot into the front room. 'Who has *one* idea? They come bouncing and rolling and thundering in – like a stampede. They come in flocks, and storms, and tidal waves. I honestly think, now that I've passed fifty, and looked mortality in the eye with Andrew, that it's a race to get those billion ideas down while I'm still alive. An actual race.'

And he pours the tea, in the middle of his own, unlikely happy ending, as a Dalek peers through the window, in the rain.

Anxiety. Sometimes, it feels like it is the defining emotion of our age. But there may be a reason for that ...

COFFEE IS KILLING US

I was an anxious child. We were an anxious family. It was the eighties, and my father regularly rehearsed us for when the bomb fell on Wolverhampton: 'As soon as we get the Four-minute Warning, we'll all get in the caravan, and drive to Wales,' he'd say. 'We'll live in the hedgerows. A man can live on just a handful of rice a day.'

Despite such a powerful and organised survival plan, the anxiety remained. It was an anxious house, with never enough money or space, and the breath of ten people condensed on the windows, and ran down the inside of the glass, like rain – and that made you feel anxious, too. Eight children, all scared and rudderless, our anxieties knotted together, like rats' tails.

But twenty-eight years on – despite graduating on to panic attacks – I have a pretty good handle on my anxiety. I basically treat myself like a nervy horse: lots of exercise, lots of sleep, lots of interesting work to keep the mind occupied, and generally avoiding being ridden hard by strangers.

I had a handle on my anxiety, that is, until this summer – when it suddenly took on a new force. There were several reasons – someone I love became troubled, work was ferocious, and it was the summer of internet trolls, and death threats. I would sit in the garden, under a parasol, in the rain, smoking and typing, seven days a week, feeling the anxiety rolling in over the clapboard fence, and dripping down from the trees.

Occasionally, I would have thoughts that would leave me breathless and flattened. The worst one was, 'When you go mad, just a single thought could break you,' which was rapidly followed by, 'And that single thought is, "Just a single thought could break you."'

This idea worked like some kind of horror key in my head – it allowed the doubling, and then quadrupling, of fear in less than a second. It multiplied endlessly – a castle full of roiling insects. Of *course* that was how you went mad. Just a single thought would break you. You got stuck in a thought and never got out of it again. Until it ended you.

Anxiety is a physical state – flooded with adrenalin, you are, essentially, constantly running for your life from the most terrifying beast, but while sitting on a chair, or cooking the tea, or talking to your children. My hands shook; my stomach was liquid. My skull was porous – I could feel the coronal suture between the frontal and temporal lobes straining, and fizzing.

My catchphrase became, around eight o'clock every night, saying, very quietly to my husband, 'I'm feeling quite anxious' – trying to say the sentence as dully as possible, so that it might not alarm the flocks of seagulls picking over the day's detritus in my head, with their hook-ended beaks, and cold gold eyes.

I become convinced that the anxiety was all tied in with the summer – partly because I was listening to The Triffids' 'Hell of a Summer' over and over: *'It's been a hell of a summer/To be lying so low/ Dogs and cats dropping down in the street.'*

The anxiety had come in with the sun, and in the calm, cold snap of autumn, it would die, like the wasps. The new term would, surely, find me calm, in a duffel coat, with my hands now still, and my head clean and clear again.

But September and October stayed unnervingly warm, and I spent the shortening evenings shaking, and Googling the side effects of anti-anxiety medications, and the prices of remote farmhouses in Wales. A friend gave me a Valium, and I put it in my purse, pretty sure that I would take it at some point in the next few weeks, and then go to my doctor and ask for more, and then leave London. At thirty-eight, anxiety had finally beaten me. The bomb had dropped, and I was going to go and live in a hedge.

And then? And then, two weeks ago, I suddenly 'remembered' something: that I was drinking a whole twelve-cup cafetiere of coffee before midday. I put the pot in front of my husband with the words, 'So – that's my usual breakfast.'

'Jesus Christ!' he said, alarmed. 'How have you managed *that*?'

'We have big cups,' I shrugged.

'You've basically been drinking *gunpowder*,' he said. 'I sometimes feel a bit edgy after one latte.'

So I quit, obviously. I resigned from being some kind of chain-smoking, caffeine-drinking lizard, and went back to my previous drink of choice: hot Bovril. Within twenty-four hours of putting the coffee pot in the basement, I'd turned back into something much more low-key, and mammalian – with small, manageable thoughts, and still hands. The seagulls are gone. My head feels perfectly solid, and untroubled.

On the bad side, I've now put on half a stone, and I'm asleep by 10.30pm; but on the good side: I am not living in a hedge. It turns out naturally anxious people should *not* drink 2,544mg of caffeine a day. But then, you probably knew that.

Following the 2012 London Olympics – which, I think I might have mentioned a few times, were ace – the next Olympics seemed to be formed in their shadow: the 2014 Winter Olympics, in Russia.

As Russia becomes ever-more intolerant, the Winter Olympics coincided with a new raft of anti-LGBT legislation prompting calls for Sochi 2014 to be a rallying point for protest. As you might imagine, I was very much in favour of this.

THE GAYEST OLYMPICS EVER

Trouble has been brewing for the 2014 Winter Olympics, since the Russian hosts brought in a slew of anti-LGBT legislation – including a ban on 'promoting' 'non-traditional relationships'.

This an interesting take on same-sex relationships, given its inference is that they were somehow invented recently – perhaps in America, by Google – rather than being so 'pre-existy' that the first time Russia tried to curb them was back in 1716, when Peter the Great tried to outlaw them in his army.

I don't know how much more 'traditional' something would have to be than 'already a massive observable phenomenon in the eighteenth century'. Perhaps you'd also have to have it recorded throughout time in a series of histories, plays, poems, 'fruity' ancient vases, etc. But, obviously, that would never happen.

Anyway. The debate went up a gear last week when Cher got involved. Yeah, that's right. Cher. When asked to take part in the Russian Opening Ceremony, Cher issued a kick-ass statement explaining that she was refusing out of solidarity with Russia's LGBT community – spurred by her own son being transgender.

There's no two ways about it – this genuinely will be a big blow to Russia. If you have already set your heart on your Opening Ceremony featuring some enormo-haired diva wearing nothing but a 12-inch piece of duct tape over her particulars, belting out 'If I Could Turn Back Time' on a fully-armed warship, then Cher pulling out means that dream is definitively dead. Who else are you going to get to do that? Lady Gaga? Madonna?

Well, obviously Lady Gaga and Madonna *would* do it, like a shot – but they've *also* spoken out against Russia's homophobic legislation. Indeed, Stephen Fry's letter to David Cameron proposed that *everyone* boycott Russia's Olympics – even the athletes.

However. Since Cameron replied with 'I believe we can better challenge prejudice as we attend, rather than boycotting, the Olympics', it was clear that – Cher aside – an LGBT-sympathetic mass Olympics walkout wasn't on the cards.

So, if we *are* going – if our solidarity is in our very presence – how can we ramp up that solidarity to the max? How can we *optimise* our support for human rights in a country where videos of gay teenage boys being tortured and murdered appear on the internet without prosecution, and 'promoting' same-sex relationships results in teachers being fired and foreigners being deported? Simple: we have to make Sochi 2014 the gayest Olympics ever:

1) Everyone must kiss. Everyone. Last month, there was a hoo-ha when two female Russian athletes kissed on the podium of the World Championships. While the athletes themselves denied that it was a protest – 'We are both married, and not having any kind of relationship,' Kseniya Ryzhova said – the pictures made front pages across the world, and prompted the obvious thought: 2014 should be a mass kiss-in! PILE ON! If every athlete at Sochi kisses their teammates – gay or straight, male or female – what more perfect way to show how, ultimately, all love is the same? It's all just humans, being there for other humans – in our short, gleeful burst of our time on Earth. Plus, for viewers at home, it allows us to play the sofa game of 'Friendly Kiss – Or Sexy Kiss?' And on top of all that: it's hot. Fun, hot, revolutionary: full house! Let's do this!

2) Rainbows. The recent Stonewall campaign – combatting homophobia in football – included sending rainbow bootlaces to every player in the Premier League. Similarly, Swedish athlete Emma Green Tregaro painted her fingernails rainbow colours, to support gay rights at the World Athletics Championships. So we should roll out rainbows *everywhere*: eyeshadow, underwear, leggings, hair. Could Pepsi-Cola work on an isotonic drink that allowed one to sweat rainbows? Or cry them? Crying rainbows of victory would be amazing.

3) Absolutely accepting the logic of Russia's argument – that homosexuality is 'non-traditional' – and taking it to its ultimate, mad conclusion. In obedient acceptance of Russia's wishes, all athletes similarly eschew *everything* 'non-traditional'. This would include: non-wooden skis, electrical ski-lifts, artificial fibres, digital clocks, the entire disciplines of both freestyle skiing and snowboarding, the participation of every female athlete and the playing of the national anthems of Canada, Bosnia-Herzegovina, Slovenia, South Africa, Qatar, Tunisia, Zimbabwe, Georgia, Libya, Romania and Australia (all adopted since the eighties, therefore not 'traditional', and therefore – by the Russian logic – 'gay'). As the world's slowest, dullest, emptiest, most dangerous and uncomfortable Olympics slowly unfolds, everyone is given their own time to have the thought: 'Progress. Hmmm. Was that necessarily a *bad* thing?'

Of course, there is an argument that, with luck on its side, Sochi 2014's human rights campaign won't need any of these things. After all, at the Berlin 1936 Olympics, during an eerily similar rise in fascism, Jesse Owens elegantly trashed Hitler's poisonous ideology simply by going out there and just … running faster than anyone else. Every gay or trans athlete who holds up a medal at Sochi 2014 will be the undeniable, living promotion of a very certain thing: human dignity and love always, in the end, outruns fascism. Because it has to.

There are various things I suspect I'll spend my lifetime writing about, over and over again: David Bowie, the Moon, progress, Benedict Cumberbatch's face, being a girl and Elizabeth Taylor. My Cumberbatch moment is coming in a minute, but, before we get there, here's the Elizabeth Taylor piece for this book. Because you can never write enough about Elizabeth Taylor.

TV REVIEW: *ELIZABETH TAYLOR: AUCTION OF A LIFETIME.* 'NOT SO VULGAR NOW, IS IT?'

What was Elizabeth Taylor? A beauty. A force of nature. A bomb that went off over and over again, shrapnel flying outward, while she carried on walking, calmly, out of the epicentre – unblinking, on whisky, in heels.

The conceit of *Elizabeth Taylor: Auction of a Lifetime* was a neat one: telling the well-known story of her life again – but this time through her jewellery. Has anyone ever been so closely associated with jewels? Richard Burton bought her not one, but the two biggest diamonds in the world, and such was her power that, the next morning, they renamed the Cartier Diamond 'the Taylor–Burton Diamond'. She named her perfume 'White Diamonds'; she demanded precious tributes from every project she worked on. Unbreakable, dazzling and elemental herself, she was obviously amused by the similarities she found in diamonds.

'All the producers she worked for were regular donors [to her collection],' a friend recalled. 'She would ring them and go [assumes little girl voice], "Ray, I haven't had my pressie yet."' And so another velvet box or bag would travel from Bulgari to Taylor: another cold handful of glitter for the hottest woman in the world.

'Look at that ice cube on your finger, dear,' an interviewer on CBS's *60 Minutes* said to her, in 1970. Taylor is wearing a diamond approximately the size of a custard cream. 'It's to keep me cool,' Taylor coos, coolly.

But why was she so obsessed with jewellery? *Auction of a Lifetime* repeatedly returned to the question: was Taylor's love of jewellery some manner of compensatory mechanism? Or did she just really love expensive shiny shit?

For a full ninety minutes, the question nagged away at the narrative. Taylor's voracious appetite for presents started at the age of eleven – when, on the last day of shooting *National Velvet*, MGM gave her a horse.

One can imagine the young Taylor in the stable, staring at the horse, and sighing: 'It's good, but . . . but I can't wear this horse on my head, at a ball. I think I'm going to go on *Swap Shop* and see if I can trade it in for a massive crown instead.'

As Taylor got older, men flocked around her and gave her jewellery as if her pheromones activated their credit cards.

'Jewellery was almost like foreplay for her,' her dealer at Bulgari said. We saw the tiara that third husband Mike Todd gave her – an item that had previously been the province of royalty – presented as the couple were getting ready for a party.

'Well, I had to thank him,' Taylor is reported as saying. 'Needless to say, we were late for the party.'

'She was always grateful for a gift,' interviewee Liza Minnelli reported, gleefully – stopping just short of doing the 'pokey finger' hand gesture for having sex in her eagerness to convey what had happened.

For Taylor, the link between sex and jewellery was ever-present. She never wanted merely the most expensive jewels – she wanted ones with infamy, too. Jewels with *inference*. By the time Taylor was with Burton – during the period they were racketing around Europe in a private jet called the *Elizabeth*, and the Pope accused them of 'erotic vagrancy' – her jewellery had a heavy, positively carnal tone.

Burton gave her the 'La Peregrina' pearl. Five hundred years old, it had been painted by Velázquez while worn by Spanish royalty – on a chain, over heavy velvets, or armour.

Taylor, by way of contrast, wore it in Monaco, with a light silk dress cut down to here. On her, its size and shape looked not regal, but obscene – a teaspoon of hardening pearlescence, dropleted on her breastbone. 'She wanted it [to hang] in a very special place on her body,' Al Durante, of Cartier, explained, having been commissioned to craft an ostentatious necklace for La Peregrina to hang off. Almost forty years later, he still blushed at the memory. 'I'm not going to go any further than that.'

Still, as she was with her beauty, so she was with her jewellery – enliveningly careless and casual with it, treating it as an endlessly renewable resource which, to be fair, to her, given her wealth, it essentially *was*. She took her beauty out in the sun; she ate and drank and denied herself nothing: she did not confine her beauty to a desultory circuit of gymnasium, beautician and spa. Likewise, she was equally relaxed and abandoned with her jewellery.

'For fun, she'd wear something in the pool,' Minnelli said. That 'something', as the following footage showed, wasn't a verruca sock. It meant Taylor – golden, freckled, carefree, astonishing at thirty-three – in the pool with rubies at her throat, ears, wrist and fingers. You wondered, idly, how many times she and Burton, hammered on gin, saw in the dawn jumping into pools, diving for stray emeralds.

The day after Burton bought her the Taylor–Burton Diamond, Taylor wore it to visit Burton's home town in South Wales.

'They went to a working men's club and plonked a chair in the middle of the floor. Elizabeth sat in it, like a queen,' the diamond's bodyguard, from Christie's, recalled. 'And then she let every woman in that room try on the ring.'

Imagine the Taylor–Burton Diamond handed around a room full of gleeful shop girls, factory workers and farmers' wives, joyously protesting the weight of it ('It's like a bloody pork chop!') as Burton, half in his cups, looked on at his wife, beaming.

Taylor's winningly slatternly way made all other jewellery-owning attitudes look loveless and dull. Drinking with Princess Margaret, Taylor saw her eyeing up the Taylor–Burton.

'That's so *vulgar*,' the Princess commented. 'Do you want to try it on?' Taylor asked. Princess Margaret slipped it on to her finger. One can imagine the slight shortening of breath – the admiring, lost, quarter-turn of the wrist.

'Not so vulgar *now*, is it?' Taylor yelped, in calm triumph. Margaret's sister – quiet and dutiful; the only woman in the world with a collection to rival Taylor's – kept her jewels in the Tower of London; cold and unworn, save in abbeys.

Taylor, meanwhile, took her jewels to parties; threw them in the pool; left them carelessly on her bed, for weeks on end. Her dog, we were told, once ate La Peregrina – then vomited it back up.

And this was, surely, the true glory of the Elizabeth Taylor Collection. As we watched it being auctioned off, a piece at a time – the emerald necklace Burton had bought her, as green as his jealousy; the sad, yellow diamond tear-drop earrings Eddie Fisher gave her, even as she cuckolded him – it looked like a collection of jewellery that had had a jolly good time, all in all.

Where would we rather have the biggest diamond in the world? In a bank vault in Geneva? Or on Elizabeth Taylor's 'fat little fingers', as she put it.

'I don't think [Taylor's jewellery] was a compensatory mechanism for something lacking in her life,' Joan Collins surmised, with a knowing smile. 'On the contrary. For her, it was just ... the icing on the cake.'

Taylor was a violet-eyed dragon, coiled on her hoard. Magpie-blooded. The best jewellery display case the world has had.

Readers of Moranthology *will recall that fully a quarter of that book was taken up with various, awe-struck, howlingly lustful encomiums to the wonder that is Benedict Cumberbatch, and his face-acting skills. Oh, how my keyboard enjoyed letting rip on a bit of Cumberbatch description! How I would rollick and roll through chronicling the rise of his deathless beauty! 'The Frumious Cumberbatch!' 'I would do him until Security pulled me off – then wank at him from behind a door!' 'DEDUCE THIS, SEXLOCK HOLMES!'*

It was all fun and games until someone got hurt. Or, to be more precise, until the person breathlessly pornographising him – me – actually met him, and had to look him in the eye, and treat him like a normal human being.

Amazingly – and this is all credit to Cumberbatch's upbringing and manners – he didn't treat me like a jailable sex case he needed to ward off with an electric cattle prod. Instead, he was gracious and funny and friendly and charming, and we ended up getting on like a house on fire. Of all the 'journeys' I've been on, it's been one of the most unlikely. And, as you will see here, part of that journey involved almost accidentally breaking into Kate Moss's house, and then getting very, very drunk, and making Benedict pretend to be a dragon.

I can't pretend it's not, on occasion, a great life.

THE FRUMIOUS CUMBERBATCH

I don't know if you remember, but sometime last summer – between the end of the Olympics and the return of *The X Factor* – it briefly became the thing to have a go at Benedict Cumberbatch for being 'a posho'.

However many times Cumberbatch tried to explain that he was 'just middle class, really', a sum kept being done, over and over: 'Harrow education' + 'called Benedict Cumberbatch' = 'A man who wipes his bum on castles'. There were a series of catty columns about it, with headlines like 'Posh off to America!' and 'Poor posh boy'.

The underlying presumption seemed to be that Cumberbatch was some dilettante princeling – stealing roles like Sherlock Holmes in *Sherlock*, and the painfully repressed landowner Christopher Tietjens in Tom Stoppard's *Parade's End*, that would otherwise have gone to working-class actors such as Danny Dyer, or Shane Richie from *EastEnders*, instead, and that this was all a great pity.

Of course, as with all these things, it blew over quite quickly – not least because it was superseded by the news that Cumberbatch had been cast in the new *Star Trek* movie, and was, therefore, about to become one of the most successful British actors of the last ten years. But I am reminded of it all today, in the back of a cab, leafing through a pile of cuttings on Cumberbatch.

'What a load of balls that was,' I muse. 'The whole posh thing. What a load of old balls. What a funny old world.'

It's a beautiful Sunday afternoon, and I have been invited to lunch with Benedict at his parents' house, in Gloucestershire. *Star Trek* is now about to open, and this is the only day Benedict has free to talk. I have made the great sacrifice, and taken a train to Swindon.

The cab driver drops me outside the house.

'Here you go,' he says.

I climb out of the car, and stare at a gigantic, honey-coloured mansion, with immaculately tended lawns. Parked in the driveway are a black London taxicab, and a vintage silver Rolls-Royce.

Last night, Benedict had offered to pick me up from the station, saying he has a 'loooooooooovely car'.

'Yes – you have, haven't you, Benedict?' I think to myself, staring. 'You've got a lovely pair.'

I crunch up the drive, carrying a massive bunch of flowers and a bottle of wine, and shout through the letterbox.

'Hello! I'm from London! I've come on holiday, to the countryside, by accident!'

Silence. I circle the house. The place is so big I can't work out where the actual front door is.

After a full three minutes of trying to break in, I decide to go and ask a neighbour for advice on how to penetrate the Cumberbatch estate. I head towards a nearby crofter's cottage.

Benedict Cumberbatch is standing in the doorway of the tiny cottage, in a pair of knackered navy corduroy slippers, watching my progress across the lawn – lavishly strewn with hyacinths – with some curiosity.

'What were you doing at Kate Moss's house?' he asks, mildly.

Ah. Kate Moss. The working-class girl from Croydon made good. That mansion is her house.

The 'posh' Cumberbatches, by way of contrast, live next door: three small rooms downstairs, three small rooms upstairs – the kitchen in old, orange pine. There are bits of odd carpet laid over the actual carpet, to protect it, and every available surface is covered in books, family photographs, or owls.

'Come in, come in,' Benedict says – tilting his head slightly to get through the low door. Even in slippers, he's 6ft, and not built for a seventeenth-century cottage. 'Thank you for coming.'

The Guinness Book of Records does not yet carry this category, but Benedict Cumberbatch is in the running for the 'Fastest Ascent to Fame Ever Recorded'.

At 8.59pm on 25 July 2010, Cumberbatch was merely a well-regarded actor who had played – to enthusiastic reviews, but little public notice – Stephen Hawking in *Hawking*, and Van Gogh in *Van Gogh: Painted with Words*. If you were a casting director, or a writer, you would be delighted to take his call; but otherwise, Cumberbatch lived a life unburdened by excess attention.

Sherlock began broadcasting at 9pm. By 9.20pm, his name was trending worldwide on Twitter. A trending fuelled by a mass outbreak of spontaneous hysteria – the fandom was instant, and visceral.

His Holmes was one of those once-in-a-generation big entrances – written by *Doctor Who*'s Steven Moffat and *The League of Gentlemen*'s Mark Gatiss, this Sherlock was fast, dark and insanely charismatic – he kicked the door in off its hinges, and didn't stop for the next ninety minutes. His first scene had him thrashing a corpse with a whip. The second had him making illative leaps in much the same way Superman flies. Looping, and high.

'I love a serial killer!' he cried, at one point, at full gallop. 'There's always something to look forward to!'

On top of this, with his blond hair newly dyed black, and lolling across his forehead, Cumberbatch's appearance took on an otherworldly hotness. Pale enough to have never seen sunlight, when he launched into his bullet-train monologues, he did it with the intensity of Paganini; or Nick Cave, with one black boot up on the monitor. There was a definite rock star element to this Holmes.

And, so, by transference, to Cumberbatch. By the end of the week, his private life was tabloid fodder. The coat he wore – a £1,000 Belstaff – a waiting-list best-seller. When the second series of *Sherlock* premiered at the BFI, a year later, fans queued outside from 6am, in the bitter cold. When he arrived, they screamed. By then, he'd been on the cover of pretty much every major magazine in Britain – Spielberg had signed him up for *War Horse*, and he was shooting *Tinker Tailor Soldier Spy*.

Looking down his subsequent list of nominations – BAFTA, Olivier, Emmy, Golden Globe – he's won more than he's been nominated for – 17 vs 15: an astonishing strike rate for someone who is still only thirty-six. And now, *The Hobbit* and *Star Trek*. And now, Hollywood.

And now: lunch.

The Veltham-Carlton-Cumberbatches are an incredibly hospitable crew.

Benedict's father's first words, on coming in from the garden – earth still on his knees – are, 'Would you like a large drink?' He pours a cripplingly strong gin, which is exactly the right thing to do.

Benedict's mother, Wanda, meanwhile, manages to combine 'cooking a Sunday roast' with 'emitting the background radiation of someone scorchingly hot in the 1960s, and who could still clearly reduce a room to rubble now, if she flashed her eyes'.

Benedict is second-generation pretendy: Google shows Wanda Ventham and Timothy Carlton in *Doctor Who*, *Carry On Up the Khyber*, *The Scarlet Pimpernel*, *The Saint*.

As there are, now, websites dedicated to young, swooning fan-love for Benedict – written by the self-proclaimed 'Cumberbitches' – so there are for Wanda and Timothy, written by the generation before.

'Is Wanda Ventham a beautiful, remarkably sensual woman? You bet!' one writes. Another describes Timothy, in *The Scarlet Pimpernel*, as 'Wearing the green coat of sex'.

As Timothy and Wanda move around each other in the kitchen, preparing lunch – Wanda spars with her husband as if he were still a young suitor, even as he sits down with an involuntary 'Ooof!' It's rather touching to watch – Benedict takes me on a tour of the house. If we weren't dallying, it would take less than a minute – it's so small.

Benedict, however, is an inveterate dallier, and so it takes a good twenty.

'They bought this house when I was twelve,' he says. 'Look. There's me, off for my first day at Harrow.'

He points at a junk-shop painting of a young Fauntleroy-type, skipping off to school in a huge sailor's hat.

'So posh,' I say.

'So posh,' he laughs.

All up the stairs are pictures of Benedict as a child. Benedict running, Benedict as a toddler. Benedict aged ten – white-blond, skinny, in tiny swimming trunks, on a rocky beach in Greece. One of the pictures shows Wanda pulling his trunks down, and kissing his bottom.

'That *is* a picture of my mother kissing my arse,' he confirms.

This was around the age he was learning to play the trumpet – the event he credits with shaping his much-commented upon mouth.

'Playing a trumpet *wounds* you,' he explains, gleefully. 'That's how this happened.' He presses his finger into his generous lower lip. 'I have trumpet mouth.'

We look around Benedict's bedroom, which is small and floral, with a well-thumbed Alan Bennett by the bed.

On the chintzy dressing table is a small china pot, with 'I Feel Pretty & Witty' painted on the lid, in curlicue script.

I'm just asking Benedict if this is his morning affirmation – 'Well, I *do* feel quite pretty,' he's saying, thoughtfully   when his mother comes upstairs, and interrupts in the way that is the birth right of all mothers. She addresses me with some urgency:

'Can you just … find him a bird?' she asks. 'You *must* be able to find him a bird. There must be *someone* in London who's suitable. I want grandchildren. Please – find my son a bird.'

It is interesting – watching Sherlock Holmes being berated by his mother for still being single. Especially as, where we are standing, we are surrounded by Wanda's collection of stuffed barn owls ('Mum's obsessed with owls') who are all staring at Benedict with pretty much the same gimlet expression as his mother.

'I'm doing all right,' he pleads – body language now that of an awkward teenager.

'I can't wait much longer,' she rejoins, firmly. *'Get a bird.* Anyway it's time for lunch. Come and have another drink.'

Wanda is, much like her owl collection, a hoot. Over a long lunch, she tells a series of anecdotes – including the day Benedict took her and Timothy on to the set of *Star Trek.*

'… and they did *take after take,*' Wanda says, in her cut-glass finishing school accent, serving up the pudding, 'reset after reset. It went on all *day.* Just to get Ben in this bloody *spaceship.* At one point, I said to them, "You know, when I was doing *UFO* [the 1970's Gerry Anderson sci-fi series] it only took me three takes to get to the *Moon*!"'

The Ventham-Carltons never really wanted their son to be an actor – they knew how precarious it was as a lifestyle; it's why they scraped together the money to send him to Harrow, for a 'proper education'. He certainly needed something to fill his days – even as a baby, Wanda describes Benedict as 'a whirlwind – he never stopped'.

'I had a very fast metabolism,' Benedict says.

'He was skeletal!' Wanda rejoins. 'And we did feed him, we really did.'

'They worried that I had a thyroid problem. I would arrive on the school steps drenched in sweat, because I would run there. I never stopped.'

However, it became obvious, early on, only one thing provided enough distraction for Benedict.

'I was a pain in the arse. Show off,' he says, pouring more wine. 'Not malevolent – just disruptive. They tried to see if I could put all my energy to good, rather than just disrupting yet another lesson doing a silly voice.'

He was given his first role, in a production of *A Midsummer Night's Dream*.

'And we all remember Benedict's Bottom,' Timothy says, with perfectly timed lugubriousness.

'And I got *Half a Sixpence*!' Benedict cries. 'I played Ann, long-suffering wife of Arthur Kipps.'

He launches into 'I Don't Believe A Word Of It' – a 36-year-old man doing an impression of his ten-year-old self, playing a role popularised by Julia Foster when she was twenty-four. It's actually brilliant: funny, indignant. He dances from one side of the room to another.

Still, the Carlton-Venthams could kid themselves acting might just be a hobby for Benedict, until Wanda took him to see Timothy, who was on in the West End at the time.

As they stood in the wings, watching, Benedict suddenly started saying, loudly, almost wildly: 'I want to go on. I want to go on!'

'We had to stop him from running onstage,' Wanda says, clearing the plates.

'But why wouldn't you?' Benedict asks, appealing to me, now. 'What kid wouldn't? Have you ever been backstage? All the sets, with the name of the production on the back, with weights on the bottom of them, to hold them steady. And in the wings, you see all that. But then you walk onstage – and you walk into a *real world*, for the people who are watching it. It's amazing.'

There is more wine, and seconds of the roast, and pudding, and seconds of pudding. Benedict picks at leftover roast parsnips – 'I'm not supposed to. I'm on the 5:2 diet. You have to, for *Sherlock*.'

And then, finally, an hour after I was supposed to leave, and woozy with red wine, we go into the other room, to do the interview.

Here's what it's like interviewing Benedict Cumberbatch: a bit like interviewing a waterfall. It won't really answer any of your questions, but it's fabulous to watch. It's not that it's trying to *ignore* or avoid your questions – God no. It is endlessly, eagerly forthcoming, and shows a touching courtesy towards the whole notion of being interviewed. It will tell you a story about being stung on the penis by a sea anemone in the same breath as discussing the panic of entering the library in Harrow for the first time: 'Because I thought, I probably won't have a lifetime long enough to read the first shelf – let alone the first room, let alone the whole fucking library. I've always been after the idea of betterment – to know *exactly everything* about that wine, and tell you about the birdsong I can hear, and to understand the world around me.'

But as you can already see, and as his mother has lamented, he is just an energy – he never stops. This is the force he plays into these huge, notably unusual characters: Van Gogh and Turing and Holmes; Tietjens in *Parade's End* with his genius; a dragon – Smaug – in *The Hobbit*; in the West End, in turn, Frankenstein, then his monster. And, soon, Hamlet, and Julian Assange, and Brian Epstein – manager of the Beatles.

As we're already late, Benedict tries to set out a schedule. He's due on set in Bristol at 7.30am tomorrow, for the third series of *Sherlock*. At pains not to give away any plot, but keen to show what his workload is like, he picks up the script and flicks through it.

'This scene is forty pages long. *It's a forty-page long deduction*,' he says. 'Basically a monologue. And I have to learn it before I go to bed.'

Pointing at the clock on the wall, which has birds instead of numbers, he says, 'So we have to stop at …' – he stares – '… half-past chaffinch. Okay?'

*

As we're already in the past – surrounded by photos – we stay there.

The conversation at lunch got us as far as Harrow, where Benedict boarded – leaving his parents' top-floor flat in Kensington, 'When Kensington was run-down; smalls hanging out in the smog, riots in Notting Hill. A two bedroom flat for £2,000 – the wallpaper the same now as it was then.'

When he got to Harrow, did he find out he was clever?

'Not that clever. Not ridiculously clever. Sharpish – I was a quick learner. A good impersonator.'

Was he bullied?

'No. Because …' he chooses his words carefully, 'my parents loved the fucking life out of me. So I felt confident about the world. Not … entitled. Just like … I could step into the world. Investigate it.'

He loved his schooldays – 'I really did. Sports and outings … I made lifelong friends. In my letters home, I wrote "I am blissfully happy" and I really meant it.'

The first and only time someone tried to bully him, it felt so alien – 'He made me feel insecure and shy, and all I wanted was to be confident and happy' – that Cumberbatch pinned him against the wall, in utter fury, and his assailant stuttered an apology.

He continued being the class clown – not, as it is with almost all future performers, to prevent bullying, but, oddly and sweetly, to get the respect and attention of younger children, instead.

'You could make younger kids go to bed and brush their teeth on time if you made them laugh,' he recalls, fondly.

The only fly in Cumberbatch's ointment was physical: 'I was a very late developer,' he says. 'Very late. Fifteen, sixteen – maybe even seventeen.' The worry was so great, he even went to the doctor. 'I was a kid until I was eighteen, really. But the one grace of an all-boys' boarding school … is that you could lie about what you'd done on your holidays. Not like a mixed school, where you had to parade your girlfriend around the playground. I was a bit Hugh Grant around women. "Good gosh er do you mind if I, erm, touch, ah, *it*? Gosh, I feel funny now." I don't hold it against my parents at all, but that's why I would never send my kids to a single-sex school. I would have *killed* for experience. Fuck the grades. I was all, "I *understand* what girls are now – where *are* they?"'

He'd already had his first kiss: 'Underwater. Mary. I was eleven. The wettest lips you could possibly kiss. I think that was definitely my first kiss. Unless I'd kissed a boy at school in a fucking play – which would ruin that very erotic Humbert Humbert-like memory I have of my first female obsession.'

In his last year at Harrow he discovered 'pot and girls and music', 'got a bit lazy' and forfeited his chance of Oxbridge. He took a year out – working for six months in a perfumier's to earn the money to teach English in Tibet. At the perfumier's he learned to prefer 'bright citruses – bergamot, vetiver'.

Once, with a severe cold, he served Richard E. Grant and watched, with horror, as a drip from his nose 'landed right on his Blenheim Bouquet as I gift-wrapped it' – the most gently dandy thespian anecdote of 2013. A month later, he was in India, watching a parade of keening mourners take the dead down to the river, to be burned.

'You taste it in the air. It's not a charming ancient tradition. You are inhaling the smoke of a burning body. Palpable – in your mouth.'

He nearly died in India: 'I got mountain sickness. Lost on a mountain. It was a pathetic expedition – Hillary-like. We were woefully underprepared. I had simply … an extra scarf my mother had knitted me, and a … piece of cheese.'

With water on his lungs, and his doctor friend warning him he was at risk of an aneurism, Cumberbatch hallucinated wildly on his way back down the mountain: 'I dreamed the stars turned to lightning.'

He looks excited as he remembers this. Suddenly, violent birdsong fills the room.

Cumberbatch looks across, to the clock on the wall.

'Shit. Shit. It's already half-past chaffinch. If we get to barn owl, I am *never* getting to Bristol tonight.'

'So you didn't die,' I remind him, briskly, 'because you are here. And here is pretty odd. Tell me a story about how unreal the last three years have been. How everything has changed since July 2010.'

Benedict thinks – for nearly a minute. The longest he's been silent all day.

'The Golden Globes,' he says, eventually. 'Meryl Streep coming up, going, "Oh my God, we're such big fans, we love you as Sherlock. How do you fucking do that shit?" And then Ted Danson, going, "Oh my God, it's fucking Sherlock!"'

Benedict mimes being trapped between Sam Malone from *Cheers* and Mrs Kramer from *Kramer vs. Kramer*, both of them freaking out, with him in the middle, mind-blown. 'Getting advice from George Clooney, on how to handle all of … this.' He spans his hands out, to represent the last three years.

As luck and Hollywood would have it, Benedict then spent autumn 2012 shooting the forthcoming *August: Osage County* with Streep – plus Julia Roberts, Juliette Lewis and Sam Shepard.

He describes acting opposite Streep – 'Her character is suffering from oesophageal cancer, smoking like a chimney, high on downers, behaving like the most monstrous matriarchal pterodactyl you can ever imagine. And none of us could act opposite her. None of us. We all, one at a time, went up to her and said, "I'm sorry, I can't act around you because … I can't stop watching you. We all want to watch you."'

The American elections occurred while they were shooting. He gets his iPhone out and shows shots of Roberts and Streep posing for their own 'Yes We Can'-style election posters. As the results came in, and Obama pulled ahead, they were all screaming at the television.

Eventually, he and Streep were the last ones up, in a Marriott hotel in Oklahoma: 'Bumping fists when he won.'

He boggles for a minute.

When the fan polarity is reversed, Cumberbatch is graceful with his fan base. He refuses to call them by their chosen name – 'Cumberbitches' – mentioning, with aching courtesy, the 'Cumberwomen', or 'Cumbergirls' instead.

'It's not even politeness. I won't *allow* you to be my bitches. I think it sets feminism back so many notches. You are … Cumberpeople.'

Recently, Cumberbatch websites have been alight with discussion over the next series of *Sherlock* – particularly since Cumberbatch was photographed, on set, making a mysterious, triangular hand signal. The speculation over the meaning of this gesture has been intense. Here, Cumberbatch looks slightly guilty for a minute – then starts laughing.

'You know what? I was just being silly. That sign is just something the lead singer of alt-J does when he plays "Tessellate". I love that band. But!' he says, springing to his own defence, 'I remember Brett Anderson [from Suede] saying, back in the day, "Isn't the point of art to deepen the mystery a bit?" You know? If you start to unweave the jumper, it's boring to look at a … ball of wool.'

It's time to go. I have one question left to ask. I have a brilliant idea. I want to look at the jumper.

'Do some now,' I say.

'What?' Benedict asks, confused.

'Some acting,' I say. 'Do some acting now.'

Sportingly willing to be a big Cumberbatch jukebox, Benedict springs to his feet.

'What do you want me to do?' he asks, with pleasing, if baffling, eagerness. It is, after all, his one day off from work.

'Do the … baddie … in *Star Trek*,' I say, with unprofessional vagueness. 'Whatever his incredibly normal and unintergalactic name is. Simon.'

'John Harrison,' Benedict says, vaguely chidingly.

And it really is the most amazing thing. We're in a tiny, peach-coloured room – the beams so low Benedict's hair almost touches them. Through the window, you can see Benedict's dad, on his knees, in the garden, as the wind moves the narcissi. This is the safest and most normal room in the world. The house still smells of Sunday lunch.

But when Benedict starts his monologue, you see, again, what Spielberg and Streep and Stoppard see in him. You see what he does in *Sherlock*, and in *Parade's End*, where he tore up the screen with only two days' preparation. This big, brilliant, slightly space-cadet kid suddenly comes into focus – painful, super-bright focus – and becomes absolutely other.

In jeans and slippers and a knackered t-shirt, Cumberbatch now looks like someone who has been to the loneliest, outermost reaches of the galaxy, and become demented. The softness disappears from his face – the skin becomes tight. He *is* a terrorist who wants to destroy the Earth. Even when he giggles, for a minute, in the middle of the monologue, he pulls it back immediately, comes in even harder – ending the speech full of cold, still hate. He *is* one of the universe's unstoppable forces.

There is a pause, during which I probably should have applauded.

'Do another!' I say, waving my wine glass at him. 'Do … the dragon.'

Smaug, from *The Hobbit*. He doesn't say anything. Just starts breathing. Breathing like a dragon. The sound of a dragon, breathing in its cave – his neck lengthens, his hands reach out for invisible things – palpable talons. I have it all on tape. I will play it you. It is amazing. It is the thing. It is the thing every actor hopes they will be, and almost never is. It is someone becoming utterly, brightly, incandescently gone.

Thursday, 2 May. Leicester Square. Premiere of *Star Trek Into Darkness*

On a perfect sunny evening, Leicester Square has essentially turned into a *Star Trek* Glastonbury. Music booms from the PA as the crowds mill. People have camped out overnight for a good view of the red carpet. Prosthetic Spock ears abound. One man has turned up in his own *Starship Enterprise* – a fibreglass shell bolted to an adult-sized tricycle. It is one of the most admirably demented items I have ever seen.

The cast turn up, one by one, to roars from the crowd. Chris Pine as Kirk, Zachary Quinto as Spock. There is the usual rhythm of name-howling, carefully rotated smiles, and flashbulbs.

But when Cumberbatch arrives – last – the audience reaction is something other. The screams are another level entirely – the wild seagull ululation of One Direction gigs, and fainting. There is a surge that has security shouting, 'All right ladies, calm *down*,' in a slightly panicked manner.

I am next to a woman from Bootle who has camped out all night with her beautifully painted portrait of the *Star Trek* crew, which she wishes to present to director J.J. Abrams. She is becoming increasingly crushed, and disillusioned. In the end, she turns, and tries to fight her way out of the crowd.

'These people aren't here for *Star Trek*,' she says, casting a hateful eye over the gleefully calling fans. 'They don't even know what *Star Trek* is. They're just here for *him*.' She jerks a disgusted thumb at Cumberbatch.

On the red carpet, Cumberbatch is slightly flustered – in the hotel, there was an incident with cufflinks, and then a tie – but is dealing with the crowds ebulliently. One girl is waving a poster that reads 'BENEDICT – I'M PREGNANT AND IT'S YOURS' – a bold new conversation-opening technique. His stylist keeps catching his eye, saying, 'Benedict – your hair,' and urging him to smooth it out of his eyes. He doesn't. The 20ft x 30ft hoarding above us, that says *Star Trek Into Darkness*, shows him, and no one else. And *everyone* is calling his name. Properly, too – and not 'Bendybum Cumbycatch' for the lols.

'Well, this is insane,' he says, quite reasonably, as he signs an autograph for a girl dressed as Captain Kirk.

3am. After-show party in Chelsea. It has been a long night. Sean Penn is apparently in here somewhere. Benedict has been at the centre of a constant circle of people telling him, in varied and increasingly slurry ways, that his life is about to change forever. He has taken all this lightly, joyfully, and with a series of vodkas. At 3am, however, he calls it a day: 'I'm going to become … non-verbal now,' he says, owlishly. He oils on to the dancefloor, and busts a move to a series of eighties gay anthems, right under the glitterball.

After our interview last week, I received a text from Benedict before the train had even pulled out of the station.

'All the things we didn't talk about!' he lamented. '*The Simpsons*, New York at New Year, Iceland ... I've seen and swam and climbed and lived and driven and filmed ... Should it all end tomorrow, I can definitely say there would be no regrets. I am very lucky, and I know it. I really have lived five thousand times over.'

More heroes, now – and the sad part of the book that is given over to obituaries. In April 2014, Sue Townsend died – taking with her the voice of one of the greatest comic creations of all time: Adrian Mole.

OBITUARY: SUE TOWNSEND

In 1982 there was no doubt who the funniest person in the world was – it was Sue Townsend, writer of *The Secret Diary of Adrian Mole*. A book by a previously unknown author that became a word-of-mouth phenomenon, sold 1.9 million copies within two years, and which contains some of the loveliest set pieces ever done in comic writing: Adrian's first drink ('I was given a glass of Bull's Blood and felt dead sensual. I talked brilliantly and with consummate wit for an hour, but then my mother told me to leave the table'), hypochondria ("Dad, I'm over the worst." My father was overcome with relief and emotion. His laughter was close to hysteria') and cowardice ('I used to be the kind of boy who had sand kicked in his face. Now I'm the kind of boy who watches *other* people get sand kicked in their face').

Since Townsend's death last week, at the age of sixty-eight, there has been no shortage of people all telling, essentially, the same story. That they were a hapless, idiot teenager who thought they were, in some way, a little bit better than everyone else in their small town, who came across *The Secret Diary of Adrian Mole* in the library, or as a Christmas present, and instantly, gleefully, identified with Adrian. Adrian – the gonkish 'intellectual' boy in a cul-de-sac in Leicester, obsessively measuring his 'thing' and writing terrible poetry as, around him, the miners strike, unemployment rises to 3 million, and Diana goes down the aisle in her 'dirty white dress'.

Pop sox, sniffing glue, BMX bikes, Toyah, Lambrini and Selina Scott – if there was an aspect of the 1980s that wasn't in *Adrian Mole*, then it wasn't, in retrospect, really an important part of the 1980s, after all. Sue Townsend owned that decade from the moment Adrian's dad heard that the Falklands War had broken out, and leapt out of bed, panicking – only to discover that the Falklands weren't 'off the coast of Scotland', as he believed, and crawled back under his duvet.

When I first read it, in 1988, I was twelve, and saw Adrian as oddly inspiring. Here was a working-class English boy reading Simone de Beauvoir, and fretting over current events on the news. No matter that he found de Beauvoir terrifying – and, also, believed she was a man – and didn't really understand politics: a depiction of the working classes that didn't involve them limiting their consumption of current affairs to Linda Lusardi on Page 3 was revelatory. Adrian sent his poetry off to the BBC; he wrote fanzines (*The Voice of Youth*), joined a band and dreamed of better things – all while being unintentionally, screamingly funny.

In a world where my available teenage role models had previously been the – let's be honest – oddly priggish, cold and unlikeable Holden Caulfield, or the surreally lavish lives of sexy teenage girls in California in *Sweet Valley High*, Adrian – wearing his rebellious red socks, getting duffed up at his comprehensive school and fretting over the demise of the Labour Party – was the first teenager I'd ever met in a book that I liked. And, more than that, made me realise that I actually existed.

For Sue Townsend made me believe I could be a writer. I had known I wanted to be a writer from the age of ten, but constantly fretted that I had no story to tell. Stories were about Southern belles caught up in the middle of civil wars; lands full of dragons; or orphaned boys with The Force, living on alien planets. Without a story like this, what would I write? What book was there left for me to shape, when my only experience was of living in Wolverhampton, reading books and wanting to get laid?

I spent years miserably trying to get over this problem – believing I might actually have to time-travel, or become magic, in order to become a writer – until I read Adrian Mole: a boy whose existence was essentially like my own. That was when I became suddenly, gloriously aware that the tiny, reedy piccolo flute-voice of a suburban boy could be just as glorious as the raging timpani and violins of Tolstoy. Every book, screenplay or piece of journalism I've written since has come from the same realisation – that simply being alive means you have a story to tell: you don't need to invent a Narnia, or go back in history, to find drama, amusement and life. It's all around you, every second – this is a world of 7 billion stories, so long as you know which bits to write down: your parents' affairs; your unrequited crushes. Angrily colouring in Noddy's hat-bells on your childhood wallpaper with a black felt-tip pen.

Money, by Martin Amis, is widely considered to be the Great British Novel of the 1980s. Personally, I think the *true* Great British Novel of the 1980s was written by a former factory worker and mother of three, who dropped out of school at sixteen, and wrote, secretly, while her children slept, about every teenager who ever lived.

Who was, in 1982, the funniest person in the world.

And in June 2014 I got a text from my friend Martin that made me instantly burst into tears. 'Fuck. Rik Mayall is dead.'

Rik – the perfect, exploding combination of handsomeness and silliness. A man who so palpably enjoyed being himself, he was like a living manual for minxishness, and joy. I have still not yet been able to rewatch any of his shows, as I miss him so much. When I was thirteen, I thought I would end up married to him. In the end, I never even met him. But he changed the way I enter a party – dressed as a man dressed as a woman, holding a bomb and shouting 'WOOF!' – forever. Love you, Rik.

OBITUARY: RIK MAYALL

As weird, home-educated kids with no friends, me and my seven siblings were obsessed with Rik Mayall – and, particularly, *Bottom* – to a degree others would dub 'unhealthy', but we saw as 'utterly life-saving'.

Centring on two loser friends – Richie Richards (Mayall) and Eddie Hitler (Ade Edmondson) – who flat-share, and are seen as utterly undesirable by the outside world, for a load of weird, adolescent and pre-adolescent kids, we saw them as far more comforting or realistic role models than others available to us at the time, such as the kooky teenagers in *Blossom*, or Bronwyn in *Neighbours*.

There are lines in *Bottom* I've used nearly every day of my life: 'That's a smashing blouse.' 'It's sexier in a booth.' 'It's *myyyyyyy* birthday' and the always useful 'Back in a mo. A *sex*-mo.' If you haven't seen these lines performed by Mayall, I urge you to YouTube them now. I suspect you will start using them, too.

Socially anxious, sexually longing and perpetually on the scrounge, Richie and Eddie were essentially two teenagers in the bodies of men – failing in the adult world and being very, very funny about it. That Mayall and Edmondson were the kings of slapstick helped – the episode where they've been illegally siphoning off next door's gas supply and, in their panic, kill an investigating gas man, is a masterclass in physical comedy. They hit him on the head forty-seven times – I counted – with a large, wobbly frying pan. It starts off funny, becomes too much, then becomes *way* too much – and then, around the fortieth 'clong' – becomes unbearably funny again.

Going too far was Rik Mayall's exquisite talent – the terrifying high-wire act of pushing things way, way further than any sane person would attempt, when all eyes are on you. His cameo as Lord Flashheart in *Blackadder* is, almost certainly, the greatest sitcom cameo of all time. He doesn't just kick the doors in – he blows the whole show up. The rest of the cast – the not-inconsiderable Rowan Atkinson, Miranda Richardson and Stephen Fry – stand around like they can't quite believe what they're seeing. Apparently, Mayall didn't do it like that in the rehearsal. Memory tells you he was a major part of *Blackadder*. In that series, he's actually onscreen for less than five minutes. That's sheer, white-light, burning charisma. He could make a sad loser, looking out of a window – mournfully – painfully funny. He could also play the world's most dashing super-hero. He had every single chop a comedy actor could ever have. And he was also, incidentally, very beautiful – pale blue eyes, amazing cheekbones – but you might never have noticed that, underneath all the utterly egoless clowning.

In the end, my brother Richie – that's his nickname, given in tribute to *Bottom*, at the tender, worshipping age of twelve – met Rik Mayall. Mayall was performing in Wolverhampton, and my brother bumped into him, in the street.

'Ah, man – can I shake your hand?' he asked. 'You meant a lot to us as kids, man.'

'Certainly!' Mayall said – putting out his hand, and shaking it with a rococo flourish. Then he assumed the sly, wheedling air of Richie Richards: 'That means you owe me a tenner now, mate. Cough up.'

Oooh, this one was controversial. But I stand by every word. Of course the way you are raised forms your view of the world. OF COURSE, this would have a bearing on how you subsequently formulate government policy ...

PRIVILEGED BOARDING SCHOOL BOYS ARE WEIRD

One of the most pointless sentences on this planet is: 'I'm just a normal person, really.'

Because *everyone* thinks they're normal. Everyone. Weird people rarely know they're weird – because they invariably hang out with other weird people.

By and large, there's just one group of people who *don't* say, 'I'm normal': very fierce drag queens. They *own* their freaky. They're proud of it. They have total perspective about their glorious cultural niche-ness. Underneath all that make-up and glitter, they're hiding precisely nothing.

Given both this, and the increasing likelihood of the Tories winning the next election, I think it is becoming a matter of urgent necessity for one particular group of people to stop pretending they're normal, and start owning *their* freakiness, too, in the manner of RuPaul: public schoolboys. Public schoolboys need to admit their utter bizarreness. For they are *far* odder than a 6ft welder in a diamante catsuit and Miu-Mius.

For a working-class peasant like me, everything about posh boys' lives makes me boggle. Let's just go in with the biggie: boarding schools. Boarding schools are beyond weird. They are from *Mars*. You're sending your children away to be looked after by an – *organisation*. A company to which you pay hundreds of thousands of pounds, but which is staffed with people you'll have barely spent twenty minutes with – and, indeed, most of them you will never have met. That sounds like some serious L. Ron Hubbard shit, right there.

The idea of outsourcing almost the entire raising of your child never fails to blow my mind – because only the posh could get away with it. If you imagine, for one minute, a flip-reversed scenario – where the working classes were regularly sending *their* kids away, across the country, to be raised in a load of caravans by a bunch of people they barely knew – Social Services would be all over it like a pigeon on a chip. They would have closed it down by the end of the month – accompanied by shots on the news of tearful children being escorted away by social workers, still clutching their teddies.

All those febrile, pivotal, delicate years where your child's mind and soul is being shaped by … *staff*. It seems *far* more dysfunctional than what happens on your average, mildly demonised council estate.

As a kid off a mildly demonised council estate, I feel sorry for those rich kids. When it comes down to it, boarding schools are just posh care homes, really. Care homes with cricket, and croissants.

And the awful societal disadvantage of boarding schools becomes clear when you run through all the issues the posh white public school political parties are traditionally 'blind' on – women, community, childcare, housing, immigration, multiculturalism. It's notable they're all things that simply disappear from your life when you leave a world of sisters, parents, babies, homes and new neighbours, and enter into a silver Hogwarts bubble made up only of boys, all like you. Boys, all like you, in an atmosphere where you're not loved for who you are, in the quiet contentment of your family – but, where, instead, you have to try and gain that same contentment by trying to *win* things – prizes, exam results, sports matches.

And now, suddenly, so many policies start to look less like exercises in administration and reason, and more like emotionally damaged people simply echoing their emotional damages. I don't claim to be a psychologist – not since I ran that 'Free Psychiatry Here!' booth at the local fair, and got shut down by the police – but I can't help but see a causal link between young boys who were sent away from everyone they loved and needed, because they had to go to a school 'that will be the making of you', and those boys – now fully grown, in government – coming up with policies that briskly and cheerfully presume people must just bite the bullet, and relocate across the country to find employment, or housing – leaving behind everyone they love and need.

Of *course* they don't understand communities – they have no home town. They were raised by an institution. This is why it was so amusing when David Cameron (Eton) thought he'd invented 'The Big Society'. When he actually *pitched* the idea of people in their local area helping each other out, and being involved in each other's lives. Everyone who didn't go to boarding school was like, 'That's what we're already doing, dude. We've been doing that for centuries. Hang around here next half-term instead of going skiing – you'll be amazed.'

And a cap on immigration is perfectly understandable when your life was predicated on attending a school for which your name was put down at birth. There's a limited guest list, you see … you can't just *expand* Eton.

Do you remember a few months ago, when there was a hoo-ha about the idea of a 'gay school' – where the majority of the pupils would be LGBT?

'That would be *weird*,' opponents said. 'Don't you think it would be *weird* for pupils to go to a school where nearly everyone was gay, or transgender, or running around in drag?'

No weirder than being the average public schoolboy. Not in the slightest.

I'm not chippy about my class, but I do think the working classes are a) different and b) well, better. I want to talk about what we bring to the table. If there is a table, of course. We were too poor for one in our house. Except for that one my dad made out of a door and some bits of wood, that time.

THE POOR ARE CLEVER

Not to beat around the bush, but if you were to catch most people in an absent moment, and press them on the intelligence levels of 'the poor', they'd probably reply, 'No offence, and it's not their fault, but they're generally a bit … thick. Yah. Sorry.'

Modern peasants – welfare claimants; people on council estates; your classic *Shameless* – are slightly dim-eyed, bovine creatures, swaddled in shapeless leisure wear, stirring only to scream obscenities at Sky Sports when their football team loses.

When you boil it right down, the dimness of the poor is indisputable, because there's nothing more stupid than being poor. That's just dim. Who wants to earn less than £60k pa? Only stupid people – that's who! Ipso facto = duh.

However. I've been both poor – one Mars Bar between ten people! You need a breadknife, and the steady, reliable hands of a brain surgeon to make that an equitable feast – and I've been rich – I've got underfloor heating now. Yeah – and I know that I am, now, definitely more stupid than I used to be. Definitely. There are whole parts of my brain I haven't had to use for years now. As soon as I went up an income bracket, I went down a small but noticeable intelligence level, because the first thing money does is takes away problems – the million small practical problems every day brings up when you have limited financial resources, but still desire to do things, and go places, and progress.

Take, for instance, television. If my television breaks down now, and can't be repaired, I'd simply order a new one, to be delivered from John Lewis. Total brain used: less than an egg-cup full.

But back when we were poor, the death of a television meant scouring the local small ads for a new one within our budget (£20), being first on the phone to buy it – 'I'm sorry love – it's already gone to a fella in Coseley' was the end of so many dreams – and then working out a way to get a 36-inch faux-teak surround television from Cannock to Wolverhampton using only buses – as we had no car at the time.

Similarly, being, say, invited to a wedding would mean a borderline military operation: calculating which cousins were of roughly similar build to each of my seven siblings, borrowing posh clothes off them in a day-long manoeuvre of visits and fervent guarantees of non-spillages or damage, asking a friend-of-a-friend-of-a-friend for a lift – usually in exchange for the promise of helping them erect a flat-pack shed the following week – etc., etc., etc.

The amount of collaboration, forward planning, charm, mental arithmetic, creativity, flexibility and iron will involved means that every day, as a poor person, is like staging a small Opening Ceremony of the Olympics, but on a budget of £9.80. Or getting shut in the Aztec Zone on *The Crystal Maze*.

It's amusing how knotty little puzzles like crosswords, and Sudokus, are the relaxing pastimes of the middle and upper classes – when the poor are engaged in real-life lateral brain-teasers every day. That's the intellectual equivalent of going to the gym to keep fit – instead of spending all day on a building site, or bed-bathing sixteen geriatric patients. It's great that everyone's getting good core strength – but some people are doing this out of necessity. Survival.

One of the things I keep meaning to do is get a t-shirt made up with the slogan 'The Working Classes Do It Differently' across the chest – because it *is* different being working class, but that difference is so often framed as simply an … absence. The working classes as merely the middle classes – but without money. A social evolutionary stage down. Nascent. Lacking.

But I was brought up aware of all the good differences of being working class – the superiorities. The working-class parents of my generation all know how to mend a clutch, build a bookcase, grow marrow from seed, sort out the gears on a bicycle, brew beer, tend the dying, rewire stereos, install a bathroom, identify every single edible thing in a woodland. Go around the Black Country Working Museum and the curators – ex-miners – will tell you how the Industrial Revolution was powered by both the workers' brawn *and* their intelligence: the terrifying, 50 per cent mortality rate in the nineteenth century reduced by the miners themselves inventing new safety devices: welding innovative safety-shackles in the evening, then sharing them for free. The same working-class creativity and collaboration that, two generations later, and fuelled by the introduction of state education, and art colleges, powered the astonishing cultural revolution of the sixties, and terraformed most of the world we live in today.

But should you point all this out, there is one last, offhand class-war dick-move that people pull.

'Oh, yes,' they will reply, facetiously. 'The working classes *are* wily – you can't deny that. They have *cunning.*'

As if there must be different words for the intelligence of the poor. As if simply 'being clever' only happens in certain wage brackets.

One of the biggest scourges of our time is 'ironic bigotry' – the modish new invention that allows one to say absolutely unconscionable things, but then end it with 'Joking!!!!', thus serving ... well, thus serving the purposes of Satan, as I explain here.

IRONIC BIGOTRY. BECAUSE ONLY A CUNT WOULD PRETEND TO BE A CUNT

The problem with progress is, you never know who is going to benefit from it. The ground-breaking cancer medicine that saves a dictator; the human rights legislation that frees a rapist. When people are driven to improve the world, they always imagine saving the good people – innocent children; kindly mothers – and not the bad. Marie Curie did not toil to save Scrooge McDuck.

But, of course, when the world gets better for kind people, it gets better for unkind people, also. The shiny, dazzling future does not, sadly, leave the ass-hats behind.

And, so, to comedy. Over the last few years, there has been a rise in a new kind of comedy – one which got its most public outing yet during Seth MacFarlane's hosting of the Oscars, three weeks ago. I'm sure you know what happened by now – the jokes about domestic assault, 'powerful' Jews, the word 'nigger', the nine-year-old African-American actress Quvenzhané Wallis still being too young to have sex with George Clooney; all topped with a song called 'We Saw Your Boobs', in which MacFarlane named every actress in the room who'd done a nude scene in a film – four of which centred around rape, or assault.

In the controversy that followed, the defence of MacFarlane was the satirisation of a more bigoted era. MacFarlane *himself* did not look at, say, multi-Oscar-winning writer, actor and director Jodie Foster, and immediately think of her breasts in the rape scene in *Accused*.

Of course not! But people *used* to. And he was just – as every good comedian should – acknowledging the historical elephant in the room.

I have noticed that comedians – white, male, straight comedians – have been acknowledging this elephant for a while, now. They have been acknowledging the hell out of it. Until MacFarlane on the Oscars, it had previously been in more select, partly concealed environments – characters in the post-modern sitcoms of Ricky Gervais, say; or edgy entertainers on the boys' clubs of *Top Gear*, or *Mock the Week*. Ironic bigotry, faux-misogyny. Pretend racism, satirical homophobia – all the comedy tropes we might, light-heartedly, group together under 'Being Satan's craven ventriloquist dummy, for cash'.

So. Here's the problem: in all these instances, the comedians were not acknowledging an elephant that wandered into the room – *they* brought the elephant into the room. All artists start with an empty page, or a silence – and this is what they wanted to talk about. Over and over. In a world of medicine and fast beats and revolution and prosthetic lungs growing in Petri dishes, and universes dying at the end of telescopes, this is what they want to talk about, time and time again. Women and niggers and puffs, and funny dwarves, and mongs.

And how this feels to anyone who has struggled with who they were born as. It is as if you had, some years ago, been in a traumatic car crash. And you had a work colleague who, every morning, greeted you with, 'Hey! How you doing? God – do you remember when you nearly died in that *terrible* car crash?'

The first few times, you would think, 'This person is acknowledging the bad things that happened to me – and I thank him.'

But by the end of the week – when he said it, *every* morning – you would be going, 'This is a raging pervert who wants to *remind* me about bad things that have happened, and see me get upset about it. This guy is nursing some kind of raging Taboo Boner. This dude has watched *Crash* too often.'

Because the thing about bigotry is that it's like the flu. Every couple of decades it mutates into a new strain that catches you by surprise. Feelings buried that deep in the bone have a terrible, prehistoric smartness – they can rewire whole blocks of their DNA in order to survive. They find new hosts, to quietly mutate in: sitcom writers. TV presenters. Sports commentators. Oscar hosts. It lives in 'banter', and 'lads being lads'. Its first symptom is saying something that makes other people awkward – then greeting the resultant wince with a peevish, hurt, 'Hey – I was just *joking*.'

Which, if I might translate this down into its absolute, finite instruction, means, 'Laugh, bitch.'

So, on the flanks of progress, ride ticks. Ironic bigotry is a parasite – it snacks on things people have wept over, and died for. When I see a straight white able-bodied millionaire making an 'ironic' joke about when a nine-year-old African-American girl will be old enough for George Clooney to have sex with her, it's a little bit like watching someone using the Universal Declaration of Human Rights to mop up their spilled beer, or write a note to their cleaner.

As it turns out, ironic hatefulness works in pretty much the same way as *real* hatefulness. In 2013, we have no need for nostalgia for jokes about uptight women, powerful Jews, horny gays, repulsive transsexuals and the weirdness of other ethnicities. Because you know what – I can remember these kind of jokes from yesterday. From ten minutes ago. From now, right now.

Right, let's get fruity. It's time to talk about pumping. When How to Build a Girl *came out – a book that centres on a teenage girl who wishes to be, in her words, 'a Swashfuckler' – I was asked to write a piece detailing my own 'sexual awakening'.*

As a consequence, in this piece, I explain to a world that has, in all truth, probably heard too much about my vagina, about how I learned all the 'Birds and Bees' stuff. As you may imagine, it was a shambles throughout, but it's still one of my favourite activities – just under 'Baked Potatoes', but above 'Second Pint of Gin'.

HOW I LEARNED ABOUT SEX

So at some point, inevitably, your parents give you The Talk. The Big Talk. The one awkward – sometimes upsetting – talk that initiates you into adulthood.

Unfortunately for me, as the child of hippies, The Big Talk wasn't about the birds and the bees – but what we would do in the case of total nuclear annihilation, instead.

'As soon as they give the Four-minute Warning, we're pegging it to Wales,' my dad explained.

It was a sunny day in 1988, and we were in the back garden, mending a puncture on my bike.

'Obviously all the other cunts will have the same idea, and the motorways will be rammed,' Dad continued, fag wedged in mouth, 'so we'll be taking the backroads. I'm thinking B4176, through Claverley. But once we get past Telford, we'll be fine.'

'Oh, good,' I said, carefully gluing the rubbery patch on to the wheel. I was glad we would be fine, once we got past Telford.

'Because most people will be dead by then,' he explained, cheerfully. 'Twenty per cent of the population gone with the first three bombs. POW! POW POW! There won't even be any screaming. Not that you'd hear, anyway – because anyone within the 25-mile blast radius will instantly go deaf. Just keep watching the news, love. If the Soviets start getting arsey, pack a suitcase. Keep it under your bed. Best to be ready. We're only ever three bad days away from the start of Armageddon. Right, that's done,' he said, standing up, and looking at the bike. 'You off to the library?'

'I suppose. While it's still *there*,' I said, morosely.

I'd got the new Terry Pratchett reserved – but it seemed rather futile to go and collect it now, given that I might die before I finished it. Perhaps I'd just go and reread *Jane Eyre*, instead.

For another two years after this Big Talk, I fully expected the *other* Big Talk – the Sex Talk – to follow it: either my mother or my father finally taking me to one side, and telling me about sex. What it was, how to do it, and how I mustn't do it until I was thirty-three, and happily married. But the talk never came. There was total radio silence.

I even tried to start it once – 'So! Sex!' I said brightly. 'What's *that* all about?'

'You've seen *Bergerac*,' my mother replied, gnomically, closing the conversation back down again, to my infinite confusion.

And that was the end of that.

Now, twenty years later, I can only presume that this was because they either presumed that a) I already knew what it was – perhaps, indeed, because of *Bergerac* – and they didn't want to patronise me or b) they'd looked at me – fat, in NHS glasses, wearing an old tartan dressing gown instead of a coat, and apt to say 'Forsooth!' when panicked – and calculated that, the Cold War being what it was, I was just very unlikely to lose my virginity before the entire Western world got wiped out, and it was a waste of their time – indeed, possibly taunting, and cruel – to tell me about something I'd never get around to doing before I was vaporised. Either way, I never got The Big Talk.

But, thankfully, whatever your parents find too difficult to talk about, popular culture will invariably find fascinating. Mum and Dad might not have wanted to talk about sex – but telly, film, literature, newspapers and pop music did. As my hormones staged a total coup over my life, I abandoned all other activities to become a full time Seeker of all the Filth Information out there. Thank you, world! Thank you for being full of rudeness!

I'd already grasped the basics thanks to the joyous, posh fucking in Jilly Cooper's *Riders* and *Rivals* – generally very useful, albeit that they made me believe that champagne was an absolutely necessary part of copulation: either drunk, deployed in blow-jobs, or just sprayed all over some hot nymphet splayed on a bed, who clearly didn't share a bunk bed with her sister, or have to worry about her only pyjamas (polyester, BHS, with a fetching teddy-bear print) having to be put in the wash afterwards.

However, all the information in Jilly Cooper novels was something that I was just going to have to *wait* to deploy, when I got near some men. As a very self-motivated girl – I had, only the other week, made myself a poncho out of a table cloth – I wanted to find some information about sex that I could get *moving* with. I wanted Sex Homework, essentially. Something I could practise, in my spare, manless time – so that, when one finally got near me, I could spring knowledgeably into action.

And this came when *Twin Peaks* was shown on British television, in 1990. Although David Lynch's cinematography and meta-narrative yadda yadda, what I found truly interesting in *Twin Peaks* was the scene where the sexy teenage Audrey Horne (Sherilyn Fenn) applies for a job as a prostitute at Twin Peaks' spooky, high-class brothel, One Eyed Jack's.

In this legendary piece of television, the owners of One Eyed Jack's ask Horne if she can prove she would be a good potential employee at the brothel. Other sexy teenage prostitutes might have replied by bringing out their CV, or perhaps talking about their Duke of Edinburgh Award scheme. Or, frankly, just saying 'I have a vag' – but Audrey Horne was far too sassy for that.

Horne took a cherry from her cocktail, popped it into her perfect, red mouth – and, ten seconds later, carefully removed from the tip of her pink tongue the stalk, now tied into a perfect knot.

This scene made an enormous impression on me: I absolutely presumed that tying a cherry stalk into a knot was something all teenage girls *had* to master – up there with algebra, and how to fill in the paying-in slip on a Nationwide Building Society savings account – and decided to dedicate myself to learning this vital craft. I feared being at a party, some years hence, where all the other women were assiduously crocheting fruit stalks with their tongues, while I stood in the corner going, 'So! Anyone know any great recipes using leftover mince? I do! BIG TIME!'

As cherries were far too luxurious an item to be on our family's shopping list – the only cherries I'd ever come across before were the ones in tins of Del Monte fruit salad – I improvised with a piece of string, and spent long hours in my room, alone, quietly gurning as I tried to tie it into a knot with my tongue.

Within a week I'd mastered the art, and was utterly triumphal – only to find that, within my house, there was a very limited audience for viewing my sex skills.

'Do you need a poo?' my sister Caz asked, as I sat with her, one night, quietly contorting my face as I worked on a particularly small piece of string. 'You look like you're in pain.'

When I exultantly spat the knotted string out into my hand, she looked at it and said, horrified, 'Is that your phlegm? There's what looks like a bit of *lung* in it. I think you have tuberculosis,' and left the room with nose and mouth covered with her jumper sleeve.

'I'm practising being sexual!' I shouted after her. A younger sibling stared at me – then started to cry.

I would like to report that knowing how to tie a cherry stalk in a knot with my mouth did, one day, pay off – bagging me a handsome lover, who subsequently blew my mind. As it turned out, the only time I ever performed the trick with a man around was twenty years later, at the after-show of an Eddie Izzard gig, in Manchester, where I was with my sister Caz, standing by the buffet.

'Remember all those years ago, when I used to tie a piece of string in a knot with my mouth?' I asked her.

'Unfortunately, yes,' she replied. 'I'm still waiting for you to cough yourself to death, to be honest.'

'I reckon I could take a piece of frisee lettuce from that salad,' I said, pointing, 'And tie *that* in a knot with my mouth.'

One minute later, I proved my point admirably as I ejected into my palm a piece of knotted lettuce. At that point, Eddie Izzard came up to us.

'I've tied a piece of lettuce in a knot with my tongue!' I told him, proudly proffering my bolus of veg and gob.

'And is that ... useful?' he asked.

And I had to admit that today, and for over twenty years, the answer had been, very much, 'No. Not really. I mean, like, never at all.'

So, by the age of seventeen, my interest in sex was still unabated. You know in memoirs by boys about being, say, football fans, where they talk about being captivated by the game at the age of eleven – and by the time they're seventeen they're travelling across the country to dedicatedly see York City at every away-fixture? I was like that – but with shagging.

By the time I was seventeen, I'd decided I wanted to be a great lay. A really amazing lay. 'See her? She's a *legendary piece of ass*,' I wanted people to say, at literary parties, pointing at me.

This is the point where you might expect me to say, 'But it proved very difficult – if not impossible.' Traditional narrative insists that this would be the part where I would begin to struggle, against the odds, for decades, in order to fulfil my dearly held dream.

But that's because traditional narratives are written by boys – who *do* find it difficult to get laid. If you're a girl, on the other hand, you can get laid *any time you like*. Seriously. Fat, badly dressed, shy, awkward – not even actually in a room with a man at all – there is nothing that can be so 'wrong' with a woman that she can't go and have sex any time she wants, merely by uttering this infallible, magic spell to a man: 'Would you like to have some sex with me?'

And this is one of the things I like about men: they're uncomplicated. Sex is fun, they think – so I would like to do it whenever I can. Why not? It was certainly how I felt about it. Yes, sex can be a potentially risky activity for a woman – but I was in a fairly closed social circle, shagging colleagues and friends of friends, and for me at least, it was less dangerous than riding a bicycle around town: I was still very shaky on the difference between 'left' and 'right', didn't understand the Highway Code, and often got distracted if a pigeon flew past. I was much safer on top of a man than on a bicycle.

And the thing was, I just quite liked the idea of gaining a lot of experience, and I was piqued by the idea that sex is the only skill where experience can be seen as a bad thing – for women, anyway. You would never denigrate a lady plumber for having fitting over a thousand toilets, or a lady pilot for having landed a thousand planes. Why, then – in a world of contraceptives, cheerfulness and feminism – was landing a thousand penises apt to have you titled a 'slag'?

So I decided not to care about being called a slag – as a writer, I simply pressed 'delete' on it, in my head, knowing how easy-to-remove words ultimately are – and embarked on a two-year pumpy quest around London. And I have to say, it was all very interesting. It wasn't *romantic*, and the sex was often quite bad, but it definitely was – as all ardently pursued hobbies are – fascinating. Also, confusing. During my Sex Quest years – I used to refer to myself as a Lady Sex Pirate, or Swashfuckler, in my head – I was given a series of bewildering pieces of advice by men.

One man told me that the secret of being a good lay was: 'Never let a hand lie idle. Always keep them both busy.'

Eager to show I was a good student, the next time we had sex I noticed that one of my hands was, indeed, lying idle – and started to pat him on the back, absently, as if trying to wind a baby.

Another man at a party noticed I was fat, and proceeded to explain to me what fat girls are 'like'.

'All fat girls,' he stated, confidently, smoking a fag, 'are good at two things. Swimming, and blow-jobs. Swimming is because they don't like any other sports, because it makes their boobies all jiggle around, and they like being weightless in the water. And blow-jobs is because you don't have to take your clothes off.'

I elegantly declined his later offer of 'a poke' – 'Soz – Aqua-Aerobics at 6am!' I said, brightly, gathering my coat. 'Gotta go and find my nose clip!'

Additionally, that man smelled of ham. In a bad way.

But I'm still very happy that I had my two years of teenage rumpeteering. Dinner parties can still be enlivened with the story of the pop star who passed out in my bed, leaving me confused as to what to do next.

Eventually, I rang his tour manager, who sounded like he'd dealt with this situation before: 'Just drag him into the corridor, and leave him there. What room you in?' he said.

'One six nine. But he's naked,' I added.

'That's okay,' the tour manager sighed. 'We can dress him tomorrow.'

And then there was the time I was with a man and we decided to bring food into our 'love play', but all there was in the hotel minibar was a miniature packet of Pringles. This initially stumped us, until he remembered reading in a survival handbook that Pringles – due to their high fat content – make amazing firelighters. Utterly distracted, we then set fire to them one by one, marvelling over their steady, potato-y light, before just having some normal sex, without any food in it at all.

And when I told these stories, my female friends started chipping in with their stories of being dirty teenage girls, too: how they were not shy, or tremulous, or scared, but bright, witty, horny girls going out and absolutely choosing to get about a bit, have sex with a man who made balloon animals, masturbating dementedly, trying out every perversion under the sun, and exploring the world through their genitals. And I thought, I'd like to write a novel about a girl like this. And then I did absolutely nothing about it.

But then, *Fifty Shades of Grey* got big. At first, I was thrilled by the idea of it – an international blockbuster about a 21-year-old girl going at it hell-for-leather with a hot boy.

'Hell yeah – really dirty books for young girls,' I thought. 'Nice one, the twenty-first century.'

But then I read the book, and completely changed my mind. For, by that point, one in three books sold that year were *Fifty Shades*, and the book had become by way of a shorthand for female sexuality. If you were into sex, you were 'A bit *Fifty Shades*'. Female celebrities lined up to be quoted on what their favourite bits of the book were.

But what I found in the book was a very niche corner of female sexuality – being presented as an everywoman coming-of-age fantasy. *Fifty Shades of Grey* is about a shy, studious, 21-year-old virgin who is repeatedly humiliated, tested, and silenced – often literally, with a ball-gag – in exchange for a go on Christian Grey's helicopter.

While I don't doubt this is what *some* women want, it's the monolithic place this book was taking up in young girls' sexual hinterlands I found disturbing. It's the opposite of independence, rebellion, curiosity, rock'n'roll, and the carefully attended forming of your own desires. Anastasia is essentially a thoughtless, desireless, empty girl who has sex happening *to* her, via a powerful and unstoppable man – and I don't think I have to spell out why I find that sexual templating deeply skeevy for, say, my own teenage daughter and her friends.

In short, although Anastasia Grey spends three whole books being fucked every which way but Tuesday, this totemic Shag Book seemed to be the very opposite of everything I, and my collection of dirty female friends, recalled about their own Sex Adventuring years, and if I may be so bold and inappropriate, what I would want my own daughters to do, when the triumphant, unignorable clarion call of their own genitals starts to rule their lives, in a few short years.

On top of all this – my dears, the solemn, unjoyous *faff* of it! The dungeons and linens and paddles and diets and doctors and waxing and waiting and whips and mind games. In a busy world that needs revolution, admin, inventiveness, glee and thrift, sex being depicted as a cross between the challenges on *I'm A Celebrity – Get Me Out of Here!* and a trolley dash around Selfridges.com seems like a deeply unnecessary complication. You know – sex is very simple. It's something cats manage to do on the shed roof, in the rain. If you *want* to, you can make it complicated – but I've had some great times in a graveyard on a picnic blanket – and, indeed, up against some bins around the back of a club – and I'd like something of that very British, make-do spirit to be represented *somewhere* in British sex fiction in 2014.

So, I wrote *How to Build a Girl* about a dirty teenage girl. Oh, it's not *just* about sex – it's about class, and pop music, and an odd love affair, and family. But I wanted to write something spirited and truthful and amusing about the two biggest words a girl can ever say – 'Yes' and 'No' – and about what *actually* happens when a virgin gets into bed with a much older man who's into S&M.

What I've actually done, I realised, even as I was writing this piece, is finally sit down, and give the Big Sex Talk to my thirteen-year-old self. Here you go, babe. Hope you like it. Just one other thing – you don't end up marrying Han Solo. Sorry. But you also don't die a virgin in a nuclear holocaust – you *definitely* end up doing it. A *lot*. So it's swings and roundabouts.

When you do the sex crime – sex – then you almost inevitably, at some point, have to do the sex time – having children.

By and large, I enjoy being a mother – it involves little travel or actual physical danger, and much of it, I have found, can be done on the sofa, usually with the telly on.

I've enjoyed most of it – pretty astonishingly, really, given that it's a 24-hours-a-day job with no pay attached. Indeed, as my children head into their teens, I would say there is only one bit that didn't *involve troubling my cervix that I actively loathed: homework.*

WE SHOULD BAN HOMEWORK

I'm not one for craven populism. I dare to say the unsayable. In my time on these pages I've suggested some pretty contentious things: jam is horrible. Fish are evil. Ketchup shouldn't be kept in the fridge. Father Christmas is the sexiest man alive.

But this week I am going to say something that I confidently expect to win 100 per cent support. I cannot imagine a single person disagreeing with me. It's this:

We should ban homework.

If one thing happens in 2015, it should be a concerted campaign to eradicate this illogical, damaging, ass-paining institution once and for all.

It is an invention universally loathed. It's slightly less popular than mouth ulcers.

For children, homework is one of their classic, immortal enemies: up there with vegetables, darkness, teeth cleaning and bedtime.

Parents, meanwhile, are doubly enraged. As former children themselves, they can't *believe* this homework stuff has come back round *again* – this time, with the added top spin of *you* now being the poor sap that has to haul their kids in from the playground, and make them give a shit about Richard II on one side of A4 paper, as your offspring scream, 'I HATE YOU! I'M TOO TIRED TO DO THIS, AND I WANT TO DIE!'

Finally – should parents and children wish to round on the people who have given them the homework – teachers – they would find that teachers are the ones who hate homework most of all. Teachers are all like, 'Don't have a go at *us*   we'd kick homework in the *nuts* if we could.'

Teachers *loathe* homework. It's yet another round of projects to be set, handed out, nagged over and marked. Homework for the kids just basically means homework for teachers, too.

And everyone is quite right to hate it – for it makes life far worse than even we imagined.

Look – these are days of rocketing child obesity, anxiety and emotional disorders. Prescriptions for tranquillisers for children have gone through the roof. I don't think I'm being too fanciful to suggest that, as soon as children complete their *seven-hour-long* academic day, they should be free to run around in the park, muck about with their friends, and have the chance to interact with their parents in a way not centred around screaming 'I HATE YOU! I'M TOO TIRED TO DO THIS AND I WANT TO DIE!' And that this would, obviously, improve the physical and mental health of British children immeasurably.

When *else* are they going to do all of that 'running around and being happy' we keep saying they need to do? The winters are long, they've got homework until 8pm, and then that big history project over the weekend. Homework means our children never really leave school. Even when they're at home, they're strapped to that bulging rucksack full of folders: still on deadlines, still producing.

And while that's never fun for any child, for some, it's utterly devastating. If you know, in your bones, that academia isn't for you, those final hours of homework mean you've spent your entire waking day doing stuff that you feel a failure in.

You have no time to go out there and find the things that you might excel at – that give you joy, and change your life. You could help your mum mend the clutch, or be taught how to cook by your dad, or hear the record that makes you form a band, or spend five hours obsessively practising free-kicks with your mates.

Instead, it's that sad chair at the kitchen table, and the slow pen across the pages as your heart revolts and, latterly, breaks.

I loathe my children's homework with a passion. When they come home from school, I want that time to be *ours*. How many hours do we all have left, of their already dwindling childhood? How many of these ultra-vivid years, where an evening – walking along a river; visiting Nan; learning how to do magic tricks; reading stories – is something you'll remember forever: will *become* you?

That my children spend these evenings exhaustedly weeping over a cardboard model of a neutron – which will just get chucked into some cupboard at school, and doesn't count in their exams – makes me feel a sad and desperate fury.

And not least because of the final awfulness of homework – that my kids are the lucky ones. That homework just about works for them, because they have a calm house, and parents who have the time – just about, if we forget that we actually wanted to listen to *Serial* while having a hot bath – to help them.

But for those children not that lucky – in a chaotic house; parents busy, or gone – homework is the cruellest reminder yet that the biggest factor in your educational attainment is, over and over, your parents' education, and class. It's the final blow to the already struggling.

Let's call homework what it really is. It's a parent-test. It's a life-vampire. It's a future heart attack. It's emptied our playgrounds, and panicked our children. It puts work into a home. I wish it death. I hope the biggest dog in the world comes and eats it.

My kids are lucky, of course. The worst thing that happens in their lives is homework, or realising, tearfully that there is no emoji for 'emoji' ('This is a DISASTER.')

For other teenagers, however, things are much more difficult. In the last few years, I have met so many who are standing on the edge of a vortex I remember from my teenage years – toes over the abyss, looking down and wondering what it would be like to fall – and I wrote this in half an hour, on a train, coming back from one particularly intense night. Beautiful girls, this is for you, with all my love.

TO TEENAGE GIRLS ON THE EDGE

I have just finished a tour where I spoke on stage, for two hours, about doubt and self-loathing, anxiety, eating disorders, hope, joy, and wanting to change both yourself, and the world – because those are the subjects of my latest book, *How to Build a Girl*. And unless I was ill, I would always sign books, and meet everyone, after.

These signings were no small things – they would go on for two, three hours. I would meet 400, 500 people a night – something not many people get to do, and which is both a rare and unusual gift, and something that can blow a hole in your heart as often as it uplifts you.

For when you are someone who talks about the bloody war of attrition that adolescence can so often be – especially for girls – you tend to get two kinds of people coming to the gigs.

Half are the ones who've already been through it – winking and hooting, 'Thank you for telling the truth. And thank *God* it's all over.'

And the other half? They are the ones still going through it. You can tell instantly, as they step up. The posture, the sleeves over the hands, something in the eyes – the girls who are struggling, right now. Some of them are hard, and tense, with overeating. Others, anorexic, feeling like starving baby birds when you hug them – a handful of brittle bamboo canes. There are arms furious with criss-cross razor lines. Studs in the ear, the nose, the tongue – where they have tried to reclaim their bodies from something, or someone, with the *snap* of a piercing gun.

Sometimes their parents are there – standing in the background, nervous, their faces anxiously projecting, 'She likes you. Please make her feel better now. Oh Christ, don't break her.'

What do I say to these girls? The ones who are having The Bad Year – The Bad Year where you cannot remember why you were happy aged twelve, and cannot imagine being happy at twenty-one? What can you say in one minute, two minutes, three minutes?

So many things. That panic and anxiety will lie to you – they are gonzo, malign commentators on the events of your life. Their counsel is wrong. You are as high, wired and badly advised by adrenalin as you would be by cocaine. Panic and anxiety are mad, drugged fools. Do not listen to their grinding-toothed, sweaty bullshit.

Here is a promise, and a fact: you will never, in your life, ever have to deal with anything more than the next minute. However much it feels like you are approaching an event – an exam, a conversation, a decision, a kiss – where, if you screw it up, the entire future will just burn to hell in front of you and you will end: you are not. That will never happen. That is not what happens. The minutes always come one at a time, inside hours that come one at a time, inside days that come one at a time – all orderly strung, like pearls on a necklace, suspended in a graceful line. You will never, ever, have to deal with more than the next sixty seconds. Do the calm, right thing that needs to be done in that minute. The work, or the breathing, or the smile. You can do that, for just one minute. And if you can do a minute, you can do the next.

Pretend you are your own baby. You would never cut that baby, or starve it, or overfeed it until it cried in pain, or tell it it was worthless. Sometimes, girls have to be mothers to themselves. Your body wants to live – that's all and everything it was born to do. Let it do that, in the safety you provide it. Protect it. That is your biggest job. To protect your skin, and heart.

Buy flowers – or if you are poor, steal one from someone's garden; the world owes you that much at least: blossom – and put them at the end of the bed. When you wake, look at them, and tell yourself you are the kind of person who wakes up and sees flowers. This stops your first thought being, 'I fear today. Today is the day maybe I cannot survive any more', which I know is what you would otherwise think. Thinking about blossom before you think about terror is what girls must always do, in the Bad Years.

And the most important thing? To know that you were not born like this. You were not born scared and self-loathing and overwhelmed. Things have been done – which means things can be undone. It is hard work. But you are not scared of hard work, compared to everything else you have dealt with. Because what you must do right now, and for the rest of your life, is learn how to build a girl. You.

And yet more advice. It's almost as though, as a woman, I live in a world where I am daily given beauty advice, and somehow feel I must fight back with my own, psychotic, scutty, no-frills whimsy.

MY BEAUTY ADVICE

As someone who is regularly asked how old they are – only for the answer to come back, 'Oh yeah – that sounds about right. *Thirty*-nine, you said? Mmmm-hmmm. You've got quite dry skin, haven't you?' – I feel it's only fair to share the beauty philosophy I have pieced together over my near four decades, although to be fair to my interlocutors, it does feel longer, it's not the years it's the mileage, and, yes, my skin *is* very dry. Sometimes, my face feels like one of those sachets of silica gel – inexplicably found everywhere these days, yet able, when placed in the same box, to suck all of the moisture out of a pair of trainers! And who knows how! Or why!

I) **Small yet regular outbreaks of adult acne simply mean you're more sexual than 'normal' people.** Feel self-conscious about the sporadic eruptions on your chin? Regularly succumb to flailing despair that you're still fighting a rearguard action with teenage acne *at the same time* as dealing with your own adolescent child's burgeoning acne? Simply remind yourself of the fact that I totally made up: adult acne means you're so pumped full of irresistible sexual pheromones and sexy sex-things that, yes, inevitably, they become dangerously overheated, and burst out on your face. Whenever, in weaker moments, you are in danger of feeling self-conscious about what appears to be a recreation of the Avebury Stone Circle around your nose, simply look everyone in the room in the eye and say, 'I apologise for being hotter and more irresistible than everyone else in here. It must be awful being you,' scream, bow, then leave. NB this exit works in almost every situation *except* when on a surveillance exercise. MI5 do *not* like this exit being used by employees.

2) **'Ringing in the changes' with your make-up is the ethos of a lunatic.** There may be those who enjoy experimenting with their make-up, and to them – I wish you nothing but joy! Delight in standing in the big Boots up town and trying on seventeen different kinds of bronzer on the side of your nose! Thrill at the prospect of experimenting with modish new make-up looks recommended in *Grazia*, such as 'Neon Murderer', 'Confused Baby-Mother' or 'Pimpy Clown'. For the rest of us, however – those who found a 'look' they liked in 1994 and are, frankly, still exhausted from the task – I say: dig in! Carry on! State your intention, loudly, to take your current make-up regime to the grave. Stipulate in your will: 'I will be buried in Rimmel eyeliner, "Hurrah! Britpop Forever!" eyeshadow and whatever the fuck foundation is under £20.' Your motto is: 'Ring in – *the same!* Experiment – with not giving a shit about experimenting! Be bold – in your obdurate belief that one kind of face per lifetime is enough!'

3) **Get excited about slowly rotting!** Over the last six months, my first big Ageing Sign has made itself apparent: a wattle. My neck has started to gently collapse, and I'm now rocking a small, dangly pleat in the middle – a little as if it's been taken over by Hyacinth Bucket, who has decided to 'treat' me to some manner of dainty neck-valance. Faced with these kind of undeniable evidences of ageing, there are only really two ways to react: a) either becoming inexplicably shocked and angry about the nature of time, like some mad drunken alien working on a Time Freezing Bomb on *Doctor Who*, and who will clearly have to be killed by the end of the episode because their plan to suspend all temporal advancement in the universe is demented, or b) thinking of yourself as your own pet, and being gently fascinated and amused by the mad-ass crazy shit that's happening to you as you march on down life's long path. Personally, I'm very fond of my wattle. I like to stroke my

wattle, when looking out of the window, and feeling reflective. If I *really* liked you, I would allow you to wibble my wattle, over dinner – so long as we were on the second bottle. I *like* having a new place grow on my body, with no effort from me – save having hunched over a laptop for twenty years while grimacing, and eating beef jerky. How exciting! Who knows what will grow next! Maybe I'll develop an erectable scaly display-ruff – or a tail that can drop off, when under threat. Everything to play for here! More jerky for me!

4) **Most of the time, it's good to be clean.** But also, I like to believe you are not the only one who finds your belly-button smell intoxicating; and there's a lot to be said for being the one in your social group who nabs the nickname 'the Musky Ox'.

5) **The cosmetics and beauty industry is valued at $19 trillion.** Yet, without exception, everyone looks at their best ten minutes after a shag, sitting on the sideboard in the kitchen, wearing an old baggy shirt, and eating cereal. Next time someone tries to sell you Botox, designer gear or lipstick, just say, 'No need, babe – I've got cornflakes and cock,' and stroll on.

One of the things about being a parent is realising you are basically farming the future. That's what you're doing: raising the next fifty years. The little people-crops you sow, and so tenderly nurture, will go on to take over the world. That's their job, and yours.

And while, as a parent, you are apt to believe that you must cram this delicate future with all you have learned and known, sometimes you are reminded that you have a built-in obsolescence. All your lessons worked for you, where you lived – in the past – but these children are going to live in the future. Perhaps, sometimes, they know a little more than you. Perhaps they can see further down the road. Perhaps you just need to back off. Perhaps the future will tell you what the future is, now.

IT'S OKAY MY CHILDREN DO NOT READ

We have decided not to drink, my friend James and I – but we are not so strong-minded about smoking.

We are sitting on the doorstep, hiding from our children – 'You don't smoke, do you, Mummy?' 'No!' – and talking about the books we have loved, in the year just passed.

James loved *Stoner* – 'I had no idea I could cry that much, just from reading words' – and I am becoming tedious about how much I loved *Moby-Dick*: 'I've spent twenty years thinking it was some Hemingway-esque bore-athon about angling – but it's actually explosive homoerotic whale-porn! Why don't they *tell* you these things?'

Laurence Sterne, Lorrie Moore, Eimear McBride – this is our real gossip: talking about authors we've long heard about, but only just got around to reading; as if they're friends of friends, just met.

And then – after an hour – we move on to the only sensitive topic we have.

'So … your kids reading much?'

Pause.

'No.'

Pause.

'Mine neither. Just the ones that are made into movies. You know. *The Hunger Games*.'

Sigh.

'Same here. Oh God. *What have we done wrong?*'

We are liberal parents. The things other parents fear – their children being gay, marrying someone of a different race, choosing a 'risky' career – aren't even worthy of a shrug. We would not give them a second thought.

But we have discovered, now, with our teenage children, that there is only one thing we truly fear – our children not reading. Reading being a thing you have to *remind* them to do – or even coerce them into.

In November, after years of literary truculence, I found myself desperately offering my youngest daughter £2 if she read *Adrian Mole, Alice's Adventures in Wonderland* or *The Hitchhiker's Guide to the Galaxy* – placing them in an enticing stack beside her bed.

She eyed them balefully, like a cat eyes the door to the vet's surgery.

'I don't really want £2,' she said, reasonably. 'I just want to watch Zoella, on YouTube.'

And why does this agonise me? Oh God – for so many reasons. Because I need us to have shared literary references – 'Don't Panic!', 'You are sleepy, like the Dormouse' – in order for us to feel like a proper family, bound together by 'our' books.

Because every book you read, as a child, becomes a whole new room in your head – and I want them to live in a mansion of people, universes and centuries, and phrases like 'Runcible spoon'.

Because there's an air about someone who's gallivanted, joyously, through a library in their early years that I revere – far more than I revere someone who has travelled the world, been born beautiful, or wears a cheap acrylic fake-fur coat like it's worth £1 million.

Because – and this is the key thing – I worry they will not manage without it. That books are *needed*. That they will *suffer* without books. That it will *ruin* them.

'Because it made us who we are, didn't it?' James says. 'Reading *saved* us. We'd be nothing without books.'

And that is true, because we were odd children – working-class, a little bullied, a little lonely – and books were like a combination of map, weapon and ladder to climb out of our bad years, and into the happy adults we became. And not only were they a survival kit, but also our greatest joy. We had the library. Endless books for free, stacked up around our beds like piles of money in a treasure house.

Why do our children not need, *or* want, our carefully collated inheritances – slowly yellowing, and dust-furred, in the bookcase?

'What have we done *wrong*?' James sighs again.

But it's cold, so we put our cigarettes out, and go in, and see what our children are doing.

They've been spending the evening recording a mockumentary of *Made in Chelsea* on their phones, and editing it on the laptop – looking up how to do so on Google. Then they play Trivial Pursuit, and watch *Hairspray* – becoming hysterical with laughter, and having to do competitive headstands, in order to calm down.

And I start thinking – why am I worrying about these children? These happy children? Why am I worried that *they* might be dumb – when they are answering quiz questions on maths and geography that leave the adults standing? Why am I worried *they* will be lesser people without literature – when their generation is unprecedentedly tolerant of different sexualities and cultures, has a plummeting use of drink and drugs, and an ability to satirise itself, and anything else, in a way that makes teenagers of the 1990s look like earnest, credulous cavemen? They live in a world of black presidents; lesbian Prime Ministers – the internet, with a billion people, and a trillion facts, at their fingertips. From their bedrooms! From the beach, or on a bus!

By way of contrast, when I was a teenager, if *I* wanted to see outsiders triumph, or witness omniscience, I had turn to those carefully hoarded novels about Jo March, or Aslan.

Perhaps it's just that their lives are *better* than books. Perhaps it is that. Perhaps you don't need novels if your life is happy. Perhaps I am a monkey, pitying a man.

MORANIFESTO
part four

So, in the last section I said I believe everyone should write a manifesto – just to finally get down on paper what they *actually* believe; find out what it all adds up to.

The following, then, is what I came up with on the subjects that intrigue *me*. You may note I've largely left out anything on policies that involve either a) maths or b) guns, as these are not my strong areas. My presumption is that, before I actually took this manifesto to the hustings, I would team up with Carol Vorderman and the Doctor, who would take over, respectively, the economy, and defence. I've looked up 'team player' on Google, and that's definitely what I'd want to be – so long as it didn't actually involve kicking or catching any balls. I instinctively close my eyes whenever balls come towards me. I think it's why I have two children.

So here it is: the actual Moranifesto. I'm only showing you mine under the condition that you then show me yours. We all have to bare our political tits together.

1) Electoral reform: i.e. the scrapping of 'First Past the Post' and introduction of some form of alternative vote/proportional representation, to end unhappy voters blindly and 'tactically' voting for parties they don't believe in, or not voting at all, thus making the entire system, to use the scientific term, 'Useless, time-wasting bullshit'.

2) State-funding of political parties – no more corporate lobbying, or self-interested sponsors – in order to rebuild voter trust. Once a party starts polling more than 7 per cent annually in opinion polls, and/or has more than 60,000 members, funding kicks in.

3) Andy Burnham to sing Hot Chocolate's 'Sexy Eyes' at the next Labour Party conference.

4) Boris Johnson to be installed as 'Store-Front' Prime Minister. While the *real* Prime Minister is some furiously untelegenic maths nerd who simply wishes to sit in a room for fourteen hours a day with a massive calculator, crunching some serious economics, Boris gets to jet around the world, being amusing, falling over, saying 'Blimey!' and riding a bicycle, a bit like Mr Bean.

He is allowed to job-share with Hugh Grant as the Prime Minister in *Love, Actually*, and/or Martin Freeman playing Prime Minister as Tim from *The Office*.

It should be noted this Store-Front Prime Minister has absolutely *no* powers – he's just there, like a political Kardashian, to give the media a series of amusing photo-ops and interviews, while someone with a brain the size of Mars, but no charisma at all, gets on with the actual 'running of the country' stuff.

5) The House of Commons to be fully insulated, lined with pine and turned into a sauna. Debating style now totally recalibrated by a) emotional vulnerability of everyone being in a towel b) searing heat making everyone very relaxed c) no speech able to go on for more than five minutes, as the speaker gets too sweaty, and has to sit back down again, as they've gone a bit dizzy.

6) Manifestos to be written with the aim of people reading them – so people actually know what they're voting for, instead of voting for a Prime Minister who 'seems nice'. This jazzing up to happen by whatever means necessary – forcing J.K. Rowling to write it, having a nudey picture of Benedict Cumberbatch in the centrefold, impregnating each page with a lickable film of beer. Democracy should be entertaining, hot, and alcoholic.

7) On the basis of the handy reckoner 'Would we invent this now?', abolition of the House of Lords. Is what we need, in the twenty-first century, a House of Lords? I mean, just the name: 'The House of Lords.' They're not who you want in an emergency. When the shit's going down with the Avengers, and Captain America's locked in a basement, and the Earth is being dragged into the Sun, and everyone's despairing, you wouldn't want Black Widow to go, 'Hang on! I know! Let's get the House of Lords in! They'll sort it out!'

The whole idea of Britain being represented by 'Lords' is weird. Lords are good for getting drunk – indeed, they are the benchmark – and a-leaping, and they have a high tolerance for fancy dress: all those ermines and gold chains require strong levels of being able to 'style it out'. But, seriously, we only tolerate them because 'Lords' sounds posh. Given their centuries-old feudal allegiances, weird sexual politics, high-bling gear and intense insularity, they are basically a souped-up version of *My Big Fat Gypsy Wedding*, but with castles instead of caravans.

Surely what we want is basically the Council of Elrond – a collection of people all eminent in their fields, taken from a proportionately representative background and paid a wage that reflects the serious and vital nature of what they do – so they're not tempted to take backhanders, and – most crucially – can afford nicer bras and stockings when they're photographed taking cocaine with sex-workers.

8) Relocation of Westminster. Again, using the handy measuring device 'Would we invent this now?', I suspect we would not start from scratch with our centre of government in an old Victorian Gothic building with a huge clock tower strapped to it, right on the banks of the Thames, where it will be at terrible risk in the event of climate-change flooding. I don't know about you, but I'd like to think we'd located the seat of administrative power in this country somewhere where there is absolutely no chance of waking up one day and seeing our Prime Minister floating down the Thames shouting, 'Help! Help! Someone get a pedalo! I'm heading towards Southend!'

Anyone who's been to the Houses of Parliament can see that, while it's an amazing tourist attraction – the medieval hall!

Famous clock! Mad old Black Rod banging on the door with a stick! – it's not a place to do business. There aren't enough offices, it's cramped and outdated, it's an insane security risk – all those shootable, bombable windows overlooking the river – and there aren't enough women's toilets, because, when they built it, women were still sitting at home wearing huge hats and saying, sadly, 'I cannot work out which I would like best – a slightly looser corset, or the vote.'

It *is*, however, an amazing place to sit in one of the eight subsidised bars and get drunk. I mean, it's awesome. On that terrace with an Aperol spritz, trying to work out if you fancy Michael Portillo or not? In that sole respect, it's peerless.

Obviously, I know that, in many ways, I'm arguing against my core values to veto a big Gothic booze-barn that's on the labels of HP Sauce as being the seat of our democracy. In another dream, that's probably what I would have invented.

But this dream is a *practical* dream, spurred on by the recent estimate that it will cost £3 billion to refurbish the Houses of Parliament to make it a *slightly* more modern building in an impractical location, that's still too small.

I'd relocate it, wholesale. I'd put it in Birmingham – the centre of the country, the safest from flooding. As a Midlands girl, I think it would be incredible healthy for the centre of government to leave London – insular, overpriced, wanky – and put it in the middle of a city with a brilliantly dry, witty, dolorous sense of humour. Politics badly needs to be in a place where it will hear someone going, 'To be fair, you look like a bit of a dick' when they're rehearsing their speeches.

London is a basket with too many eggs in it – media, politics, business, the City – and it would be healthy to put the big old emu egg of government in a second basket, 120 miles up the M1. The resistance to its relocation tells you everything you need to know about how government views 'the regions' – this presumption that civilisation ends north of Hampstead. If it *does*, then this is an *excellent* reason to spend that £3 billion on building a fabulous, fit-for-purpose modern Parliament – with things like crèches, public spaces and maybe even living quarters – to cut down on all those expenses claims. It would *bring* 'civilisation' to 'the regions'.

The current Houses of Parliament can then be turned into luxury flats and sold for vast profit – because that's just what we do with everything. Probably even Dame Judi Dench, eventually.

9) Energy security. See How Wind Turbines Keep Us Free, page 337.

10) Banning of the phrase 'hard-working people'. Man, that's a phrase I could happily never hear again. 'hard-working people.' Although it's understandable, in a capitalist economy, why 'hard-working people' is the default phrase politicians use when talking about people – it is their effort, and financial contribution to the economy, which is most valued, and visible – it is a bit arse-about-tit, in terms of priorities.

Firstly, it neatly ignores anyone who isn't in work – students, the sick, the disabled, full-time carers and the unemployed who, we *must* remember, aren't all sitting on a pile of empty Kestrel cans cackling, 'Haha I love being on the dole, me. I'm doing it just to screw people who *are* employed over,' but the majority of whom are desperately looking for work so they can enjoy having more than £57.90 a week, in order to indulge in such luxuries as a coat, or a bus fare.

And secondly, the presumed financial contribution from someone who is, above all else, 'hard-working' and tax-paying, is not all it seems.

For, if you 'work hard' at a job which makes you ill, anxious, depressed or unfit – if 'working hard' for those extra hours means you don't have time to exercise, and rely on ready-meals – you could negate your tax value pretty quickly.

Currently, nearly half the British population takes prescription drugs – cholesterol-lowering statins, ACE inhibitors for high blood pressure, or painkillers: nearly one in five women in economically deprived areas is being prescribed antidepressants. Eight million people in Britain suffer from anxiety disorders.

The cost of these medicines to the NHS was £15 billion in 2013. On top of this, we spend nearly £9 billion on Type 2 diabetes – a disease which is largely and easily preventable, through good diet and a bit of moving around, but which currently results in 135 amputations a week. Amputations! In the twenty-first century!

Look again at what 'hard-working' means – what politicians mean when they say it. It means 'working two jobs if you have to'. It means 'taking nightshifts'. It means 'working zero-hours contracts'. It means 'relocating your entire family across the country if that's where the work is'. It means 'accepting whatever job you are offered at the Job Centre, or having your benefits withdrawn'. It means prioritising being a wage-earner above your own wellbeing. It means saying, 'That job would make me miserable, and ill – it means I will not see my family, and I will be anxious, and withdrawn' is unacceptable.

But given the above cost of people living miserable lives – and that's *before* we calculate time off work, and the knock-on effects on loved ones' health and ability to work, if they must stay at home and care for someone ill – there's a fairly sizeable argument to say that people would be of more benefit to their country – or, at least, be a considerably smaller burden – if the onus was put on being a content and healthy citizen, rather than a hard-working one. Plus, it allows someone in a low-paying job, who is healthy, feel they are 'contributing' as much to society as someone in a high-paying job. It allows pride, and value, to be attached to things that are not just financial.

So much of the NHS's budget goes on what is, essentially, the medicalising of social problems. Elderly 'bed-blockers', repeat emergency admissions for the mentally ill, obesity, diabetes, the Friday night carnage of the pissed. All problems that could have been addressed, earlier down the line, with the spending of hundreds of pounds, now costing tens of thousands of pounds when they present to A&E, and result in long-term admissions and expensive treatments. At the moment we are currently spending billions on fixing loneliness, depression, anxiety and self-loathing, because there is no real value put on being a healthy and happy person – merely a 'hard-working' one.

The fact that we don't have, at the forefront of our planning departments' priorities, building estates, towns and cities that work as brilliant machines to keep us healthy, and inspired, and happy, is another depressing waste of time, and energy, and resources.

Currently, we tend to dismiss the bland, monoculture architecture and planning of most twenty-first-century urban spaces as nothing more harmful than 'boring'. But research conducted by cognitive neuroscientist James Danckert discovered that when people are bored, they don't merely become dispirited. Instead, they register higher levels of cortisol – the stress-related hormone, which is linked to anxiety, strokes, heart disease and diabetes.

Boredom is also linked to increased involvement in risky behaviour – gambling, drinking and taking drugs. Suddenly, the high street of a depressed area – full of cheap off-licences and betting shops; and A&E on a Friday night – a carnage of drunken, high people rolling in from 11pm onwards – all seem part of the same story.

But yet we still build cities that make the citizens ill, and cost the NHS billions.

I would have the health and care services – both physical *and* mental – work as part of the consultation process on any sizeable building development – malls, town centres, housing. Have them help, from day one, to build cities that actively keep people healthy, stimulated, connected, and never too far from a public toilet (see page 30, The Real Purpose of Starbucks).

11) Complete legalisation of sex-work (see page 209)

12) Recognising that the BBC is just as important a part of Britain as our economy, our health and our weather, and entirely removing it from political purview. No curtailment of the licence fee – instead, the opposite: its expansion as an opt-in to everyone in the *world*, thus making it a truly global broadcaster.

13) Acknowledging the past. I once spent a very interesting afternoon with the BBC historian Dan Cruickshank. At the time, I had a massive intellectual and genital crush on him, and was wearing a very low-cut top – in order to suitably convey this to him. Over the course of our conversation, he became gradually more and more discombobulated and sweaty – all, I believed, due to my repeatedly leaning forward, tittily, and saying, 'So – tell me more about seventeenth-century bricks, Mr Cruickshank.'

Finally, he turned bright red and stood up.

'Wow,' I thought. 'I really *am* very powerful, sexually, right now. He's going to take this to the bedroom. *Yowsa.*'

'I'm terribly sorry,' Cruickshank said, leaning on a chair. 'But I must go. I'm going to Iran tomorrow to look for the Tower of Babel, and I think my anti-malaria shots are making me feverish. I feel most peculiar. Goodbye.'

And he staggered away from me, my love, and my bosoms, in order to lie down with an ice pack on his head.

However, *before* I destroyed him with my allure, he'd given me a brilliant, potted history of our country – one that has made me, subsequently, see everything through new, Cruickshank History Spectacles.

In essence, Cruickshank said, pointing out of the window of the hotel we were standing in, whenever you see a beautiful, white Georgian building – the golden crescents in Bath, the stucco confections of London – these were buildings almost certainly built on slave money. In all those beautiful English novels, whenever a character has made his money in 'the Indies', that would almost certainly have been slave money, too.

Ever since, when I am walking down a British street, this is what I see: the real cost of these beautiful buildings. It's like having the receipts nailed to the door. Really, they might as well be built of bone – the white, white render made of crushed bone – because that's the currency they were paid for in. Ravishing, but deadly – like white piles of sugar, or cocaine. We effected an astonishing piece of bad alchemy – turning incalculable suffering into things that make us swoon, and, in our rapture, never asking after their history.

It's rightly humbling to become aware of this – after all, when we see the Pyramids we know that their awesome beauty was only possible because of immense cruelty. We know this about the buildings of the Aztecs – and, indeed, the stadiums for the 2022 World Cup, currently being built in Qatar (current death toll: 1,200). And yet, in our Western cities, there are no lessons where we are given Cruickshank History Spectacles, and can see what we are made of.

And to know what we are made of – how we came to be the privileged country we are today – is important. It is the perfect inoculation against insularity, jingoism, and that dumb, feverish brand of fuck-them-all patriotism we fear when we look at the rise of UKIP, proto-fascist parties and the hard right. A little bit of history is the vaccine against misplaced superiority, and that unpleasant, festering, ill-informed sense that to be a Briton is to be innately superior.

In terms of both race relations in our own country, and our foreign policy abroad, it would be healthy for everyone in this country to have a deep understanding of why we are, now, such a rich and advanced nation. We don't need to become uselessly self-flagellating about it – the world will always be, to a certain extent, *Game of Thrones*, and when we started founding our Empire we had different standards of morality, and different concepts of the value of humanity. We have been on a long road out of colonialism, slavery, witchcraft, child labour, feudalism, *droit de seigneur*, capital punishment, beheadings and believing the Sun revolved around the Earth.

But if we look at the deep anger and fear in both our own citizens of colour – at risk of radicalisation, feeling 'other' – and the powerful distrust our foreign policy inspires in other countries, we could open up a new space for conversation by acknowledging that their sense of our history is very different from our own – and with good reason. Very, very early on in the game, we stole a huge advantage at the expense of other nations, and it would only be suitable, as a courteous nation, to admit this.

And the sense of urgency in this matter – the need to talk honestly about the reality of history, and the origins of current social and economic power – is so much more noticeable in America.

The first time I went there, when I was seventeen, I went to Seattle, at the height of grunge, to interview Courtney Love. It was a dazzling September day, and I stood on an intersection at 9am, looking down to the bay – surrounded by skyscrapers, and the then-newfangled coffee shops.

I expected to be blown away by being in America – home of rock'n'roll, Patti Smith, Studio 54, Truman Capote, Niagara Falls and Crosby, Stills, Nash & Young singing in Laurel Canyon. I expected to feel the giddying thrill of a new continent bursting with invention, hope and space.

At the very, very least, I thought I'd be vibing off being in the city of *Frasier*. *Frasier!* With Niles! ('A latte – with just a *whisper* of cinnamon.')

Instead, all I could think about was what had been there 300 years ago. The clearances, and the death marches; the buffalo skulls piled 20 metres high.

Meanwhile, 2,500 miles south, boats were arriving with millions of stolen people – all being poured into founding this massive, roaring continental powerhouse that now, for better or for worse, sets the economic, military, cultural and moral climate of the Earth.

I stood on that street corner and felt an unbearable sadness, a profound sense I shouldn't be there, and the itchy embarrassment of being another liberal white girl basically going all *Dances with Wolves* when confronted with America. I went out, searched fruitlessly for a proper cup of tea, and then went back to my hotel room and read P.G. Wodehouse, and pretended I was back in Britain.

Whenever I told the story afterwards, I always felt unbearably pious – 'And that was when I realised America was built on genocide and slavery! I dunno if you guys ever knew that???' – and would have to couch it in terms of me being a massive dick.

But then, twenty years later, when social media and Twitter blossomed into life, that feeling I'd had on the intersection of 2nd Avenue and Pike Street gave me an understanding of the sudden, super-heated firestorms that would suddenly rage over race issues.

America's history lies, like a subterranean methane lake, under the thin crust of its present. The gas perpetually rises and, sparked by the slightest thing, ignites – burning everything around for days.

No one is calling for the dismantling of America – or, indeed, Europe. But we do need to be aware. And awareness doesn't need to be brutal, or abject, or alienating. Awareness can be like revelation – it can inform you, and uplift you, and motivate you. It can be the start of new and brilliant things.

In this respect, culture is trying. In the last fifteen years, Hollywood – still the global teller of stories – has increasingly focused on telling the same story, over and over again, like some feverish monomyth begging to be unpicked; like a dream we desperately need to analyse. The classic Hollywood blockbuster repeatedly nags at the same tropes: the Earth – precious, and familiar – is being attacked by alien forces with unfathomably superior weaponry and technology. The aliens seem not to have human emotions – they have simply come for our resources: be it oxygen, land or flesh. They cannot be reasoned with – there is never a diplomatic solution to an action movie. It's just simple, all-out war – with one side having to be annihilated.

And this mono-story does seem to be a desperate attempt at telling the story of the invasion of America, and/or founding of European empires, abroad. The aliens – with their weaponry, and technology; no diplomacy, only annihilation – are playing the role of European invaders. And white male heroes play the role of the defending native populations. With the tiniest flick of the switch – just a small inversion of the tropes – our huge, entertaining, but increasingly repetitive and boring blockbusters could be retooled to tell our real history – as with the making of the long-mooted telling of the slave rebellion in Haiti (see page 307, *12 Years a Slave*).

Not knowing our history is one of those problems that could be largely solved by culture – a couple of dozen TV shows/films/albums would tell the stories far better than any government initiative. But politics would have to do the groundwork in making sure there were enough people of colour in positions of power, and with big enough budgets, to commission these projects in the first place. With Hollywood so incredibly white right now – 94 per cent of the Oscars Academy is white – culture cannot cure this problem alone, without a very firm, correcting redistribution of power.

Again, we find that the answer to our problems is a fundamentally right-wing mindset – letting people come up with their *own* solutions to problems – but one that needs a left-wing, state-ist push: making sure the playing field is level, and those in need are given the power, resources and infrastructure they require to effect change.

It's almost like this theory I have about right-wing vs left-wing being obsolete is a coherent theory.

14) Complete protection of abortion rights (see page 222).

15) Restoration of the Victorian drinking fountain network, in order to save the 13 billion plastic water bottles thrown away every year. It's not just an environmental concern – bottled water is 500 times more expensive than tap water. Neither the planet, nor ordinary people, can afford for most water to be available only in non-reusable plastic bottles, when the Victorians had this problem licked in 1898.

16) Business. Currently, too many of our big multinationals gain massive profits at the expense of the state: by paying the minimum wage, or placing employees on zero-hours contracts, their employees must claim top-up benefits/housing benefits simply in order to survive. This hugely inflates our welfare bills, while the multinationals continue to enjoy vast profits – which they then often don't pay tax on, should they choose to register their businesses in tax havens/abroad.

At the moment, the only pressure against this kind of corporate behaviour are ad hoc internet campaigns, aimed at shaming the companies in question. And while I enjoy re-Tweeting a petition about Amazon/Tesco as much as the next person, it does rather feel as if this is an issue that could be addressed in a slightly more 'let's do something about this' way.

What we need is some kind of official Quality Employer mark, whereby companies would be rewarded for running their businesses in such a way that both doesn't put pressure on the Welfare State, and contributes to taxation in the country that has educated their workforces, and provided the infrastructure (roads, rail, policing, healthcare) that allows their businesses to thrive.

Given that there *is* a lobby system, perhaps the Quality Employer companies would be the only ones allowed to hire government ministers/advisers as consultants. They would have proved themselves to be assets to the community – and therefore accorded the access that, currently, any company is afforded, if they wang enough cash at it. Maybe they would be given fast-track planning permission for new buildings, or put through a system that reduced red tape for imports/exports. The key thing would be to reward any company that behaved with an old-fashioned sense of care towards the employees who give their lives to it, and pride in contributing to the taxation system of the country it works in.

I would publish a yearly league table of companies' tax returns, and render their payments as physical purchases: 'John Lewis paid for six cancer wards, pensions for 4,000 widows and the new municipal swimming pool in Croydon! Yay, John Lewis!' I would make paying your tax *competitive*. I would make it *sexy*. Yeah. John Lewis wanted to be taxed hard, all night long. I would do you, John Lewis.

So … yeah. That's what I think.

I mean, that's what I think *right now*. Who knows what I'll think in six months, or a year. I hope I'll think differently about some things – because I'll have learned more about them. It would be mad if I didn't. All political beliefs should be based on the understanding they will change, and improve. Planting your feet firmly in the ground at seventeen, or twenty-six, or forty-one, and saying, 'This is what I will believe – FOREVER!' is the first sign of someone indicating that, at some point, they intend to stop thinking. I wouldn't trust those people as far as I could throw them. And I have very poor upper-body strength. I call monkey bars 'failure bars'.

Let me be clear – even though I've written a manifesto here, if I were elected on a landslide victory, I wouldn't walk into Parliament tomorrow and rigidly enact all of these policies. Unless someone Double Donkey Dared me, of course – which is, as we all know, the dare you cannot decline.

No. What I've tried to do here is … start a conversation, instead. Open up a clearing in the woods, with very firm notices pinned on trees – 'THIS IS A PLACE FOR POLITE CONVERSATION ONLY, THANK YOU', and 'LET US HAVE A MORAL IMAGINATION ONCE MORE' – and then welcome everyone in who has that … *restless* feeling, too.

If I began this by standing on stage, in a cape, intoning 'A change is going to come' – simply because it felt quite exciting – I'd like to end by making a speech a bit like the one Michael Sheen made in 2015 – where he stood in the rain, passionately defending the future of the NHS.

If you want to imagine I actually *am* Michael Sheen, absolutely feel free to. I do most of the time. It makes me fancy me.

Many times in human history we have achieved extraordinary things, on impossible deadlines, while facing utter horror.

During the Second World War – the defining historical event of the last century – the cross-discipline of state management and rapid technological advances allowed astonishing leaps: first on the battlefield – allowing us to end the rolling, mechanised charnel houses of the Nazis – and then in our homes, streets and cities, as the planned implementation of social and technological progress resulted in the most dizzying rises in living conditions ever recorded.

We know that, with our backs to the wall – when we are under pressure – we, as a species, are capable of incredible cooperation across all spheres. Back then, no effort was too great, no plan too ambitious, no investment too much – as to put a limit on our expectations was, simply, to die: to see civilisation crushed by fascism.

Well, we are at war now. We are at war with our own unhappiness, and obsolescence.

We're at war with anxiety, and depression, and hopelessness, and apathy, and despair; we're at war against the idea of millions of people waking up every day and being too scared to say who they are, or who they love, or what they think. We're at war with the idea that the children in some countries must be sacrificed for the comfort of children in others.

We're at war with the terrible possibility we might get to a point in the not too distant future – maybe just ten years, almost certainly fifty – where we look at a problem we finally *cannot* solve, and go, 'Oh Christ. We really fucked it. We really, really fucked it.'

No one wants to be Charlton Heston crying over the Statue of Liberty, buried in the sand. That is always a bad day in the 'So – how did that all pan out?' factory.

When someone says they cannot change these things, as their hands are tied – because of cataclysmic events in the economy, banking system or commerce – then I would point out that these were things that were invented, by humans. They can be uninvented and reinvented a million times over – before breakfast, if necessary. They are merely systems born of ideas – not acts of God, or forces of nature, or physics. Once, they did not exist. If necessary, at some point in the future, they cannot exist again. If they are not fit for purpose. If they are not to the ultimate, fast betterment of humanity.

Because the job of politics is to defend and uplift and represent and improve the people – not lie helplessly between other, competing forces saying, 'If things were different, we would change things.'

We must *make* things different. We must *change* them. That is, simply, our job.

For the ultimate purpose of politics should be to enable people to experience as much joy as possible before they die. We are only here a tiny wink of time – a snap of the fingers; barely enough time to get a proper round in. It's a heartbreaking flash, really. You just start to work out what trousers suit you, or how to talk to the people you really love, and then you're dead.

That is why, when, as sometimes happens in politics, it is casually accepted that a whole generation will be raised under austerity; or a whole country's economy will go to the wall; or those running, as fast as they can, away from a war are told they must simply … return to the war, as we can offer them no solutions here, I cannot help but grit my teeth.

There is no afterlife. This is it. To dismiss entire lives – those millions of heartbreaking flashes – as being irretrievably at the mercy of 'unsolvable problems' is, frankly, in an age of impossible miracle and wonder, *balls*. It should make the blood pump – but not in anger.

The blood should pump to the heart and the head, instead; it should make you tilt your chin upwards, and narrow your eyes, and go, slowly, 'Nah – I don't reckon. I think we probably *could* solve this, if we really wanted.'

However and whatever we decide we want our future to be, we must be remorseless – in our kindness.

We must be iron – in our demand that life be joyful.

We must not dare waste a second of our only, exploding existence, thinking that, 'It will be better ... later' is *ever* a fit thing to say. If we say these things cannot be done, we are in denial of humanity. We are perversely proud to be small. And we are not. Trying. Hard. Enough.

EPILOGUE

This next piece has to come last in the book, for two reasons.

Firstly, because it's the piece that, by far, received the biggest response I've ever had – partly because it is, obviously, a profound and powerful piece of writing, but mainly, I suspect, because it was re-Tweeted by Adele, who has 23 million followers. The results of being re-Tweeted by someone iconic with 23 million followers are interesting. Many of the responses I got were greatly moving – 'Your piece has left me in tears.' 'Thank you for saying to my teenage daughter what I could not say myself.'

But most of them were along the lines of: '@AdeleOfficial @caitlinmoran – Adele we love you in BRAZIL! Come play for your fans IN BRAZIL! I cry for you! I sing your song very much! BRAZIL LOVE YOU!' '@caitlinmoran PLEASE tell @AdeleOfficial I DIE FOR HER! It would make my LIFE!'

I have enjoyed wielding this supposed power. 'No – Adele will NOT come and play in Brazil – as she says you don't actually love her ENOUGH', I will Tweet back, every so often, when bored. Or, 'Adele is looking at your profile picture – and thinks you would look BETTER in a scoop-necked top. The v-neck isn't doing it for you. ADELE HAS SPOKEN. ATTEND THE WORDS OF ADELE!'

And the second reason why this piece had to be last is very simple: it's a posthumous letter. It is written from beyond the grave. It is the last thing I will ever say. Even with my natural optimism about my immortality, I know that, once you're dead, there's nothing more to say.

MY POSTHUMOUS LETTER TO MY DAUGHTER

My daughter is about to turn thirteen and I've been smoking a lot recently, and so – in the wee small hours, when my lungs feel like there's a small mouse inside them, scratching to get out – I've thought about writing her one of those 'Now I'm Dead, Here's My Letter Of Advice For You To Consult As You Continue Your Now Motherless Life' letters. Here's the first draft. Might tweak it a bit later. When I've had another fag.

Dear Lizzie

Hello, it's Mummy. I'm dead. Sorry about that. I hope the funeral was good – did Daddy play 'Don't Stop Me Now' by Queen when my coffin went into the cremator? I hope everyone sang along and did air guitar, as I stipulated. And wore the stick-on Freddie Mercury moustaches, as I ordered in the 'My Funeral Plan' document that's been pinned on the fridge since 2008, when I had that extremely self-pitying cold.

Look – here are a couple of things I've learned on the way that you might find useful in the coming years. It's not an exhaustive list, but it's a good start. Also, I've left you loads of life-insurance money – so go hog wild on eBay on those second-hand vintage dresses you like. You have always looked beautiful in them. You have always looked beautiful.

The main thing is just to try to be nice. You already are – so lovely I burst, darling – and so I want you to hang on to that and never let it go. Keep slowly turning it up, like a dimmer switch, whenever you can. Just resolve to shine, constantly and steadily, like a warm lamp in the corner, and people will want to move towards you in order to feel happy, and to read things more clearly. You will be bright and constant in a world of dark and flux, and this will save you the anxiety of other, ultimately less satisfying things like 'being cool', 'being more successful than everyone else' and 'being very thin'.

Second, always remember that, nine times out of ten, you probably aren't having a full-on nervous breakdown – you just need a cup of tea and a biscuit. You'd be amazed how easily and repeatedly you can confuse the two. Get a big biscuit tin.

Third, always pick up worms off the pavement and put them on the grass. They're having a bad day, and they're good for... the earth or something (ask Daddy more about this; am a bit sketchy).

Fourth, choose your friends because you feel most like yourself around them, because the jokes are easy and you feel like you're in your best outfit when you're with them, even though you're just in a t-shirt. Never love someone who you think you need to mend – or who makes you feel like you should be mended. There are boys out there who look for shining girls; they will stand next to you and say quiet things in your ear that only you can hear and that will slowly drain the joy out of your heart. The books about vampires are true, baby. Drive a stake through their hearts and run away.

Stay at peace with your body. While it's healthy, never think of it as a problem or a failure. Pat your legs occasionally and thank them for being able to run. Put your hands on your belly and enjoy how soft and warm you are – marvel over the world turning over within, the brilliant meat clockwork, as I did when you were inside me and I dreamed of you every night.

Whenever you can't think of something to say in a conversation, ask people questions instead. Even if you're next to a man who collects pre-seventies screws and bolts, you will probably never have another opportunity to find out so much about pre-seventies screws and bolts, and you never know when it will be useful.

This segues into the next tip: life divides into AMAZING ENJOYABLE TIMES and APPALLING EXPERIENCES THAT WILL MAKE FUTURE AMAZING ANECDOTES. However awful, you can get through any experience if you imagine yourself, in the future, telling your friends about it as they scream, with increasing disbelief, 'NO! NO!' Even when Jesus was on the cross, I bet He was thinking, 'When I rise in three days, the disciples aren't going to believe this when I tell them about it.'

Babyiest, see as many sunrises and sunsets as you can. Run across roads, looking both ways, to smell fat roses. Always believe you can change the world – even if it's only a tiny bit, because every tiny bit needed someone who changed it. Think of yourself as a silver rocket – use loud music as your fuel; books like maps and coordinates for how to get there. Host extravagantly, love constantly, dance in comfortable shoes, talk to Daddy and Nancy about me every day and never, ever start smoking. It's like buying a fun baby dragon that will grow and eventually burn down your f***ing house.

Love, Mummy.

Join the Debate!

If you have enjoyed *Moranifesto*, visit Caitlin's YouTube channel where she discusses themes from the book and invites you to join the conversation by recording your own One Minute Manifesto. The best ones will be featured on the channel.

Find out more visit www.caitlinmoran.co.uk

 Tube 'Caitlin's Moranifesto'

 @Caitlinmoran